ON BEING STONED

ON BEING STONED

STONED

A PSYCHOLOGICAL STUDY OF MARIJUANA INTOXICATION

By CHARLES T. TART, Ph.D.

Associate Professor of Psychology
University of California, Davis

SCIENCE AND BEHAVIOR BOOKS
Palo Alto, California

This book is dedicated to the one hundred and fifty marijuana users who overcame their fear that this study was a police trap, and so gave of their time and experience to make this book possible.

Library of Congress Card Number 79-153848
ISBN 0-8314-0027-7

Contents

Foreword

THE RESEARCH reported in this book is both innovative and relevant. At a time in our culture when there is a growing concern about drug abuse among the young, and the use of marijuana is increasing more than it ever has in our country's history, it is fortunate that someone has seriously attempted to investigate the psychological and subjective effects of marijuana. This book should prove valuable for the interested layman who is curious about such effects and also for the scientist who may be stimulated to carry the results of this research further.

It is important for anyone to note before reading this book that the content is a careful study of the personal *experience* encountered when marijuana is used. This important fact sets this book apart from those primarily dealing with the pharmacology, medical implications, social desirability/undesirability, or the legal problems of marijuana, and is the very reason that Dr. Tart's approach breaks new ground in this controversial area. His method has been quite simple and straightforward, yet it is one which has too long been ignored in modern behavioristic psychology in a misguided attempt to be "scientific" by avoiding subjective experience. Dr. Tart has asked persons who themselves have used marijuana what different kinds of experiences they have had. His instrument has been a carefully constructed questionnaire that has proved to be extremely useful in gathering a very large amount of data from the persons who should know best what the experience is like— those who have actually taken the drug. The personal account of the subject cannot be ignored despite some imprecision in measurement. Each individual person may use his own standards for interpreting the experience or measuring the intensity, but there is no substitute for a report by the person who has been there. Indeed, this experiential aspect of the effect, especially with psychedelic drugs, may in the long run prove to be the most valuable. Far more important than laboratory conditions far removed from the actual social usage of marijuana is what happens to the person in his own consciousness, how he interprets this, and how it influences his actual life.

Another reason this book is a valuable contribution to our knowledge about marijuana is that it helps to answer a very important question often not even asked by many who are the most concerned about marijuana usage. This question is: Why do so many otherwise lawabiding people risk their freedom and reputation to use this illegal drug? The data in this book show consistent agreement that most of the subjective experiences reported by users—for example, sensory intensification of musical appreciation, gustatory enjoyment, and sexual activity—are extremely pleasurable. Dr. Tart has attempted to establish a subjective scale to help quantify such effects. Because pleasure is the reason most people use the drug, it should certainly be studied and not ignored in research on the effects of marijuana.

From a strictly scientific point of view, this research has great value by opening up new questions that are researchable. Once it has been established that certain types of subjective experience do in fact occur consistently, psychophysiological correlates can be measured, such as various EEG brain waves, pulse, blood pressure, and skin potential. Some of the positive effects reported might have practical clinical application, such as stimulation of appetite, decrease in depression, enhancement of refreshing sleep, and certain types of problem solving. Hopefully, Dr. Tart's work will stimulate future research to test these hypotheses.

Dr. Tart's pioneering effort points the way toward the future in other ways as well. This book is a creative step forward in better understanding the range of human consciousness. The method of studying actual subjective experience is an indispensable tool for future research into altered states of consciousness. There are important implications not only for the effects of marijuana, but also for research in hypnosis, sensory isolation, EEG feedback, and the major psychedelic drugs such as LSD, mescaline, and psilocybin. In the next twenty years there will certainly be a growing interest in altered states of consciousness triggered by all these approaches. It is important to remember that the experience, and not the technique, is what will motivate this interest. Better understanding of the effects of marijuana may lead to other methods, perhaps safer and less objectionable from a legal standpoint, for achieving similar effects.

This book should make an important contribution to man's seemingly irresistible urge to explore his own consciousness. Twenty years from now its value can be assessed from the perspective of the research that will follow. I would guess that Dr. Tart's work will be judged to have had considerable influence.

Walter N. Pahnke, M.D., Ph.D.
Director of Clinical Sciences
Maryland Psychiatric Research Center

A Fable

ONCE UPON A TIME, *not so very long ago, there was a rich and powerful Kingdom called Middle America. It was progressive and beautiful, and its people were a contented lot.*

The Kingdom was surrounded on three sides by (almost) impassable mountains, and on the fourth by a broad river perpetually shrouded with dense fog. There were legends that some citizens, called Travelers, had gone to places "outside" the Kingdom, but the solid citizens considered these as tall tales or crazy things; all that one needed was in the Kingdom, so why would anyone want to go "outside," even if such a thing were possible and safe?

The King and his Government took a more serious view, and long ago made Traveling unlawful because it was Dangerous. Special Constables policed the boundaries of the Kingdom.

For many years some of the impoverished citizens and outcasts had talked of Traveling to a land called Muggles, which they claimed was on the other side of the Foggy River; but these poor citizens were simply thrown in prison by the Constables, and nobody cared very much about them.

Then as time went on, more and more citizens talked about the joys of Traveling to the land of Muggles, and these citizens were Merchants, Princes, Solicitors, Tradesmen, and, especially, the Young. More Constables were hired, and the Ministers of the government warned the populace of the menace of Traveling; but still more and more citizens traveled.

Great outcries arose from the good citizens for something to be done. Some cried out that Traveling to Muggles was a menace that was sapping the strength of the Kingdom. Others cried out that those who traveled were sick in their minds and should be helped, whether they wanted help or not. Some, who claimed to be Travelers, raised their voices and said it was a good thing to travel to the land of Muggles. Some said it was not the King's business whether a citizen traveled to Muggles or not.

In the midst of the Confusion and Outcry, some thoughtful citizens asked, "What say our Scholars? What can we make of this Traveling?

*How can we understand those who say it is Good and those who say it
is Bad? How can we wisely spend the Kingdom's gold to Do Something
when we are confused as to what is happening?"*

*The Scholars looked at their books and their papers, and quarreled
among themselves. Some books said that Traveling to Muggles was Bad,
and the Doctors wrote of sick people they had treated who had been to
Muggles at one time or another. Some books said that it was Good, Ineffa-
ble, Beautiful, and the Ultimate Truth. Some books about Traveling to
Muggles, written by citizens who had been there once or twice, were clearly
Confused. Other books were clearly written by crazy people. Artists wrote
of the paintings of Muggles. Philosophers wrote of the sublime philosophy
of Muggles, but did not mention the paintings. Religious people wrote
of the teachings of Muggles, but did not mention the paintings. What
could one make of this? Perhaps the Crazies were mainly writing about
craziness, the Philosophers mainly about philosophy, the Religious about
teachings, and no one was saying much about Muggles at all?*

*As the outcry of the citizens rose higher, the King's Ministers dispensed
gold to the Scholars, and commanded them to find out the Real Truth
about Traveling to Muggles.*

*Now as any man knows, there are Scholars and Scholars. Some did
one thing with their gold, others did other things.*

*The school of Scholars most in power at that time was known as
the Externalist School. They knew that men may lie, and so reasoned
that what a man says is of little importance, but what he does is Hard
Data. The means of Traveling to Muggles was to immerse oneself in the
Foggy River. As "swimming" was unknown in the Kingdom, this seemed
an insane act that might lead to drowning; but the Scholars of the Externalist School set out to study it in their Laboratories. Skilled Craftsmen
constructed large tanks, which were filled with water from the Foggy River.
Ordinary citizens (those who claimed to have traveled to Muggles were
considered too biased to use) were held under the water for various times
and their behavior observed. Short immersions had little effect, but longer
immersions caused Wild Movements, Increased Respiration, and Strange
Sounds. Thus the Externalist Scholars produced the Hard Data on what
Traveling to Muggles did to people.*

*Some said, "This is certainly true, but why do citizens risk the wrath
of the constables for this? Perhaps there is more Truth to be found elsewhere?"*

*A few Scholars of other schools used experienced Travelers in their
tanks of water and found very different results, but theirs is a minor tale,
as there were so few of them.*

*This book is the work of a Scholar of Another School who believed
that while men could lie, many men would also try to tell the Truth as*

best they could. He read the books of the Scholars and talked with many experienced Travelers, and asked himself, "What could we find out if many experienced Travelers to the land of Muggles were all asked the same questions, instead of letting each talk only of the things he loves?" So he tested many experienced Travelers, and, after eliminating those few who readily told bizarre stories, he found there was Meaningfulness in what they said. Now this Scholar has made a Map of the whole land of Muggles, so perhaps new Royal Expeditions and Studies can find their way to the Important Places in Muggles and bring back Knowledge and, perhaps, Riches.

Introduction

I have long been impressed with the need so many people seem to have of occasionally altering their state of consciousness, of radically changing the way in which their minds function. Alcohol, prayer, meditation, sacred dances, fasting, revivals, hypnosis, drugs—these and many other techniques have all been used by people in various cultures for pleasure and insight, worship and diversion, work and healing. Yet practically all of our science and philosophy is based on what seems sensible to our ordinary state of mind, and the existence of these other states is largely ignored by being relegated to the realms of the abnormal and the illogical. It is only in the last few years that psychologists and other scientists have begun to pay serious attention to altered states of consciousness and to ask questions about what they are like, how they affect behavior, what function they have for the individual and his culture, and how they might supplement traditional methods of gaining knowledge.

In spite of the attention now starting to be focused on altered states of consciousness, we know very, very little about most of them.

When I began focusing my researches on altered states of consciousness some years ago, I found myself in a similar position to the scholar of the fable, who wanted to know about the land of Muggles.* It was clear that the mind could indeed function in non-ordinary ways, but beyond that fact things were not so clear. Some "travelers" told consistent stories about some of the states of consciousness they had experienced, and I could feel certain enough about them to plan "expeditions," research projects to investigate some aspect of that state in detail. For other states, the tales were wild and improbable, inconsistent, and clearly reflecting whatever ax the particular traveler had to grind.

The literature on marijuana was especially confusing. Even when it purported to be medical or scientific literature, much of it was full

_____
*"Muggles" was one of the slang terms for marijuana when it was first introduced into this country in the 1930s.

of propaganda, pro or con. Lurid individual tales of marijuana intoxication contradicted the laboratory studies of its effects. For reasons detailed in Chapter 2, the individual anecdotes were often hopelessly confused by the personalities of the writers, and the conditions of the laboratory studies were so unusual as to have no applicability to the ordinary use of marijuana. How could I profitably explore particular features of this strange country of marijuana intoxication when the overall map of the landscape was so confused and useless? I might expend great effort on what was truly a trivial feature.

The study described in this book is an attempt to get an overall look at marijuana intoxication as it occurs in the ordinary world (insofar as California and America represent the ordinary world!). What happens to the minds of experienced users when they smoke marijuana? What do they experience? What are the frequent and infrequent, important and unimportant experiences? How do they relate to how "high" or "stoned" the user is? Are they affected by his overall drug experience, his educational background, etc.? Knowing these general effects—the overall lay of the land—then we can concentrate our research efforts on the important aspects of marijuana intoxication.

The study that gathered this information is, as far as I know, unique in its approach. Staying with our analogy, I treated experienced marijuana users as explorers of the marijuana state and then systematically collected, compared, and analyzed their reports. Since it is an initial attempt at this sort of thing, it can be done in an even better fashion a second time around, and, ordinarily, I would like to have repeated the study with improvements before publishing this report.

But the times are *not* ordinary, and so I am publishing this without waiting for the replication that would make the figures a little more precise and eliminate an occasional mistake in the effects of some background factors. A certain amount of justifiable technical criticism will result and, hopefully, will help myself or others to carry out an improved version of this study. Because the times are not ordinary, however, I suspect a great deal of *a*-rational criticism of this book will also occur. Marijuana is not a subject being discussed in intellectual isolation; emotions about its use are heated, both pro and con, to put it mildly. Pressures to change existing laws are very high, and legislators ask for scientific studies of the effects of marijuana to base such changes on, so every study on this subject receives a great deal of partisan criticism or acclamation in addition to the usual scientific scrutiny. To those with a fixed position that marijuana use is harmful and marijuana users are deviates or mentally ill escapists of some sort, this book will be unwelcome. I have not argued for or against the legalization of marijuana, but the effects that experienced users describe are generally very interesting and pleasant. Thus some critics will see the tone of the book as "pro-pot," even though I have attempted to be neutral and simply describe results.

I am presenting this study, then, because the subject of marijuana intoxication is so important today and because the information contained herein will answer many questions about what it is like to be high on marijuana (and, therefore, why people use it) in a way that no other current studies will. Too, my knowledge of what most of the studies being funded by various agencies are like indicates that there are no studies going on now which will provide better answers to these questions. I regret to say that most of the new studies going on are subject to many of the same criticisms that make the older ones irrelevant to the real world, as discussed in Chapter 2.

Because of the importance of the subject and the uniqueness of this approach, I think this book will be useful or informative to three different audiences. First, researchers may use these findings as a guide to profitable research. Second, people who are curious about what being stoned on marijuana is like but who do not use it themselves—parents, educators, physicians, legislators—will be able to get a good picture of what it is like and why people use marijuana in spite of the legal penalties. Third, marijuana users themselves will be able to compare their personal experience with that of users in general, with the result, according to many of the users who contributed to this study, that they will be able to experience more effects and acquire more control over their state.*

Again I stress that this is basically a scientific book; I have attempted to present objectively descriptions of what experienced users feel about marijuana intoxication, without arguing for or against marijuana use or letting my own feelings about marijuana distort the writing. I have feelings, of course. My own survey of the scientific and other literature puts me in agreement with Kaplan (1970) that the known dangers of marijuana use are very small, while the known social cost of the present legal structure—branding millions of Americans criminals, clogging the courts with victimless crimes, creating disrespect for the law among the young, and enforcing the laws at huge expense—is tremendously high. Thus I see some form of legalization-under-control of marijuana as socially desirable. I have, however, attempted to keep these personal feelings completely out of the book.

A tremendous amount of data is contained in this book. Although I have checked the manuscript against the computer data printouts in several ways to eliminate error and inconsistency, the sheer size of the

---

*Because readers of these last two types are sometimes put off by numbers and statistics, I have disposed of all these complexities in a page of explanation following this section.

undertaking makes it inevitable that an occasional error or inconsistency may be apparent to the diligent reader. I would appreciate his writing me about any such inconsistencies, so they may be corrected in a subsequent printing.

This study could not have been carried out except for the assistance of a number of people in the data collection, analysis, and write-up stages, all of whom I wish to thank; namely, Joan Crawford, Lois Dick, Dee Kindelt, Carl Klein, Arthur Hastings, Wanda Meyer, Mary Moore, Donna Sedgwick, Marlene Shinazy, Penny Smail, and my wife Judy. This research was supported by the United States Public Health Service, grant MH16-810. All opinions expressed in this book are my own and do not necessarily reflect those of the above people or the Public Health Service.

A Note to the Non-Scientist Reader

In order to conveniently present exact findings to the researchers who read this book, there are lots of parentheses filled with numbers and simple statistics.

If you aren't interested in the *exact* findings, or if numbers and statistics turn you off, there's a simple way to avoid any problem: ignore them. Everything has been written in plain English, and the numbers confined to parentheses for just this reason!

If, on the other hand, you haven't a formal background in statistics but would like to know what the probability figures in the parentheses (such as "$p < .05$") mean, it all boils down to this: how do you know when a difference in the way two groups of people answer a question is a meaningful, *significant* difference, and how do you know when it results only from the random variation you get whenever you deal with people's responses?

You never know for *certain* which is which, but a statistical test is an objective way of being reasonably sure, one way or the other. Statistical tests use the known mathematical properties of numbers to let you decide when a difference is probably due to chance, and when a difference is so large that chance seems unlikely. The exact mathematics aren't of interest to the general reader, but only the outcome, the probability figure. If the outcome of a particular test could have happened by chance only five or fewer times in a hundred trials (conventionally expressed in this book as $p < .05$, probability equal to or less than $5/100$),* we begin to doubt that this is chance variation. It probably represents a real difference between the groups. If the probability is even smaller that the outcome is due to chance, say less than one in a hundred ($p < .01$) or less than one in a thousand ($p < .001$), we can feel quite certain that we are dealing with real, important differences.**

Thus in this book the lower the probability figure in parentheses, the greater the difference between the groups being compared.

---

*More exactly, the sign should be $\leq$ rather than simply $<$, but this simplification will be used throughout the text.

**Statistical tables available to me only go up to the .0005 level. When I use the notation $p \ll .0005$, the difference is even more significant; when I use $p \lll .0005$, it is *super*significant. For the technically minded, I use $p \ll .0005$ when chi square is greater than or equal to 50, and $p \lll .0005$ when chi square is greater than or equal to 100, with four degrees of freedom in each case.

PART *I*

STUDYING MARIJUANA INTOXICATION

CHAPTER 1

Marijuana

ONE OF THE MOST persistent and unusual aspects of human behavior, observable in all cultures and through all of history, is man's dissatisfaction with his ordinary state of consciousness and the consequent development of innumerable methods for altering it. Our normal pattern of thought and feeling, useful in many ways, never seems to be enough for some people.

The reasons for this search for better states of consciousness are many, ranging from desires for greater knowledge to religious, hedonistic, and power motives. The belief that our ordinary state of consciousness is of only utilitarian value and not suitable for insights into basic questions about the meaning of life has been one of the most important motives. Some men have been successful in achieving higher states of consciousness; others have failed. Techniques have been innumerable: religious ceremonies, meditation, hypnosis, self-hypnosis, asceticism, fasting, dancing, yoga exercises, and drugs, to name a few. Some of the men who have succeeded in altering their state of consciousness, such as the Buddha, are revered by hundreds of millions of people. Others have been outcasts of society or considered insane because their views were too different from those of their contemporaries. Still others have gone truly insane in the course of their search.

Our scientific understanding of altered states of consciousness is minuscule in comparison with what we do not know and the importance of these states. (For a survey of the scientific literature on them, see Tart, 1969.)

Drugs have been an important means of inducing altered states of consciousness throughout history. Cultures have embraced or rejected this means. Proponents have touted it as the shortcut to enlightenment, while critics, both ordinary men and those considered spiritual giants, have called it an escape, a pseudo-enlightenment.

Our culture today is one of the most drug-oriented cultures in history; we go by the millions to our doctor (or our dealer) for pills to pep us up, calm us down, wake us up, put us to sleep, relax our tensions, make us forget, or enlighten us. As a whole our cultural attitudes toward drugs are irrational to the point of absurdity. We mightily praise some drugs whose detrimental effects are enormous and well known, such as alcohol, and condemn other drugs about which we know very little. Scientific knowledge about drugs has generally been of little consequence in affecting social attitudes and usage.

This book is an attempt to broaden our knowledge about one of the most widely used and poorly understood drugs in our culture today, marijuana.

THE PLANT

Marijuana is the term given to preparations of the flowering tops, leaves, seeds, and/or stems of the Indian hemp plant, *Cannabis sativa L.* The preparation, for eating or smoking, is commonly called marijuana, marihuana, Mary Jane, hemp, pot, grass, shit, and dope, with usage depending on fashions and subcultures.

Cannabis sativa grows wild all over the world and is a very hardy plant. It is extensively cultivated in many areas, and research of optimal techniques of cultivation has been extensive (Drake, 1970). The plant is desired for its fibers, which are used for rope, as well as for its drug value. Attempts to increase fiber content and decrease drug content of the plant by mutation have succeeded only in increasing the drug content (Warmke & Davidson, 1941-43, 1942-43, 1943-44).

The drug potency of the plant depends on the particular strain of plant, cultivation techniques, soil, and climate. Different parts of the plant have different concentrations of the drug. Much of the marijuana generally available in the United States today is what is called in India *bhang*, and is the least potent mixture, made from poor quality plants or from the lower leaves of better plants. Stems and seeds are generally separated out from marijuana by users, as they contain practically none of the desirable ingredients of marijuana. The seeds are also widely reputed to contain substances that induce headaches if smoked.

A more potent grade of marijuana, termed *ganja* in India, consists of the flowering tops and upper leaves of carefully bred plants. The most potent marijuana preparation, generally termed hashish or, colloquially, hash (*charas* in India), consists only of the sticky resin scraped from the tops of mature and carefully bred plants.

Hashish is often treated as a separate drug, but there is no good scientific evidence to indicate that it is chemically different. By virtue of its containing far more active ingredients by volume, however, the

user either can get intoxicated with much less hashish than ore
marijuana or can get more intoxicated by using an equal amount. W.
ever I refer to marijuana effects in this book, I am including those
hashish.

Techniques of Use

Marijuana is eaten or smoked. Most American users prefer smoking
because (1) less marijuana is required for a given degree of intoxication;
(2) effects begin within a few minutes after smoking and end within
three or four hours, as compared to an hour or more for onset and
a duration of six to twelve hours when eaten; (3) more precise control
of the level of intoxication is possible, as the user can stop smoking
when the desired level is reached; and (4) more aftereffects and unpleasant effects are associated with eating marijuana because of the possibility
of overdose. Smoking is done by making a cigarette (commonly called
a joint or reefer) or by using a pipe, often a waterpipe to reduce the
harshness of the smoke. The smoke is held in the lungs as long as possible
to maximize absorption.

Active Ingredient(s)

Marijuana is a complex substance and has long resisted analysis
as to its active ingredients. The reader interested in the chemistry and
pharmacology of marijuana should see Mechoulam (1970) and Wolstenholme (1965).

In the last few years one of the major active ingredients has been
identified and named tetrahydrocannabinol (THC).[1] Human subjects
given synthesized THC under laboratory conditions report many effects
similar to those reported for natural marijuana, and a number of workers
feel that THC may be the only active ingredient in marijuana. Numerous
studies of the effects of synthetic THC on animals and humans are being
funded by the federal government. Experienced users, however, insist
that different samples of marijuana differ somewhat in *qualitative* as
well as quantitative effects; some marijuana has a much stronger sedative
effect, some tends to make people very silly, and so on. This suggests
that there are other active ingredients than THC in marijuana, and
research should not concentrate too exclusively on THC, in spite of the
pharmacological and medical convenience of working with a pure drug
instead of a natural mixture (Weil, 1969).

---

[1]Technically this is named 1-Δ^1-*trans*-THC. Due to an ambiguity in the system for giving chemical
names, it is sometimes refered to as 1-Δ^9-*trans*-THC in some literature.

Pharmacology

Little is understood of the chemical fate of marijuana once it is absorbed into the human body. Older research with marijuana extracts on animals, the usual method of establishing basic pharmacological information, has been fraught with methodological difficulties. Many physiological effects appear in animals that do not appear in humans, species differ markedly from one another, and different individuals of the same species often show opposite effects. It is not known whether the dosages used were really comparable to those used by humans. Ongoing research with synthetic THC may begin to add to our knowledge, but at present we know practically nothing about the pharmacological action of marijuana.

PHYSIOLOGICAL EFFECTS ON HUMANS

The most striking thing that can be said about the physiological effects of marijuana on humans is that there are practically no observable effects of consequence. Weil, Zinberg, and Nelson (1968) found that marijuana increases heart rate somewhat and causes a dilation of conjunctival blood vessels (somewhat bloodshot-looking eyes). They found no evidence of dilated pupils, even though law enforcement officers typically use this as a test for intoxication.

Marijuana seems to be a rather unique drug in having such profound psychological effects with virtually no readily observable physiological changes.

Effects on Human Performance

The performance capabilities of intoxicated users have been investigated in a number of older studies, but because of methodological shortcomings, discussed fully in Chapter 2, they have yielded little reliable information.

Two recent studies, both methodologically very good, found essentially no measurable changes in performance. Crancer and his colleagues (1969) tested *experienced* users for performance in a driving simulator. When intoxicated on marijuana, they were not significantly different in *overall* performance than under control (non-intoxicated) conditions, although there were significantly more speedometer errors. Speedometer errors have not been found to correlate with actual driving performance in normal drivers, however. When the same subjects were intoxicated on alcohol, they made large numbers of errors on almost all aspects of the driving simulation tests.

Weil and his colleagues (1968) found that *experienced* marijuana users showed no significant losses in performance on some simple motor and intellectual tasks; indeed, they sometimes showed a slight improvement when intoxicated. Naïve subjects who had not smoked marijuana before the laboratory experiment did not get "high," i.e., felt none or few of the experiential effects of marijuana, but showed significant impairments on a variety of tasks.

I doubt that alterations of simple sensory and motor tasks will be found associated with marijuana intoxication. *Subtle* alterations may be found by sophisticated analyses, such as Weil and Zinberg (1969) found for speech patterns, but the effects of marijuana seem to be primarily on the more complex intellectual functions, as detailed in this book. These are probably detectable only by asking users about them and/or by administering psychological tests, which are sensitive to complex alterations of mental functioning.

Psychological Effects

In one sense this entire book is a description of the psychological effects of marijuana intoxication, so no attempt will be made to deal with them in this introduction.

Addiction

An addicting drug, such as heroin, generally requires the user to continually increase his dosage because of the tolerance he builds up to the drug, produces acute distress if the user does not get his dose at the regular time, and produces extreme distress, which can result in death or severe withdrawal symptoms, if the drug is completely taken away from the user.

Much nonsense has been promulgated in the past by narcotics agencies and medical groups about the addicting properties of marijuana. There is no evidence of addiction. Emphasis today is laid on the fact that marijuana produces a "psychological dependence." This is a nonsensical use of the English language, for psychological dependence simply means that people tend to repeat enjoyable experiences.

Experienced users can stop using marijuana at any time with no distress or physiological symptoms. Once they learn how to get intoxicated, they require less, not more, marijuana.

Occasional users who are mentally ill may use excessive amounts of marijuana or become temporarily dependent on it, but this says something about mental illness rather than marijuana.

Similarly, no reliable evidence exists that marijuana use causes users to try dangerous narcotics like heroin. Persons predisposed to narcotic addiction become addicted whether or not they have used marijuana. The vast majority of marijuana users never get involved with narcotics, even though the need to deal with pushers, who may also sell narcotics, gives them ample opportunity.

LEGAL STATUS OF MARIJUANA

The possession of marijuana or its extracts is a serious offense in every state of the United States and its territories. Penalties vary widely from state to state. Although reform movements are under way, the prescribed penalties in many states are still extremely harsh. Years of imprisonment are frequently mandatory for the possession of the smallest detectable amounts of marijuana.

Penalties for selling or giving away marijuana are even more severe. Since many users also buy marijuana as a favor for their friends, they are generally liable to these higher penalties.

The actual structure of the laws is exceptionally complex, and some will be changed shortly. By far the best review of existing laws and their social consequences has been made by Kaplan in his recent book, *Marijuana, the New Prohibition* (1970). Smith's (1970) book also contains excellent discussions of the social issues revolving around marijuana use.

EXTENT OF USE

In spite of the severe penalties attached to possession and sale of marijuana, use today is very widespread. Given the sorts of pleasurable effects reported later in this book, it seems likely that use will continue to increase.

No definite survey of incidence of use can be made because there is always a (realistic) tendency of wary users to deny their use. Nevertheless, a large number of surveys of drug use on college campuses have been made (Kaplan, 1970; Pearlman, 1968). It is now a rare college campus that does not have a significant number of marijuana users, and on many campuses users themselves estimate over 50 percent of the students use marijuana occasionally, primarily at social events. An unpublished study that I carried out in collaboration with one of my graduate students, Carl Klein, found that from 1967 to 1968 the percentage of students who used marijuana at a conservative West Coast university doubled, and various formal and informal estimates of that population since have confirmed that a majority of the students have tried marijuana. (Further details of this study are presented in Chapter 28.) This seems typical. Drug-education programs sponsored by schools and government agencies are viewed with scorn and amusement by users, since their own and friends' experiences with marijuana convince them that the instructors are ignorant or lying. This is an unfortunate effect, as the attitude may be generalized to warnings about drugs that really are dangerous, such as hard narcotics and amphetamines.

Marijuana use is by no means confined to college campuses. In a survey of young adults (eighteen and over) in San Francisco, Manheimer, Mellinger, and Balter (1969) reported that 13 percent had used marijuana at least once. Conservative estimates in the press usually figure that several million Americans have tried marijuana, although it is not clear how many use it with any regularity.

Difficult political, moral, and religious problems arise when an act generally condemned and illegal spreads at such a rapid rate. This book is not the place to go into them, but the interested reader will find some good discussions in Aaronson and Osmond (1970), Krippner (1968), and Kaplan (1970).

Leaving aside considerations of social and political problems, what sort of reliable, scientific knowledge do we have about the effects of marijuana? What do users experience that makes the risk of prison worthwhile?

The following chapter discusses the nature of marijuana intoxication and explains why previous scientific work has gained very little reliable knowledge about it. The remainder of the book describes the method and results of the present study as an attempt to answer the question of what marijuana smokers experience.

CHAPTER 2

The Nature of Drug-Induced
States of Consciousness

PEOPLE SELDOM do something without a rationale explicitly or implicitly guiding their actions. Although I have tried to avoid theorizing as much as possible in this book, there was a theoretical rationale that led to the initiation of the present study. The theory presented here is applicable to most altered states of consciousness, although this presentation focuses on marijuana intoxication. Application of this theory to more powerful psychedelics, such as LSD, mescaline, or psilocybin, should take account of the fact that an even greater range of effects is potentially available with these drugs than with marijuana.

The condition of being under the influence of marijuana—of being in a state of *marijuana intoxication*—is one of many altered states of consciousness potentially available to man (see Tart, 1969). But what exactly do we mean by a *state of consciousness*, and more specifically, what do we mean by the particular state of consciousness we call marijuana intoxication?

A simple answer to this is that marijuana intoxication is a reorganization of mental functioning that comes about from the ingestion of marijuana. For reasons explained in detail later, however, to define a state of consciousness in terms of its obvious initiating procedure, while "objective" and "operational," can be very misleading. Some people, for example, smoke marijuana and experience no discernible effects; are such people in the same state of consciousness as someone who smokes marijuana and says time goes slowly, sounds are more beautiful, and his body is filled with energy?

A state of consciousness is a hypothetical construct invoked to explain certain observed regularities in behavior and experience. That is, we start out by observing a number of people about whose functioning there is something presumably *different*. Each of these people reports experiences and exhibits behaviors that are unique, a product of the individual's personality and the particular situations we observe him in. If, however, we can discern a certain common patterning of functioning in all of these people, a common pattern superimposed on their individual uniqueness, we may hypothesize something to explain this common pattern. This hypothesized something might be a common personality trait, belief system, physical attribute, or, in terms of our interest, a common state of consciousness. Particularly, if we know that all the observed individuals ingested marijuana just before we began observing them, we will be tempted to say that the common pattern of functioning we observe is the result of their all being in a state of marijuana intoxication.

Note, however, that it is the empirically observed common pattern of functioning[1] that is the crucial defining operation of the state of consciousness; the fact that they had all ingested marijuana serves secondarily to specify something we think to be a *cause* of the hypothesized state of consciousness.

What, then, are the properties of this hypothesized state of consciousness, marijuana intoxication? How do we discover these properties?

Clearly the way to answer this is to give marijuana to a number of people and observe what is common in their experience and behavior. Unfortunately, the observation process is much more complex and full of pitfalls than we would expect.

Much of our usual experience with the effects of drugs on consciousness misleads us into expecting fairly simple relationships. If, for example, you give a strong dose of barbiturates or other sedatives to a person, he almost always goes to sleep. Hence we describe the state of consciousness (or lack of it) induced by barbiturates as a barbiturate-induced sleep. There is little variability across subjects, and our observational process is simple.

With a psychoactive drug like marijuana, on the other hand, the variability across subjects is very high, and the observation process itself may systematically bias what we observe, as will be detailed in the next section. It may even turn out that different people might experience different states of consciousness from using marijuana, that is, the observed patterns of experience and behavior fall into *several* distinct patterns rather than a single pattern common to all individuals. We generally consider alcohol intoxication, for example, as a single state, yet on a second thought there are clearly some individuals who have very different experiences with alcohol from those the majority of us have. A drug may thus stimulate a reorganization of functioning, but the nature of

---

[1]Note that a pattern of functioning is not the same thing as the observed effects per se. Different restructurings of mental functioning may lead to the same overt effect in some cases; the report that one event followed rapidly after another could stem either from a change in experienced time rate or from falling asleep between events. Relationships between observed effects determine the overall pattern.

the new pattern may be determined by factors other than the nature of the drug per se.

Let us consider in detail the question of why a given individual, taking marijuana (or any other psychoactive drug, for that matter) at a particular time and place, might experience the particular things that he does.

VARIABILITY OF DRUG-INDUCED STATES

Our common experience with many drugs inclines us to think along the line that "Drug A has effects X, Y, and Z." This is generally adequate for most drugs. Heavy doses of barbiturates make a person drowsy. Penicillin cures certain diseases. Amphetamines stimulate people.

When it comes to drugs whose effects are primarily psychological, however, the tendency to think that drug A has effects X, Y, and Z can be very misleading and introduces confusion. That type of statement attributes certain sorts of invariant qualities to the chemical effect of the drug on the nervous system. When dealing with psychoactive drugs such as marijuana or LSD, however, both scientific research and the experience of users have made it clear that there are very few "invariant" qualities that are somehow inherent in or "possessed by" the drug itself. Rather, the particular effects of a drug are primarily a function of a *particular* person taking a *particular* drug in a *particular* way under *particular* conditions at a *particular* time.

Potential Effects Model

The conceptual scheme used in this book for understanding the variability of effects with psychoactive drugs may be called the *potential effects model*. Basically, the observable effects of a psychoactive drug such as marijuana are of three types. First are what might be considered *pure drug effects*, i.e., effects almost always manifested when a particular drug is taken, regardless of person, place, situation, and time. Such effects are probably due primarily to the chemical nature of the drug as it interacts with common characteristics of human body chemistry. With many psychoactive drugs, pure drug effects are only a small portion of the total effects possible.

Potential drug effects are effects that are made *possible* by the ingestion of a particular psychoactive drug but that will not manifest (become noticeable to the user or an observer) unless various non-drug factors operate in the proper manner; i.e., potential effects manifest only under certain conditions. These conditions will be discussed at length below. These potential effects constitute the majority of effects for a drug such as marijuana.

Insofar as potential effects constitute the bulk of effects for marijuana intoxication, it is misleading to talk about the effects of marijuana per se, as is commonly done. Rather, we must speak of the effects of marijuana on certain types of people under certain types of conditions. (A third category of effects under this model is not, properly speaking, drug effects at all, but *placebo effects*, or pure psychological effects. These are effects brought about by non-drug factors entirely. If the particular configuration of non-drug factors necessary to produce a particular placebo effect occurs frequently under conditions usually associated with taking a particular drug, the effect will probably be, erroneously, ascribed to the drug.)

Factors Controlling Potential Effects

We shall consider all of the current known classes of factors, which will determine how a particular individual reacts to a psychoactive drug at a particular time, before looking at the problem of variability from one time of drug intoxication to another.

Drug factors include the chemical composition of the drug, the quantity used, and the method of administration.

Marijuana has a very complex *chemical composition*. Some investigators feel that THC is the only active chemical of importance; others feel there may be other active chemicals or chemicals that, while not active in isolation, may modulate the effect of the THC. For marijuana use outside the laboratory, the possibility of significant adulteration exists. These adulterants may have no effect themselves, simply reducing the potency of the marijuana, or they may modify the intoxicated state, as when marijuana has been soaked in opium or LSD. Certain active adulterants are valued by some users, disliked by others. As users generally test samples of marijuana offered for sale, they often have an opportunity to reject marijuana with adulterants that produce undesirable effects.

Authoritative figures on the extent and type of adulteration of marijuana cannot be obtained, but most users feel it is usually rare for marijuana in the United States to be actively adulterated.[2] The more powerful psychedelics purchased illicitly, on the other hand, are usually significantly adulterated (Cheek, Newell, and Joffe, 1970).

The *quantity* of marijuana taken at a given time is important in determining effects, but not as important as we might expect. Experi-

---

[2]Ironically, users generally feel that increased government crackdowns on marijuana usually result in more adulteration as dealers attempt to pass off the poor quality marijuana then available as higher quality material.

enced users have a great deal of control over the effects (see Chapter 17), and can sometimes increase or decrease their level of intoxication at will.

An important consideration with respect to *quantity* and *method of administration* of the drug used at a particular time is whether the user himself has control of the method and quantity. Marijuana users typically smoke marijuana and control their level of intoxication as desired by the amount they smoke. Many users consider smoking the ideal method of administration for this reason. Eating marijuana usually requires about three times as much marijuana to reach a given level, takes effect more slowly, lasts longer, is more variable in effects, and is much more frequently associated with overdoses and unpleasant effects. For some users, eating marijuana or taking a capsule in the laboratory produces some anxiety in and of itself, because they know they will have less control of the level of intoxication.

Long-term factors affecting a particular period of intoxication include the culture (and subculture) of the user, his particular personality characteristics, his physiological characteristics, and the skills he has learned for controlling his intoxicated state in earlier drug use.

Cultural background is a very important factor about which little is precisely known. Attitudes toward various drugs vary tremendously from culture to culture, and this prevailing cultural climate may have a strong effect on the user. Classical Islamic culture, for instance, prohibits the use of alcohol but sanctions marijuana use. Our American culture as a whole believes marijuana produces undesirable and dangerous effects, and this knowledge may very well influence an individual user at times, in spite of subcultural support of marijuana smoking. In our culture, feelings of paranoia (e.g., fear that there may be a policeman watching) are frequent and normal, although experienced users generally treat them rather objectively rather than getting concerned about them in a maladaptive fashion.

Personality affects marijuana reactions. Users commonly believe, for example, that authoritarian people, who are not open to new ways of perceiving and thinking, either get no effects at all from smoking marijuana or have very unpleasant effects. They try to maintain their ordinary way of perceiving and thinking against the drug effects. There is a large psychological literature on the way in which personality factors affect reactions to a wide variety of psychoactive drugs other than marijuana.

Overall *physiological functioning* shows very similar patterns in healthy individuals; i.e., their bodily reactions to a given drug are similar enough to not be important. For some drugs and/or for some individuals, however, unique physiological factors might cause special reactions. I know of no solid information on this for marijuana, but it should be kept in mind as a potential source of variability.

Learned drug skills are particularly important in marijuana intoxication. A neophyte commonly must use marijuana several times before becoming aware of its effects; he must learn to recognize certain subtle effects that indicate he is intoxicated (see, e.g., Becker, 1953). With increasing experience and contact with other marijuana users, the neophyte learns of other effects that he may try to experience himself and of techniques for controlling his intoxication experience (see Chapter 17). He may learn to reproduce many of the usual effects of intoxication without actually using marijuana, as in "contact highs" (feeling intoxicated just by being with intoxicated companions) or "conditioned highs" (feeling intoxicated to some extent by the action of preparing to use marijuana).

Immediate user factors include several factors that assume particular values for hours to days before using a drug, such as mood, expectations as to what will happen, and desires for particular happenings.

Mood is particularly important with a drug like marijuana, as many users report the intoxicated state amplifies whatever mood they were in before taking the drug (see Chapter 16). If they were happy, they may become very happy; if they were sad, they may become particularly gloomy. An experimental study that picked student subjects just before exams, for example, might find that marijuana depressed people.

Mood interacts with *expectation*, the user's beliefs about what the drug can and will do to him. This, in turn, derives from what he has heard about the drug, the situation he will be in, and his own past experience.

The user's *desires* may or may not be congruent with his expectations; he may want to have insights about himself or find a new appreciation of beauty, but he may expect that the drug will not do this, or will make such an experience unlikely, given the circumstances.

The experiment or situation includes the immediate factors surrounding the taking of the drug, such as the physical setting and social interactions. In the experimental situation, both the formal instructions and the implicit demands given a subject can strongly influence the user-subject's reactions.

The *physical setting* in which the drug is taken can have important effects. If it is cheerful, warm, esthetically pleasing, it may help create a positive mood in the intoxicated state with consequent effects on a variety of other drug phenomena. If the physical setting is cold, sterile, or ugly, negative emotions may be amplified. Effects that only manifest if the user relaxes his control would not manifest in a setting that makes the user insecure. Experienced drug users may attempt to turn inward and ignore unpleasant aspects of the physical setting, with varying degrees of success.

Social events include all interactions with companions, experimenters, other subjects, and casual droppers-in. A major way of controlling marijuana intoxication is the direction of attention; interactions with others also direct attention, and this can have a major effect on what the user experiences and how he behaves. Strangers, people the user does not trust, manipulative people, and the like can produce strong negative, paranoid reactions. Warm, cheerful, enthusiastic, interested people have an opposite effect.

The *formal instructions* given in an experimental situation ("We are here in order to study X by doing Y") further shape the user-subject's expectations as to what will and should happen, provide norms for behavior, and a goal to be sought. All reports of experiments specify the formal instructions to the subjects; they are indispensable to understanding the results. Unfortunately, most experimental subjects now know that experimenters frequently lie to them or mislead them with instructions, implying that the subjects are dumb, unimportant, or untrustworthy. This does not make for an honest experimenter-subject relationship, and may encourage the subject in turn to lie or mislead the experimenter.

This brings us to the problem of the *implicit demands* of the experimenter, what Orne (1959, 1962) has called *demand characteristics* and Rosenthal (1966) has called the problem of *experimenter bias*. Briefly, when psychologists and psychiatrists began copying the methods of the physical sciences, they took up the idea of the *neutral observer*, whose presence did not itself affect the experiment. It is now clear, however, that an experimenter, in addition to his formal instructions, which are available for public assessment, makes all sorts of covert, implicit demands on his subjects to perform in a certain manner. These demands are *not* open to public examination and so cannot be fully evaluated for their effect on any given experiment. Particularly, the experimenter frequently has an a priori belief or hypothesis as to how an experiment *should* turn out, and this belief can be covertly communicated to the subjects. Since subjects are there to "help science," they often modify their behavior or experiences—unconsciously, semiconsciously, or consciously—to do the "right" thing (or the "wrong" thing if they are in a negative mood). I believe we shall see a major reformulation of the methods of the social and psychological sciences in the next decade as we realize that experimenters *interact* with subjects, that they are themselves one of the variables in the experiment, and that science is a *human* activity. The bases for this change are nicely summarized in Kuhn (1962), Lyons (1971), Maslow (1966), Polanyi (1958), and Rosenthal (1966).

Most of the scientific literature on LSD demonstrates the effect of experimenter bias. Researchers who believed that LSD was a "psychotomimetic" constantly reported psychotic-like reactions among their subjects. Researchers who believed LSD was mind-expanding or psychedelic saw these beliefs confirmed. Both groups were partially right. What they did not realize was that they had unconsciously acted in ways to make their beliefs come true. They both demonstrated *some* of the potential effects of LSD, but were mistaken in thinking they had demonstrated pure drug effects or invariant effects.

Selective Amplification, Inhibition, Interaction

None of the above factors affects the intoxicated state in isolation. Some may be important at one time, others unimportant. Users may choose to concentrate on some of these factors, amplifying their effect, or try to inhibit others, with varying degrees of success. Some of the factors may interact at a given time. A cold and sterile setting, an angry or unfriendly experimenter, and a poor mood on the subject's part can all combine to produce negative effects beyond the subject's ability to control.

The ranges and combinations of these important factors are enormous, which means that the variety of drug intoxication effects is correspondingly large. We know little about exactly *how* important some of these are, or *how* they interact. Some *extreme* values of these factors, however, do produce known effects.

For example, suppose we wanted to know how to produce a pleasant marijuana experience or an unpleasant one. Table 2-1 summarizes some extreme values of controlling factors that will maximize the probability of a "good trip" or a "bad trip." If all the controlling factors take one or the other of the extreme values, success in manifesting the potential effects that constitute a "good" or "bad" trip is highly likely. If some factors take on "good trip" values and others "bad trip" values, the outcome is uncertain.

Feedback Modification of Intoxication

It should be stressed that the user is not a passive object to which a certain configuration of controlling factors can be applied and, as a consequence, certain results will automatically manifest. The user is monitoring his own state of consciousness; he may deliberately seek to intensify the effects of certain factors and diminish those of others in order to obtain effects he considers desirable.

This applies both to specific effects and the level of intoxication. If a room is depressing, the (free) user will leave it. He may select music that will remind him of (and thereby induce) certain experiences, or he may seek out companions more intoxicated than himself in order to raise his level of intoxication by means of a "contact high" (see Chapter 17). The effects of all controlling factors are constantly subject to modification by the actions of the user.[3]

Variability over Time

Any or all of the above controlling factors may vary from one period of intoxication to the next, and many are likely to vary considerably over longer time periods. While long-term factors may generally stay relatively constant for a given user, they *can* change; as when the user associates with a new subculture. For example, many students who have used marijuana extensively get interested in meditation and, once associated with a formal meditative discipline, are often told that the "spiritual" experiences they have had with marijuana are unreal and diversionary, so that they no longer value such sorts of experience.

The increasing skill in control and wider range of possible effects as a drug user becomes more experienced are particularly important. A given user taking marijuana for the tenth time is, in many ways, a very different person from when he took it for the first time.

THE LEVEL OF INTOXICATION

In the previous discussion, we have treated marijuana intoxication as something that is simply present or absent; but, in fact, it may be present in various degrees, from the lowest degree possible for a user to recognize that he is intoxicated, up to the maximum level of intoxication he may obtain. Variation in level from time to time constitutes another source of variability, as well as being of interest in its own right.

In studying drug-induced states of consciousness, it is tempting to assume that the level of intoxication is specified by the dosage of the

---

[3]The great importance of the user's modification of his effects was strikingly (and humorously) demonstrated to me some years ago when, as a graduate student, I participated in an experimental study in which psilocybin (a psychedelic drug similar to LSD) was administered. I had to take a "symptom check list" type of test, sort a bunch of cards into true and false piles. Each card had a phenomenon on it, such as "I feel dizzy." As I started to sort these, it became clear that, by reading the card several times, I could make the effect manifest. So if I read a card that said, "My palms are sweating green sweat," I would decide that that would be interesting to experience, and, sure enough, in a few seconds I could see green sweat on my palms! If I read a negative effect, such as "I feel anxious and afraid," I would immediately toss that card in the false pile, and the effect wouldn't happen.

Table 2-1
Values of Variables for Maximizing Probability of "Good" or "Bad Trip"

	VARIABLES	GOOD TRIP LIKELY	BAD TRIP LIKELY
Drug	Quality	Pure, known.	Unknown drug or unknown degree of (harmful) adulterants.
	Quantity	Known accurately, adjusted to individual's desire.	Unknown, beyond individual's control.
Long-term factors	Culture	Acceptance, belief in benefits.	Rejection, belief in detrimental effects.
	Personality	Stable, open, secure.	Unstable, rigid, neurotic, or psychotic.
	Physiology	Healthy.	Specific adverse vulnerability to drug.
	Learned drug skills	Wide experience gained under supportive conditions.	Little or no experience or preparation, unpleasant past experience.
Immediate user factors	Mood	Happy, calm, relaxed, or euphoric.	Depressed, overexcited, repressing significant emotions.
	Expectations	Pleasure, insight, known eventualities.	Danger, harm, manipulation, unknown eventualities.
	Desires	General pleasure, specific user-accepted goals.	Aimlessness, (repressed) desires to harm or degrade self for secondary gains
Experiment or situation	Physical setting	Pleasant and esthetically interesting by user's standards.	Cold, impersonal, "medical," "psychiatric," "hospital," "scientific."
	Social events	Friendly, non-manipulative interactions overall.	Depersonalization or manipulation of the user, hostility overall
	Formal instructions	Clear, understandable, creating trust and purpose.	Ambiguous, dishonest, creating mistrust.
	Implicit demands	Congruent with explicit communications, supportive.	Contradict explicit communications and/or reinforce other negative variables.

drug, and this has been done in most laboratory studies. With respect to marijuana (and other psychedelic drugs), however, comments of users indicate that dosage is only an approximate, and sometimes quite fallible, guide to level of intoxication. Neophytes may ingest very large quantities of marijuana without feeling any effect. Experienced users generally report they can become very intoxicated on quantities of marijuana that are small compared to what they originally required. Further, not only will using the same amount of marijuana from the same supply result in different degrees of intoxication for a user at different times, many users have special techniques for raising or lowering their level of intoxication by psychological means.

Users commonly evaluate the potency of marijuana offered for sale by smoking a fixed quantity of it and rating the level of intoxication thereby attained. In the present study I formalized this procedure by asking users to rate, on the basis of their extensive experience, the *minimal* level of intoxication necessary to experience various intoxication effects. That is, certain effects may be experienced at all levels of intoxication, others in the moderate and high levels, others only at the high levels. The minimal-level model, then, assumes there is a threshold level of intoxication below which a certain effect cannot usually be experienced and above which it can be experienced (assuming other conditions are right for a potential effect). Once this minimal level is passed, the effect is potentially available at all higher levels. For example, slowing of time is practically never reported at very low levels of intoxication, but is usually reported at moderate and higher levels. This model is further discussed in Chapter 24.

The theoretical rationale for self-reporting of depth of an altered state of consciousness may be found in detail elsewhere (Tart, in press). Briefly, in the course of his marijuana use, a user finds that certain phenomena become available when using more marijuana and that the progression of phenomena with increasing dose follows a fairly regular sequence through most of the times he has become intoxicated. In the future he can then examine what is happening to him, survey the phenomena he can and can't experience, and estimate his degree of intoxication from this.[4] I have found this kind of self-estimation of level to be extremely useful in the study of hypnosis (Tart, 1970a), and Franken-

---

[4]For example, one of my informants, an engineer, reports that he can scale his level of intoxication on a ten-point scale by whether or not certain phenomena are available. He uses *zero* as non-intoxicated; *one* as a level where he feels a little different but nothing is clear enough for him to be sure he is intoxicated; *two* as the lowest degree of clear intoxication manifested by a full feeling in his head, clearer and more beautiful sounds, and calmness; *five* for the level where he first experiences time slowing down; *eight* for clear shortening of the memory span; and *ten* for the maximum level of intoxication, where he has large visual distortions and may begin to feel ill.

haeuser (1963) has found estimates of intoxication correlate very highly with dosage levels for nitrous oxide intoxication.[5]

STUDYING MARIJUANA INTOXICATION

In spite of all the sources of variability and uniqueness discussed above, we still commonly talk of marijuana intoxication as *a* state, implying that there is a relatively common pattern superimposed on the varied manifestations that result from using marijuana. Our present information as to what that pattern is, is very poor.

We presently have two sources[6] of information about marijuana. On the one hand, we have individual anecdotes of marijuana users. These are valuable but cannot be generalized very reliably. We don't know how much of what is reported is a product of marijuana intoxication and how much of the individual writer. On the other hand, we have clinical and laboratory experiments. These are as limited in applicability to the state of marijuana intoxication in general as are the anecdotal accounts, for the reasons detailed in the next section; the laboratory or clinic is an unusual constellation of conditions, which accentuates certain potential effects and inhibits others in a way that is atypical of the general use of marijuana.

The ideal study of the nature of marijuana intoxication should proceed in a number of stages. First, we must determine the *range* of effects; i.e., what are *all* the various effects supposedly associated with marijuana intoxication?

Second, since it is impractical to study everything at once, we must determine which of these effects in the total range are *important*. We may determine importance on theoretical grounds, which will vary with our own background and beliefs; or we may, somewhat more objectively, decide to study the frequent effects and let the rarer ones wait.

Third, we may set up controlled experiments to investigate each important effect in isolation. What causes it? How does it relate to dosage? Do different personality types experience it with important variations? Is it adaptive or nonadaptive for certain individuals?

---

[5]A simplifying assumption underlying the present study is that there is *one* state of consciousness, marijuana intoxication, common to all users and that it varies in a continuous fashion. It is possible that there are several states across individuals and/or that there may be qualitative alterations in patterns large enough to be called a different state of consciousness for a given individual (Tart, in press). The latter possibility cannot be properly investigated with the present data.

[6]The user has a third source of information, his own experiences, and may consider our other two sources quite secondary to this. If he is interested in understanding the nature of marijuana intoxication in a general sence, however, he should realize that his own experience is limited just as the other two sources are; namely, it is a selection from the total range of potential effects determined by his own personality characteristics and life situation.

Fourth, we may study the relationships between important effects. Must effect X always appear before effect Y? Does B inhibit A? Does investigator M always observe effects N, O, P and investigator Q always observe effects R, S, and T? Why?

Finally, all this knowledge may be put together for a general theoretical understanding of what marijuana intoxication is. As with any scientific theory, this understanding will then be judged on its informational usefulness (does it "make sense" and order the observations conveniently?) and its ability to predict further observations (i.e., if it orders all presently known facts elegantly and can't handle the next new fact, it's not very good).

In steps three and four, it is important to remember the restricting effects of the laboratory; i.e., the gain in precision of observation may be offset by the narrowing of the range of potential effects observed and the distortions caused by experimenter bias. However, if we know the range and importance in advance, from steps one and two, we can compensate for the restrictions of the laboratory to a great extent; we will be careful not to overgeneralize and misapply laboratory findings.

THE SCIENTIFIC LITERATURE ON MARIJUANA

There is a vast medical and scientific literature on marijuana, dating back over half a century. The reader interested in perusing this should consult Gamage and Zerkins' *A comprehensive guide to the English-language literature on cannabis* (1969).

It is traditional in a scientific book for the author to thoroughly review all other scientific literature on the subject. I shall not do this, for this literature represents work that is generally methodologically unsound, so no solid conclusions can be drawn from it.

Most of this literature rather uniformly attributes almost every human ill imaginable to marijuana intoxication. It is rather reminiscent of the medical literature on masturbation in the last century. As a first methodological warning sign, the intelligent reader might wonder why the practice of marijuana smoking is so widely indulged in if all its effects are negative?

More formally, let us consider the literature in two categories, the medical literature and the experimental literature.

The medical literature to date on marijuana consists primarily of clinical observations of patients identified as marijuana smokers by physicians treating them. Because marijuana was used before the patient came to the physician, marijuana is considered the cause of the disease. The logic of this is fallacious. Cause and effect cannot be established simply because one thing precedes another unless all other preceding events can be eliminated as possible causes. For example, various medical disorders prevalent among people of underdeveloped nations where marijuana smoking is widespread are attributed to its use. We could equally well reason that the medical conditions in underdeveloped nations lead to marijuana smoking, or that they have nothing to do with it. Thus practically all the medical literature on marijuana is useless, being moralizing under the guise of medicine.

This is a particularly regrettable situation. It seems a priori likely that prolonged use of any drug would have some effects on the body (good or bad), and we very much need factual medical knowledge of marijuana's effects.

The experimental literature on marijuana, with an occasional and notable exception, represents research carried out under a set of circumstances that are almost certain to produce results that have practically no applicability to the normal use of marijuana; i.e., they emphasize certain potential effects that are atypical of our society's normal use of the drug.

Some of the most notable atypicalities of the experimental research to date are as follows.

Control of the drug has been in the hands of the experimenter. The subject usually had to take one of a number of unknown substances in an unknown dosage. This can produce a good deal of anxiety and an intensified need for control and defense. As discussed earlier, marijuana users prefer to control their own level of intoxication. (User control of dosage could be allowed, even if it is somewhat less convenient for the experimenter.) Note also that subjects in many laboratory studies of marijuana have been given what are, judging by the effects reported in Chapter 11, overdoses, i.e., dosage levels they would not choose for themselves because of the probability of unpleasant symptoms and loss of control.

Physical setting has usually been a hospital or laboratory, typically ugly and impersonal. The social sciences generally, in their pursuit of "objectivity," have adopted cold and impersonal settings in order to gain it. In reality this gains a particular set of limiting conditions, not objectivity. Scientists are just beginning to become aware of how physical settings affect people (Sommer, 1969).

Social setting often paralleled the physical setting. Experimental personnel tended to be impersonal, evasive in answering questions, and manipulative of the subject. There were seldom the sort of people the experienced user would have chosen for companions. They were often typical of our culture in that they considered drug use "bad" or "sick."

Learned drug skills were typically non-existent in that *naïve* subjects were almost universally used because their reactions were supposedly "uncontaminated." Thus much of subjects' reactions in such experiments represented coping activities of naïve people under stress in an unknown situation. The effects of coping may have been much more prominent than many drug effects and may have been mistaken for them. Studying adaptation to drugs is fine and necessary *if* the experimenter realizes that that is what he is studying, a realization rare in the literature.

Implicit demands, difficult as they are for a reader of the literature to judge, often seem to have been negative in that "sick" or "maladaptive" reactions were expected. Aside from the unknown degree to which such demands might have been communicated by the verbal interaction of the experimenter with his subjects, such practices as keeping psychiatric attendants nearby, locking the subject in a room and keeping him under surveillance, and having subjects sign legal release forms prior to the experiment, seem sufficient to communicate strong expectations of adverse effects to subjects.

Orne and Scheibe (1964) carried out a classical study demonstrating that demand characteristics of sensory deprivation experiments might be responsible for many of the effects supposedly resulting from the "drastic" treatment of depriving a person of sensory stimulation for prolonged periods. Because the procedure in so many sensory deprivation experiments parallels that in laboratory studies of marijuana and other psychedelic drugs, it is worth reporting this study in some detail.

Two groups of normal male college students, naïve as to what sensory deprivation was about, took part in the experiment. The experimental group reported individually to the hospital where the experiment was to be held and were greeted by an experimenter dressed as a physician. The experimenter interviewed the subject about his medical history, including dizziness, fainting spells, and so forth. A tray of drugs and medical instruments, labeled "Emergency Tray," was clearly visible in the background. No reference was made to it unless a subject asked about it, in which case he was told that this was one of the precautionary measures taken for the experiment and that he had nothing to worry about.

Instructions for the four-hour experimental period, termed "sensory deprivation," were given. They included the fact that a physician was always available should anything untoward develop, and pointed out that if the subject couldn't take it, he could push a button, labeled "Emergency Alarm," to summon assistance.

The subject then had his blood pressure and pulse taken to further reinforce the "medical" atmosphere and was asked to sign a form that released the sponsoring organization, all affiliated organizations, and their personnel from legal consequences of the experiment.

The actual experimental treatment, spending four hours in a small, well-lighted, comfortably furnished room, had nothing to do with sensory deprivation. Except for the observation window through which the subject could be observed, it was essentially a normal room and all that happened to the subject was that there was no one to talk with for four hours.

A second group, the control subjects, were greeted by the same experimenter but he wore ordinary business clothes and acted in a less officious manner. There was no "Emergency Tray" in the interview room, nor was a medical history taken. The subject was told he was a control subject for sensory deprivation studies. The procedures typical of such studies were described to him, such as white noise on earphones, translucent goggles to block out all patterned vision, soft beds to reduce touch sensations, and rules prohibiting physical movement. There was no "Emergency Alarm" button in the experimental room.

Each control subject then spent four hours in the experimental room; experimental conditions were thus the same except for the demands.

Both groups were interviewed after the experimental period and given various psychological tests.

The experimental group showed a number of significant changes on the psychological tests typical of those found in sensory deprivation studies. Further, this group reported many more classical sensory deprivation effects than the control group, including more perceptual aberrations, feelings of intellectual dulling, unpleasant emotions, spatial disorientation, and restlessness. Thus many of the effects commonly attributed to a "powerful" treatment, sensory deprivation, can be obtained by the implicit demands in experimental instructions.

I fear that the reader who is not himself a physician or psychologist (i.e., who accepts such experimental conditions as "normal") will find the above description of experimental conditions rather ludicrous. How can we expect to find anything but unpleasant and unusual reactions under such circumstances? I regret to say that such conditions have been standard for almost all the research that has been done on marijuana intoxication or studies of other psychedelic drugs.

Indeed, practically all the conditions outlined in Table 2-1 as maximizing the probability of a "bad trip" are standard conditions in laboratory studies of marijuana. This was not a result of deliberate malice on the part of earlier investigators, of course, but stemmed from inadequate knowledge of the importance of non-drug factors and from the pervasive belief in "pure" drug effects.

Future experimental studies of marijuana intoxication should note the importance of the many controlling factors discussed above and report their values in particular studies. If this is done, we may begin to round out our overall picture of marijuana intoxication. Further, these controlling factors should be systematically varied. Different environments, varying from cold and sterile to warm and esthetically pleasing along various dimensions, can be tried. Experimenters and experimental personnel can be deliberately selected in terms of their personal attitudes toward drug use in order to assess how important this parameter is, and so on.

On a very practical note, political pressure is now very strong for scientists to produce better knowledge about the effects of marijuana in order to guide changes in legislation. If experimental results are to be socially relevant, priority must be given to studies carried out under conditions comparable to the ordinary use of marijuana today. Overdosing a naïve person under very stressful conditions is not very relevant to answering questions about the dangers of marijuana, for an overdose of multitudes of common substances under stressful conditions can produce adverse effects. Experimental research *can* be both valid and relevant. I hope it will be.

The previous scientific literature on marijuana intoxication, then, generally represents sets of conditions under which an extremely limited range of potential effects is likely to emerge. This set of potential effects is quite unrepresentative of the effects ordinarily associated with marijuana intoxication. The old research literature can be of some scientific value in detailing the effects of marijuana on people under conditions of high stress.

THE PRESENT STUDY

The present study is intended to begin to provide answers to the first, second, and fourth questions discussed earlier under the general question of how do we scientifically study marijuana intoxication. That is, it is intended to investigate: (1) the range of effects associated with marijuana intoxication under its usual conditions of use; (2) the importance of such effects in terms of which effects are frequent and which infrequent; and (3) the relationships of these effects to level of intoxication, to some important background factors, such as education, and the relationships of some of the effects to each other.

By asking experienced users to report on various intoxication effects in the course of their last six months' marijuana experience, all the various controlling factors, which determine potential effects, will have obtained most possible values many times, so the range can be determined.

By knowing these sorts of things about the ordinary use of marijuana, we may then estimate whether a given experimental study's results may be generalized to non-laboratory conditions, and, more importantly, we may plan future experimental studies from this base to be relevant to normal marijuana use.

Also, because of the lack of scientific information about the entire range of marijuana effects, the data of the present study provide a unique kind of information about the experiential effects of marijuana intoxication that cannot be obtained elsewhere. They are of considerable interest to the reader who simply wants to know "What do people experience when they use marijuana?" and to the marijuana user who would like to compare his experiences with those of others.

It should again be emphasized that the present study is itself limited; the marijuana users studied were mostly young college students or rather well-educated older users, and the results should not be glibly generalized beyond such groups. I hope that this study will serve as a stimulus to better and broader studies that will supersede it, both general studies and intensive laboratory research.

SUMMARY

Most psychological effects of psychoactive drugs such as marijuana are primarily *potential* effects; i.e., the drug action makes certain experiences and actions possible *if and only if* various non-drug factors are just right.

This means there is a tremendous range of experiences possible with marijuana, depending on conditions.

Previous experimental and medical studies of marijuana have been carried out under such an unusual and restrictive range of conditions that their results have little applicability to the ordinary use of marijuana in our culture today.

The present study, by inquiring about intoxication experiences of many experienced users over a long period, provides information on nearly the total range of potential effects, because the many controlling factors have varied over most possible configurations in that time.

This study thus provides basic data on the range of intoxication experiences, their relative frequency or rarity, their relationship to level of intoxication, and the effects of various background factors on them. This information provides an answer to the question "What is it like to be high on marijuana?" and provides experimental and psychological guidelines for making future experimental research more relevant and profitable.

Note that the method of the present study can provide valuable data on the *general* effects of marijuana intoxication in experienced users, but it is not suited to investigate questions about individual differences among users. Some users, for example, might experience primarily cognitive alterations while others might experience primarily sensory enhancements. Individual differences are an important topic for future study.

CHAPTER 3

Method of the Study

THE PRESENT STUDY had a variety of origins, all centered around my long term interest in altered states of consciousness. For several years I had read many anecdotal accounts of what it was like to be intoxicated on marijuana,[1] talked with many students and acquaintances (hereafter referred to as pilot subjects and informants) about what being intoxicated was like, and tried to do some theorizing that would make some sense and order out of the many phenomena reported. What little sense I have been able to make out of things in terms of theorizing has been presented in Chapter 2. This theorizing also made it clear that a systematic look at the overall phenomenology of altered states of consciousness was vital. The present study is an initial systematic look for one state of consciousness, marijuana intoxication.

For several years I took systematic notes on various phenomena reported for marijuana intoxication, and, based on these, a large questionnaire was made up. The questionnaire used the current language of marijuana users ("heads") as much as possible. It was distributed with a covering letter that was intended to be friendly and to induce cooperation among users both in filling out the questionnaire and in passing questionnaires along to other users. The text of the letter is given below.

To: ANYONE WHO HAS SMOKED MARIJUANA
    MORE THAN A DOZEN TIMES

I usually start a letter with "Dear So-and-so," but somehow greetings like "Dear Marijuana Smoker," "Dear Head," "To whom it may concern," or anything else like that sound pretty bad, so I'm skipping the greeting and getting right down to the point.

One of my main research interests as a psychologist is the area of altered states of consciousness. I am particularly interested in investigating the psycho-

---

[1]Well-written anecdotal accounts may be found in Andrews and Vinkenoog (1967), Anonymous (1969), Bloomquist (1968), de Ropp (1967), Ebin (1961), Goode (1969), Hollander (1967), Rosevear (1967), Simmons (1967), and Solomon (1966).

logical effects of marijuana, both for their intrinsic interest and for comparison with other altered states of consciousness. Reading the (scant) scientific literature on marijuana is disappointing, for most everything is on the order of, "Gee whiz, I smoked (or ate) grass, and I saw all sorts of pretty pictures which can't be described, and gee whiz, etc., etc., etc." That's very nice for a start, but not very specific!

From preliminary talks with people who smoke marijuana, it is obvious that there are many and varied effects, and that it would be of great psychological interest to know what they are. Scientists, as a whole, know practically nothing about the experience of smoking marijuana. You do. The ideal way to expand our knowledge about these effects would be to have people smoke it under a variety of conditions, with known amounts and qualities of grass, and then report on it. Even a rudimentary knowledge of the legal situation, though, tells you genuine laboratory research on marijuana is virtually impossible.

So I'd like to enlist your help as an expert; you've been there and, I hope, you would like to see us really know something about marijuana experiences on a scientific level, instead of just an anecdotal level. Enclosed is a questionnaire. It has a few basic questions about how much you've used marijuana, other drug experiences, and so on, to get a little background. Then the main part consists of over two hundred statements about possible experiences during the marijuana high that have been selected from preliminary surveys. I would like you to fill out the questionnaire and rate each of the described experiences in terms of how frequently it happens to you and how stoned you have to be to experience it. This is explained more fully in the questionnaire.

If you will help by carefully filling in this questionnaire and by passing more of these questionnaires on to other heads, what will you accomplish? The following kinds of questions can be answered from analyzing this data. What sorts of experiences occur when stoned, with what frequency? How are they related to how stoned you are? What kinds of differences are there between individuals? Are there several different patterns of going up, or does everybody go up the same way? How is the marijuana experience related to experience with other drugs? How is it related to how long people have been smoking? Are there certain more basic factors that account for a lot of the specific experiences? And many other things.

O.K., I'm going to learn a lot, and so will the scientific community when the results are published. What will *you* learn? The same thing. I don't like the kind of research (of which there is too much today) where the all-knowing scientist manipulates his stupid subjects. You're acting as the expert, the explorer, and you should be able to learn a lot for your trouble in helping me. Now, I can't get your name and mail you anything (that would run the paranoia level too high!), but it is common practice in science to send reprints of research results to anyone who requests them. If you will drop me a card in about a year (it takes that long to analyze everything and get it published), I will send you a copy of the results. No need to be paranoid on that, as I will get lots of reprint requests from people who have nothing to do with this study.

While we're on the subject of paranoia: you are able to help in this study on the basis of your *past* experience. I am *not* advocating that anyone smoke marijuana or do anything illegal in order to be able to fill out this questionnaire, but naturally you don't want to put your name on it! Note also that it is not illegal to fill out a questionnaire. The questionnaire comes with a stamped, return envelope so you can return it to me anonymously. The data from the questionnaires will be punched on IBM cards, and the original questionnaires destroyed as soon as possible.

The way these questionnaires are being distributed also insures your anonymity. I don't know any marijuana smokers by name, so I am simply putting these questionnaires out in places where marijuana smokers may have a chance to pick them up, and just handing them to people who might or might not know smokers, until this finally reaches you, with me having no idea of the route. In turn, please take as many questionnaires from whatever source you get this as you think you can pass on to other marijuana smokers. The more returns I can get, the more revealing this research will be.

I'm asking for about an hour or two of your time. In return, you will eventually know a lot more about the psychological effects of marijuana, and the scientific community will learn even more (considering the starting level); hopefully this knowledge will eventually result in more rational attitudes toward marijuana use.

If you can't fill this out, through lack of time or experience, please pass this material and any other sets of it you have along to someone who can.

Many thanks!

Sincerely yours,

CHARLES T. TART, PH.D.

Because most users experience a variety of intoxication phenomena by the third or fourth time they use marijuana, I selected the cutoff of a dozen uses to define an "experienced" user. As noted in Chapter 4, all the users who returned the questionnaire were far above this minimal cutoff.

THE QUESTIONNAIRE

The questionnaire consisted of three parts: (1) instructions; (2) background information questions (reported on in Chapters 4 and 5) covering such things as age, sex, occupation, education, history of drug use, and so forth; and (3) 220 descriptions of effects the users might have experienced. (The questionnaire is reproduced in full in Appendix B.)

Instructions for Filling Out the Questionnaire

The following instructions were attached to each questionnaire:

Do *not* put your name on this questionnaire or otherwise identify yourself.

The first two pages of the questionnaire are self-explanatory questions about your background, how much you've used pot, and your experiences with other drugs.

The rest of the questionnaire consists of statements describing a wide variety of experiences people have reported having while stoned. These descriptive statements have been taken from a wide variety of different people's accounts, and it is unlikely that any single person has experienced all of the things described.

The statements are grouped into categories, such as Vision Effects, Hearing Effects, changes in Space-Time Perception, and so on. Some descriptive statements are relevant to more than one such category, but they are only listed under one, in order to keep this questionnaire as short as possible.

Each statement describes a particular kind of experience, for example, "I can see more subtle shades of color." The sense of each statement is that whatever effect is described, it is considerably stronger or somehow different when stoned than if you were experiencing it straight. That is, some of the things described can be experienced to some degree when straight but are reported to be much more intense or different when stoned. Even if the statement does not include the phrase "than when straight," this comparison is implicit in all the statements.

For each descriptive statement, you are to make two ratings.

The first is how frequently you have experienced that particular effect when stoned, judging against all the times you have been stoned in the last six months.[2] Circle the answer category that most closely describes how often you experience that effect. The categories, reproduced under each description, are:

Never = you have never experienced this effect.

Rarely = you've experienced it at least once, but it's not at all frequent.

Sometimes = you experience it between about 10 percent and 40 percent of the time.

Very Often = you experience it more than about 40 percent of the time.

Usually = if you experience it practically every time you get stoned.

These rating categories are approximate, so while you should use your best judgment you need not try to count over all your experiences!

The second rating to make for each descriptive statement is one of *how* stoned you have to be to experience it (if you have experienced it at all; if you haven't, don't rate this for that statement). That is, there is an assumption that some sorts of things can be experienced if you're just a little stoned, while other things can't be experienced unless you're very stoned. There is a minimal degree of "stonedness" that you have to be at to experience a particular effect. The "How Stoned?" scale under each descriptive statement runs from Just, which is the smallest degree to which you could be stoned and *know* that you were

---

[2]The experience of the last six months is used rather than *all* your experience to cut down inaccuracies due to memories' fading. It may be that there are changes in how frequently you experience various things as you get more experience in being stoned, but this can be analyzed for in comparing the responses of new heads and old heads. If, however, you haven't been stoned very much in the past six months, use *all* your experiences for estimating frequencies.

stoned, to Maximum, which is the most stoned you've ever been after smoking a lot of high quality pot.

It is possible to think about the "How Stoned" rating as relating to the amount of pot you smoke (or eat), but this is only a rough parallel because of the variations in the quality of pot. Thus this rating scale is defined in terms of your own perception of how stoned you have to be to experience the described effect, and you are asked to make five discriminations of your degree of stonedness, with Just and Maximum at the low and high ends of the scale, and Fairly, Strongly, and Very Strongly as intermediate points.

To take an example, the first descriptive statement is, "I can see new colors or more subtle shades of color than when I'm straight." You might have this happen to you about half the times you get stoned (ignoring for the moment *how* stoned you are over all these times in the last six months), so you would circle the Very Often category. Then, thinking about how stoned you have to be to experience it, you might feel that it doesn't happen to you unless you're very stoned, so you'd circle the Very Strongly category. Thus you would be saying that you can't experience (or haven't experienced) this when you've been just stoned, or fairly stoned, or even when strongly stoned; but when you're very strongly stoned or maximally stoned you can experience the change in color perception.

It may be that you've experienced a particular effect at several degrees of "stonedness," but what you're rating here is the *minimal* level of stonedness you must be to experience it.

There is one other category on the "How Stoned" scale, marked LSD. You are to circle this category *only* if you have experienced that effect after having taken one of the very powerful psychedelic drugs like LSD, DMT, DET, mescaline, peyote, psilocybin, or STP. Thus there will probably be a number of things described that you've never experienced with pot but have with one of the more powerful psychedelics (if you've had any of the more powerful psychedelics).

There are a few questions where the two scales "Frequency" and "How Stoned" don't apply, and space is left for a descriptive answer.

There are a number of experiences that occur when stoned for which the opposite also occurs frequently; e.g., sometimes colors may be more intense and sometimes they may be duller. A bracket has been put in the left-hand margin whenever two questions are linked this way. Thus, you might find colors get brighter sometimes at a minimal degree of Very Stoned, and also that colors get duller frequently at a minimal degree of Just.

Finally, space has been left at the end for you to describe any effects you get from being stoned that haven't been mentioned in this questionnaire. In making up this questionnaire it was attempted to mention *everything* that people may have written about as happening while stoned, but some things have undoubtedly been missed, so this is your chance to complete the list!

Please rate the statements as accurately as you can. Whenever you feel that the way the statement is phrased doesn't quite fit your experiences, feel free to write in an explanation. If a statement makes no sense at all to you, put a ? beside it and skip it. It is understood that many of the experiences of being stoned are difficult to express in words!

Answer this questionnaire while straight, and when it is complete, seal it in the attached return envelope (do *not* put a return address on it!) and mail. The envelope is already addressed and stamped.

It is so commonplace and trite on psychological questionnaires to say "Thank you" that I hesitate to say it, but I really do appreciate your filling this out!

Possible Effect Descriptions

Figure 3-1 shows part of the first page of the actual questionnaire. Each possible effect statement (referred to simply as "question" or "item" from now on) was presented in this way, with a few exceptions, described later.[3]

VISION SENSE:

1. I can see new colors or more subtle shades of color than when I'm straight.

Frequency?	Never	Rarely	Sometimes	Very Often	Usually	
How Stoned?	Just	Fairly	Strongly	Vy Strongly	Maximum	LSD

2. Colors get duller, not as vivid.

Frequency?	Never	Rarely	Sometimes	Very Often	Usually	
How Stoned?	Just	Fairly	Strongly	Vy Strongly	Maximum	LSD

3. There is a sensual quality to vision, as if I were somehow "touching" the objects or people I am looking at.

Frequency?	Never	Rarely	Sometimes	Very Often	Usually	
How Stoned?	Just	Fairly	Strongly	Vy Strongly	Maximum	LSD

4. When I look at *pictures* they may acquire an element of visual depth, a third-dimensional aspect that they don't have when straight.

Frequency?	Never	Rarely	Sometimes	Very Often	Usually	
How Stoned?	Just	Fairly	Strongly	Vy Strongly	Maximum	LSD

5. The world looks flat; it lacks the third dimension of depth.

Frequency?	Never	Rarely	Sometimes	Very Often	Usually	
How Stoned?	Just	Fairly	Strongly	Vy Strongly	Maximum	LSD

6. I see fringes of colored light around *people* (not objects), what people have called the "aura."

Frequency?	Never	Rarely	Sometimes	Very Often	Usually	
How Stoned?	Just	Fairly	Strongly	Vy Strongly	Maximum	LSD

7. I see fringes of colored light around *objects* (not people), what people have called the "aura."

Frequency?	Never	Rarely	Sometimes	Very Often	Usually	
How Stoned?	Just	Fairly	Strongly	Vy Strongly	Maximum	LSD

FIGURE 3-1. FORMAT OF THE QUESTIONNAIRE

---

[3]In retrospect, I believe I should have used a 7- or 10-point scale for frequency and intoxication levels, as I had forgotten the tendency of people to avoid extreme categories on any scale.

VALIDITY PROBLEMS

For the present study to produce valid, accurate information about the nature of marijuana intoxication, we must feel reasonably certain that the possible effect descriptions mean what they seem to mean and that the respondents answered without bias or error, i.e., that they were careful in giving their answers and did not deliberately distort their answers in any fashion.

In wording the possible effect descriptions, I compromised between using standard English and drug-culture argot. I used the latter only when it was clear, as "stoned" or "high" for intoxicated. I avoided other argot terms like "far out," which have come to be used so ambiguously as to be worthless for communication. Thus the possible effect descriptions generally seem clear as to what they mean. For those few which may be unfamiliar to non-drug users, I have included brief explanations and/or references at appropriate places in the text.

A second language difficulty is that there are a variety of effects that users insist cannot be put into words, even approximately. These have necessarily been left out of the present study.

What about careless answering, or deliberate bias in answering designed to create an overly favorable picture of intoxication?

Three steps were taken to reduce this problem. First, the sympathetic tone of the covering letter and instructions hopefully reduced the need for the users' justifying themselves. Second, my promise to get results back to them made accurate reporting favor the users' self-interest. Third, a validity scale, described in the next section, was used to eliminate overly careless or bizarre questionnaires from the analysis.

While eventual replication of the present results by others is the final test of validity, the above steps, plus my knowledge of marijuana intoxication acquired from pilot subjects and informants, gives me confidence that the present results are reasonably accurate.

Validity Scale

Fourteen of the 220 items constituted a validity scale. These were descriptions, scattered randomly through the questionnaire, of "possible effects" which I had never heard of or had heard of only extremely rarely, which seemed extremely unlikely to occur, and (one) which had been used in studies of hypnosis as a validity item (Orne, 1959).

No single improbable answer can necessarily disqualify a questionnaire, because the respondent may actually have experienced an improbable effect. The a priori decision was made to disqualify any questionnaire with six or more positive responses on the validity scale, as this would be an extremely improbable occurrence, warranting suspicion.

The 14 items of the validity scale, together with the percentages of the 150 final respondents[4] rating each frequency category, are shown in Table 3-1. The a priori rules for counting an answer as a point on the validity scale are indicated by the boxes around certain response categories for each item. For example, if a user answered item 26 by circling Very Often, it would count a point on the validity scale, but not if he circled Never, Rarely, or Sometimes.

For the 150 questionnaires used for analysis, the mean validity scale score was only 1.5, so the final group of users did not show a bizarre patterning of answers on this scale, and we may presume they were careful in filling out their questionnaires.

DISTRIBUTION OF QUESTIONNAIRES

Because of the severe legal penalties attached to the possession, use, or sale of marijuana it was important to assure the users' anonymity in order to get any returned questionnaires. The distribution technique consisted of my handing large stacks of questionnaires to students and acquaintances whom I thought might be marijuana smokers and/or who might have friends who were marijuana smokers, and asking them to keep passing them on to other users. This worked very well. Many times students walked into my office and asked for more to pass out. In this way I had no names of anyone and could not even tell if the people I thought were smokers actually filled out a questionnaire. Users who completed the questionnaire simply put it in the attached, stamped return envelope and mailed it to me.

Data Reduction

All properly filled out and acceptable questionnaires returned by a cut-off date several months after distribution were coded onto IBM cards and magnetic tape for later processing at the computer centers of the University of California at Davis and at Berkeley.

SUMMARY

A large questionnaire was constructed on the basis of readings and informal interviews with marijuana users. It was distributed, along with a sympathetic covering letter, in a fashion that ensured anonymity of the respondents. Only experienced marijuana users were asked to fill out and return the questionnaire.

---

[4]A number of returned questionnaires were rejected because of high validity scale scores or other reasons, as discussed in Chapter 4. Validity score data on rejected users are not included in Table 3-1.

For each of more than two hundred possible intoxication effects, the user was asked to rate how frequently he had experienced that effect in the last six months of use and the minimal degree of intoxication necessary to experience it.

TABLE 3-1

VALIDITY SCALE ITEMS

Q NO.	ITEM	PERCENTAGE OF USERS ANSWERING:[a]				
		Nvr	Rly	Smt	VyO	Uly
26	I have difficulty hearing things clearly, sounds are blurry and indistinct.	61%	23%	13%	1%	1%
42	I salivate quite a lot when stoned.	44%	30%	13%	5%	5%
54	Objects seem to tilt toward the left.	80%	10%	3%	1%	1%
57	The force of gravity seems to alternate between pushing me up and pushing me down.	56%	14%	17%	5%	5%
72	When there is any trembling in my body, the upper half of my body trembles much more than the lower half.	69%	7%	10%	5%	3%
87	My scalp itches a lot if I have smoked too much grass.	80%	13%	6%	1%	1%
97	My non-dominant hand (left if you're right-handed and vice versa) becomes partially paralyzed, unusable.	86%	9%	2%	1%	0%
102	I tremble a lot in my hands for a while *after* having been stoned.	71%	20%	7%	0%	1%
104	Smoking grass makes me cough hard while inhaling and holding my breath.	14%	42%	32%	9%	2%
132	My mind goes completely blank for long periods (15 minutes or more) even though I'm not asleep . . .	56%	27%	13%	2%	0%
166	I almost invariably feel bad when I turn on, regardless of how I felt before I turned on.	47%	36%	9%	1%	1%
180	I have lost control and been "taken over" by an outside force or will, which is hostile or evil in intent, for a while.	79%	14%	4%	0%	0%
181	I have lost control and been "taken over" by an outside force or will, which is good or divine, for a while.	63%	16%	9%	5%	1%
187	When stoned I lose most of my sense of ego identity and usually take on the identity of my like-sexed parent (father for males, mother for females).	79%	10%	7%	0%	1%

[a]A given row may not add to exactly 100% because of users' skipping that item and/or rounding errors. The scored direction for counting on the validity scale is given in the boxed responses.

CHAPTER 4

One Hundred and Fifty Experienced Marijuana Users

APPROXIMATELY 750 QUESTIONNAIRES were sent out. Of those returned by the cutoff date several months later, three were rejected because of high scores on the validity scale, as explained earlier, and several others were rejected because the respondent indicated that he had been intoxicated with marijuana *while* he was filling out the questionnaire. A number of partially completed questionnaires were also returned with notes that they were just too long for the user to complete. Verbal comments by students around campus also indicated that the primary reason they had not completed the questionnaire was its length. One hundred and fifty usable questionnaires were left. Thus the 150 respondent users are a verbal lot, sufficiently motivated to help science that they would fill out a lengthy questionnaire.

As the data below will indicate, this is primarily a young, student population. How representative it is of any other specific population is unknown.[1] As the primary purpose of the present study was to discover the major experiential effects of marijuana intoxication, to study the effects of some important background variables, and to specify the *range* of phenomena, rather than produce exact figures for a specified population, this lack of knowledge about the generality of the present sample is not a serious drawback. Again, however, the reader should be cautioned against overgeneralizing the exact figures presented later.

Some further comments should be made about generalization of the effects in this study to other populations. In terms of the model for drug intoxication effects presented earlier, it is clear that the intellectual level, social learnings and expectations, and values of a given population may strongly affect what they will experience during marijuana intoxication. The present sample is highly educated (in college

---

[1]It is my personal impression from informal and teaching contact with many students that the sample, while rather avant garde for 1968, would be fairly typical now. A Gallup poll taken as this book went to press reported that 42 percent of college students polled said they had used marijuana, compared with only 5 percent when the same question was asked in 1967 (see *Newsweek*, January 25, 1971, p. 52).

or already graduated) and intelligent, is coping successfully with modern American culture (by virtue of most being in college or holding down a job), and thus may be fairly representative of what Americans who have made a fair adaptation to the Establishment may experience when intoxicated with marijuana. It probably is poorly representative of what happens when slum dwellers, depressed minority groups, or people in different cultures use marijuana, or what happens when the mentally ill use marijuana. Remember, too, this is an experienced group, so the effects reported are not applicable to those who are just beginning to use marijuana.

IMPORTANT BACKGROUND VARIABLES

Area of Residence

The residential area of the users was determined by inspection of the postmark on the returned questionnaire. The users were from California for the most part (67 percent), some from the East Coast of the United States (11 percent), and the remainder from various miscellaneous or undetermined locations.

Age

Age was distributed as shown in Table 4-1. The vast majority of the users were in the 19–30 age range.

TABLE 4-1

AGE DISTRIBUTION

AGE RANGE	PERCENTAGE OF USERS
16 or younger	1%
17–18	10%
19–20	23%
21–22	22%
23–24	16%
25–30	15%
31–40	7%
41–50	5%
51 and older	1%

Occupation

Occupation was classified into six categories, shown in Table 4-2. The majority (67 percent) of the users were students, with academics and mental health professionals being the next largest classifications.

TABLE 4-2

OCCUPATION

OCCUPATION	PERCENTAGE OF USERS
Students	67%
Academics, Teachers	7%
Mental Health Professionals	6%
Professionals, other	5%
Non-professional	15%
Unclassifiable	1%

Note.—The percentages in this table do not add up to exactly 100% due to rounding errors and/or some users' skipping the question.

Sex, Marriage, Offspring

It was possible to identify 49 percent of the respondents as men and 27 percent as women. However, on a number of questionnaires in the first distributions, the blank for sex of the respondent had been inadvertently left off, so 23 percent of the users could not be classified. Of the whole group, 71 percent were single, 19 percent were married or living with a semi-permanent mate, 8 percent were divorced, and 1 percent were widowed. Most (81 percent) had no children.

Educational Level

Table 4-3 shows the educational level of the users. This is a highly educated group, the vast majority having at least some college training and 21 percent having some graduate education.

Political Affiliations

Table 4-4 presents the political affiliations of the users. Most indicated no affiliation or Democrat.

TABLE 4-3

EDUCATIONAL LEVEL

EDUCATIONAL LEVEL	PERCENTAGE OF USERS
High school	6%
College, 2 years or less	35%
College, 4 years or less	37%
MA degree or some graduate training	13%
PhD, EdD, or MD degree or graduate training beyond the MA level	8%
Unclassifiable	1%

TABLE 4-4

POLITICAL AFFILIATION

POLITICAL AFFILIATION	PERCENTAGE OF USERS
Democrat	24%
Republican	5%
Left-wing	5%
Right-wing	0%
Miscellaneous	23%
No political affiliation indicated	43%

Religious Affiliation

Religious affiliation is presented in Table 4-5. Most users did not give any affiliation. Of those who did, the psychedelic churches (i.e., those advocating the use of psychedelic drugs as part of their sacraments), such as Timothy Leary's League for Spiritual Discovery, and various Oriental religions, such as Subud, were almost as frequent as traditional affiliations.

Arrests

One question asked whether the users had ever been arrested and, if so, for what and whether they were convicted. Twenty-five users (17 percent) indicated they had been arrested, and the various offenses are summarized in Table 4-6.

TABLE 4-5

RELIGIOUS AFFILIATION

RELIGIOUS AFFILIATION	PERCENTAGE OF USERS
Protestant	11%
Catholic	4%
Jewish	11%
Oriental, mystical	5%
Psychedelic churches	7%
No affiliation	60%

TABLE 4-6

ENCOUNTERS WITH THE LAW

TYPE OF OFFENSE	NUMBER OF USERS	
	ARRESTED	CONVICTED
Political and Nuisance Offenses	6	3
Traffic Violations & Parking Tickets	5	4
Drunkenness or Illegal Possession of Alcohol	3	3
Miscellaneous Misdemeanors	4	1
Third-degree Burglary	1	0
Possession of Marijuana	5	2
Selling Marijuana	1	1

The category "Political and Nuisance Offenses" includes being arrested for participating in civil rights demonstrations, loitering, and trespassing.

Five of the users had been arrested for possession of marijuana, and one for selling marijuana.

All in all, the users are a generally law-abiding lot except for their use of marijuana.

Personal Growth

The users were asked, "*Do you regularly practice any sort of meditation or other non-drug discipline for spiritual or personal growth? If so, what?*" The responses are tabulated in Table 4-7. Irregular or non-disciplined practices labeled "meditation" or "contemplation" by the users were put in the "informal meditation" category here.

TABLE 4-7

GROWTH PRACTICES

DISCIPLINE	PERCENTAGE OF USERS
Informal meditation	16%
Formal meditation, oriental form	13%
Formal meditation, occidental form	3%
Conventional psychotherapy	2%
New therapies (encounter, Gestalt, etc.)	5%
Other disciplines	5%
None	57%

Note.—The percentages in this table do not add up to exactly 100% due to rounding errors and/or some users' skipping the question.

Marijuana Use

A number of questions dealt with the overall use of marijuana by the group. Responses to "*How long have you been smoking pot or hash?*" are presented in the first column of Table 4-8. Most of the users have smoked marijuana from one to two years, but some have used it for more than eleven years. If we take the midpoint of each category (assume fifteen years for the eleven-plus category), this group of users represents a total of 421 years of marijuana use.

The users were asked their average frequency of use in all the time they had used marijuana. Users with less than six months' experience were instructed to skip this question. Monthly or Weekly use are the modal patterns in this group, as shown in Table 4-9. By an approximation, described fully in Chapter 5, these figures may be combined with length-of-use figures to give an estimate that this group of 150 users has used marijuana approximately 37,000 times altogether.

Asked for their frequency of use in the preceding six months (the time base over which effects were to be rated), the users replied as shown in the second column of Table 4-9, with Monthly and Weekly use still being the modal responses. The Total and Last Six Month frequencies of use do not differ significantly from each other. The respondents use marijuana about as often now as they ever did.

Other Drugs

The users were asked how often they had used various major psychedelic drugs *before* starting to use marijuana, *after* starting to use mari-

TABLE 4-8

USE OF MARIJUANA AND ALCOHOL

LENGTH OF USE	MARIJUANA PERCENTAGE OF USERS	ALCOHOL PERCENTAGE OF USERS[a]
$\leq$ 6 months[b]	3%	3%
$\leq$ 1 year	21%	2%
$\leq$ 2 years	34%	7%
$\leq$ 3 years	19%	14%
$\leq$ 4 years	6%	11%
$\leq$ 5 years	4%	10%
6 to 10 years	5%	17%
11 years or longer	6%	21%
Never used alcohol		13%
No response	2%	3%

[a]The percentages in this column do not add up to exactly 100% due to rounding errors and/or some users' skipping the question(s).
[b]$\leq$ means less than or equal to.

TABLE 4-9

FREQUENCY OF USE OF MARIJUANA AND ALCOHOL

	MARIJUANA		ALCOHOL	
FREQUENCY OF USE	TOTAL PERCENTAGE OF USERS	LAST 6 MOS. PERCENTAGE OF USERS	TOTAL PERCENTAGE OF USERS	LAST 6 MOS. PERCENTAGE OF USERS
Occasionally	7%	11%	33%	40%
Once/month or more	35%	28%	34%	26%
Once/week or more	40%	42%	21%	12%
Almost every day or more	16%	19%	2%	7%
No response	3%	1%	11%	15%

Note.—The percentages in some columns of this table do not add up to exactly 100% due to rounding errors and/or some users' skipping the question(s).

juana, and during the last six months. Table 4-10 presents this data. The category "psychedelics" was presented on the questionnaire as including LSD, mescaline, peyote, psilocybin, DMT (dimethyltriptamine), and DET (diethyltriptamine). Other drugs are listed separately.

TABLE 4-10

FREQUENCY OF USE OF OTHER DRUGS

| | BEFORE USING MARIJUANA | | | AFTER USING MARIJUANA | | | IN LAST SIX MONTHS | | |
| | TIMES USED | | | TIMES USED | | | TIMES USED | | |
DRUG	0	1–5	6+	0	1–5	6+	0	1–5	6+
Psychedelics	76%	15%	3%	27%	38%	31%	51%	33%	11%
Exotic Psychedelics:									
STP (DOM)	49%	3%	0%	45%	7%	0%	45%	7%	0%
MDA	49%	3%	0%	46%	5%	1%	45%	7%	0%
PEACE	48%	3%	0%	46%	4%	1%	44%	6%	1%
Amphetamines or Methadrine									
(orally)	58%	8%	6%	35%	22%	15%	42%	15%	15%
(injection)	51%	3%	0%	47%	4%	3%	50%	3%	0%
Hard Narcotics	30%	1%	1%	25%	5%	3%	25%	7%	0%

Note.—The percentages in this table do not add up to exactly 100% due to rounding errors and/or some users' skipping the question(s).

With chi-square analyses of the distributions, the respondents have used major psychedelic drugs and oral amphetamines[2] more frequently since starting to use marijuana ($p < .001$ for each comparison). Contrary to popular myth, use of hard narcotics is quite low and does not show a statistically significant increase from before to after marijuana use.

Psychedelic Drugs and Marijuana

The users were asked, "*Do you think your experiences (if any) with any of these other psychedelic drugs have affected or changed the quality of your experiences with pot? If yes, how?*" Twenty-eight percent of the users replied that there had been no change in their marijuana experiences as a result of taking other drugs, 26 percent that normal marijuana phenomena were more vivid or could be experienced more easily, 12 percent that new experiences were possible on marijuana that were not available before, and 3 percent that their marijuana experiences were not as satisfactory or enjoyable any longer. Differences in marijuana effects between users and non-users of psychedelic drugs will be investigated in detail in later chapters.

---

[2]In retrospect, asking about oral amphetamines was poorly done, as the question does not distinguish the typical college student who uses low doses to help himself study from the high-dose user who wishes to radically alter his state of consciousness.

Marijuana and Alcohol

The 150 users were asked, for comparison purposes, *"How long have you been drinking alcoholic beverages in sufficient quantity to change your consciousness (i.e., drinking to get 'tipsy' or drunk rather than just having a little wine or beer with meals for the taste)?"* The second column of Table 4-8 presents their replies. The respondents have clearly been using alcohol to alter their state of consciousness much longer than marijuana (*p* < .001), a difference that may represent desirability, but more likely represents the easier availability of alcohol to young people at the time the respondents were growing up.

The users were also asked about their frequency of use of alcohol for changing their state of consciousness, and this data is presented in the third and fourth columns of Table 4-9. For both total use and usage in the last six months, marijuana has been used more frequently (*p* < .001 in each case).

To further investigate feelings of preference for marijuana and alcohol for altering consciousness, the users were asked, *"If pot were as available legally as alcohol, about what percentage of the time would you choose alcohol to alter your state of consciousness rather than pot?"* Table 4-11 shows that the users generally would choose marijuana in a free-choice situation. Supporting this is a suggestive tendency (*p* < .10) for the respondents to be using alcohol less frequently in the last six months than in their total alcohol-drinking career.

TABLE 4-11

USE OF ALCOHOL RATHER THAN MARIJUANA

PERCENT OF TIMES ALCOHOL WOULD BE CHOSEN RATHER THAN MARIJUANA	PERCENTAGE OF USERS
0%, Never	43%
≤ 25%	37%
≤ 50%	13%
≤ 75%	2%
≤ 100%	3%

Note.—The percentages in this table do not add up to exactly 100% due to rounding errors and/or some users' skipping the question.

SUMMARY

In general, we may describe our 150 users as a predominantly young, highly educated group of California college students, with a high interest in self-improvement (meditation or therapy), considerable experience with other psychedelic drugs, and little experience with narcotics. Most of them used marijuana once a week or more during the six-month period covered by this study.

CHAPTER **5**

Methods of Analysis

ALL OF THE CHAPTERS in Part II, Phenomenology of Marijuana Intoxication, are organized along the same general plan, for the convenience of the reader. I shall outline the basic plan, give definitions of terms, and present descriptions of methods here.

BASIC PLAN

General Format

Each chapter consists of the results of potential effect descriptions (questions, items) dealing with a single area, such as vision, thought processes, etc. Within each chapter are subgroupings of related questions.

For each question I have given: (1) the actual wording used in the questionnaire; (2) the percentage[1] of users responding in each of the frequency of occurrence and minimal level of intoxication categories; and (3) differences in the effect related to the background variables when such differences were statistically significant.

When the wording of a question does not completely explain the nature of the effect, I have added explanatory comments, based on my interviews with pilot subjects and informants. Many effects deal with areas of knowledge that are not generally well known even among scientists, such as those concerning meditation or ostensible paranormal phenomena, so I have given literature references to guide the reader seeking more understanding. I have tried to avoid speculation and interpretation as much as possible and to stick to the basic findings.

Each chapter also contains a section on additional effects, a ranking of effects according to increasing minimal levels of intoxication, a sum-

---

[1]I have generally used percentages rather than actual numbers for clarity of presentation. All statistical tests, however, were performed on the raw data to avoid the slight rounding errors involved in using percentages.

mary of background factors modulating the effects, and a general summary.

Terminology

It is impossible to write about these phenomena in a readable style without using descriptive adjectives. To avoid the ambiguity usually inherent in quantity adjectives, I have used a standard set of them, which are defined in Table 5-1. Whenever other adjectives than those defined are used, I am speaking generally rather than describing the exact form of the data.

To illustrate: if an intoxication effect is described as "very characteristic" and "primarily beginning to occur at Moderate levels," this

TABLE 5-1

DEFINITION OF TERMS

TERM	DEFINITION
Frequency of Occurrence Terms	
"Rare"	$\geq 75\%$ indicate *Never, Rarely*
"Infrequent"	$\geq 50\%$ indicate *Never, Rarely*
"Fairly Frequent"	$\leq 50\%$ indicate *Sometimes, Very Often, Usually*[a]
"Common"	$\geq 50\%$ indicate *Sometimes, Very Often, Usually*
"Very Common"	$\geq 75\%$ indicate *Sometimes, Very Often, Usually*
"Characteristic"	50% indicate *Very Often, Usually*
"Characteristic"	Bottom third of distribution
"More" ⎱ Characteristic" "Very" ⎰	Middle third of distribution
"Most" ⎱ Characteristic" "Extremely" ⎰	Top third of distribution
Levels of Intoxication Terms	
"Low"	Questionnaire term *Just*
"Moderate"	Questionnaire term *Fairly*
"Strong"	Questionnaire term *Strongly*
"Very Strong" ⎱ "Very High" "Maximum" ⎰	Questionnaire term *Very Strongly* Questionnaire term *Maximum*

[a]*Infrequent* and *Fairly Frequent* are not always identical in practice because of variable numbers of users' skipping particular questions.

indicates that more than 50 percent of the users rated this effect as occurring Very Often or Usually when they have been intoxicated in the last six months, and my judgment of the distribution of responses on minimal levels of intoxication is that the Moderate ("Fairly Stoned") level is the most representative[2] level indicated.

Linking

Many pairs or sets of question called for statistical comparison because of obvious similarity or because they described converse effects. This was always done by a chi-square test of the distributions. I have usually presented graphical results when they would be illustrative, as well as the probability figures.

Many other links exist that I have not analyzed in the text. The reader interested in particular comparisons may perform such analyses himself from the percentage data presented for each item. Only slight errors will result from using percentages rather than the raw data I worked from.

Background Variables

The background information on the first page of the questionnaire was used to divide the users into a number of groups, and every question was subjected to a chi-square analysis for differences in the distributions among the groups. Only significant ($p < .05$) differences are presented in the text.

The groups compared were as follows:

Males versus *females*. Forty-nine percent of the users were men, 27 percent women. The remainder were not used in male-female comparisons because this question was inadvertently left off some of the questionnaires.

Older and *younger* users were defined as those 25 years of age or older versus those from 16 to 24.

Educational Level was compared for the *College-educated* (at least some college up to and including bachelor's degree or equivalent) versus the *Professionals* (graduate training or master's or doctor's degrees). The users with only a high school education were too few (6 percent) to constitute a group for valid analysis and so were omitted from the educational level comparison.

---

[2]While it would have been possible to assign the intoxication levels the values of 0, 1, 2, 3, and 4 and use the arithmetic mean as the average value, I did not want to make the questionable assumption of equal intervals between categories. Also, many of the distributions were highly skewed, so I would judge the most representative intoxication level as half-way between two of the defined levels. In practice, a correlation between my judgments and arithmetic means would be extremely high.

Frequency of use of marijuana in the last six months was broken into three groups: the *Occasional* user ("occasional" or "less than once/month" on the questionnaire), the *Weekly* user ("once/week or more"), and the *Daily* user ("almost every day or more"). With a three-way classification, it was found that some of the frequency and intoxication level categories had to be combined to avoid having too many cells with low expected frequencies for the chi-square tests,[3] so all analyses with three-way classifications were done against frequencies of Never, Rarely/Sometimes, and Very Often/Usually. Similarly, levels were uniformly condensed into Just, Fairly/Strongly, and Very Strongly/Maximum.

Because a given degree of marijuana use in the last six months might mean different things for one user who had followed that pattern for ten years and for another who had used it for just one year, a three-way analysis was also made for *total marijuana use*. Categories were *Heavy Total* users, *Moderate Total* users, and *Light Total* users. These categories were obtained in the following way. Using the number of uses per month as a basic unit, the self-rated frequency of use over the user's whole use-history was assigned the value of 20/month ("almost every day or more"), 8/month ("once/week or more") or 2/month ("once/month or more" plus "occasionally"). Total length of time in years that the users had used marijuana was weighted as 1 for one year or less, 2.25 for three years or less, and 6 for more than three years.

The combinations of these weightings are shown in Table 5-2. They fell into three natural groupings, which were designated the Heavy (21 percent of the users), Moderate (44 percent), and Light (32 percent) Total users. A few users did not provide enough information to be classified.

Users and *Non-users of Psychedelics* were classified on the basis of whether they had *ever* used LSD, mescaline, peyote, psilocybin, dimethyltriptamine (DMT), diethyltriptamine (DET), STP (2, 5-dimethoxy-4-methylamphetamine), MDA (3, 4-methylene dioxy-amphetamine) or PEACE (a supposedly psychedelic drug of unknown composition). Seventy-two percent of the users had tried at least one of these powerful psychedelic drugs at least once.

---

[3]The technical question of how many cells in a chi-square table can have expected frequencies below a certain value is still hotly debated in the psychological literature. Rather than arbitrarily combine the data on every question in ways to eliminate low expected values, I have used the uniform rules above, plus the rule, used only rarely, that in any chi-square table with more than four cells having expected frequencies of less than five I would combine whichever end category eliminated the largest number of low cells with the adjacent category, i.e., Never or Just with Rarely or Fairly, etc. If this was not sufficient, the analysis was thrown out. Allowing as many as four cells to have low expected values is a fairly liberal position, but seemed appropriate in an initial exploration of an important area.

TABLE 5-2

DIVISION FOR TOTAL MARIJUANA USE:

WEIGHTING FACTORS

FREQUENCY OF USING MARIJUANA IN TOTAL USE PERIOD	LENGTH OF TIME MARIJUANA HAS BEEN USED		
	ONE YEAR OR LESS	THREE YEARS OR LESS	FOUR OR MORE YEARS
Almost every day	20	45	120
			Heavy Total Use
Once a week or more	8	18	48
Once a month or more or occasionally	2	4.5	12
		Light Total Use	

The final background analysis, dealing with commitment to personal growth, divided the users into *Meditators*, the *Therapy and Growth Group*, and *Ordinary Users*. Meditators were so classified if they indicated that they *regularly* practiced some form of meditation. They comprised 16 percent of the users. The Therapy and Growth group were those who indicated they had been in regular psychotherapy (2 percent) or the new growth-oriented therapies (5 percent), such as Gestalt therapy (Perls, Hefferline, & Goodman, 1951) or encounter groups (Schutz, 1967). Ordinary users may have tried meditation exercises or the like occasionally, but did not indicate any regular, systematic approach to personal growth as the other two groups did.

Additional Effects

This section includes any further phenomena, volunteered by the users at the end of the questionnaire, that were not already covered in one of the regular questions. These have not been included in any tabulations or analyses, and are added in each chapter to further indicate the *range* of effects.

Levels of Intoxication

Except when there are too few effects of a given type to warrant it, each chapter has all the effects discussed ordered by the representative minimal level of intoxication. Categories are the five divisions of level of the questionnaire (Just, Fairly, Strongly, Very Strongly, Maximum) and levels halfway between these. Relevant effects from other chapters also appear in the graphs.

Within each level, effects are ordered in terms of the arithmetic mean of the intoxication levels reported, from lowest at the bottom to highest at the top. *Within* a level, chi-square tests of the distributions practically never reach significance. Overall differences in levels for the phenomena of a particular chapter were tested by a chi-square test using the lowest level (by arithmetic mean) effect within each level category as the entry for that level. They were usually extremely significant.

Variations in type style are also used in these graphs to indicate the frequency of occurrence of an effect. Characteristic phenomena are in bold capital letters, common are in bold lower case, infrequent (fairly frequent is combined with infrequent here) in small capitals, and rare phenomena are set in capitals with lower case letters. Thus if one wants to know what is very likely to happen at various levels for a given category of phenomena, one can look only at the characteristic or common effects (in boldface). If one wants to flesh this out with what may also happen if psychological factors assume the correct values, all the phenomena may be looked at.

I have occasionally inserted question marks after particular phenomena on the graphs, indicating that comments of informants raise some doubts as to its fitting into the minimal level model, i.e., it may cease to be available after some higher level.

Modulating Factors

Each chapter contains a table summarizing the effects of all significant background factors. I have combined the categories of frequency of use of marijuana in the last six months, total marijuana use, and psychedelic drug use into a single category of *more drug experience* for convenience here. The reader who needs these separated can go back to the original item descriptions in the text.

Almost all background variables had relatively linear effects. Where they did not, the text in this section mentions the fact, and they are not included in the table.

Statistical Notes

In addition to the various statistical considerations mentioned above, it should be realized that about 5 percent of the significant differences reported herein are due only to chance, i.e., are not really reflecting a genuine effect. In the many thousands of comparisons made in this large mass of data, 5 percent will come out at the .05 level of probability by chance alone. I debated on whether to try to eliminate these false positives, but the only way would be by the criterion of whether the differences "made sense" to me. Rather than impose my judgment on the data, I have let it stand. As the main purpose of this study is to stimulate research rather than provide final answers on the nature of marijuana intoxication, these occasional false positives will be weeded out by lack of confirmation in future studies.

PART II

PHENOMENOLOGY OF MARIJUANA INTOXICATION

CHAPTER 6

Vision

MAN IS PRIMARILY a visual animal, both in terms of vision's being his primary and generally most efficient way of perceiving his environment, and in terms of visual styles' influencing his thinking, imagining, and conceptualizing. Changes in visual experience while intoxicated on marijuana are thus of particular interest. We shall first consider phenomena related to visual perception of the external world, then those related to visual imagery and hallucinations.

PERCEIVING THE EXTERNAL WORLD

Form and Organization

A very characteristic effect of marijuana intoxication is increased perceptual organization ("meaningfulness"): "*I can see patterns, forms, figures, meaningful designs in visual material that does not have any particular form when I'm straight, that is just a meaningless series of shapes or lines when I'm straight*" (6%, 6%, 29%, 37%, 19%).[1] The modal minimal level of intoxication for this is Strongly (3%, 25%, 37%, 17%, 5%). The College-educated experience this more frequently than the Professionals ($p < .05$).

A common effect that also reflects this increased perceptual organization of the visual field is "*Things seen are seen more sharply in that their edges, contours stand out more sharply against the background*" (13%, 13%, 31%, 30%, 11%). The contrary effect, "*My vision tends to be somewhat blurry; if I try to examine something visually, I can't focus as sharply as when straight*" (32%, 29%, 25%, 9%, 3%) occurs much less frequently ($p < .001$), as shown in Figure 6-1. Blurriness of vision is associated with higher levels of intoxication (1%, 13%, 18%, 21%, 11%) than sharpening (6%, 41%, 24%, 10%, 2%), as shown in the figure ($p < .001$).

---

[1] For all items, frequency of occurrence data is always presented in the order Never, Rarely, Sometimes, Very Often, Usually, and intoxication level data in the order Just, Fairly, Strongly, Very Strongly, Maximum. These will not always add up to 100 percent because of variable numbers of respondents' skipping various questions and/or rounding errors.

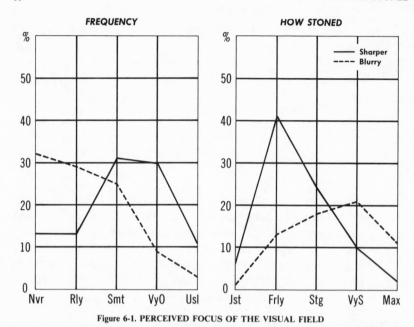

Figure 6-1. PERCEIVED FOCUS OF THE VISUAL FIELD

Note.—In interpreting the "How Stoned" graphs, note that the percentage of users plotted at each level is the percentage indicating that level as their minimal level of intoxication for experiencing that particular effect. Thus, a drop in the curve with increasing minimal level of intoxication does not mean that fewer users experience that effect at higher levels, but that fewer give a higher level as their minimal level for experiencing that effect.

Visual blurriness is reported somewhat more frequently by women than by men ($p < .05$), and is reported as occurring at lower minimal levels of intoxication by Occasional users in comparison to Weekly or Daily users ($p < .05$, overall).

A fairly frequent effect that also illustrates reorganization of the visual field is "*The face of another person will change even as I watch it, so he keeps changing from one different person to another*" (36%, 21%, 23%, 11%, 6%). This is a high-level effect (2%, 3%, 11%, 19%, 17%), although many (47 percent) users did not rate level. Users of Psychedelics experience it more frequently than Non-users ($p < .01$). Meditators experience it more frequently than Ordinary Users ($p < .05$), with neither group significantly differing from the Therapy and Growth group.

Color

Like form, color is an important aspect of visual organization, and perceptual changes here are common: "*I see new colors or more subtle shades of color than when I'm straight*" (10%, 18%, 30%, 19%, 21%). The contrary effect, "*Colors get duller, not as vivid,*" is rare (62%, 23%, 8%, 3%, 1%), as shown in Figure 6-2 ($p < .001$). Color perception is enhanced at low levels of intoxication (17%, 31%, 27%, 7%, 4%). Most users (67 percent) could not rate the minimal level for color dulling (6%, 13%, 6%, 5%, 3%), and this distribution of levels does not differ significantly from that reported for color enhancement.

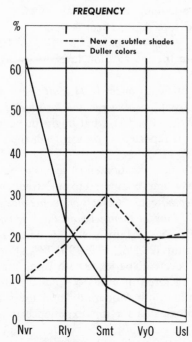

Figure 6-2. PERCEIVED COLORS WHEN STONED

The Therapy and Growth group tends not to see new colors as frequently as the Meditators and Ordinary Users ($p < .05$, overall). The Professionals have to be more intoxicated than the College-educated for colors to get duller ($p < .05$).

Depth

An important element of visual organization is the dimension of perceived *depth*. Four items deal with changes in perceived depth. We shall describe each separately before considering their interrelationships.

A common effect is *"When I look at pictures they may acquire an element of visual depth, a third-dimensional aspect that they don't have when straight"* (13%, 12%, 34%, 23%, 15%), which begins in the low-middle range of intoxication (4%, 26%, 32%, 12%, 7%). One of my informants, known for his excellent phenomenological description of marijuana intoxication (Anonymous, 1969), describes how dramatic this can be: if, while intoxicated, you look at a color photograph or picture postcard of a scene with natural depth in it, and look with one eye through a pin-hole close enough to the picture so that its borders cannot be seen, the two-dimensional representation will suddenly turn into three dimensions, as if you were looking at the actual scene.

A converse and rare depth effect is "*The world looks flat: it lacks the third dimension of depth*" (55%, 27%, 9%, 5%, 1%). Most users (61 percent) did not rate the intoxication level for this (4%, 8%, 15%, 7%, 5%).

A fairly frequent depth effect is "*Visual depth perception changes, so that near objects seem much nearer and far objects seem much further away*" (32%, 19%, 29%, 11%, 5%), what might be called a *magnification of visual depth*. This is reported as occurring in the higher intoxication levels (1%, 14%, 25%, 17%, 6%).

The visual depth magnification effect seems to be a long-term effect, persisting steadily over time, compared to an infrequent effect that might be termed a *visual depth jiggle*: "*Objects or people may seem to get visually nearer or further as I look at them without their actually moving at all*" (39%, 23%, 21%, 10%, 5%). Many users (46 percent) did not rate the intoxication level for this (2%, 9%, 17%, 19%, 7%), although it is generally perceived at higher levels. Experience with using marijuana modulates this effect, whether factored in terms of total use or frequency of use in the last six months. Both Moderate Total users and Weekly users need to be more intoxicated for this experience than Light or Heavy Total users in the one case ($p < .05$) or Occasional or Daily users in the other case ($p < .01$).

All four of these intoxication effects on visual depth perception are compared in Figure 6-3. The illusion of depth in flat pictures and the general magnification of depth both occur more frequently than the world's appearing flat or the depth's changing even as the user looks (jiggling) ($p < < < .001$), and the jiggling of perceived depth requires a higher intoxication level ($p < .02$).

Centrality

Two common phenomena represent an increased centrality of vision, enhancement of the focused object at the expense of peripheral objects: "*Things outside the center of my visual field, things in the periphery of my vision look different when I'm not looking directly at them than when I look directly at them. E.g., I might see a door as open when I'm not looking directly at it, but when I look directly at it, it is closed*" (19%, 21%, 32%, 19%, 7%) and "*My visual perception of the space around me*

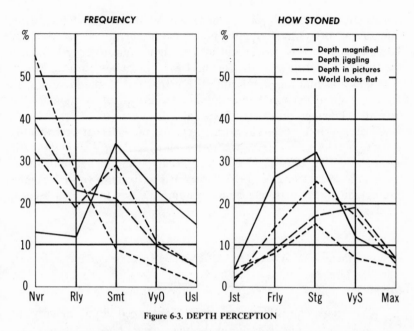

Figure 6-3. DEPTH PERCEPTION

Note.—For guide to interpreting the "How Stoned" graph, see note on Figure 6-1.

is changed, so that what I'm looking at is very real and clear, but everything else I'm not focusing on visually seems further away or otherwise less real or clear" (23%, 15%, 27%, 19%, 13%). Both have a modal level of intoxication of Strongly (3%, 23%, 29%, 17%, 5% and 4%, 17%, 25%, 17%, 6%, respectively). Neither the frequency of occurrence nor level of intoxication distributions differ for these effects.

Several background factors affect whether things in the periphery change. Younger users and Non-users of Psychedelics report this phenomenon as occurring more frequently ($p < .05$, $p < .01$, respectively) compared to Older users and Users of Psychedelics. Further, Users of Psychedelics are more variable in their ratings for this than Non-users ($p < .05$) and generally require higher levels of intoxication.

With respect to increased centrality of vision, Daily and Weekly users must be more intoxicated than Occasional users ($p < .05$, overall).

Sensuality, Aliveness

Another common phenomenon is *"There is a sensual quality to vision, as if I were 'touching' the objects or people I am looking at"* (22%, 16%, 31%, 19%, 9%), which occurs at higher levels of intoxication (5%, 14%, 23%, 25%, 5%). This is reported more frequently among the College-educated than among the Professionals ($p < .05$). This effect is also reported most frequently among the Heavy Total users (modal frequency category is Very Often/Usually), next most frequently by the Moderate Total users, and least frequently by the Light Total users ($p < .01$ for the Heavy-Moderate, $p < .01$ for the Heavy-Light comparison, Moderate-Light not differing significantly). Further, the Moderate and Light Total use groups report higher minimal levels of intoxication for this than the Heavy group ($p < .05$, overall).

The final infrequent effect on perceiving the external world is *"Everything I look at seems to vibrate or pulse, as if it had a life of its own"* (23%, 31%, 29%, 8%, 7%), which occurs at the higher intoxication levels (1%, 5%, 15%, 23%, 19%). Users of Psychedelics report a higher level of intoxication (mode at Maximum) for this than Non-users ($p < .05$).

VISUAL IMAGERY AND HALLUCINATION

Imagery

A very characteristic phenomenon is enhanced visual imagery: *"If I try to visualize something, form a visual image, I see it in my mind's eye more intensely, more sharply than when straight"* (12%, 3%, 22%, 25%, 35%). This begins occurring in the low-middle ranges of intoxication (13%, 33%, 24%, 11%, 3%).

A specific illustration of this is the common effect, *"I have more imagery than usual while reading; images of the scenes I'm reading about just pop up vividly"* (15%, 11%, 24%, 27%, 15%), which also occurs at the lower levels of intoxication (13%, 33%, 22%, 4%, 2%). The Weekly users have to be somewhat more intoxicated to experience this than the Occasional users ($p < .05$), with a suggestion that the Daily users do not have to be as intoxicated as the Weekly users ($p < .10$). While the general enhancement of visual imagery occurs more frequently than visual imagery accompanying reading ($p < .01$), the distribution of levels of intoxication does not differ significantly.

A related phenomenon, described fully in Chapter 15, *"When thinking about things while stoned, there are visual images that just automatically go along with thinking,"* a very common effect, which occurs at Moderate levels of intoxication.

Auras

Two frequent phenomena stand midway between perceptual alteration of real phenomena and hallucination: *"I see fringes of colored light around objects (not people), what people have called the 'aura'"* (46%,

21%, 20%, 8%, 1%), and "*I see fringes of colored light around* people (*not objects), what people have called the 'aura'*" (50%, 23%, 19%, 5%, 1%).[2] Many users (57 percent, 59 percent, respectively) did not rate the level of intoxication for this, but for those who did, it was generally rated in the highest ranges (1%, 4%, 15%, 10%, 13%, and 3%, 2%, 9%, 12%, 15%, respectively).

Seeing an aura around *objects* is somewhat more common in the Younger group than in the Older group ($p < .05$); more common in Heavy Total users of marijuana than in Moderate ($p < .05$) and Light Total users ($p < .05$); more common in Users of Psychedelics than in Non-users ($p < .05$). Seeing auras around *people* is also more frequent in Users than in Non-users of Psychedelics ($p < .001$).

Hallucination

Pure visual hallucination is an infrequent phenomenon: "*With my eyes open, I can see things that aren't there, i.e., for which there is no real visual basis. E.g., if you look at stains on a wall and see a design, that's an illusion; you are altering something there. This question deals with seeing something when there's* nothing *there, such as seeing a pattern or object on a perfectly blank wall*" (33%, 23%, 27%, 7%, 9%). Although many (45 percent) users did not rate intoxication level, when it does occur this is a high-level phenomenon (1%, 6%, 10%, 20%, 18%). It is reported more frequently in the Younger Group ($p < .01$), and more frequently in the Heavy and Moderate Total use groups compared to the Light Total use group ($p < .05$ overall).

ADDITIONAL EFFECTS

A number of users wrote in additional visual effects in the final part of the questionnaire.

Three users mentioned stroboscopic effects on vision: (1) "Old-time movie effect, where people move in phases as in a movie running too slow" (Sometimes, Strongly); (2) "I see in frames like a movie, only slowed down" (Rarely, Strongly); and (3) "Vision distorted as if seeing world with big strobe light flickering overhead" (Sometimes, Maximum).

"I see movement in things that I focus on, a matchbook cover with a geometrical design shifted like a light show movie; the more stoned, the bigger they are of movement" (Sometimes, Fairly).

"I find a continuum which starts with things' being two-dimensional

---

[2]Readers interested in this rather exotic effect may see Ellison (1962) and Kilner (1965). Most of the writing on this subject is mystical, but the above references do attempt some objective treatment of the phenomenon.

and progressing to deep three-dimensional. I find I can stop anywhere on it" (Usually, Maximum).

"I can see the texture of the air in little swirling dots" (Usually, Just).

"Things inanimate, like a pile of clothes, seem to come to life;" (Sometimes, Strongly).

"Much more fun to watch color TV or newscasts" (Sometimes, Fairly).

"Am able to see mythical, angel-like creatures, which seem to be personal spirits" (Rarely, Maximum).

"Figure-ground shifts become more frequent and easier to control when stoned" (Sometimes, Strongly).

"I get more, and more pronounced, afterimages" (Rarely, Strongly).

"Aesthetic perception augmented re Cezzane [sic]: see interview with Allen Ginsberg, Paris Review #37" (no specification of frequency or levels).

LEVELS OF INTOXICATION FOR VISUAL PHENOMENA

The grouping of visual phenomena by intoxication levels is presented in Figure 6-4 and is highly significant ($p \lll .0005$). At the lowest levels, vision may sharpen up, patterns may appear, and colors

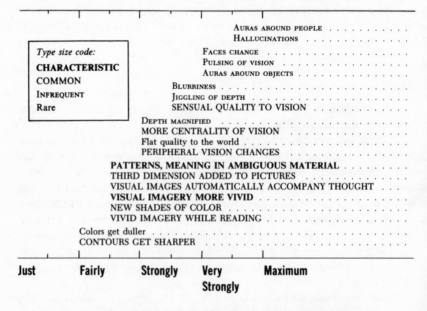

FIGURE 6-4. INTOXICATION LEVELS, VISUAL PHENOMENA

may be affected. Further up, visual imagery is enhanced, and vision may become more central with depth magnified. Between Strongly and Very Strongly intoxicated, a sensual quality is frequently added to vision, and the external visual world may become unstable, with blurring and jiggling in depth. As one goes higher, vision may pulse, faces may change, auras may appear around objects, and at the highest level the maximal alteration of the visual world may occur with hallucinations and auras around people.[3]

MODULATING FACTORS

Table 6-1 summarizes the effects of background factors that have relatively linear effects. Imagery automatically accompanying reading and visual jiggle appear to have a curvilinear relationship to drug experience, occurring more frequently and at lower levels of intoxication with moderate experience than with little or much experience.

In general, more drug experience goes with sensuality and unusual visual experiences, and with more intoxication required for the possibly undesirable effects of blurriness and pulsing of vision.

SUMMARY

In general, the specific changes in visual perception brought about by marijuana intoxication may be seen as particular manifestations of a general change in what we might call the *visual pattern-making process*. It is common to assume that we passively "see" what is out there, that the qualities of the visual world are inherent in the physical properties of objects and space. Modern psychological investigations have made it clear that seeing is a very active and complex process in which we *construct* the visual world from the flux of visual sensations reaching us. That is, patterns, forms, objects, recognizable people, etc. exist in our minds as a construction from visual data. We are so used to doing this automatically that it seems as if the visual world were given. This active nature of visual perception is true of all sensory modalities.

The patterns that are formed from visual data are organized into a degree of complexity and familiarity that is optimal for surviving in the world around us. Detecting a potential predator concealed in some bushes has survival value; seeing a potential predator in every ambiguous visual input is not conducive to survival of the organism. Thus we may

---

[3]In general, intoxication effects that are two levels or more apart in this type of graphical plot will be different enough to reach statistical significance.

TABLE 6-1

EFFECTS OF BACKGROUND FACTORS ON VISION

BACKGROUND FACTORS	EFFECTS	
More drug experience	More frequent: Sensuality of vision Auras, objects Auras, people Hallucinations Face changes More intoxicated for: Blurriness Pulsing of vision Peripheral vision changes More centrality of vision	Less frequent: Peripheral vision changes Less intoxicated for: Sensuality of vision
Older		Less frequent: Peripheral vision changes Auras, objects Hallucinations
More educated	More intoxicated for: Colors duller	Less frequent: Patterns in ambiguity Sensuality of vision
Males		Less frequent: Blurriness
Meditation	More frequent: Face changes	
Therapy & Growth		Less frequent: New colors

conceive of some optimal level (actually a dynamic range)[4] of pattern-making activity, of organization of ambiguous (and not so ambiguous) visual data into meaningful percepts. Raise this level too high and we have illusion or hallucination. Lower this level too much and we have stupidity.

Marijuana intoxication seems to raise the level a fair amount, more so with increasing levels of intoxication. Thus patterns form from ambiguous material, contours are sharpened, central visual phenomena are

---

[4]The "optimal" level is quite situation-specific; depth jiggle, for example, may be quite amusing and enjoyable during a relaxed evening at home (safe conditions) but might be a pronounced disadvantage while working at some crucial task that required very accurate depth perception.

enhanced at the expense of peripheral phenomena, depth is magnified and more subtle shades of color are perceived. With eyes closed, visual imagery is enhanced.

Such a raising of level of the patterning mechanism is a two-edged sword. On the one hand, it may genuinely result in perceiving useful patterns and meanings that would have been overlooked. On the other hand, meaning may be falsely attributed to phenomena that have no such meaning. Many users seem to be aware of this combined advantage-disadvantage of marijuana intoxication and to compensate for it by requiring more data than usual before making a judgment or carrying out a consequent action. Others naïvely accept everything seen while intoxicated as true. This same dual aspect of raising the level of pattern-making activity applies, of course, to all sense modalities and cognitive processes.

Whether the proportion of naïveté and sophistication is any different from that of ordinary people in everyday life is a moot question.

CHAPTER **7**

Hearing

MAJOR EFFECTS

Acuity

The most characteristic effect of marijuana intoxication is an auditory one: "*I can hear more subtle changes in sounds; e.g., the notes of music are purer and more distinct, the rhythm stands out more*" (1%, 0%, 4%, 25%, 70%), which is experienced very often or usually by almost all users and occurs at a low level of intoxication (27%, 51%, 17%, 3%, 0%).

Two other items also deal with perceived auditory acuity. A very characteristic effect is "*I can understand the words of songs which are not clear when straight*" (4%, 10%, 20%, 29%, 37%), which also occurs at the lower levels of intoxication (19%, 45%, 25%, 5%, 1%). This is an experience clearly relevant to understanding rock music, which seems incomprehensible to many ordinary people. A rare effect on auditory acuity is "*I have difficulty hearing things clearly; sounds are blurry and indistinct*" (61%, 23%, 13%, 1%, 0%), a very high level effect (6%, 5%, 6%, 9%, 10%, but note that 64 percent could not rate this). The interrelationships between these three acuity effects are plotted in Figure 7-1. Hearing more subtle changes in sounds occurs more frequently than understanding the words of songs better ($p < .001$); and the latter effect, in turn, occurs more frequently than blurring of sounds ($p < .001$). Subtle changes in sounds and understanding songs have the same distribution of levels of intoxication, but the level for sound blurring is much higher than either of these phenomena ($p < .001$ in both cases).

One of the acuity phenomena is affected by background variables. Moderate Total use of marijuana is more frequently associated with understanding the words of songs better than Heavy Total use ($p < .05$), even though this is a very frequent phenomenon with Heavy Total users (mode at Very Often/Usually), with a suggestion ($p < .10$) that

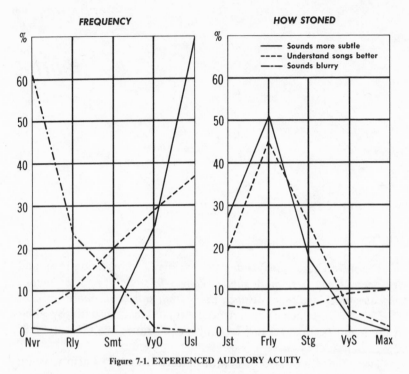

Figure 7-1. EXPERIENCED AUDITORY ACUITY

Note.—For guide to interpreting the "How Stoned" graph, see note on Figure 6-1.

Light Total users also understand the words of songs better more frequently than Heavy Total users but do not differ from Moderate Total
users. Users of Psychedelics also experience this more frequently than
Non-users ($p < .01$).

Sound and Space

Another very characteristic effect also relates to the user's perception
of music: *"When listening to stereo music or live music, the spatial separation between the various instruments sounds greater, as if they were physically further apart"* (13%, 4%, 23%, 31%, 29%), which occurs at Moderate
levels of intoxication (7%, 32%, 35%, 7%, 1%). A more extreme effect
on the relation of sound to space, occurring less frequently ($p < .01$)
and at higher levels ($p < .001$), as shown in Figure 7-2, is *"With my
eyes closed and just listening to sounds, the space around me becomes
an auditory space, a place where things are arranged according to their
sound characteristics instead of visual, geometrical characteristics"* (16%,
13%, 25%, 19%, 21% and 7%, 18%, 25%, 17%, 7%). One user offered

a rich example, which happened to him when listening to stereo music on headphones: "Ordinarily I tend to hear high sounds as located further up in my head than low ones, and, with stereo, the sounds move back and forth along an axis between my ears, giving a two-dimensional display. When I'm stoned, the sounds also move back and forward in my head, depending on their quality, so I experience a beautiful three-dimensional sound space. Overtones and complex notes 'twist' the space in an indescribable way."

Several background factors affect the experience of auditory space. Users of Psychedelics experience auditory space somewhat more often ($p < .05$) than Non-users. The College-educated need to be somewhat more intoxicated than the Professionals to experience it ($p < .05$). The Moderate Total users need to be more intoxicated than either the Light Total users ($p < .05$) or the Heavy Total users ($p < .05$), with the Light and Heavy Total users both peaking sharply at the Fairly/Strongly level. Meditators tend to rate all intoxication levels about equally and average a lower minimal level, while ordinary Users and the Therapy and Growth group peak sharply at the Fairly/Strongly level ($p < .05$, overall).

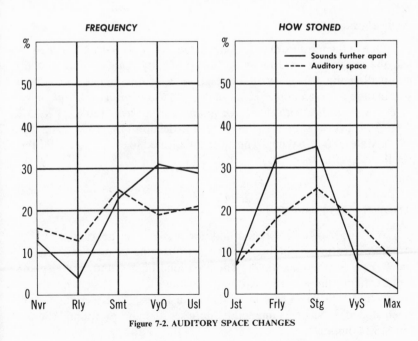

Figure 7-2. AUDITORY SPACE CHANGES

Note.—For guide to interpreting the "How Stoned" graph, see note on Figure 6-1.

Auditory Imagery

A common effect is imagery enhancement: "*If I try to have an auditory image, hear something in my mind, remember a sound, it is more vivid than when straight*" (16%, 7%, 26%, 27%, 20%), which occurs at Moderate levels of intoxication (9%, 33%, 27%, 7%, 3%). The Meditators and the Therapy and Growth group experience it less often than the ordinary users ($p < .01$, overall), as do the older users ($p < .05$). Further, Meditators report a somewhat higher level of intoxication for this experience than the other two groups ($p < .05$, overall).

Hearing Your Own Voice

One source of sound commonly heard to change by marijuana users is their own voices: "*The sound quality of my own voice changes, so that I sound different to myself when I talk*" (15%, 19%, 27%, 17%, 19%), mostly at the Strong level of intoxication (5%, 18%, 31%, 19%, 7%). Comments by my informants indicate that this is probably a perceptual change, not an actual change in voice quality. It occurs more frequently among the Younger group ($p < .05$).

Synesthesia

One of the most exotic phenomena associated with drugs is synesthesia, the experience of another sensory modality than the one actually stimulating the person. Visual sensation in conjunction with auditory stimulation is a common effect of marijuana: "*Sounds have visual images or colors associated with them, synchronized with them*" (20%, 23%, 33%, 16%, 7%). It occurs at high levels of intoxication (1%, 10%, 25%, 19%, 19%). Males report having to be more intoxicated to experience synesthesia than females ($p < .05$).

ADDITIONAL EFFECTS

A number of users offered additional effects on hearing.

Two mentioned ringing sounds: (1) "Ringing in my ears" (Sometimes, Very Strongly), and (2) "There's a loud buzz sound, like airplane motors, filling the air" (Sometimes, Maximum).

"When I listen to certain kinds of music (especially serious music) when stoned, it becomes incredibly more sensual and profound" (Sometimes, Maximum).

"When listening to music, my mind can become completely absorbed by sound to the extent that my body is writhing, but entirely disconnected from my mind" (Sometimes, Very Strongly).

"While chanting *mantras*, rhythmic continuity is more sensuous and secure" (no specification of frequency or level).

"Admiration for the intrinsic knowledge musicians and composers have of the effect of their sounds on people's total being" (Very Often, Fairly).

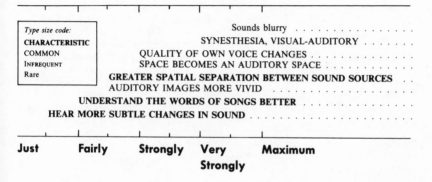

FIGURE 7-3. INTOXICATION LEVELS, AUDITORY PHENOMENA

LEVELS OF INTOXICATION FOR AUDITORY PHENOMENA

Figure 7-3 orders the various auditory effects by level of intoxication. Overall differences are very significant ($p \lll .0005$). Experiential enhancement and enrichment of sounds appears at the very low levels of intoxication and progresses to vivid auditory images and changes in space perception in accordance with sound in the middle ranges of intoxication. Synesthesia may appear above this, and the rare effect of sounds' becoming blurry and indistinct may appear at the next-to-highest possible level.

MODULATING FACTORS

Table 7-1 summarizes those background factors that have a relatively linear effect.

TABLE 7-1

EFFECTS OF BACKGROUND FACTORS ON HEARING

BACKGROUND FACTORS	EFFECTS	
More drug experience	More frequent: Auditory space More intoxicated for: Auditory space	Less frequent: Understanding words of songs better
Meditation	More intoxicated for: Auditory imagery better	Less frequent: Auditory imagery better Less intoxicated for: Auditory space
More educated		Less intoxicated for: Auditory space
Older	More frequent: Auditory imagery better	Less frequent: Own voice changes
Males	More intoxicated for: Synesthesia	

Although several background factors have a relatively linear effect on the phenomenon of experiencing space as an auditory space, total marijuana use has a curvilinear effect. Moderate Total users have Very Strongly/Maximum indicated as the minimal level almost as frequently as Fairly/Strongly, while the Light and Heavy Total users peak sharply at Fairly/Strongly.

Overall, auditory effects are infrequently affected by background factors.

SUMMARY

In general we may note that effects on sound perception are some of the most characteristic effects of marijuana. Every effect here but one was at least common; one (subtle changes in sounds) was the most characteristic effect found in the entire study, and many others were characteristic. Further, all of these effects were perceived as emotionally pleasant or cognitively interesting, leading to greatly enhanced enjoyment of sound and music. The only exception was the blurring of sounds, which was one of the rarest effects in the study, occurring primarily at very high levels of intoxication, and was never experienced at all by most users.

The earlier discussion (Chapter 6) about perception as an active pattern-making process is applicable here, as it is to all sensory modalities. A primary experiential effect of marijuana intoxication is to make slight, ordinarily unnoticed nuances of sounds into *meaningful* variations. The question of whether this would produce a verifiable increase in auditory acuity by objective standards (say, in understanding the words of songs better) is quite intriguing.

CHAPTER 8

Touch, Temperature, Taste, and Smell

TOUCH AND TEMPERATURE

MAJOR EFFECTS

A very characteristic effect of marijuana intoxication is *"My sense of touch is more exciting, more sensual, when stoned"* (4%, 9%, 21%, 31%, 34%), which occurs at the lower-middle levels of intoxication (9%, 35%, 37%, 9%, 3%). Meditators experience this at a lower level ($p < .01$, overall).

A variant of this effect, also characteristic, is *"Touch sensations take on new qualities that they don't have when straight"* (5%, 9%, 30%, 30%, 25%), with the minimal necessary level of intoxication again being primarily in the Fairly and Strongly range (9%, 37%, 30%, 13%, 4%). Meditators show a lower and more variable level of intoxication for this ($p < .05$, overall).

Two linked common phenomena help to specify these new touch qualities: *"Some surfaces feel much smoother, silkier than when straight"* (11%, 10%, 39%, 25%, 13%), and *"Some surfaces feel much rougher, more irregular than when straight; the roughness or graininess forms interesting patterns"* (14%, 13%, 37%, 25%, 11%), which are reported with essentially the same frequency. The minimal level of intoxication for both is the Fairly-Strongly range (5%, 36%, 31%, 9%, 3% and 5%, 29%, 31%, 13%, 3%, respectively). The College-educated experience increased roughness more frequently than the Professionals ($p < .01$), and the College-educated need to be somewhat more intoxicated to experience either smoothness ($p < .05$) or roughness ($p < .01$).

Tactual Imagery

An enhancement of tactual imagery is common: *"I can experience vivid tactual imagery, imagine what things feel like and feel their texture very vividly in my mind"* (19%, 20%, 27%, 24%, 9%). Heavy Total users experience this most often, Moderate Total users next most often, and Light Total users least ($p < .05$, overall). This effect occurs at Strong levels of intoxication (3%, 19%, 31%, 17%, 7%).

Temperature

A sense ordinarily included with touch is temperature. A common effect is *"The temperature of things, their warmth or coldness, takes on new qualities"* (19%, 12%, 32%, 25%, 12%), which occurs in the middle ranges of intoxication (3%, 21%, 35%, 16%, 3%). This is reported more frequently by the College-educated than by Professionals ($p < .01$).

Weight

Another common effect closely related to touch is the kinesthetic sense of the weight of objects: *"Objects seem heavier, more massive, when I lift them when stoned"* (21%, 21%, 29%, 15%, 11%). The opposite effect, *"Objects seem lighter, less massive, when I lift them"* (31%, 30%, 24%, 5%, 3%) is infrequent, as shown in Figure 8-1 ($p < .001$). The modal levels of minimal intoxication for both effects are Fairly to Strongly, and do not differ from one another (7%, 26%, 25%, 15%, 1% and 5%,

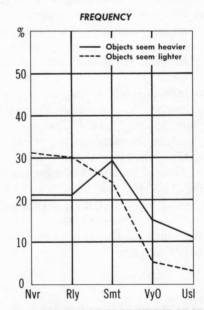

Figure 8-1. KINESTHETIC SENSE OF WEIGHT OF OBJECTS

17%, 22%, 12%, 3%, respectively), although many (41 percent) users did not rate the level on objects seeming lighter.

Women and Non-users of Psychedelics experience increased massiveness of objects somewhat more frequently than men and Users (*p* < .05 for each comparison). The Professionals need to be somewhat more intoxicated than the College-educated to experience this increased heaviness (*p* < .05).

ADDITIONAL EFFECTS

"Touch becomes more erotic with friends than usual" (Sometimes, Strongly).

"Sensation increases with amount and then becomes less pleasurable and more physically objectionable" (Usually, Just).

"When I am starting to get stoned, I feel a tingling at the end of my fingertips" (Usually, Strongly).

"Touching of objects and areas (walls, etc.) with eyes closed brings many enjoyable and fantastic experiences to my mind" (Usually, Strongly).

"When being touched, I feel that figures are being described in space rather than 'on' my skin" (Sometimes, Fairly).

"My skin feels exceptionally sensitive" (Usually, Fairly).

"Much prefer hot weather to cold, since cold is especially uncomfortable when stoned" (Very Often, Strongly).

LEVELS OF INTOXICATION FOR TOUCH PHENOMENA

All the effects of marijuana intoxication on touch may occur in the Fairly to Strongly range, with no significant differences between the two adjacent levels, so they are not plotted.

MODULATING FACTORS

The relatively linear effects of several background factors are summarized in Table 8-1.

TASTE

MAJOR EFFECTS

The second most characteristic quality of marijuana intoxication is "*Taste sensations take on new qualities that they don't have when straight*" (3%, 3%, 15%, 29%, 49%). This occurs at Low levels of intoxication (17%, 49%, 22%, 5%, 1%). Not too surprisingly, then, an extremely

TABLE 8-1

EFFECTS OF BACKGROUND FACTORS ON TOUCH

BACKGROUND FACTORS	EFFECTS	
More drug experience	More frequent: Tactile imagery	Less frequent: Objects seem massive
More educated	More intoxicated for: Objects seem massive	Less frequent: Surfaces feel rough New temperature qualities Less intoxicated for: Surfaces feel smooth Surfaces feel rough
Males		Less frequent: Objects seem massive
Meditation		Less intoxicated for: New touch qualities Touch more sensual

characteristic effect of marijuana is *"I enjoy eating very much and eat a lot"* (1%, 5%, 18%, 31%, 44%), which also occurs at low intoxication levels (22%, 44%, 26%, 4%, 1%). Users of Psychedelics report this as occurring less frequently than Non-users ($p < .05$).

Taste Imagery

As with other senses, sensory imagery is a common experience (15%, 15%, 37%, 17%, 16%): *"If I try to imagine what something tastes like, I can do so very vividly"* occurs at Moderate minimal levels of intoxication (11%, 31%, 29%, 11%, 1%), with Meditators reporting this less frequently than Ordinary Users or the Therapy and Growth group ($p < .05$, overall). Users of Psychedelics and Meditators do not have to be as intoxicated for this experience ($p < .05$ in each case).

Sweets

The data confirm a popular belief that marijuana smokers like sweets: *"I crave sweet things to eat, things like chocolate, more than other foods"* is a common effect (16%, 26%, 25%, 15%, 17%), which occurs at Low levels of intoxication (11%, 41%, 23%, 5%, 0%). The Light and Heavy Total users peak sharply at Fairly/Strongly on level of intoxication here, while the Moderate Total users are more variable ($p < .05$).

Components of Taste

A fairly frequent effect is *"Tastes become divided into several components, instead of an overall taste. E.g., a bite of bread may taste salty on one part of your tongue and sour on another part at the same time"* (43%, 15%, 25%, 11%, 5%). Although many (47 percent) users did not rate this for level, it is an effect occurring at fairly strong levels (3%, 12%, 20%, 15%, 3%). It is interesting to raise the question whether this is an actual perception of the several discrete tasting organs in the mouth functioning separately instead of their usual blending together, or whether it is imagery added to taste sensations.

Miscellaneous Taste Phenomena

An infrequent phenomenon is *"There is an exceptionally long time delay between starting to chew food and the time the taste actually reaches my consciousness"* (49%, 18%, 15%, 10%, 3%), which occurs at Strong levels of intoxication (1%, 11%, 19%, 13%, 3%, noting that 55 percent did not rate this). This delay is more frequent among Non-users of Psychedelics ($p < .01$). We may be dealing more with a time phenomenon than a taste one here, perhaps a differential delay between "outside" sensory input (taste) and internal feedback of what the body is doing (chewing).

Because it has frequently been noted that marijuana produces dryness of the mouth, the item *"I salivate quite a lot when stoned"* was included in the questionnaire as a Validity Scale item. As it may be that some users do indeed salivate a lot, however, the data on it are presented here for what they are worth to future investigators. This effect is infrequent (44%, 30%, 13%, 5%, 5%) and rated at Moderate levels (10%, 17%, 17%, 3%, 2%, with 51 percent not rating). Light and Moderate Total users have Never as their modal frequency of occurrence, with Heavy Total users having Rarely/Sometimes as the mode ($p < .01$, overall). A question to consider, then, is: Does long, heavy marijuana use alter the dryness usually considered an invariable physiological effect?

The final phenomenon of taste investigated is also infrequent: *"If I belch, I retaste the food in my stomach, and it tastes very good"* (51%, 17%, 15%, 6%, 3%). It also occurs at Moderate levels of intoxication (8%, 15%, 11%, 3%, 1%). It occurs more often with Heavy Total users ($p < .05$, overall) and with Meditators ($p < .01$, overall).

ADDITIONAL EFFECTS

"When eating, the texture and temperature are important" (Texture: Very Often, Strongly; Temperature: Very Often, Fairly).

"Throat dry and special taste that lingers (I don't think it's the taste of grass, but rather the sense of taste when stoned: most foods taste the same, anyway, when stoned)" (Usually, Fairly).

"Want to have cigarette (tobacco), but don't enjoy it" (Usually, Strongly).

LEVELS OF INTOXICATION FOR TASTE PHENOMENA

Figure 8-2 shows various taste phenomena by level of intoxication. Overall differences are highly significant ($p \ll .0005$). Starting at the Fairly intoxicated level, there is an enhancement of taste and increase in appetite. Somewhat higher, taste imagery may be enhanced. Above that there may be a time delay between chewing and tasting, and at the level midway between Strongly and Very Strongly tastes may break into components.

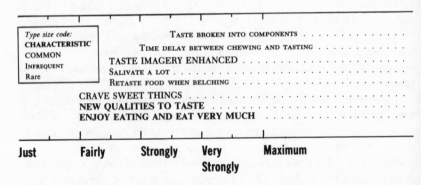

Type size code:	TASTE BROKEN INTO COMPONENTS . . . .
CHARACTERISTIC	TIME DELAY BETWEEN CHEWING AND TASTING . . . .
COMMON	TASTE IMAGERY ENHANCED . . . .
INFREQUENT	SALIVATE A LOT . . . .
Rare	RETASTE FOOD WHEN BELCHING . . . .

CRAVE SWEET THINGS . . . .
NEW QUALITIES TO TASTE . . . .
ENJOY EATING AND EAT VERY MUCH . . . .

Just   Fairly   Strongly   Very   Maximum
                                          Strongly

FIGURE 8-2. INTOXICATION LEVELS, TASTE PHENOMENA

MODULATING FACTORS

The background factors having relatively linear effects are summarized in Table 8-2, namely, Drug Experience and Meditation. Both those with more drug experience and Meditators would seem to be more involved with tasting and eating generally.

A craving for sweet things in preference to other foods is common but affected by total marijuana use in a non-linear fashion; Light and Heavy Total users both indicate Fairly/Strongly as a modal level of intoxication for this, but the Moderate use group, while also having a mode at Fairly/Strongly, also frequently indicates Just and Maximum as minimal levels for experiencing this.

TABLE 8-2

EFFECTS OF BACKGROUND FACTORS ON TASTE

BACKGROUND FACTORS	EFFECTS	
More drug experience	More frequency: Retaste food when belching Salivate a lot	Less frequency: Delay between chewing and tasting Enjoy eating, eat a lot Less intoxicated for: Vivid taste imagery
Meditation	More frequency: Retaste food when belching	Less frequency: Vivid taste imagery Less intoxicated for: Vivid taste imagery

SUMMARY OF TASTE EFFECTS

In general, we may say that the main perceived effect of marijuana on taste is enhancement of taste qualities and (a consequent?) increase in appetite. As one informant put it, "On pot every man becomes a gourmet; good food tastes remarkably good, crappy food is awful!" This effect might be put to practical medical use where a patient is seriously underweight.

SMELL

MAJOR EFFECTS

Although smell is a relatively neglected sense in modern man, some alterations in smell sensations are reported by marijuana users.

A common experience is *"Smells become much richer and more unique when stoned"* (13%, 17%, 35%, 23%, 12%), which occurs at Moderate levels of intoxication (5%, 30%, 33%, 14%, 3%). This occurs more frequently among Heavy Total users of marijuana and Users of Psychedelics than among Light or Moderate Total users ($p < .05$, overall) or Non-users of Psychedelics ($p < .05$).

An almost synonymous common experience is *"Smell sensations take on new qualities that they don't have when straight"* (15%, 13%, 45%, 15%, 11%), which also occurs at Moderate levels (3%, 31%, 33%, 17%, 1%). This also occurs more frequently among Heavy Total users of marijuana ($p < .05$, overall).

Smell Imagery

Smell imagery enhancement is fairly frequent: "*If I try to imagine what something smells like, I can do so much more vividly than when straight*" (31%, 24%, 29%, 7%, 5%), which occurs at Strong levels of intoxication (3%, 18%, 25%, 13%, 3%).

Smell Components

A rare effect is "*When I smell something, different components of the smell seem to register at different physical locations in my nose*" (61%, 23%, 9%, 1%, 1%), which occurs at higher levels of intoxication (1%, 7%, 8%, 11%, 3%, with 69 percent not rating). It is interesting to compare this with the experience of taste being broken down into different locations in the mouth (see page 83); this is done in Figure 8-3. This effect occurs more frequently with taste than smell ($p < .001$), but levels of intoxication do not differ significantly.

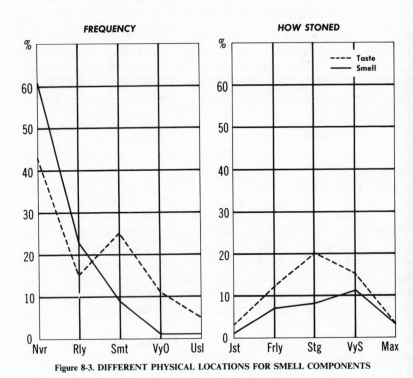

Figure 8-3. DIFFERENT PHYSICAL LOCATIONS FOR SMELL COMPONENTS

Note.—For guide to interpreting the "How Stoned" graph, see note on Figure 6-1.

LEVELS OF INTOXICATION FOR SMELL PHENOMENA

Intoxication levels for olfactory phenomena all run from midway between Fairly/Strongly to midway between Strongly/Very Strongly, with the differences in levels not significant.

MODULATING FACTORS

The two qualities of smell alteration affected by background factors are smells' becoming more unique and richer, and smells' taking on new qualities, both of which occur more frequently among users with more drug experience.

SUMMARY OF SMELL EFFECTS

In general, the main perceived effect of marijuana intoxication on the sense of smell is an experiential enhancement, making smells richer and more unique.

CHAPTER 9

Space and Time

SPACE

EXPERIENCES, EVENTS, do not just *happen*; they happen to a *person* at a *place* at a *time*. This chapter will deal with many important changes in the perception of and orientation to the matrix of space and time during marijuana intoxication. Some 11 items specifically dealt with this in the questionnaire, and another 11 items from other sections are clearly relevant, as well as all the effects on Memory discussed in Chapter 14. The question of the *person* who experiences things in the space/time matrix will be dealt with in Chapter 18.

PERCEPTION OF SPACE

Distance

The third most characteristic effect of marijuana intoxication is "*When I walk someplace, my experience of the distance covered is quite changed (e.g., not being aware of the space between, just seeming to suddenly be there or, conversely, feeling that it takes an immense number of steps to cover the distance*" (1%, 3%, 18%, 45%, 33%). The minimal level of intoxication is generally Low to Moderate (7%, 27%, 41%, 19%, 3%). The Therapy and Growth group and the Meditators have to be less intoxicated for this ($p < .01$, overall) than the ordinary user.

Even when the user is not moving about himself, distances change: "*Distances between me and things or me and other people seem to get greater; they are further away*" (13%, 15%, 44%, 17%, 9%) is a common effect, which, occurs at Moderate to Strong levels of intoxication (3%, 17%, 27%, 19%, 8%). The converse effect, "*Distances between me and other things or people seem to get shorter; they are closer*" is also common (23%, 20%, 43%, 7%, 3%) as a mid-range effect (4%, 17%, 27%, 19%,

3%). As shown in Figure 9-1, distances' seeming greater occurs somewhat more frequently ($p < .01$), but levels of intoxication for these linked effects do not differ significantly.

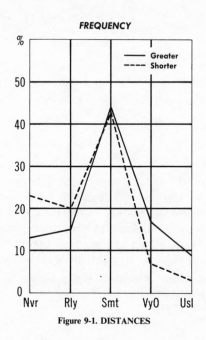

Figure 9-1. DISTANCES

The college-educated need to be somewhat more intoxicated than the Professionals for distances to seem shorter ($p < .05$).

Spatial Orientation

Spatial orientation may be completely lost temporarily: "*I get so lost in fantasy or similar trips in my head that I completely forget where I am, and it takes a while to reorient after I come back and open my eyes*" is common (15%, 22%, 37%, 19%, 8%) but occurs mainly at the very high levels of intoxication (1%, 3%, 20%, 33%, 24%). This is reported as occurring less often by the Daily users ($p < .05$, overall). Two related phenomena, dealt with fully in Chapter 11, are "*I have lost all consciousness of my body during fantasy trips, i.e., gotten so absorbed in what was going on in my head that my body might as well have not existed for a while*" and "*I have lost all consciousness of my body and the external world and just found myself floating in limitless space (not necessarily physical space).*" The experience of floating in limitless space is infrequent and is reported as occurring significantly less frequently than losing consciousness of the body per se during fantasy ($p < .001$) or losing consciousness of the body sufficiently to need to reorient ($p < .05$). None of the three phenomena differ significantly in levels of intoxication, all being very high-level phenomena. The latter two items are probably variants of the same phenomenon.

Quality of "Empty" Space

An infrequent but rather dramatic phenomenon is "*The space or air around me takes on a solid quality; it is no longer 'empty' space*" (41%, 21%, 26%, 7%, 2%), which occurs at relatively high levels of intoxication (0%, 3%, 15%, 19%, 13%) for those who could rate it. My informants indicate that this phenomenon may take a visual form, with the air or space taking on faint, vibrating colors, or a "tactual" form in that the air or space "feels" solid even though there is no visual change; space, rather than being a nonperceptible abstraction, becomes an immediate experience. The Weekly users report this most often (mode at Rarely/Sometimes), with both Occasional and Daily users having a modal occurrence rate of Never ($p < .05$, overall). The Meditators experience it more frequently than the Therapy and Growth group or the ordinary users ($p < .05$, overall). The Professionals need to be more intoxicated than do the College-educated to experience the air becoming solid ($p < .05$).

Related Phenomena

Related phenomena of space, dealt with in other chapters, are the visual effects of Chapter 6, such as pictures' acquiring a third dimension, the world's looking flat, visual centrality, and visual jiggle; and the auditory restructuring of space, greater separation between sound sources, and space becoming an *auditory* space, dealt with in Chapter 7.

SPACE PHENOMENA AND LEVELS OF INTOXICATION

Figure 9-4 presents the various perceived alterations of space by levels of intoxication. The overall differences in levels are highly significant ($p <<< .0005$). At the lowest levels of intoxication no changes in space are generally reported. At Moderate levels, distances frequently change, and sound sources seem further apart. As one goes higher, visual qualities of space may become less important as organizing factors, and perceived space may be unstable (jiggle); and at the very highest levels of intoxication, awareness of ordinary space may disappear completely, with the user lost in fantasy or floating in a purely mental space.

TIME

PERCEPTION OF TIME

Passage of Time

One of the most characteristic effects of marijuana intoxication is *"Time passes very slowly; things go on for the longest time (e.g., one side of a record seems to play for hours)"* (1%, 3%, 21%, 43%, 31%). The effect begins to occur at Moderate levels of intoxication (4%, 29%, 37%, 21%, 4%). The only background variable modulating this characteristic effect is total marijuana use; Heavy Total users must be more intoxicated to experience this ($p < .05$, overall).

An even more radical alteration of time is the common effect, *"Time seems to stop; it's not just that things take longer, but certain experiences are outside of time, are timeless"* (17%, 17%, 37%, 20%, 6%). Priestley (1964) has dealt with this phenomenon and calls it the experience of archetypal time. It generally does not begin to occur until very high levels of intoxication are reached (1%, 6%, 17%, 21%, 25%). It is reported as occurring more frequently by Females ($p < .05$). Non-users of Psychedelics experience it at higher levels of intoxication than Users ($p < .05$).

The converse of time's slowing or stopping is *"Time passes very rapidly; things finish almost before they seem to have gotten started,"* an infrequent effect (28%, 29%, 32%, 7%, 1%) of the middle levels of intoxication (6%, 16%, 19%, 18%, 7%). Females experience this more frequently than Males ($p < .05$), and Heavy Total users more frequently than Light or Moderal Total users ($p < .05$, overall). The Therapy and Growth group must be more intoxicated to experience time as passing rapidly than the Meditators ($p < .01$) or the Ordinary Users ($p < .01$).

The interrelationships between time passing rapidly, slowly, or stopping are shown in Figure 9-2. Time passing slowly is more frequent than time stopping ($p \ll .001$), and time stopping occurs more frequently than time passing rapidly ($p < .001$). While the distributions of minimal levels of intoxication do not differ significantly for time passing slowly or rapidly, the experience of time stopping occurs at higher levels of intoxication ($p \ll .001$ for either comparison).

An aspect of time passing more slowly has already been presented in the phenomenon of a long delay between chewing something and tasting it (see page 83); this delay phenomenon occurs far less frequently ($p \lll .001$) than a general slowing of time, but at approximately the same level of intoxication.

Time stopping—archetypal time—was also investigated with respect

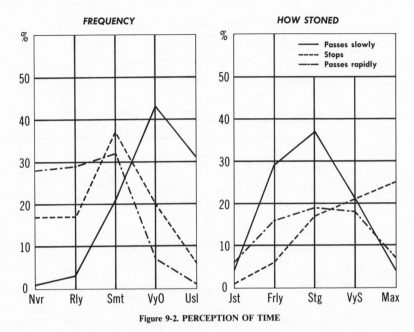

Figure 9-2. PERCEPTION OF TIME

Note.—For guide to interpreting the "How Stoned" graph, see note on Figure 6-1.

to shift in identity in the item *"Some events become archetypal, part of the basic way Man has always done things . . . ,"* which is dealt with fully in Chapter 18. It occurs about as frequently as time stopping, but at lower levels of intoxication ($p < .01$).

Events and the Passage of Time

Not only is it characteristic of marijuana intoxication for time to seem to pass more slowly; it is common for events to fit more smoothly into this slowed time: *"Events and thoughts flow more smoothly; the succession of events in time is smoother than usual"* (12%, 16%, 38%, 20%, 11%). This begins to occur at Moderate levels (8%, 30%, 31%, 13%, 1%). The Therapy and Growth group has to be more intoxicated to experience this increased smoothness of flow ($p < .05$, overall).

The converse common effect, *"Events and thoughts follow each other jerkily; there are sudden changes from one thing to another"* (13%, 23%, 35%, 19%, 5%) occurs at significantly higher ($p < .001$) levels of intoxication (6%, 13%, 34%, 19%, 7%), as illustrated in Figure 9-3.

Meditators experience jerkiness in the flow of time less often than ordinary users ($p < .05$) or than the Therapy and Growth group ($p < .05$). Users of Psychedelics need to be more intoxicated to experience this jerkiness ($p < .05$).

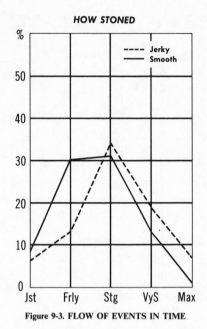

Figure 9-3. FLOW OF EVENTS IN TIME

Note.—For guide to interpreting the "How Stoned" graph, see note on Figure 6-1.

Here-and-Now-ness

Two time phenomena may be alterations in the perception of time per se or possibly consequences of some of the changes described above. A characteristic effect is *"I give little or no thought to the future; I'm completely in the here-and-now,"* and a related very common effect is *"I do things with much less thought to possible consequences of my actions . . ."*; both are dealt with fully in Chapter 15.

Déjà Vu

"While something is happening, I get the funny feeling that this sequence has happened before, in exactly the same way. Even though I logically know that it couldn't have happened before, it feels strange, as if it's repeating exactly (this is called a déjà vu *experience and should not be confused with a false memory)"* is a common experience (21%, 23%, 37%, 16%, 3%), which occurs at the middle level of intoxication (4%, 16%, 27%, 20%, 7%). While this is a phenomenon of memory by conservative standards, it would certainly influence a user's view of the nature of time. Some users, for example, interpret *déjà vu* as evidence for reincarnation. Similarly ostensible precognition (see page 100), while

occurring rarely, could also strongly influence a user's view of the nature of time.

In terms of a human experience, and particularly a marijuana user's experience, the common physical view of time as an impersonal abstraction flowing along at a constant rate, with only the present being real, is inadequate, for some people may experience: (1) the past and future as being as real as the present at times; (2) the rate of time flow changing radically; (3) time stopping (archetypal time); and (4) events fitting smoothly or jerkily into the flow of time.

Note also that all memory effects (Chapter 14) are relevant to time effects, but they will not be discussed here.

LEVELS OF INTOXICATION FOR TIME PHENOMENA

Figure 9-4 presents various time phenomena ordered by levels of intoxication. The overall ordering is highly significant ($p <<< .0005$). As with space, there are no alterations of time commonly occurring at the very low levels of intoxication, but beginning between Fairly and Strongly, time is usually experienced as slowing. Going a little higher, the user is quite likely to feel much more in the here-and-now and

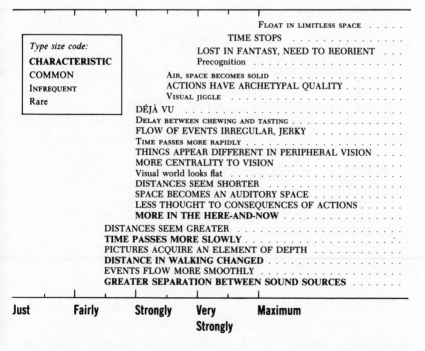

FIGURE 9-4. INTOXICATION LEVELS, SPACE AND TIME PHENOMENA

may give less thought to the consequences of his actions. At higher levels actions take on an archetypal quality, and at the highest levels time may seem to stop, in that actions seem somehow removed from time, not a part of the inevitable flow.

ADDITIONAL EFFECTS

"Time moves discontinuously" (Usually, Strongly).
"The world is more real" (Usually, Fairly).

LEVELS OF INTOXICATION FOR SPACE AND TIME PHENOMENA

Space and time form a tightly interwoven matrix in experience, so in some ways the division of space and time phenomena in the above discussions has been artificial. Figure 9-4 presents both space and time phenomena by level of intoxication, a significant overall ordering ($p \lll .0005$).

As the marijuana user becomes moderately intoxicated, the space/time matrix of experience seems to change; distances he moves around in change in size, time slows down, and sound begins to have some structuring effect on the space/time matrix. As he becomes strongly intoxicated, a variety of effects on his visual perception of the space of the world around him may occur, typically of the sort that involve him more in the space/time matrix (here-and-now-ness, centrality of vision, distances affected by his interest in objects). Moving into the high levels of intoxication, space may take on a structure or texture rather than being an abstract thing, and actions may take on an archetypal quality as the ordinary character of time becomes less binding on experience. He may sometimes become so lost in inner thoughts and fantasies that it takes some time to reorient to where he is. At the highest levels, time may seem to stop, actions to be out of the framework of physicalistic time, and he may also completely lose touch with the ordinary space/time continuum and experience floating in limitless space.

In general, the higher in level of intoxication one goes, the less binding the ordinary space/time matrix is on experience. One methodological difficulty created by this is that the descriptions of experiences at high levels can become less adequate, for language was evolved within the context of a quite rigid space/time matrix.

MODULATING FACTORS

A summary of the effects of various linearly-acting background variables is presented in Table 9-1. The effect of these background variables is quite complex.

TABLE 9-1

EFFECT OF BACKGROUND FACTORS ON SPACE AND TIME

BACKGROUND FACTORS	EFFECTS	

More Drug Experience	More frequent:
	Time flows rapidly
	Space becomes an
	  auditory space
	Precognition
	Actions archetypal
		Less frequent:
		Delay between chewing
		  and tasting
		Totally in here-and-
		  now
		Lose track, need to
		  reorient
		Lose consciousness of
		  body during fantasy

	More intoxicated for:
	Time flows slowly
	Jerkiness of events
	Visual centrality
	Space becomes an
	  auditory space
		Less intoxicated for:
		Less thought to
		  consequences of
		  actions
		Time stops

Meditation	More frequent:
	Air, space solid
		Less frequent:
		Jerkiness of events
		
		Less intoxicated for:
		Totally in here-and-
		  now
		Walking distance
		  changed
		Space becomes an
		  auditory space

Therapy & Growth	More intoxicated for: Events flow smoothly	Less intoxicated for: Walking distance changed
More Educated	More intoxicated for: Air, space solid	Less intoxicated for: Space becomes an auditory space Distances seem shorter
Males	More intoxicated for: Actions archetypal	Less frequent: Time stops Time flows rapidly
Older		Less intoxicated for: Float in limitless space

Frequency of use has a curvilinear effect on the experience of air or space as taking on a "solid" quality; Weekly users have a modal report of Rarely/Sometimes, while the mode for both Daily and Occasional users is Never.

SUMMARY

A major set of perceived effects of marijuana intoxication is the alteration of the space/time matrix in which all experience is set. This characteristically takes the form of increased attention to the present at the expense of the past and future (here-and-now-ness). Spatial dimensions may alter, and such alteration is affected by sound, music, and the user's attention. At the high levels of intoxication, experiences are increasingly less structured by the ordinary physical space/time matrix. At the highest levels, time may seem to stop, the user may experience archetypal time, where he is part of a pattern that man has always been part of, and he may temporarily lose consciousness of the ordinary space/time framework altogether, thus having experiences, which are inadequately communicated by language.

CHAPTER 10

Ostensible Paranormal Phenomena (ESP)

PHENOMENA PURPORTING to be paranormal in nature—i.e., involving the transmission of information (extrasensory perception, ESP) or power (psychokinesis, PK) across space or time when known physical carriers would not be operative—were often reported in pilot interviews with marijuana users, so a number of questions were devoted to this in the main study. A questionnaire study can only deal with *ostensible* paranormal phenomena, i.e., with phenomena that the experiencers themselves judge to be paranormal. Whether such phenomena would appear to be genuinely paranormal in terms of laboratory standards is unknown; judging by previous studies of self-reported ESP instances (Anonymous, 1958; Green, 1960, 1966; Gurney, Myers, & Podmore, 1886; Membership Committee, American Society for Psychical Research, 1967; Prasad and Stevenson, 1968; Sidgwick et al., 1894), some of the ostensible ESP would be discounted by a scientific investigator and some would turn out to be well evidenced and worthy of investigation. Thus the figures given below for paranormal phenomena are probably too high in terms of actual paranormal phenomena,[1] but do reflect the incidence of ostensible paranormal phenomena in our 150 marijuana users. It is, of course, the experiencer's own judgment of the paranormality of an experience that may radically alter his belief system, not the judgment of a hypothetically expert scientist. Thus ostensible paranormal phenomena are an important aspect of marijuana intoxication.

First, it should be noted that most of the users (76 percent) believe in the reality of ESP; their responses to the question, "*I believe in the existence of extrasensory perception (ESP), i.e., that people can sometimes*

---

[1]Although paranormal phenomena are not accepted as real by a large number of scientists, this is primarily a matter of belief system clash ("Since it can't occur, why should I waste my time looking at the evidence?"), or what Kuhn (1962) has called paradigm clash. The reader interested in a survey of the findings of modern parapsychology may consult the following references: Broad (1962), Heywood (1959), Johnson (1953), Murphy (1962), Rao (1966), and West (1954). While laboratory research has established the reality of some paranormal phenomena beyond doubt, the overenthusiastic and uncritical acceptance of these phenomena by the young is muddying the waters.

acquire knowledge about things happening at a distance in space or time, or about other people's thoughts, when there is no possibility of this knowledge having been acquired through the known senses (sight, hearing, etc.)" are tabulated in Table 10-1.

TABLE 10-1

BELIEF IN ESP

LEVEL OF BELIEF	PERCENTAGE OF USERS
Believe strongly	46%
Believe somewhat	30%
Haven't made up my mind	15%
Disbelieve somewhat	6%
Disbelieve strongly	3%
No response	1%

Note.—The percentages in this table do not add up to exactly 100% due to rounding errors and/or some users' skipping the question.

MAJOR EFFECTS

Telepathy

A specific question dealing with marijuana experiences was *"I feel so aware of what people are thinking that it must be telepathy, mind reading, rather than just being more sensitive to the subtle cues in the behavior."* This was a fairly frequent occurrence (30%, 22%, 31%, 12%, 4%), usually occurring at moderately high levels of intoxication (6%, 11%, 21%, 19%, 5%). Heavy Total users of marijuana report it more frequently than Moderate Total users ($p < .05$) or Light Total users ($p < .05$), with the Light and Moderate Total users peaking sharply at Rarely/Sometimes and not differeing significantly from each other. Users of Psychedelics need to be somewhat less intoxicated to feel they experience telepathy ($p < .05$).

A related phenomenon, dealt with fully in Chapter 12, is *"I empathize tremendously with others; I feel what they feel; I have a tremendous intuitive understanding of what they're feeling,"* a very common phenomenon, which occurs at Moderate levels.

Precognition

The experience of precognition is a rare phenomenon: *"I can foretell the future by some kind of precognition, more than just predicting logically from present events*" (64%, 19%, 11%, 1%, 1%); and while most (71%) of the users did not rate the minimal intoxication level for this, those who did gave it a quite high rating (3%, 3%, 7%, 11%, 3%). Heavy Total users report precognition more frequently than Moderate Total users ($p < .01$) or Light Total users ($p < .05$). Similarly, Daily users report precognition more frequently than Weekly users ($p < .05$) or Occasional users ($p < .01$), with a suggestion ($p < .10$) that Weekly users also experience it more often than Occasional users.

Magic, Psychokinesis (PK)

The converse of extrasensory *perception*, a sense of paranormally affecting the world, was investigated with "*I can perform magical operations that will affect objects or people while stoned*," and appears to be a very rare effect (83%, 6%, 6%, 1%, 0%). The few users rating level of intoxication indicated this as a high-level effect (1%, 1%, 3%, 5%, 3%). Daily users reported it occurring more frequently than Weekly users ($p < .05$) or Occasional users ($p < .01$). The users were also asked to describe examples of this; of the twelve who wrote descriptive comments, five users gave comments which were not readily understandable, suggesting a communications gap. One user expressed clearly a semantic problem inherent in the question: "I believe that magic is just 'doing' on a higher level of awareness. It is 'magic' to the spectator who does not expect or understand it. I have to be very stoned in order to be able to concentrate and flow at the same time to a sufficient degree to perform magic. 'Magic' tricks can be very funny and very beautiful, also astonishing. Maybe dangerous, too."

Two other users indicated that their experiences depended on how you defined magic; one described chanting *mantras* (Govinda, 1960) with others as a magical way of affecting them; another, "using subliminal suggestion in a soft voice across the room."

Of the phenomena reported that resemble those reported in the parapsychological literature: (1) two were of increased telepathic rapport ("playing guitar with a friend so well it seems magic," and "I can be 100 percent accurate about stating peoples' signs (sun), I can predict peoples' movements, social groupings"); (2) two involved being able to paranormally affect another user's level of intoxication ("I can get other people higher by *more* than ordinary communication—can feel as if I exude a force that draws their consciousness to me and higher, more than gaze and conversation alone," and "I can bring people 'up' if I want to—people who are close to me emotionally"); and (3) one involved a sensing of the *prana* force described in Chapter 11 ("Sometimes while stoned we play a game in which one person will hold his hand near another person's body. This will cause the person to feel a tingling, or other feeling in this area. Sometimes the affected person may have his eyes closed").

The frequencies of occurrence of these three paranormal phenomena are shown in Figure 10-1. Telepathy is reported more frequently than precognition ($p < .0005$) or magical operations ($p \ll .0005$), and in turn, precognition is more frequent than magical operations ($p < .001$). There is a parallel to laboratory work with the paranormal, where contemporary time ESP (telepathy, clairvoyance) studies are most often significant, precognition studies are not significant as often, and psychokinesis (usually "willing" dice faces to come up in a certain pattern) is a rare bird (Rao, 1966). The levels of intoxication for the three phenomena do not differ significantly, although the test is not very adequate due to the small number of users rating the precognition and magical operation items.

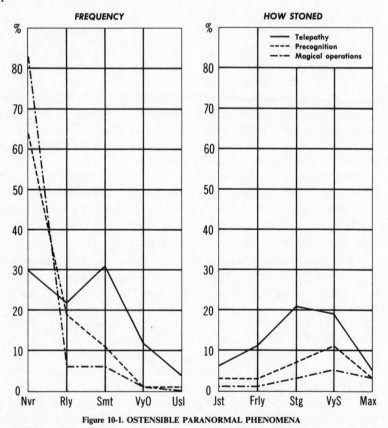

Figure 10-1. OSTENSIBLE PARANORMAL PHENOMENA

Note.—For guide to interpreting the "How Stoned" graph, see note on Figure 6-1.

Out-of-the-Body Experiences

A phenomenon rare in the pilot data, but of particular interest to me because of some intriguing laboratory findings (Tart, 1967, 1968), is the so-called "out-of-the-body" experience (OOBE) *"Have you ever had the experience of being 'located' outside your physical body, i.e., of you being at a different location in space than the one you knew your body was at? Dreams aren't included here, or situations where you just lose consciousness of your body. This is where you consciously feel located at a different place and know at the time that you are conscious but at a different location. Has this happened to you?"* The last sentence ended in several modifiers, *"at all?" "while stoned?" "happened before started smoking grass,"* and *"happened after started smoking grass."* The users were also asked to describe any such experiences. Fifty-three percent of the users indicated they had never had such an experience, 23 percent (34 users) that they had had it once, and 21 percent (32 users) that they had had multiple experiences; 3 percent did not answer.

Because OOBEs are not familiar to the general scientific reader, half a dozen examples will be given from the comments of 57 users who added some explanatory note to their positive response. This will illustrate the range of phenomena connected with OOBEs, a range similar to that reported generally for spontaneous occurrences of this phenomenon (Crookall, 1961, 1964a, 1964b; Green, 1968).

A rather classical example was reported by a 29-year-old electronics technician:

> It occurred one noon hour where I work. I was meditating when I perceived that I was looking down on myself, then looking at the roof of the buildings. The ground passed under as if I was flying, it became a blur then blue and then land again. I then found myself in a Lapp hut with an old shaman who was an old woman. She was brewing a tea of bird twigs and mumbling. The return was instantaneous. Someone at work shook my shoulder and I was back. At the time I did not know she was a Lapp. This came out after I described the kit and costume to my wife who is Scandinavian. We later researched it in several picture books on the Lapp culture.

OOBEs often involve seeing one's own physical body from an outside point of view. Of the 57 who added comments 19 percent specifically mentioned this. An example, also involving the rarer activity of the physical body continuing to operate in a complex manner, was reported by a 23-year-old user:

> I was riding my motorcycle home from school (with girl passenger). While I was operating all the controls (of the motorcycle), I was watching my motorcycle with the girl and me from a distance of about six to eight feet above our physical existence. I had no noticeable physical sensations

such as feeling while operating the motorcycle, though I seemed to be functioning fairly well. Physical sound didn't register either. I thought I was hearing wonderful, powerful, colorful, emotional, free music. The whole experience was remarkably enjoyable.

Accidents are often associated with OOBEs, presumably in a causative manner. A 36-year-old assistant manager reports:

Knocked unconscious in fall—saw crowd collect around own body from above, saw self lying on pavement. Perception and cognition very sharp for three days afterward.

While a defining characteristic of an OOBE is that one perceives the self as being at a different location from the physical body while knowing simultaneously that one is not dreaming, occasionally perceptual and cognitive changes occur in addition during the OOBE that indicate another state of consciousness is operative. The next three examples further illustrate such phenomena.

A 26-year-old teacher reports:

I sometimes view my body and the sequence of functions it follows in a particular environment from some operator's or observer's vantage above and behind my body. "The whole scene" is then more obvious to me in that I have a sense of 360° perception rather than 180–200°. I am now conscious of what is actually behind me.

A 22-year-old clerk reports:

Once on an acid trip in an apartment in San Francisco, a friend and I changed places. I was inside his head looking at my body and my face and hearing my voice *when he talked.* He was looking from my body into his face, and when I spoke it was with his voice.

As a final example of OOBE phenomena, a 44-year-old psychiatrist reports a fairly frequent sort of OOBE that involves "visiting" a sort of world that is clearly unlike the known physical world:

I left my own body, went into "another dimension" (?), where I found other people, all young (I was 42) playing games of "switch the body"—an experience like taking off your clothes and playing in the nude—very freeing—seemed somewhere in outer (or another) space.

Several background factors, which affect the reporting of OOBEs, are noted in Table 10-2, with significance levels for the obtained distributions.[2]

Fewer males tend to report OOBEs, but of those who do, multiple

---

[2]Because all users did not answer all parts of this question on OOBEs, the totals in various tables are slightly discrepant.

TABLE 10-2

BACKGROUND FACTORS AFFECTING THE REPORTING
OF OUT-OF-THE-BODY EXPERIENCES

	NUMBER OF USERS ANSWERING		
BACKGROUND VARIABLE	No OOBEs	One OOBE	Multiple OOBEs
Sex			
Males	46	8	17
Females	20	14	7
			$X^2 = 8.629, p < .05$
Meditation			
Meditators	14	6	3
Therapy & Growth	4	3	9
Ordinary	62	25	20
			$X^2 = 13.099, p < .05$
Psychedelics			
Users	54	23	28
Non-users	26	11	4
			$X^2 = 4.927, p < .10$

experiences are more common than with females. The Therapy and Growth group tends to report both more OOBEs and more multiple OOBEs overall. Similarly, there is a suggestion that Users of Psychedelics tend to report more OOBEs and more multiple OOBEs than Non-users.

Table 10-3 presents responses to the *"while stoned?"* part of the question.

TABLE 10-3

OUT-OF-THE-BODY EXPERIENCES
WHILE STONED

OOBEs WHILE INTOXICATED	NUMBER OF USERS
Never while intoxicated	27
Once	17
Multiple experiences, *all* with marijuana intoxication	5
Multiple experiences, some with marijuana, others without	14
Once, with LSD	6
Multiple experiences, with LSD	6

An infrequent phenomenon possibly related to OOBEs is "*I have lost all consciousness of my body and the external world and just found myself floating in limitless space (not necessarily physical space).*" This is dealt with fully in Chapter 11.

Although OOBEs are well-known in parapsychological literature as occurring "spontaneously" (in the sense of cause unknown) or being caused by serious accident or illness (Crookall, 1961, 1964a, 1964b; Eastman, 1962; Green, 1966; Muldoon and Carrington, 1956), the majority (73 percent) in this sample were in conjunction with marijuana intoxication or LSD use. More than twice as many users (38) indicated that their OOBEs began *after* they had started using marijuana as indicated they started *before* (14), a highly significant ($p < .001$) difference if one assumes the proportion should be equal before/after on the null hypothesis that marijuana use does not foster this experience. Twice as many Meditators report that their OOBEs occurred *before* marijuana use as after, however, with the proportion equal for the Therapy and Growth groups and more than three to one in the opposite direction for the Ordinary Users ($p < .01$, overall). The younger users also report that their OOBEs occur after starting marijuana use much more frequently than before, significantly different from the older group ($p < .05$), but this may only reflect the fact that the younger users have not had as much time for the experience to happen to them.

OOBEs are often interpreted as having profound religious significance by the users. An example is given in Chapter 19, Spiritual Experiences, although the user did not report this as an OOBE for the present question. Some other ostensibly paranormal phenomena, generally considered so exotic and far out that even modern parapsychologists have not dealt with them to any appreciable extent, are the sensing of energy in the body (*prana, ki*) and the sensing of *chakra* centers, dealt with in Chapter 11; the perception of auras around people, dealt with in Chapter 6; and the rare phenomenon of feeling possessed, dealt with in Chapter 17.

LEVELS OF INTOXICATION FOR OSTENSIBLE PARANORMAL PHENOMENA

All ostensibly paranormal phenomena and related phenomena have been grouped by level of intoxication in Figure 10-2. The overall grouping is highly significant ($p <<< .0005$). Between the Fair and Strong levels, feelings of intuitive understanding of people commonly occur, and this may progress to a feeling of telepathic contact as the user moves up toward the Very Strong level. At high levels, feelings of energy in the body and the spine may occur, along with (rarely) precognition and the ability to magically affect others. Up to this point we have been

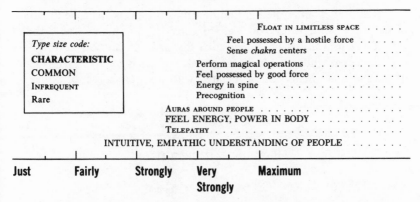

FIGURE 10-2. INTOXICATION LEVELS, OSTENSIBLE
PARANORMAL PHENOMENA

dealing largely with the ostensible paranormal extension of sensing and manipulating abilities in the known world. At the highest levels, we deal with infrequent and rare phenomena no longer relating to the physical world.

MODULATING FACTORS

The various background factors affect ostensible paranormal phenomena in a relatively linear fashion. They are summarized in Table 10-4. In general, more drug experience is associated with more frequent experience of practically all the paranormal phenomena covered in the present study. Meditators have more frequent experience with energetic phenomena, and the Therapy and Growth group seems to have more frequent experiences with OOBEs and some energetic phenomena.

SUMMARY

After allowing that general credulousness and specific drug-induced credulousness have probably raised the apparent incidence of paranormal experiences in this group of marijuana users, it is still clear that the proportion of users reporting such phenomena is much higher than in surveys of general populations, which have found a low incidence of 2 percent (Holland) and a high incidence of 22 percent (Germany) (Anonymous, 1958; Green, 1966; Membership Committee, American Society for Psychical Research, 1967; Prasad and Stevenson, 1968). Indeed, the incidence of personal experience of ostensibly paranormal phenomena is as high in the present sample as that reported for members of a society specifically interested in promoting the scientific investigation of the paranormal, the American Society for Psychical Research (Membership Committee, 1967).

Researchers interested in finding subjects especially prone to paranormal experience would do well to consider marijuana users. Either marijuana use affects judgment such that a large number of ordinary experiences are judged to be paranormal, or there is a very high incidence of paranormal phenomena associated with marijuana use, or both.

TABLE 10-4

EFFECTS OF BACKGROUND FACTORS ON OSTENSIBLE
PARANORMAL PHENOMENA

BACKGROUND FACTORS	EFFECTS	

More Drug Experience	More frequent:
	   Telepathy
	   Precognition
	   Magical operations
	   Auras around people
	   Energy in spine
	   Sense *chakra* centers	

		Less intoxicated for: Telepathy

Meditation	More frequent:
	   Energy in body
	   Energy in spine
	   Sense *chakra* centers
	   OOBEs before using
	      marijuana	

Therapy & Growth	More frequent:
	   OOBEs
	   Multiple OOBEs
	   Energy in body
	   Possessed by good
	      force	

Males	More frequent:
	   Multiple OOBEs
		Less frequent:
		   OOBEs

Older		Less frequent:
		   OOBEs after starting
		      to use marijuana
		
		Less intoxicated for:
		   Float in limitless space

CHAPTER 11

The Body

THE HUMAN BODY is something that is treated with great ambivalence in our culture. On the one hand, it is a frail thing and a source of sin and evil; on the other, a glorious creation and source of joy. Some people neglect their bodies entirely; other focus on them to the point of pathology (hypochondriasis). Our attitudes about what we put into our bodies are also extremely ambivalent; we pump them full of every food fad that comes along, alcohol, stimulants, tranquilizers, and, for some, drugs such as marijuana. Some of the dangerous drugs we put in our bodies receive great praise (alcohol, as a prime example); others, shocked horror. As well as being a reference point for many of our experiences, the body is thus a focus of many ambivalent attitudes, and it is particularly interesting to see what the effects of marijuana intoxication are on the perception of one's own body.

We shall deal with changes in the perception of the body under three semi-distinct categories: (1) changes in the ordinarily perceived aspects of the body, such as its size and strength; (2) the body in motion; and (3) changes in the perception of the internal workings of the body, which are normally not in awareness.

CHANGES IN PERCEPTION OF THE ORDINARY BODY

Direction of Attention

Perception of one's body is more affected by the direction of attention during marijuana intoxication than ordinarily; a common effect is "*If I am paying attention to some particular part of my body, the rest of my body fades away a lot, so the part I'm attending to stands out more sharply*" (13%, 15%, 37%, 27%, 6%). About as common is "*I lose awareness of most of my body unless I specifically focus my attention there, or some particularly strong stimulus demands my attention there*" (13%, 24%, 39%, 17%, 5%). This latter effect is more common among

Non-users of Psychedelics ($p < .0005$). Both effects begin to occur primarily at the Strong and higher levels of intoxication (2%, 19%, 29%, 26%, 7% and 3%, 17%, 28%, 20%, 14%, respectively). The older users do not need to be as intoxicated to lose awareness of their bodies if they are not focusing there ($p < .05$).

This phenomenon manifests in more extreme form with *"I have lost all consciousness of my body during fantasy trips, i.e., gotten so absorbed in what was going on in my head that my body might as well not have existed for a while,"* a common phenomenon (10%, 21%, 36%, 20%, 10%) of the very high levels of intoxication (1%, 7%, 19%, 27%, 29%), experienced less frequently by Daily users ($p < .01$, overall). An even more extreme version of this phenomenon, but still fairly frequent, is *"I have lost all consciousness of my body and the external world, and just found myself floating in limitless space (not necessarily physical space)"* (25%, 29%, 30%, 10%, 4%), which occurs at maximal levels of intoxication (1%, 2%, 11%, 21%, 31%). The younger users need to be more intoxicated to experience this ($p < .05$).

The relationships between these four phenomena dealing with awareness of the body are plotted in Figure 11-1. Totally losing awareness of the body and the world, and experiencing oneself floating in limitless space occurs less frequently than the other, less extreme ways of losing awareness of the body ($p < .0005$, overall). With respect to level of intoxication, the body fading from awareness unless attended to and the focused part of the body standing out more happen at essentially the same levels of intoxication. The two phenomena of totally losing awareness of one's body occur at higher levels of intoxication ($p << .0005$, overall) than the previous phenomena, but these two do not differ from one another.

Given that the perception of one's body is highly affected by the deployment of attention while intoxicated on marijuana, what are some of the specific changes?

Pain

A common effect is *"Pain is easy to tolerate if I keep my attention elsewhere"* (21%, 10%, 34%, 13%, 12%), with the linked opposite effect, *"Pain is more intense if I concentrate on it,"* which occur with essentially the same frequency (23%, 11%, 23%, 17%, 15%), an excellent illustration of the importance of deployment of attention. Both experiences occur at essentially the same Strong levels of intoxication (7%, 13%, 28%, 15%, 1% and 6%, 19%, 26%, 9%, 2%, respectively).

The phenomenon of pain being more intense if concentrated on is affected by several background variables. It is reported more frequently

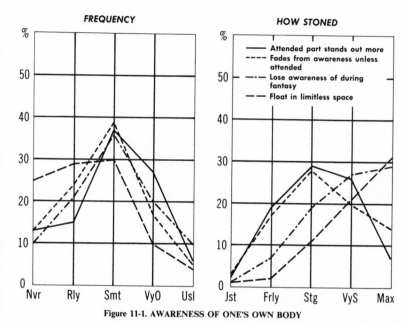

Figure 11-1. AWARENESS OF ONE'S OWN BODY

Note.—For guide to interpreting the "How Stoned" graph, see note on Figure 6-1.

by the younger users ($p < .05$), by the College-educated ($p < .05$), and by Non-users of Psychedelics ($p < .05$). The older users need to be more intoxicated to experience this ($p < .05$), while the Heavy Total users experience this at lower levels of intoxication than the Light or Moderate Total users ($p < .05$, overall).

Lightness and Heaviness

A common experience is *"With my eyes closed, my body may feel very light or even feel as if I float up into the air when stoned"* (16%, 16%, 41%, 19%, 8%), which begins to occur at Strong levels of intoxication (3%, 13%, 30%, 21%, 15%). According to my informants, having the eyes closed is not necessary to experience much lightness, but is necessary to feel as if one were actually floating. This experience is more common among the College-educated ($p < .01$).

The opposite phenomenon, *"My body feels abnormally heavy, as if it weighed much more"* (26%, 31%, 31%, 7%, 5%), is fairly frequent, but does occur significantly less frequently than lightness ($p < .005$), albeit at essentially the same levels of intoxication (3%, 10%, 28%, 18%, 13%). Heaviness is reported as occurring more frequently by the younger users ($p < .05$).

It is of interest to compare these phenomenological increases and decreases in the weight of one's own body with those earlier mentioned for objects, namely, objects' seeming heavier and objects' seeming lighter, discussed in full in Chapter 8. Figure 11-2 compares all four phenomena. Objects seem heavier more frequently than lighter, but one's own body seems lighter more frequently than heavier. Further, increased heaviness is more frequently attributed to objects than to one's own body ($p < .05$), but lightness is more frequently attributed to one's own body than to objects ($p < .0005$).

In terms of levels of intoxication, overall differences among these four phenomena are quite significant ($p < .0005$). While the levels are not different for objects feeling lighter or heavier, or for the body feeling lighter or heavier, a higher level of intoxication is generally needed for the body to feel heavier compared to objects feeling heavier ($p < .0005$). The same is true for body vs. object lightness; the user must generally be more intoxicated for his body to feel light than for objects to feel light ($p < .01$).

Body Size

One's own body may change in perceived size: "*My body feels larger than usual*" occurs infrequently (37%, 21%, 29%, 9%, 1%), as does the opposite effect, "*My body feels smaller than usual*" (44%, 25%, 21%, 3%,

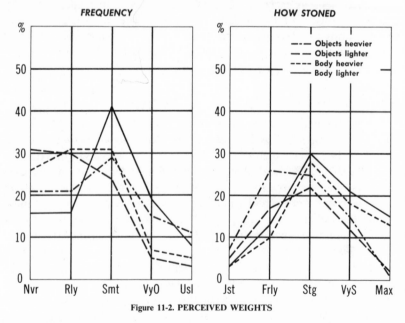

Figure 11-2. PERCEIVED WEIGHTS

Note.—For guide to interpreting the "How Stoned" graph, see note on Figure 6-1.

0%). Both may begin to be experienced at Strong levels of intoxication (1%, 9%, 21%, 23%, 4% and 1%, 7%, 17%, 18%, 3%, respectively, with many users not being able to rate these). The body's feeling smaller than usual is experienced more frequently by the College-educated ($p < .05$) than by the Professionals, and less frequently by Light Total users ($p < .05$, overall). Males need to be more intoxicated than Females to experience the body's feeling smaller ($p < .05$).

Irritating Effect of Smoking

An infrequent effect is a direct physiological effect of the irritating components of marijuana smoke: "*Smoking grass makes me cough hard while inhaling and holding my breath*" (14%, 42%, 32%, 9%, 2%). Thus, frequently, marijuana smokers use water pipes or *hookahs* to cool the smoke and dissolve out some of the irritating ingredients. No rating of intoxication levels was asked for, as the quantity and quality of smoke inhaled seem to be the primary factor determining irritation, although some of my informants indicated that if they are fairly intoxicated or higher, they can ignore the irritation of harsh smoke more easily and so are less likely to cough. Note that this item was scored one point on the Validity scale if a user answered Never.

Strength

A pair of experiences relate to strength: "*I feel much stronger when stoned (regardless of whether actually physically stronger or weaker)*" is reported infrequently (37%, 28%, 25%, 7%, 1%), with Heavy Total users experiencing this more often than Moderates ($p < .05$), and Moderate Total users experiencing it more often than Lights ($p < .05$). These feelings of strength begin occurring at Strong levels of intoxication (4%, 13%, 25%, 13%, 3%, with 43% not rating).

The converse effect, "*I feel much weaker when stoned (regardless of whether actually physically stronger or weaker)* occurs just often enough to be rated a common effect (27%, 21%, 33%, 11%, 6%), and occurs significantly more frequently than feeling stronger ($p < .05$), albeit at essentially the same levels of intoxication (5%, 17%, 25%, 14%, 6%).

Tremor

The final and quite infrequent effect on the ordinarily perceived body is "*My muscles develop actual physical tremors (large enough to see visually)*" (51%, 23%, 17%, 4%, 3%), which may occur at the Stronger and higher levels of intoxication in the minority of users who could rate this (1%, 7%, 11%, 14%, 11%).

These last few phenomena bring us to a consideration of the moving body in contrast to the relatively static experiences above.

THE BODY IN MOTION

Relaxation and Restlessness

One of the most characteristic effects of marijuana intoxication is *"I get physically relaxed and don't want to get up or move around"* (1%, 3%, 24%, 49%, 23%), which typically begins to occur at Moderate levels of intoxication (12%, 37%, 29%, 12%, 8%). While this occurs primarily at the Fairly and Strongly levels for Occasional and Daily users, many Weekly users also indicate Very Strong and Maximal for this effect ($p < .05$, overall). One informant commented on this to the effect that marijuana is naturally tranquilizing; the Weekly user is busy learning about all the things he can do when intoxicated, the Occasional user hasn't learned to exert himself like the Weekly user to overcome this tranquilizing effect, and the Daily user has already explored what he can do and is content to be relaxed.

The opposite effect, *"I get physically restless so that I want to move around a lot"* is common (16%, 25%, 40%, 13%, 5%), more so in the young users and the College-educated, compared to the older users ($p < .05$) and the Professionals ($p < .01$). It also occurs at Fair to Moderate levels of intoxication (13%, 29%, 26%, 7%, 5%). It occurs far less frequently ($p <<< .0005$) than feeling relaxed and not wanting to move, as shown in Figure 11-3.

Coordination

In spite of this tendency to sit around and relax, if the user moves about, he characteristically finds his movement seems exceptionally well coordinated: *"When I move about or dance, my motions seem exceptionally smooth and well coordinated"* (7%, 9%, 28%, 33%, 20%). This is reported as occurring more frequently by females ($p < .05$) and by Non-users of Psychedelics ($p < .01$). It begins to occur at Moderate to Strong levels of intoxication (7%, 31%, 37%, 13%, 1%), with Weekly users needing to be more intoxicated than Occasional or Daily users for this ($p < .05$, overall).

The converse effect, *"When I move about or dance, my motions seem awkward and uncoordinated"* is infrequent (25%, 31%, 27%, 8%, 5%). It may begin to occur from Moderate Levels of intoxication and higher

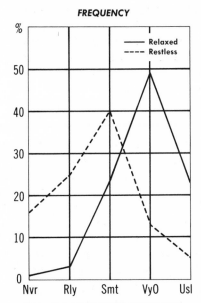

FREQUENCY

Figure 11-3. DESIRE FOR MOVEMENT

(7%, 17%, 19%, 17%, 8%). It is reported as occurring *less* frequently by Light Total users ($p < .05$, overall), Occasional users ($p < .05$, overall), and Non-users of Psychedelics ($p < .01$). The Professionals need to be more intoxicated to experience this awkwardness ($p < .05$). It is an important research problem to determine whether this is an actual decrement in coordination or simply an altered perception of one's own movements, possibly related to time alterations.

A more extreme version of poor coordination is "*My sense of balance gets very erratic, making it seem difficult to walk or even maintain a sitting position.*" This is a fairly frequent effect (29%, 35%, 28%, 6%, 1%) in that few users have not experienced it at all, but even fewer experience it Very Often or Usually. It is reported as occurring more frequently by females ($p < .05$). It generally occurs at Very Strong levels of intoxication (2%, 4%, 11%, 35%, 14%), with older users having to be less intoxicated to experience it ($p < .05$).

The relationships between these three effects on the quality of movement are plotted in Figure 11-4. Movement seeming exceptionally well coordinated occurs significantly more frequently than movement being uncoordinated and jerky ($p << .0005$) or than the sense of balance being lost ($p <<< .0005$). There is no significant difference in frequency of occurrence between awkwardness and erratic balance. Exceptional smoothness of movements occurs at lower levels of intoxication than awkwardness ($p < .0005$) and, in turn, awkwardness occurs at lower levels of intoxication than balance becoming lost ($p < .0005$). In general, marijuana intoxication seems at first to make movements feel smoother and more coordinated, but at very high levels of intoxication this may reverse and may sometimes culminate in experiential loss of the sense of balance.

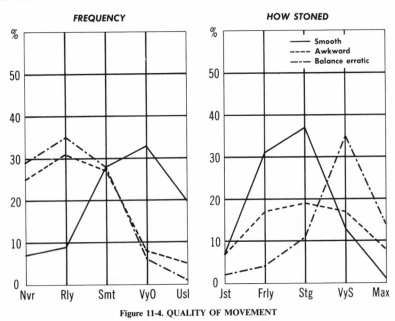

Figure 11-4. QUALITY OF MOVEMENT

Note.—For guide to interpreting the "How Stoned" graph, see note on Figure 6-1.

PERCEPTION OF INTERNAL PROCESSES

Shape of the Body and Location of the Self

We shall first consider an infrequent effect that stands as a bridge between the perception of the ordinary body with modifications and a more radical shift toward new internal perceptions. "*My perception of how my body is shaped gets strange; the 'felt' shape or form doesn't correspond to its actual form (e.g., you may feel lopsided, or parts of your body feel heavy while others feel light*," a fairly frequent effect (29%, 29%, 32%, 6%, 2%), which may begin to occur at Very Strong levels of intoxication (1%, 9%, 15%, 24%, 13%). This is of particular interest also in its relation to identity; the constancy of our perceived body can lend a stability to our sense of identity. Indeed, many people will readily localize their own consciousness in some part of their body more than others, and this may also change during marijuana intoxication. "*The location of my consciousness, the physical locale of the part of me that seems most me, has moved to different parts of my physical body from those it occupies while straight*" is reported, albeit infrequently (55%, 17%, 18%, 3%, 2%) and at Strong levels of intoxication by those users who could rate it (1%, 5%, 12%, 13%, 6%). The College-educated need to be more intoxicated than the Professionals to experience this ($p <$ .01).

Note that the rather high incidence of out-of-the-body experiences in this sample, already discussed in Chapter 10, represents an even more radical change in the experienced location of consciousness with respect to the body.

Interior Perceptions

General awareness of internal organs and processes was investigated with "*I become aware of parts of my body that I am normally unaware of, can't become aware of when straight, such as internal organs.*" This is an infrequent effect (35%, 23%, 27%, 11%, 2%), which may begin to occur at Strong levels of intoxication (1%, 3%, 19%, 21%, 13%), and is higher for Males than Females ($p < .05$). The converse effect. "*My body gets very numb, without feeling,*" however, occurs almost as frequently (42%, 29%, 22%, 5%, 1%) and at similar intoxication levels (0%, 3%, 16%, 19%, 17%). Males experience numbness slightly more often than Females ($p < .05$), but need to be more intoxicated to have the experience ($p < .01$).

That both increased perception of internal organs and bodily numbness occur, with about equal frequency and at the same levels of intoxication, serves to underscore the importance of psychological and situational factors in determining which of many potential effects may manifest at any given time.

We shall now consider some particular types of awareness of internal organs and processes, starting with the most frequent.

Warmth

"*I feel a lot of pleasant warmth inside my body*" is a common effect (13%, 13%, 34%, 25%, 13%), which begins to occur at Moderate to Strong levels of intoxication (9%, 23%, 33%, 17%, 1%).

Beating of the Heart

"*I am much more aware of the beating of my heart*" is also common (11%, 19%, 41%, 18%, 10%), more so with females ($p < .05$). It may begin to occur at Strong levels of intoxication (5%, 22%, 34%, 19%, 6%), with the Professionals needing to be less intoxicated to experience this ($p < .05$).

Breathing

"*I become very aware of my breathing and can feel the breath flowing in and out of my throat as well as filling my lungs*" is also common (21%, 18%, 40%, 15%, 5%), more so with the College-educated ($p < .05$). It may begin to occur at Strong levels of intoxication (6%, 13%, 33%, 18%, 6%). Meditators may experience this at lower levels of intoxication than the Therapy and Growth group or ordinary users ($p < .01$, overall), probably because so many techniques of meditation involve becoming more aware of the flow of breath.

Defecating and Urinating

"*When defecating or urinating, I become aware of the internal organ processes involved that I can't be aware of when straight.*" This is an infrequent effect (43%, 16%, 21%, 13%, 5%), which is reported more frequently by Heavy Total users ($p < .05$, overall). It is also experienced more frequently by the Therapy and Growth group ($p < .05$, overall). It may begin to occur at Strong and higher levels in those who experience it (1%, 7%, 19%, 17%, 5%).

Sexual Orgasm

Note also that "*Sexual orgasm has new qualities, pleasurable qualities, when stoned,*" is a characteristic effect. It is discussed fully in Chapter 13.

Most of the above experiences have a known physiological basis. We now come to a group of experiences which cannot be readily conceptualized as resulting from increased awareness of known physiological processes.

Vibration, Energy, Chakra Centers

The most common of these is "*I get feelings in my body that are best described as energy, force, power of some sort flowing*" (21%, 13%, 35%, 21%, 9%). Both the Meditators and the Therapy and Growth group experience this somewhat more often than Ordinary Users ($p < .05$, overall). It may begin to occur at Strong and higher levels of intoxication (4%, 10%, 25%, 26%, 7%). This experience is reported more frequently by Users of Psychedelics ($p < .05$).

A more general phenomenon that does not specifically interpret unusual internal feelings as energy or force is "*I feel a vibration or tingling sensation in some or all of my body that I can tell is not an actual muscle tremor by looking at my body,"* a common effect (27%, 15%, 32%, 17%, 7%). It is reported about as frequently, and at similar levels of intoxication (1%, 10%, 24%, 25%, 7%), as sensations of force or energy. It is also of interest to note that these tingling feelings are reported more frequently than actual muscle tremors ($p < .0005$).

There is an occult theory, known mainly in its Indian form in the West (Garrison, 1964) but occurring in the occult traditions of many lands (Blofeld, 1970; Chang, 1963; Evans-Wentz, 1958; Frager, 1970; Govinda, 1960; Muses, 1961), that there is some sort of psychical energy that flows through man's body, and particularly through the nerves such as those in the spinal cord. This energy has been called a variety of names, such as *prana* in India, *ki* in Japan (Westbrook & Ratti, 1970), *magnetic fluid* (Mesmer, 1774), and *odic force* (von Reichenbach, 1968). While proof of the physical reality of such a force is highly debatable, it is clearly a phenomenological reality. Since experiences with some sort of energy were mentioned by informants in designing the present study, the two previous questions were included to deal with this phenomenon. The phenomenon of an aura around people (Chapter 6) is also considered a manifestation of this energy in some occult systems.

Two more specific questions deal with the common statement in occult philosophies that the spinal cord is the main channel for this energy to flow through and that there are special centers (*chakras* in Yoga literature, *latifa* in Sufi literature; see Shah, 1968) in the body, primarily lying along the spinal cord, in which this energy may activate special sorts of experiences; i.e., if the energy flows into one of these centers, special psychological and/or spiritual experiences are manifested. An example will be given below.

"I become very aware of my spine and feel energy flowing through it" is a rare effect (59%, 17%, 14%, 2%, 3%), which may occur at Very Strong and Maximal levels of intoxication (3%, 4%, 7%, 14%, 7%). It is reported more frequently by Meditators ($p < .05$, overall) and by Users of Psychedelics ($p < .05$).

"I become aware of chakra *centers along my spine and feel changes in my state of consciousness as energy flows through the* chakras" is also a rare effect[1] (65%, 14%, 6%, 3%, 1%), which may occur at Very Strong and Maximal levels of intoxication (2%, 2%, 2%, 8%, 8%) in the few who have experienced it. It occurs more frequently among Heavy Total users ($p < .05$, overall) and among Meditators ($p < .01$, overall).

One of my informants, asked to describe an experience with *chakra* centers in detail, replied:

---

[1]It is interesting to note that most users (89 percent) apparently knew what *chakras* were, for few skipped this question completely as they had been instructed to do if a question made no sense to them. This reflects the tremendous rise of interest in metaphysics and the occult among the young.

I occasionally try various Yoga breathing and meditation exercises when I'm stoned. Several times I've tried one of inhaling slowly and deeply, picturing a flow of energy coming in with my breath and going right on down to the base of my spine. I hold my breath for half a minute to a minute, all the time picturing an accumulation of energy in the root *chakra* at the base of the spine. As I slowly exhale I picture this energy as flowing up my spine, all the way up to my brain. The several times I've done this have convinced me that *prana* is real and powerful enough so I've decided to stop fooling around with it. The first few breaths I'm picturing, imagining all this, but then it becomes real and I can *feel* the energy, the *prana*, flowing up my spine. My consciousness is changed in distinct jumps as it goes up my spine; and by the time the *prana* flows into my head, there is a very distinct jump, and I'm suddenly more stoned, and 25 percent more stoned than I usually am for smoking whatever quantity of grass I've had. I'll stay more stoned as long as I keep up the exercise, but drift back down in a minute or two after I stop. I can't really describe the nature of the particular sorts of consciousness I experience as the energy jumps up along the spinal cord. . . .

Figure 11-5 summarizes the relationships between the four questions dealing with perception of non-physical energies. Awareness of a general tingling or vibration, or feelings of energy or force in the body, both occur commonly; awareness of energy flowing in the spine or of *chakra* centers occurs much less frequently ($p <<< .0005$, overall). Both of the latter two phenomena also occur at significantly higher levels of intoxication than the former two ($p < .05$, overall).

Nausea and Sickness

Two rare phenomena complete the items dealing with the body. *"I get dizzy or nauseated, so much so that I wonder if I will get sick"* occurs rarely or not at all for the vast majority of users (47%, 41%, 8%, 1%, 1%). Actual sickness, *"I have gotten very nauseous and vomited"* is significantly ($p < .0005$) rarer (80%, 15%, 2%, 0%, 1%). Of the users who could rate these effects, these were generally considered the very highest-level phenomena (1%, 1%, 6%, 13%, 21% and 1%, 0%, 1%, 5%, 8%, respectively). My informants indicate that the usual way feelings of nausea are dealt with is to lie down, divert one's attention, and wait for them to pass. Usually one or two experiences with nausea are sufficient to teach a user what his overdose level is, and he will avoid smoking enough marijuana to reach that level in the future.[2]

---

[2]In many of the laboratory studies of marijuana or one of its active ingredients, tetrahydracannabinol (THC), nausea is frequently reported by subjects, suggesting that the experimenters may be overdosing them. While such findings are of interest in a purely scientific sense, they are not representative of the ordinary use of marijuana.

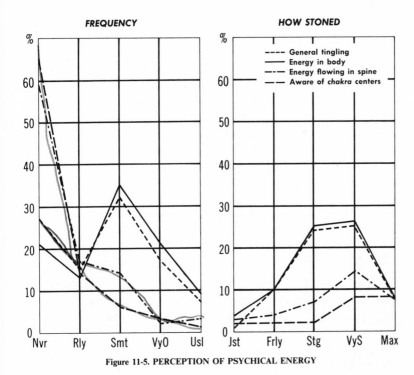

Figure 11-5. PERCEPTION OF PSYCHICAL ENERGY

Note.—For guide to interpreting the "How Stoned" graph, see note on Figure 6-1.

ADDITIONAL EFFECTS

Many additional effects were volunteered for the body:

"When I'm walking it seems as if the world is rolling under me and I'm remaining still" (Very Often, Fairly).

"I become much more aware of my body temperature" (Usually, Fairly).

"Pains in the chest" (Sometimes, Fairly).

"I feel like I am controlling a huge machine (my body) from my eyes" (Sometimes, Very Strongly).

"After much pot, my head feels as if it were about to explode" (Sometimes, Very Strongly).

"My whole body is surrounded by a ghost body about six inches thick (all rounded); when I close my eyes, I fill out" (Sometimes, Very Strongly).

"I can feel the blood rushing through my veins, pulsating throughout my entire body" (Usually, Just).

"Body consciousness includes large amount of space all around actual physical body" (Usually, Fairly).

"Parts of my body begin to *feel* as if they're moving wildly, faster and faster, in geometrical patterns. Actions I perform are repeated over and over in my mind, so that I feel that my body is racing about (i.e., I chew my food and suddenly my mouth is moving in fast, set patterns), even though I'm doing this slowly or not at all" (Very Often, Very Strongly).

"My feet and legs immediately become cold and numb when stoned and become progressively number and colder as my 'stonedness' increases in magnitude. When exceptionally stoned, I sometimes feel no contact with my skin. I've received surface injuries and not felt them. Heat and cold are difficult to perceive. I've walked in snow barefoot and not felt cold" (Very Often, Strongly).

"I become keenly aware of unrelaxed muscles and sphincters" (Sometimes, Very Strongly).

LEVELS OF INTOXICATION FOR BODILY EXPERIENCES

The various phenomena are arranged by levels of intoxication in Figure 11-6. The overall ordering is highly significant ($p <<< .0005$).

Effects on the perception of the user's body begin between the Fairly and Strongly intoxicated levels, and at first consist primarily of alterations in the perceived interaction of the body with external objects, i.e., the touch and muscle senses. As the user gets higher, sexual orgasm characteristically acquires new, pleasurable qualities, and a variety of internal processes may become accessible to awareness if attention is turned there. From this level up, the experienced body becomes more and more affected by the direction of attention rather than by the inherent physical structure of the body.

Between the Strong and Very Strong levels of intoxication, very unusual sorts of perceptions may begin to occur, which become more pronounced at higher levels, namely, sensations of vibration and energy inside the body, as well as the increased possible awareness of internal organs. The size and shape of the user's body may seem to change and the location of his consciousness in his body alter. Between Very Strongly and Maximally intoxicated, he may lose all awareness of his body during fantasy, and a few users may become aware of the *chakra* centers along the spine. At the maximal levels the user may feel nauseated, although this is rare, and even more rarely may actually vomit as a result of this nausea.

MODULATING FACTORS

Background factors affecting perception of the body, which had relatively linear effects, are summarized in Table 11-1.

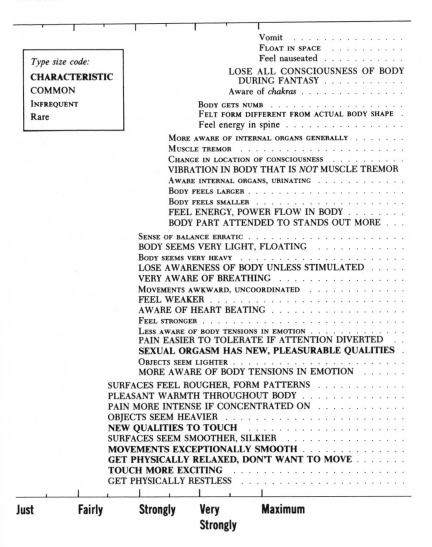

Type size code:
CHARACTERISTIC
COMMON
Infrequent
Rare

Vomit . . . .
Float in space . . . .
Feel nauseated . . . .
LOSE ALL CONSCIOUSNESS OF BODY
DURING FANTASY . . . .
Aware of *chakras* . . . .
Body gets numb . . . .
Felt form different from actual body shape .
Feel energy in spine . . . .
More aware of internal organs generally . . . .
Muscle tremor . . . .
Change in location of consciousness . . . .
VIBRATION IN BODY THAT IS *NOT* MUSCLE TREMOR
Aware internal organs, urinating . . . .
Body feels larger . . . .
Body feels smaller . . . .
FEEL ENERGY, POWER FLOW IN BODY . . . .
BODY PART ATTENDED TO STANDS OUT MORE . . .
Sense of balance erratic . . . .
BODY SEEMS VERY LIGHT, FLOATING . . . .
Body seems very heavy . . . .
LOSE AWARENESS OF BODY UNLESS STIMULATED . . . . .
VERY AWARE OF BREATHING . . . .
Movements awkward, uncoordinated . . . .
FEEL WEAKER . . . .
AWARE OF HEART BEATING . . . .
Feel stronger . . . .
Less aware of body tensions in emotion . . . .
PAIN EASIER TO TOLERATE IF ATTENTION DIVERTED . .
SEXUAL ORGASM HAS NEW, PLEASURABLE QUALITIES .
Objects seem lighter . . . .
MORE AWARE OF BODY TENSIONS IN EMOTION . . . . . .
SURFACES FEEL ROUGHER, FORM PATTERNS . . . .
PLEASANT WARMTH THROUGHOUT BODY . . . .
PAIN MORE INTENSE IF CONCENTRATED ON . . . .
OBJECTS SEEM HEAVIER . . . .
NEW QUALITIES TO TOUCH . . . .
SURFACES SEEM SMOOTHER, SILKIER . . . .
MOVEMENTS EXCEPTIONALLY SMOOTH . . . .
GET PHYSICALLY RELAXED, DON'T WANT TO MOVE . . . .
TOUCH MORE EXCITING . . . .
GET PHYSICALLY RESTLESS . . . .

Just   Fairly   Strongly   Very   Maximum
Strongly

FIGURE 11-6. INTOXICATION LEVELS, BODY PHENOMENA

Both more drug experience and experience with meditation are associated with more frequent experience of energy in the body and some of its exotic concomitants such as *chakra* centers.

Feeling physically relaxed and not wanting to move is mostly reported at Fairly/Strongly as a minimal level of intoxication, but Weekly users have a significant number of responses at Very Strong/Maximum for this. The same pattern occurs for Weekly users on levels of intoxication for movement being exceptionally smooth.

TABLE 11-1

EFFECTS OF BACKGROUND FACTORS ON PERCEPTION OF THE BODY

BACKGROUND FACTORS	EFFECTS	

More Drug Experience	More frequent:
	  Body feels smaller
	  Feel stronger
	  Aware of internal
	    organs when
	    defecating
	  Feel energy in spine
	  Aware of *chakra*
	    centers
	  Movements awkward
	  Feelings of energy in
	    body
		Less frequent:
		  Lose awareness of
		    body parts not
		    focused
		  Pain more intense
		  Movement
		    exceptionally
		    smooth, coordinated
		  Lose consciousness of
		    body in fantasy
		
		Less intoxicated for:
		  Pain more intense

Older	
	
	More intoxicated for:
	  Pain more intense
		Less frequent:
		  Pain more intense
		  Body feels heavier
		  Physically restless
		
		Less intoxicated for:
		  Float in limitless space
		  Lose awareness of
		    body parts not
		    focused on
		  Balance erratic

More Educated	
	
	More intoxicated for:
	  Movements awkward
		Less frequent:
		  Pain more intense
		  Body feels light
		  Body feels smaller
		  Hyperaware of
		    breathing
		  Physically restless
		
		Less intoxicated for:
		  Location of
		    consciousness moves
		  Aware of heart beating

Males	More frequent:
	  Body feels numb
	
	More intoxicated for:
	  More aware of internal
	    organs
	  Body feels numb
	  Body feels smaller
		Less frequent:
		  Aware of heart beating
		  Movements
		    exceptionally
		    smooth, coordinated
		  Balance erratic

TABLE 11-1 (*Continued*)

BACKGROUND FACTORS	EFFECTS

Meditators	More frequent:
	  Energy in body
	  Energy in spine
	  Aware of *chakra*
	    centers
	
	                      Less intoxicated for:
	                        Hyperaware of
	                          breathing

Therapy & Growth	More frequent:
	  Aware of internal
	    organs when
	    defecating
	  Energy in body

SUMMARY

Except for various enhancements of touch sensation, physical relaxation, and smoothness of movement, there are practically no characteristic effects of marijuana intoxication on the perception of the user's body, i.e., while there are many potential alterations of the perception of the body, few of them are highly likely unless specific psychological and situational factors bring them out.

In general, the perception of the body becomes less determined by actual structure and more affected by the deployment of attention during marijuana intoxication. The body and its parts may fade partially or completely from awareness if not concentrated on, and the user may totally lose awareness of his body and be immersed in some internal experience or fantasy. When attention is deployed properly (voluntarily or by circumstances), a wide variety of perceptions of the internal workings of the body are possible, including many processes which one cannot normally be aware of. It is also common for various feelings described as energy, force, or power to be sensed within the body.

The only bodily effect of marijuana intoxication that is decidedly unpleasant, nausea, is a rare effect, usually coped with by the user's diverting his attention; actual sickness is extremely rare.

These experimental alterations of bodily perception could be of great theoretical importance to psychosomatic medicine and the study of the relationship of identity to the body.

CHAPTER 12

Social Interaction

MUCH MARIJUANA use is carried out in the company of other users. This results not only in a variety of effects on interpersonal relations, but the gestalt configuration of a group of users at any given time can strongly affect each user's individual experiences.

We shall consider social effects under three semi-distinct categories: (1) overall characteristics of groups of intoxicated users; (2) perceptions of the quality of social interaction; and (3) some negative effects on social interaction.

OVERALL CHARACTERISTICS OF INTOXICATED GROUPS

Quieting Effects

An extremely characteristic effect of marijuana intoxication, in comparison to alcohol intoxication, is "*I am less noisy and boisterous at parties than when drunk or tipsy on alcohol*" (7%, 2%, 16%, 15%, 51%). One informant remarked, "When the cops walk into a party and everybody is yelling, arguing, and reeling around, they don't bother you; but if everybody is sitting around quietly talking or listening to music, they hassle you because they're pretty sure you're stoned!" Moderate Total use is associated with a higher frequency of this than Light, and Light with a higher frequency than Heavy ($p < .05$, overall). Quietness begins to occur at Low levels of intoxication (23%, 27%, 20%, 9%, 1%).

This sort of quietness is characteristic even without a comparison with alcohol intoxication: "*I am less noisy and boisterous at parties than when straight*" (5%, 9%, 30%, 23%, 29%). This is reported less frequently by the Occasional users ($p < .05$, overall). Users of Psychedelics do not need to be as intoxicated to experience this ($p < .05$), and the effect generally begins at Moderate levels (16%, 30%, 29%, 11%, 3%).

Being less noisy than when intoxicated on alcohol is more frequent ($p < .0005$) than being quieter than when straight, as shown in Figure 12-1, but they occur at essentially the same levels of intoxication.

FREQUENCY

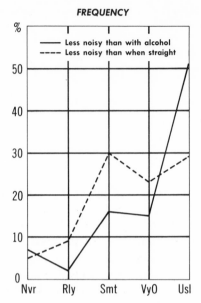

Figure 12-1. NOISINESS AT PARTIES .

This general quieting effect of marijuana intoxication in social groups generally is further reflected in the very common effect, "*I talk a lot less than when straight*" (5%, 11%, 49%, 21%, 13%), an effect that begins to occur in the Moderate to Strong ranges of intoxication (11%, 21%, 38%, 16%, 7%). The converse effect, "*I talk a lot more than when straight*" is a common effect (12%, 23%, 45%, 13%, 5%), which begins in the Moderate levels of intoxication (15%, 33%, 29%, 4%, 2%), but it occurs significantly less frequently ($p < .01$) and at lower levels of intoxication ($p < .0005$) than talking less, as shown in Figure 12-2.

The Meditators less often report that they talk more when intoxicated ($p < .05$, overall). The College-educated need to be more intoxicated to talk more ($p < .05$), as do Users of Psychedelics ($p < .01$).

Sociability

"*I become more sociable: I want to be with and interact with people more*" is a common effect (5%, 17%, 45%, 19%, 12%), but its converse, "*I become less sociable; I want to be by myself*" is just as common (7%, 19%, 49%, 17%, 7%). The latter effect occurs at higher levels of intoxication than the former (16%, 48%, 25%, 3%, 1% and 11%, 22%, 30%, 15%, 10%, respectively, $p < .0005$), as shown in Figure 12-3. Of the people at a marijuana party, the ones sitting by themselves may often be more

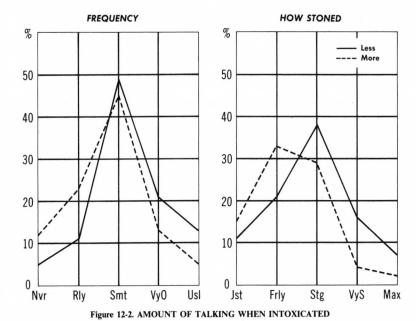

Figure 12-2. AMOUNT OF TALKING WHEN INTOXICATED

Note.—For guide to interpreting the "How Stoned" graph, see note on Figure 6-1.

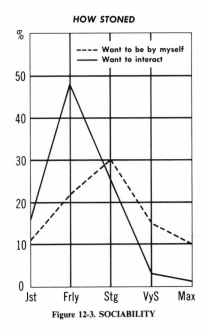

Figure 12-3. SOCIABILITY

Note.—For guide to interpreting the "How Stoned" graph, see note on Figure 6-1.

intoxicated than the ones conversing. The Meditators report higher levels
of intoxication for wanting to be by themselves ($p < .05$, overall).

Changes in Overt Behavior

Before considering the more specific ways in which social interaction
is altered among intoxicated users, it is of interest to wonder how much
an outside (non-intoxicated) observer would notice as different in the
actual social interaction of intoxicated users. It is a common experience
that *"Others (who were straight at the time) have not noticed that I've
been stoned (applies to other people who were your friends and would
have told you if they'd noticed)"* (11%, 9%, 34%, 21%, 14%). This is reported
as occurring more frequently by the older users ($p < .01$). The relationship between educational level and this effect is complex, as presented in Figure 12-4. The differences between the distributions are
significant ($p < .01$).

The users were asked to rate the *highest* level of intoxication at
which others have not noticed they were intoxicated. This was primarily
the Strong and Very Strong levels (5%, 15%, 27%, 23%, 5%); thus, users
can be experiencing a wide variety of powerful effects without outside
observers (friends who were straight at the time) being able to notice
any differences in their external behavior. Heavy Total users indicate

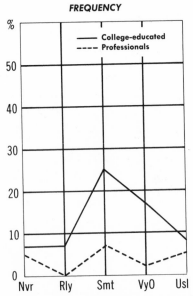

Figure 12-4. EDUCATIONAL LEVEL AND UNNOTICEABILITY
OF INTOXICATION

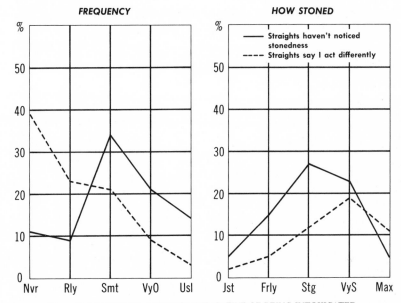

Figure 12-5. EXTERNAL BEHAVIOR INDICATIVE OF BEING INTOXICATED

Note.—For guide to interpreting the "How Stoned" graph, see note on Figure 6-1.

higher levels for this unnoticeability (Very Strong/Maximum) than Moderate and Light Total users ($p < .05$, overall), as do Users of Psychedelics ($p < .05$). More drug experience apparently allows the user to appear normal at very high levels of intoxication.

The converse of unaltered external behavior is *"Others (who were straight at the time) have told me that I act very differently when I'm stoned,"* an infrequent effect (39%, 23%, 21%, 9%, 3%), which may begin to occur at Very Strong levels of intoxication (2%, 5%, 12%, 19%, 11%). As shown in Figure 12-5, acting noticeably different when intoxicated occurs less frequently than no noticeable differences ($p << .0005$), and at higher levels ($p < .01$).

The unawareness of friends that they are intoxicated is often amazing to users; as one informant, a 40-year-old psychologist, put it, "Several times I've gone home stoned, not tremendously so but pretty stoned, and my wife, who knows me incredibly well, hasn't noticed a thing. I stand there seeing all these obvious changes in my experience, and it's just incredible that she doesn't notice!"[1]

Given these general qualities of marijuana intoxication on social groupings, namely, a general quieting effect, let us now examine what

---

[1]This apparent rarity of changes in external behavior should be carefully noted in terms of research methodology; insofar as it is true, behavioristic approaches to this area will waste a lot of time.

changes in social interaction are reported when the user chooses to interact with others.

QUALITY OF SOCIAL INTERACTION

Game Playing

A very characteristic effect of marijuana intoxication is "*I find it very hard to play ordinary social games when stoned*" (6%, 7%, 21%, 35%, 27%), i.e., various kinds of polite social chit-chat and the like seem hollow and worthless, not worth engaging in. They are "seen through," as later descriptions of effects will indicate. This is reported less frequently by Heavy Total users ($p < .0005$, overall), suggesting some Heavy Total users have learned to function quite easily in ordinary social settings. The College-educated also experience this difficulty more frequently ($p < .05$). This effect begins to occur by Moderate levels (13%, 32%, 24%, 13%, 5%).

On the other hand, it is common for users to report "*I can play elaborate games and get very involved in the games*" (14%, 25%, 34%, 17%, 9%), beginning at Moderate to Strong levels (13%, 31%, 30%, 8%, 1%). Light Total users have to be more intoxicated for this ($p < .05$) and Users of Psychedelics less intoxicated ($p < .05$). The social games played while intoxicated are not always elaborate, however; "*when stoned with others, I play 'childish' games; i.e., we interact with each other in ways which are very enjoyable but which people would ordinarily consider childish*" is a very common experience (5%, 15%, 51%, 22%, 7%). As one informant put it, "Kids have a lot of fun just doing groovy things like skipping; and if you're stoned with your friends and somebody says 'Wouldn't it be neat to skip down the road?' we may do it and have a ball. We care less that some dumb-ass old authority figure is sitting around and frowning and saying, 'Grownups don't skip!' " Playing childish games may occur in the Moderate to Strong levels and higher (9%, 31%, 37%, 15%, 1%).

Figure 12-6 plots the interrelationships of these three aspects of social game playing. Difficulty in playing ordinary games is more frequent than playing childish games ($p < .0005$), and playing childish games is more frequent than playing elaborate games ($p < .01$). Playing childish games tends to occur at higher levels than finding it hard to play ordinary social games ($p < .05$), but there are no other significant differences in level of intoxication.

There are a number of alterations in the perception of social interaction that lie behind the change in overall social interaction, which we shall now consider in decreasing order of frequency.

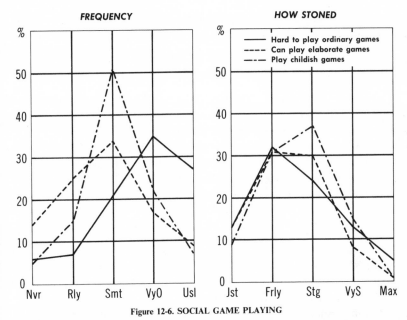

FREQUENCY **HOW STONED**

— Hard to play ordinary games
---- Can play elaborate games
–·– Play childish games

Figure 12-6. SOCIAL GAME PLAYING

Note.—For guide to interpreting the "How Stoned" graph, see note on Figure 6-1.

Insights into Others

A characteristic effect is "*I have feelings of deep insights into other people, how they tick, what their games are, when stoned (regardless of whether they check out later)*" (7%, 7%, 31%, 34%, 21%). These feelings occur in the Moderate to Strong levels (10%, 35%, 39%, 6%, 2%). A related phenomenon, discussed fully in Chapter 6, is "*The face of another person will change even as I watch it, so he keeps changing from one different person to another.*" Some informants indicate that sometimes this is a purely illusory experience on the part of the perceiver, but other times it seems a veridical "illusion" in that it allows insights into the perceived person's character, literally seeing one of the other "persons" within him. Another common, related phenomenon, discussed fully in Chapter 15, is "*I learn a great deal about psychological processes, what makes people tick. . . .*"

Not only do users characteristically feel as if they have insights into others, they very commonly empathize with them: "*I empathize tremendously with others; I feel what they feel; I have a tremendous intuitive understanding of what they're feeling*" (7%, 11%, 40%, 25%, 18%). This begins to occur at Moderate to Strong levels of intoxication (12%, 31%, 35%, 10%, 1%). A more extreme form of this, discussed in Chapter 10, is the infrequent feeling of telepathic rapport with others. Indeed, this can reach the point of feeling merged with another person, or being at one with the world, as discussed in Chapter 18.

Profundity

Another very common effect influencing social interaction is "*I feel the things I say in conversation when stoned are more profound, more appropriate to the conversation, more interesting*" (5%, 13%, 37%, 27%, 15%). This occurs at Moderate to Strong levels (9%, 38%, 31%, 11%, 1%). While most Users of Psychedelics indicate this happens at Fair and Strong levels, Non-users are more variable, indicating Fairly and Very Strongly as main levels ($p < .05$).

Subtlety and Humor

A related characteristic effect is "*I appreciate very subtle humor in what my companions say, and say quite subtly funny things myself,*" dealt with in Chapter 15. Similarly, the common effect "*I giggle a lot when stoned . . .*" is dealt with fully in Chapter 16.

Another related phenomenon, dealt with in Chapter 15, is "*Commonplace sayings or conversations seem to have new meanings, more significance.*"

Group Unity

Our group of marijuana users, then, may be sitting together feeling as if they have increased insight into one another, empathizing more fully with one another, being more childlike and open, and saying more profound things. Thus it is not surprising to find that a very common effect of marijuana intoxication is "*When stoned with a group of people, the group takes on a much greater sense of unity, of real social relationship, than when straight; i.e., I feel much more part of a group instead of one person simply in the presence of other people*" (7%, 17%, 30%, 25%, 21%). As with the other social effects, this begins to occur at Moderate to Strong levels of intoxication (15%, 35%, 29%, 10%, 0%).[2]

Contact Highs

There is one particularly interesting social effect occurring in groups of users, which further illustrates the importance of psychological variables in affecting the nature of the intoxicated state: "*Being with people who are much higher than I am (as from their being on acid or much*

---

[2]Note, however, that marijuana intoxication does not inevitably create group feelings; if some group members do not fit in or seem "phony," this will kill any feelings of closeness or group coherence.

more stoned on grass) gets me higher even though I don't smoke any more grass." This is a common effect (13%, 13%, 32%, 23%, 15%), which may occur even at the lowest levels of intoxication (23%, 22%, 26%, 5%, 2%).

Related Phenomena

Other relevant phenomena for understanding social interaction are the loss of short-term memory, the feeling that this does not seriously impair the user's ability to carry on an intelligent conversation, and the feeling of having said things that were not actually said (discussed in Chapter 14), as well as various alterations in other cognitive phenomena (discussed in Chapter 15).

NEGATIVE EFFECTS ON SOCIAL INTERACTION

There were four effects studied that seem predominantly negative. The first of these is *"I feel isolated from things around me, as if there were some kind of barrier or glass wall between me and the world, muting everything coming in and partially isolating me,"* a common effect (29%, 21%, 33%, 14%, 3%). The Meditators experience this less often ($p <$ .01, overall). It may occur at the Strong and Very Strong levels (4%, 11%, 22%, 21%, 9%).

Another infrequent effect is *"I get somewhat paranoid about the people with me; I am suspicious about what they're doing"* (20%, 38%, 31%, 7%, 4%). Non-users of Psychedelics experience it more frequently ($p <$ .01). This also may occur at the Strong and Very Strong levels (9%, 15%, 21%, 24%, 7%). The Meditators tend to experience paranoid feelings at lower levels of intoxication ($p <$ .05, overall).

What may be an even more extreme cutting-off from social relationships is the rare phenomenon, *"Other people seem dead, lifeless, as if they were robots, when I'm stoned"* (49%, 27%, 18%, 5%, 0%). This effect may begin occurring from the moderately intoxicated level on up in the users who could rate it (3%, 11%, 13%, 14%, 6%). Users of Psychedelics may experience it at lower levels ($p <$ .05).

An infrequent negative effect of the group on the user is *"I am very strongly influenced by the social situation set up by my companions, so I will do whatever they are doing, even if it is something I don't want to do or wouldn't do normally"* (33%, 38%, 23%, 3%, 0%). This is reported as occurring more frequently by Males ($p <$ .05). Weekly users also have it occur more frequently than Occasional or Daily users ($p <$ .05). In retrospect, this question is hard to interpret, as it does not specify how undesirable the actions are that a group might pressure the user into doing. A highly relevant question, dealt with fully in Chapter 17, is "*I lose control of my actions and do antisocial things (actions that harm other people) that I wouldn't normally do.*" This is one of the rarest phenomena reported, with 77 percent saying Never, 22 percent Rarely, and only one user saying Sometimes. Thus the question on social influence must deal primarily with actions ordinarily unacceptable to the individual, but not necessarily harmful.

ADDITIONAL EFFECTS

Four users mentioned increased feelings of love and compassion toward others: (1) "Increased feelings of tenderness and compassion toward people I'm with, and toward animals, if any present" (Very Often, Strongly); (2) "I become less evaluative of myself and others, more loving" (Usually, Fairly); (3) "I am more concerned with other people's happiness" (Very Often, Fairly); and (4) "If there is some particular person whom I have not cared for, if I get the opportunity to be around him while I'm stoned, I often gain understanding of him and feel very close to him afterwards. The person need not also be stoned" (Very Often, Strongly).

"Feel that many statements made by other people are, more often than not, ambiguous" (Very Often, Strongly).

"When I am with others we tend to share fantasies" (Very Often, Strongly).

"I am more tolerant of other people's beliefs and ideas" (Usually, Fairly).

"I tend to become a member of a group: laugh when they laugh, listen when they listen" (Sometimes, Strongly).

"People seem more violent when I am stoned" (Sometimes, Maximum).

"I enjoy listening to stories about people" (Usually, Strongly).

"I feel much more political" (Very Often, Just).

"A feeling that my friends are different when they're stoned" (Usually, Just).

"Think you would like to turn others on" (Rarely, Maximum).

"Say something and then realize no one heard you—this is frightening, for you're with people and they didn't notice you at all" (Sometimes, Very Strongly).

"I dislike people, especially men who are with me—I see them differently, more clearly, it seems" (Very Often, Fairly).

"An ability to communicate ritual messages" (Usually, Strongly).

"I am aware of multi-level communication; i.e., people are communicating more things than their words express, and often the messages aren't related, or one is used to communicate another" (Very Often, Strongly).

"A good way to get to know someone more quickly" (Very Often, Fairly).

"I tend to want to be with familiar people who are as stoned as I" (Usually, Maximum).

"Can relate better to my own children" (Very Often, Fairly).

"Strong desire to be alone, bordering on narcissism" (Very Often, Strongly).

"Experience extreme withdrawal" (Sometimes, Just).

"Loneliness has a pleasant rather than an undesirable quality" (Usually, Just).

LEVELS OF INTOXICATION FOR SOCIAL INTERACTION

The effects of marijuana intoxication on social interaction by level of intoxication are summarized in Figure 12-7. The overall ordering of levels is highly significant ($p <<< .0005$).

Beginning at Low to Moderate levels, there is a general reduction of loudness and noisiness as the pattern of social interaction begins to change from ordinary interaction to that characteristic of groups of intoxicated users. Ordinary social games become harder to play; users become more sociable and talk more. Thought processes begin to alter so the users feel they have insights into others and interact more subtly, especially with respect to humor. A strong feeling of group solidarity commonly occurs in this Moderate to Strong range of intoxication. Generally, at these low levels, users feel social interaction is greatly enhanced.

As the users begin to enter the Strong ranges and higher, however, *inner* experience often begins to predominate over social interaction. When social interaction continues, it is usually felt to be very profound. At the highest ranges it includes occasional feelings of telepathic contact and merging with others. Because of the increasing intensity of inner experiences, however, from the Strong level up, many users become less sociable, more wrapped up in themselves. Many of my informants comment that when marijuana is first smoked at a social gathering, there is a lot of interaction, conversing, group discussion, good feeling, but if a lot is smoked, a fair number of people will often begin to withdraw into themselves or become involved in intense dialogues with another user rather than take part in the general group interaction.

Thus low levels of intoxication seem to facilitate and deepen social interaction among users, whereas higher levels may either deepen it further or result in withdrawal from the group.

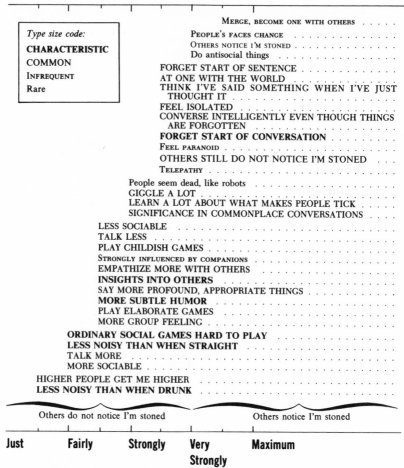

FIGURE 12-7. INTOXICATION LEVELS, SOCIAL EFFECTS

MODULATING FACTORS

Table 12-1 summarizes the effects of relatively linear background factors on social interaction effects.

Two phenomena were not affected linearly by frequency of use. Weekly users more frequently report being strongly influenced by their companions. They also need to be more intoxicated to believe they've said something when they haven't.

SUMMARY

In terms of its effects on users' perceptions, marijuana acts as a potentiator of social interaction in the Low to Moderate intoxication

TABLE 12-1

EFFECTS OF BACKGROUND FACTORS ON SOCIAL INTERACTION

BACKGROUND FACTORS	EFFECTS	
More Drug Experience	More frequent: People's faces change Less noisy than when straight Telepathy More subtle humor	Less frequent: Think said something when just thought it Feel paranoid Hard to play ordinary social games
	More intoxicated for: Talk more People haven't noticed I'm stoned Giggle a lot Forget start of conversation	Less intoxicated for: Quieter than when straight Insights into others People seem like robots Say more profound things Play elaborate games Telepathy
Meditation	More frequent: People's faces change Merge with others Feel one with world	Less frequent: Talk more Feel isolated
	More intoxicated for: Less sociable	Less intoxicated for: Feel paranoid
More Educated		Less frequent: Ordinary games hard to play
		Less intoxicated for: Talk more Merge with others
Older	More frequent: People haven't noticed I'm stoned	
		Less intoxicated for: Talk more Merge with others
Males	More frequent: Strongly influenced by companions	Less frequent: Giggle a lot
	More intoxicated for: Forget start of sentence	

levels. Users feel more empathy toward and insights into others, play childish and elaborate games, feel that their conversation is often profound, and commonly experience strong feelings of group unity.

At high levels of intoxication, marijuana may have two different effects on users because of the intensification of inner experiences. The user may become less sociable and withdraw from a group in order to more fully appreciate the inner experiences he is having or, if he continues to interact, may feel that the interaction becomes exceptionally profound, including such things as merging with another person or feeling so aware of another that it seems like telepathic communication.

Negative effects on social interaction are mostly infrequent or rare.

CHAPTER 13

Sexuality

GIVEN THE COMMON American stereotype of the "sex-crazed dope fiend," it is interesting to see what effects on sexuality are perceived by marijuana users themselves.

MAJOR EFFECTS

Desire for Sex

A common effect is *"My sexual drive goes up when stoned; I have more need for sex"* (18%, 21%, 28%, 21%, 12%). This may begin to occur at the Moderate to Strong levels of intoxication (11%, 25%, 32%, 8%, 2%). Users of Psychedelics experience this at lower levels of intoxication ($p < .0005$), as does the Therapy and Growth group ($p < .05$, overall).

The converse effect *"I have much less sexual drive when stoned; it's difficult to arouse me even in a situation which would normally arouse me"* is rare (42%, 34%, 15%, 5%, 2%). When it occurs, it is at the strong levels and higher (6%, 11%, 17%, 13%, 7%). The Professionals experience this loss of sexual need at lower levels of intoxication ($p < .05$).

A very common effect is *"I have no increase in sexual feelings unless it's a situation that I would normally be sexually aroused in, and then the sexual feelings are much stronger and more enjoyable"* (7%, 11%, 27%, 23%, 24%). Users of Psychedelics report this more frequently ($p < .05$) than Non-users. It generally occurs at Moderate to Strong levels (17%, 28%, 27%, 8%, 2%).

The relationships of these three alterations of sexual need are plotted in Figure 13-1. Sexual need going up when the situation is appropriate is reported more frequently than need per se going up ($p < .01$), and sexual need per se going up is more frequent than its going down ($p \ll .0005$). Most of my informants commented that sexual *drive* or *need* does not go up, but rather the knowledge of how intensely gratifying sex is when intoxicated serves to make any perceived sexual drive more attention getting and desirable when intoxicated.

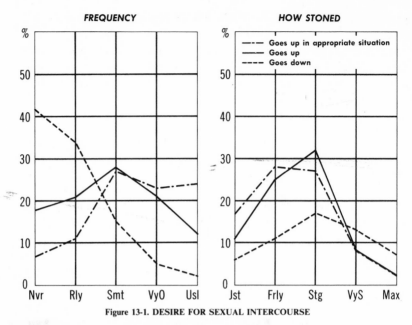

Figure 13-1. DESIRE FOR SEXUAL INTERCOURSE

Note.—For guide to interpreting the "How Stoned" graph, see note on Figure 6-1.

With respect to levels of intoxication, they are the same for sexual desire per se going up and for sexual desire going up when the situation is appropriate, but sexual desire going down occurs at higher levels of intoxication ($p < .01$ with respect to desire per se, $p < .0005$ with respect to desire in appropriate situations). My informants indicate that sexual intercourse at very high levels of intoxication can be an ecstatic, overwhelming experience, but at these levels chances are good that the user will be absorbed in his own inner experiences and not get interested in making love with someone.

Contact with Partner

A very common experience is "*When making love, I feel I'm in much closer mental contact with my partner; it is much more a union of souls as well as bodies*" (9%, 9%, 31%, 20%, 25%). This closeness occurs more frequently among Users of Psychedelics ($p < .0005$) and the College-educated ($p < .05$). It generally begins to be experienced at the Moderate and Strong levels (7%, 27%, 35%, 9%, 3%). The Heavy Total users and the Daily users both experience this closeness at lower levels of intoxication ($p < .05$ in each case).

The converse effect, "*When making love, I feel rather isolated from my partner; I'm wrapped up in my intensified sensations and not really very aware of my partner's reactions and feelings"* occurs infrequently (25%, 29%, 28%, 7%, 2%) and at Strong levels (5%, 13%, 25%, 15%, 7%). Feeling isolated from one's sexual partner occurs much less frequently than feeling closer ($p \ll .0005$) and at higher levels of intoxication ($p < .05$), as shown in Figure 13-2.

Qualities of Orgasm

One of the factors that enhance love-making when intoxicated on marijuana is the characteristic effect, *"Sexual orgasm has new qualities, pleasurable qualities, when stoned"* (6%, 9%, 22%, 27%, 28%). This occurs somewhat less often, albeit still very frequently, for the Meditators ($p < .01$, overall) and the Professionals ($p < .01$). Most users experience these new qualities of orgasm by the Strong level of intoxication (8%, 21%, 37%, 8%, 8%).

Among the various qualities potentially going into orgasm enhancement that my informants are able to describe, one or several of the following may be experienced as part of an orgasm when intoxicated: (1) prolongation of orgasm (possibly an effect of time slowing); (2) feelings of energy flowing and/or exploding or erupting in the body; (3) feelings of energy interchange with one's sexual partner, both flows

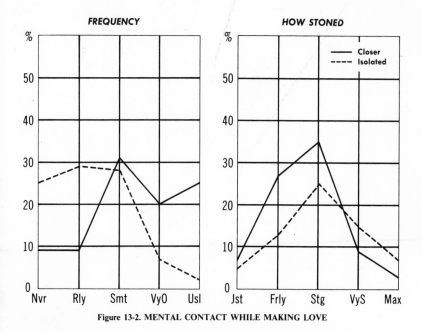

Figure 13-2. MENTAL CONTACT WHILE MAKING LOVE

Note.—For guide to interpreting the "How Stoned" graph, see note on Figure 6-1.

before orgasm and explosive interchanges through the genitals and whole body during orgasm; (4) absolutely total immersion in the orgasm, no distractions of any sort; (5) the orgasm taking place as ecstatic sensations through most of the body rather than being confined to the genital area; (6) merging of identity with one's sexual partner during orgasm, with a sharing of sensation and joy; (7) feelings that the energy interchange during orgasm balances and replenishes each partner's own vital energies, rather than depleting them—more so than when not intoxicated; (8) greater awareness of the bodily feelings leading up to orgasm, with a consequent ability to time one's movements in a way that will maximize the pleasurable qualities of the orgasm; (9) the ego temporarily disappearing, the body taking over, the orgasm happening rather than being produced; and (10) the feeling that the orgasm (and shared feelings with the sexual partner) are happening on a much vaster, wider scale than those consciously experienced, that this is an event of much greater magnitude or significance than the ego is able to sense or comprehend.

Because a number of informants indicated they are aware of what seems to be organ sensations in genitals and gut that are normally not in awareness, it is interesting to compare this report of new qualities to sexual orgasm with two more general changes in sensation, namely, touch sensations taking on new qualities (Chapter 8) and becoming aware of internal organs and processes that are normally not accessible to consciousness (Chapter 11). The relationships are plotted in Figure 13-3. New qualities of orgasm do not occur more frequently than new touch qualities, but they do occur much more frequently than awareness of normally unsensed internal organs ($p \ll .0005$). New touch qualities begin to occur at lower levels of intoxication than orgasm enhancement ($p < .05$), and increased awareness of internal organs at higher levels than orgasm enhancement ($p < .0005$). Apparently the sheer intensity of sexual orgasm may result in internal organ sensations connected with it that ordinarily occur at higher levels of intoxication.

Related Effects

There are a number of related intoxication phenomena, dealt with in preceding and subsequent chapters, that indicate, in conjunction with pilot interview data and comments of informants, some other specific ways in which sexual contact and intercourse can be altered. These will be briefly listed below.

". . . *sensual quality to vision* . . ." (Chapter 6). Looking at one's lover can be like touching him or her.

". . . *face of another . . . will change even as I watch it* . . ." (Chapter 6). One woman can become another woman, many women, all women, Woman.

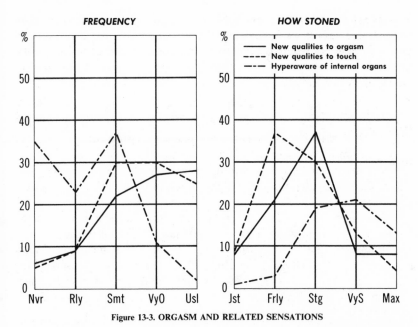

Figure 13-3. ORGASM AND RELATED SENSATIONS

Note.—For guide to interpreting the "How Stoned" graph, see note on Figure 6-1.

"*Touch sensations take on new qualities . . .*"; "*. . . touch more exciting, more sensual . . .*"; "*. . . surfaces feel smoother, silkier . . .*"; and "*. . . surfaces rougher . . . graininess forms interesting patterns . . .*" (Chapter 8). All of these changes in touch quality apply particularly to a lover's garments, skin, hair, mouth, genitals.

"*Taste . . . new qualities . . .*" and "*Smell . . . new qualities . . .*" (Chapter 8) apply to kissing and oral-genital contacts.

"*I empathize tremendously . . . feel what they feel . . .*" (Chapter 12). Your lover's joy is your joy; your lover's pain is your pain.

"*. . . so absorbed . . . in a person . . . felt as if I were that . . . person . . .*" (Chapter 18). Total blending, merging with one's lover.

"*Some events become archetypal, part of the basic way man has always done things . . .*" (Chapter 18). Instead of John Smith and Mary Jones making it in John's apartment in California on a particular night, Man and Woman Blend Together, in Now and Eternity, Here and Everywhere, an integral part of the Blending of Maleness and Femaleness of the Universe.

Note also that sexual fantasy, as well as real sexuality, can be markedly enhanced by marijuana intoxication. Imagery in all sensory modalities is generally enhanced, so fantasy preceding actual sexual contact or masturbation can be much more intense and exciting than ordinarily. New and pleasurable qualities to orgasm can occur with masturbation as well as actual sexual contact. My informants indicate, however, that as greatly enhanced as fantasy and masturbation are, that enhancement generally does not begin to compare to the enhancement of real sexuality.

Being a Better Lover

The final item dealing with sexuality was "*I feel as if I'm a better person to make love with when stoned.*" This is a common experience (26%, 12%, 20%, 12%, 20%). Although many users (44 percent) did not rate the minimal level of intoxication for this, those who did generally considered it a Moderate- to Strong-level effect (8%, 15%, 20%, 9%, 3%). The College-educated indicated higher levels of intoxication for this than the Professionals ($p < .05$).

The users were asked to explain *why* they were a better person to make love with when high on marijuana. Thirty-nine males and twenty-one females wrote brief explanations. These have been summarized in several categories in Table 13-1.[1] The number of users giving particular reasons is broken down by males and females, and by those of each sex who indicate Rarely/Sometimes or Very Often/Usually for categorizing themselves as a better lover when intoxicated.

TABLE 13-1

REASONS FOR BEING A BETTER LOVER

QUALITY	NUMBER OF MALES		NUMBER OF FEMALES	
	Rly/Smt	VyO/Uly	Rly/Smt	VyO/Uly
Less inhibited, more arousable	6	6	5	6
More contact with, responsiveness to lover, gentler, more giving	6	17	5	12
More sensual, stronger sensations, feelings	2	7	2	2
More control, capacity, coordination	5	4	0	1
More here-and-now, archetypal, spontaneous	3	4	0	1
Prolonged duration of love-making	0	1	0	0
Harder, longer-lasting erection	0	1	—	—
Miscellaneous	5	0	0	0

[1]Note that this table includes one or more answers from each user, and so is not amenable to valid statistical treatment. A valid table, using the main or first answer of each user only, was prepared, but as no differences between males and females reach statistical significance, it will not be presented here.

The first category, *less inhibited, more arousable*, represents answers such as the following: ". . . generally more open to my partner, less inhibited by sexual conventions . . ."; or "I'm usually somewhat inhibited when straight but not when stoned . . ."; or ". . . many of my inhibitions and petty thoughts are transcended by a much stronger desire to unite deeply with my partner"; or "Because *I'm* grooving to it more, because I'm frigid and when stoned I get close to coming, I'm more willing to experiment and please the other person."

It is important to clarify the above descriptions of reduction of sexual inhibitions by noting that my pilot interview subjects and later informants all commented to the effect that this reduction was not an aphrodisiac effect in the usual understanding of the word. Rather it was a selective lowering of inhibition. If the situation was appropriate, if the user really wanted sexual relations with someone else, marijuana would lower inhibitions; but if someone the intoxicated user does not like to be with attempts seduction or sexual manipulation, they will seem even more repulsive and undesirable than normally.

By far the most frequent reason for being a better lover when intoxicated, especially if the sexual partner is also intoxicated on marijuana, is feelings of *tremendously enhanced contact* with one's partner, sharing of feelings, being more sensitive, gentle, giving. A poignant expression of this was given by an eighteen-year-old male student: "When I am stoned and making love, sometimes I can be so much a part of my partner that it hurts and makes me feel very alone when we are apart . . ."; or "My own sensations are so acute that I want the person I love to feel it also . . ."; or "I feel closer physical and mental communication (actually both become one)."

The third category, *increased sensuality* and intensity of sensations, has already been illustrated above.

More control, capacity, or coordination is expressed in such comments as ". . . my movements are relaxed, confident . . ."; or "My actions are more fluid—heightened emotion and passion . . ."; or ". . . can do much more because I feel stronger . . ."; or ". . . can last as long as I'm stoned without tiring . . ."

More here-and-now-ness, spontaneity, sometimes leading to a totally archetypal experience is illustrated by: "The act and the communion become reduced to the most basic and, at the same time, expanded to the most elevated and consecrated form of experience possible . . ."

Increased experiential duration of orgasm and *increased erectile potency* are both illustrated by one student: "Potency seems to be incredibly augmented, such that an infinite orgasm could seem possible. I have had as many as seven orgasms in the span of one night, having been extremely stoned. My organ seems immense (when flaccid) and seems that it would swell to immeasurable proportions . . . my erection seems to be harder than steel . . ."

Note however that 26 percent of the users indicated they were never a better lover when intoxicated. As one user put it, "While I find it rather more pleasurable than not (the act itself), I feel that it is not *complete* somehow, because it becomes a purely sensual thing. This feeling of sensuality is tremendously vitalizing, but I find myself enjoying this so much that I wonder if my partner is aware of it in me; I am not aware of his pleasure, only my own, and this fact that neither of us can communicate this to each other makes it a selfish act . . . We both prefer not to have sex when stoned because of this." Another user, who indicates he is sometimes a better lover when intoxicated, points out the importance of direction of attention in this respect: "When I'm stoned, sex seems more natural and less inhibited. I seem to flow right into things—doing without thinking. But, I have heard later from the chick (on occasions) that I was out to gratify myself, not her. This type of self-gratification love-making usually happens when I occasionally go on a grass ego-trip. But there have been many times when we both are gratified; this result, fortunately, is the more frequent."

ADDITIONAL EFFECT

"Sexual orgasm entails a strong feeling of physical union, two making *one flesh* where I touch my partner" (Sometimes, Maximum).

LEVELS OF INTOXICATION FOR SEXUAL EFFECTS

Various phenomena affecting or characterizing sexuality on marijuana are summarized by level of intoxication in Figure 13-4. The overall stratification by level is highly significant ($p \lll .0005$).

Beginning at the Moderate to Strong levels, there is commonly more desire for sex (especially if the situation is appropriate), enhancement of sense qualities that add to sexual pleasure, especially touch, and the feeling that one becomes a better lover, usually with more feeling or empathy for one's sexual partner. At the Strong level there are new qualities to orgasm and, rarely, the desire for sex may diminish. If sexual desires are acted out, though, rather than the user getting caught up in internal fantasies and experiences, the sexual act becomes particularly profound at this and higher levels. Actions may become archetypal, all sorts of new sensations may arise from the body, and, near the maximal levels, the sexual partners may experience merging with one another, becoming one.

The potential sidetracking of sexual desires into a more general form of intimate contact was well described by one female user: ". . .

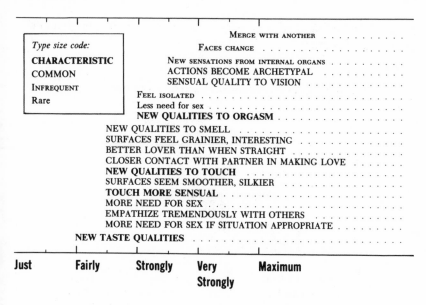

	MERGE WITH ANOTHER . . . .
Type size code:	FACES CHANGE . . . .
CHARACTERISTIC	NEW SENSATIONS FROM INTERNAL ORGANS . . . .
COMMON	ACTIONS BECOME ARCHETYPAL . . . .
INFREQUENT	SENSUAL QUALITY TO VISION . . . .
Rare	FEEL ISOLATED . . . .

Less need for sex . . . .
NEW QUALITIES TO ORGASM . . . .
NEW QUALITIES TO SMELL . . . .
SURFACES FEEL GRAINIER, INTERESTING . . . .
BETTER LOVER THAN WHEN STRAIGHT . . . .
CLOSER CONTACT WITH PARTNER IN MAKING LOVE . . . .
NEW QUALITIES TO TOUCH . . . .
SURFACES SEEM SMOOTHER, SILKIER . . . .
TOUCH MORE SENSUAL . . . .
MORE NEED FOR SEX . . . .
EMPATHIZE TREMENDOUSLY WITH OTHERS . . . .
MORE NEED FOR SEX IF SITUATION APPROPRIATE . . . .
NEW TASTE QUALITIES . . . .

Just	Fairly	Strongly	Very Strongly	Maximum

FIGURE 13-4. INTOXICATION LEVELS, SEXUAL EFFECTS

If I am *very* stoned (especially if both of us are) sometimes the mind just won't turn off, and even in the middle of a kiss there may come an overwhelming sense of peanut butter, roses, lakes, psychology, or goodness knows what. At times like these—fortunately it has usually happened to both of us at the same time—it is very pleasant just to talk and/or hold one another. Sexual attraction has become replaced or become less important than affection and simple contentment in the other's nearness. . . ."

MODULATING FACTORS

All the background factors affecting sexuality had relatively linear effects. They are summarized in Table 13-2. An interesting pattern seems to distinguish the group with much drug experience from the more educated group. The high drug experience group reports increased frequency of a variety of sensual enhancements and closeness to their sexual partners, while the more educated group does not have as much sensual experience, but has some of it at lower levels of intoxication, as well as reporting themselves to be better lovers at lower levels. The more educated group also experiences increased closeness to their sexual partners less frequently. This may reflect a generation gap in some ways, as the more educated are generally older than the rest of the users in the present sample, and may have many more inhibitions about sensuality and sexuality.

TABLE 13-2

EFFECTS OF BACKGROUND FACTORS ON SEXUALITY

BACKGROUND FACTORS	EFFECTS	

More Drug Experience	More frequent:
	    Actions become arche-
	        typal
	    New smell qualities
	    Faces change
	    Vision sensual
	    More need for sex if
	        situation appropriate
	    Closer to partner	

		Less intoxicated for:
		    Vision sensual
		    More need for sex
		    Closer to partner

Males	More intoxicated for:
	    Actions become arche-
	        typal
	    Awareness of interal
	        organs	

Meditators	More frequent:
	    Merge with another
	    Faces change
		Less frequent:
		    New qualities to
		        orgasm

More Educated		Less frequent:
		    Closer to partner
		    New qualities to
		        orgasm
		    Surfaces rougher
		    Vision sensual
		
		Less intoxicated for:
		    Merge with another
		    Surfaces rougher
		    Surfaces silkier
		    Need sex less
		    Better lover

Older		Less intoxicated for: Merge with another

Therapy & Growth	More intoxicated for:
	    New touch qualities
	    Touch more sensual
		Less intoxicated for:
		    More need for sex

SUMMARY

For practically all experienced users, marijuana intoxication greatly intensifies the sensations experienced in sexual intercourse. A minority feel that this takes something important away from sexual intercourse, namely, contact with their sexual partner as they become immersed in their own intensified sensations. For the great majority, however, marijuana seems to be the ideal aphrodisiac. Sex is generally desired more, but with others who would be likely sexual partners anyway; there is usually no drive toward sex unless the overall situation seems right to the user. Desire is then intensified, sexual sensations enhanced, and feelings of greater contact, responsiveness, sharing, desire to give, and empathy with one's sexual partner are often experienced.

While many aspects of human experience, particularly when intoxicated on marijuana, are difficult to describe, my informants and the user-respondents indicate this is particularly true for sexual experience. So much is beyond words. The descriptions above deal only with some of the partially describable aspects.

CHAPTER 14

Cognitive Processes: Memory

EFFICIENT AND ACCURATE access to memories is central to adaptive human action, both in terms of keeping track of the nature of immediate situations (intermediate- and short-term memory) and in keeping immediate action congruent with long-term values and knowledge (long-term memory).[1] With marijuana intoxication, the user perceives a variety of alterations in memory functions—enhancements, decrements, and falsifications.

MAJOR EFFECTS

Long-Term Memory

"*My memory for otherwise forgotten events is much better than when straight when I consciously* try *to remember*" is a fairly frequent effect (22%, 24%, 29%, 15%, 5%), which begins to occur at Moderate to Strong levels of intoxication (6%, 25%, 29%, 9%, 1%). The converse effect, "*My memory for otherwise forgotten events is much worse than when straight when I* try *to remember*" is an infrequent effect (27%, 28%, 22%, 11%, 7%), which also occurs at Moderate to Strong levels (4%, 19%, 21%, 17%, 5%). The College-educated experience this worsening more frequently than the Professionals ($p < .05$). The young experience worse memory primarily at Fairly and Very Strong levels, whereas the older users experience it primarily at the Strong level ($p < .05$).

Aside from consciously trying to recall things, a common effect is "*I* spontaneously *remember things I hadn't thought of in years, more so than straight* (*does not apply to consciously* trying *to remember things*)" (13%, 24%, 37%, 17%, 7%). This is more frequent among the young users ($p < .05$). It begins to occur at the Strong levels (6%, 18%, 37%, 17%, 3%).

---

[1]The terms long-, intermediate-, and short-term memory are not used in an exact technical sense in this chapter, but more generally to indicate memory span over years or days, minutes, and seconds.

The relationships of these three aspects of long-term memory are shown in Figure 14-1. Spontaneously remembering the past occurs more frequently ($p < .01$) than recall becoming poorer, and recall becoming poorer occurs at higher levels of intoxication than recall becoming better ($p < .05$).

Comments from my informants suggest that the nature of poor recall is one of selection; many memories are available, but they are often the wrong ones, not those the user wants.

Intermediate- and Short-Term Memory

A very characteristic effect of marijuana intoxication is "*My memory span for conversations is somewhat shortened, so that I may forget what the conversation is about even before it has ended* (*even though I may be able to recall it if I make a special effort*)" (3%, 7%, 29%, 49%, 11%). It begins to occur at Strong and Very Strong levels (4%, 15%, 39%, 30%, 8%). Heavy Total users need to be more intoxicated to forget the start of the conversation ($p < .05$).

Going from intermediate- to short-term memory, a common effect is "*My memory span for conversations is very shortened, so that I may forget what the start of a sentence was about even before the sentence is finished* (*although I may be able to recall it if I make a special effort*)"

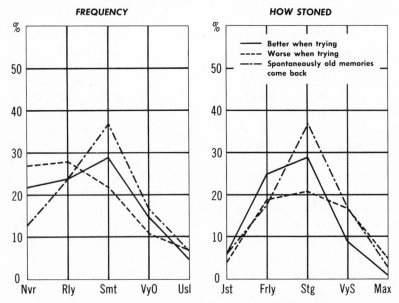

Figure 14-1. INTOXICATION EFFECTS ON LONG-TERM MEMORY

Note.—For guide to interpreting the "How Stoned" graph, see note on Figure 6-1.

(8%, 24%, 31%, 31%, 5%). This drastic shortening of memory span begins to occur at the Strong and Very Strong levels (3%, 9%, 28%, 29%, 22%), with males needing to be more intoxicated than females to experience this ($p < .05$).

In spite of this drastic shortening of immediate memory, it is also a common effect that "*I can continue to carry on an intelligent conversation even when my memory span is so short that I forget the beginnings of what I started to say; e.g., I may logically complete a sentence even as I realize I've forgotten how it started*" (6%, 20%, 43%, 24%, 5%). This effect also begins to occur at the Strong and Very Strong levels (5%, 13%, 33%, 29%, 9%). The college-educated experience this beginning at higher levels than the Professionals ($p < .05$), and the Weekly users at higher levels than the Daily or Occasional users ($p < .05$).[2]

The relationships of these three alterations of intermediate- and short-term memory are presented in Figure 14-2. Forgetting the start of the conversation occurs more frequently than forgetting the start of

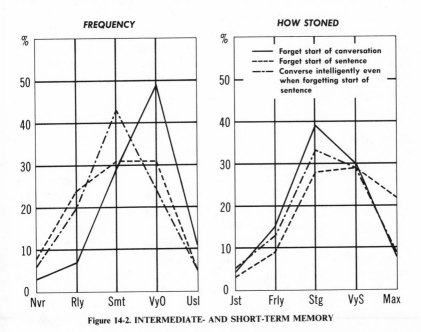

Figure 14-2. INTERMEDIATE- AND SHORT-TERM MEMORY

Note.—For guide to interpreting the "How Stoned" graph, see note on Figure 6-1.

---

[2]My informants indicate that this is an objective effect, for many of them have had the experience of talking to a straight person while they were intoxicated, forgetting the start of many of their sentences, but having no indication from the straight person that their speech was noticeably impaired. Whether this says something about the intoxicated state or the intelligence required to carry on normal conversation is an interesting question.

one's sentence ($p <$ .0005) or than being able to converse despite a shorter memory span ($p <$ .0005). Forgetting the start of one's sentence occurs at higher levels than forgetting the start of the conversation ($p <$ .01), and forgetting the start of one's sentence is rated as beginning at somewhat higher levels than being able to converse intelligently despite a shortened memory span ($p <$ .05).[3]

Two related items dealt with elsewhere also illustrate the shortening of intermediate- and short-term memory. Finding that thoughts slip away before they can quite be grasped (Chapter 15) occurs less frequently than either forgetting the start of the conversation ($p <<$ .0005) or the start of one's sentence ($p <$ .01), and at intoxication levels midway between these two phenomena, albeit not significantly different from either of them. Forgetting to finish a task one has started (Chapter 17) occurs more often than forgetting the start of one's sentence ($p <$ .01), but with about the same frequency as forgetting the start of the conversation. It occurs at lower levels of intoxication than forgetting the start of the conversation ($p <$ .01) and much lower levels than forgetting the start of one's sentence ($p <$ .0005).

In sum, there is often an increasing shortening of intermediate- and short-term memory span with increasing levels of intoxication, as much as forgetting the start of a sentence one is speaking at Strong and Very Strong levels, but it is commonly felt that this does not necessarily have any effect on the intelligibility of the user's conversation.

False Memories

A mild version of a user's memory playing him false is "*I think I've said something when actually I've only thought about saying it, more so than when straight.*" This is a common effect (18%, 24%, 36%, 19%, 3%), which may occur at the Strong and Very Strong levels (3%, 9%, 26%, 34%, 8%). Users of Psychedelics report it as occurring less often ($p <$ .05) and at higher levels of intoxication ($p <$ .05) than Non-users. Light Total users experience this mistake more frequently ($p <$ .05, overall), and Weekly users need to be more intoxicated to experience this than either Daily or Occasional users ($p <$ .01, overall).

"*I think something is a memory when it turns out to be a fantasy, something I just made up but fooled myself into thinking was a memory at the time (not the same as* déjà vu)" is a rare effect (47%, 27%, 20%,

---

[3]Being able to converse intelligently even though the beginnings of one's sentence may be forgotten, should, strictly speaking, occur at the same levels of intoxication as forgetting the start of one's sentence. This was not exactly so in the last difference mentioned above, probably because the slight ambiguity in the wording of the first question allowed it to include somewhat less drastic shortenings of memory span.

3%, 0%),[4] which may occur at the very high levels of intoxication (3%, 6%, 13%, 17%, 8%). Light Total users need to be more intoxicated for this ($p < .05$).

The experience of *déjà vu* (Chapter 9), a common effect beginning to occur at the Strong levels of intoxication, has already been described; this is another instance of poor operation of the memory process, for either a current situation falsely has the quality of "memory" attached to it, or an actual memory is not being completely labeled as a memory. It seems to *feel* like a memory without *really* seeming to be one.

The relationships between these three falsifications of memory functioning are shown in Figure 14-3. Believing a fantasy to be a memory occurs much less frequently than thinking one has said something when he has not ($p < .0005$) or *déjà vu*. Although *déjà vu* occurs at somewhat lower levels of intoxication than the other two effects, the differences do not reach statistical significance ($p < .10$ at the greatest).

Thus while the "quality" attached to contents of consciousness that identifies them as a memory may be frequently affected by marijuana intoxication, it is seldom that this is affected strongly enough for the user to actually mistake a fantasy for a memory, i.e., he may frequently

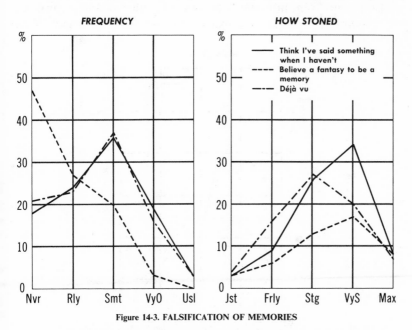

Figure 14-3. FALSIFICATION OF MEMORIES

Note.—For guide to interpreting the "How Stoned" graph, see note on Figure 6-1.

[4]The rounding-off process lets the figures in Never and Rarely add up to only 74 percent here, but the originals round off to 75 percent, thus the "rare" classification.

experience things *seeming* like memories but he does not necessarily believe it.

Memory for Periods of Intoxication

If memory functions *during* the intoxicated state seem to alter, what happens to the memories *of* the intoxicated state?

"*My memory of what went on while I was stoned is good afterwards, better than if I had been straight all the time*" is a common effect (19%, 25%, 31%, 14%, 9%), which begins to occur at the Moderate and Strong levels (13%, 24%, 25%, 13%, 1%). It is reported as occurring more frequently by females ($p < .05$), and by the College-educated ($p < .05$). The Daily and Weekly users have this improved memory more frequently than the Occasional users ($p < .01$, overall).

The converse, "*My memory of what went on while I was stoned is poor afterwards compared to what I would have remembered had I been straight*" is also a common effect (18%, 24%, 24%, 16%, 17%), which begins to occur at Strong levels (7%, 14%, 28%, 15%, 13%). It occurs as frequently as improved memory, but at higher levels of intoxication ($p < .0005$), as shown in Figure 14-4.

Comments from informants make it clear that a good deal of the poor memory for periods of intoxication is not ordinary forgetting but

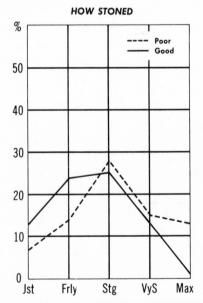

Figure 14-4. MEMORY FOR PERIODS OF INTOXICATION

Note.—For guide to interpreting the "How Stoned" graph, see note on Figure 6-1.

what has been termed "state-specific memory." The events of the intoxicated state are stored in memory, but they cannot be retrieved in an
ordinary state of consciousness. The next time the user becomes intoxicated, however, he can remember many of the things from previous
periods of intoxication that he could not remember in his ordinary state.

Thus the forgetting of periods of intoxication are a combination,
in unknown degree, of genuine forgetting (no initial storage and/or no
possible way of retrieval) and state-specific storage of memories.

A specific aspect of memory for periods of intoxication relates to
the results of reading during such periods.

"If I read while stoned, I remember less *of what I've read hours later
than if I had been straight"* is a common effect (15%, 11%, 19%, 14%,
29%), which may begin at Moderate levels of intoxication (13%, 29%,
23%, 23%, 5%, 1%). It is experienced less frequently by Meditators and
the Therapy and Growth group ($p < .05$, overall) and more frequently
by the younger users ($p < .01$).

The converse effect, *"If I read while stoned, I remember* more *of
what I've read hours later than if I had been straight"* is infrequent (41%,
25%, 16%, 6%, 3%) and, when it occurs, begins at the Low and Moderate
levels (15%, 18%, 10%, 3%, 1%). It occurs less frequently among the
Light Total users ($p < .001$), the Occasional users ($p < .05$), and the
Non-users of Psychedelics ($p < .05$). The Therapy and Growth group

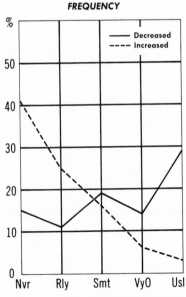

Figure 14-5. MEMORY OF READ MATERIAL

experience increased memory for read material *more* often ($p < .05$, overall).

Figure 14-5 shows that decreased memory occurs much more frequently than increased memory ($p << .0005$). The levels of intoxication do not differ significantly.

ADDITIONAL EFFECTS

"I remember the most obvious things and laugh to think I could have forgotten them" (Rarely, Strongly).

"Relive childhood experiences" (Usually, Fairly).

LEVELS OF INTOXICATION FOR MEMORY PHENOMENA

The overall relation of various phenomena to levels of intoxication is shown in Figure 14-6. The overall ordering is highly significant ($p < < .0005$).

At the lowest level, memory for material read is infrequently improved, but it commonly begins getting worse by the Fair level of intoxication. Moving up toward Strongly intoxicated, memory for periods of intoxication is good, but long-term memory may become better or worse, depending on (currently unknown) psychological variables. Memory becomes somewhat erratic and impaired from the Strong level up; while very old memories may spontaneously return, the user may easily

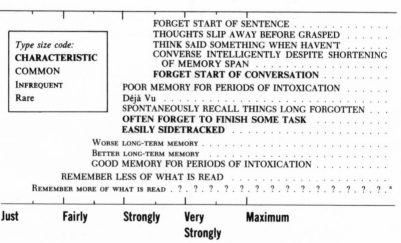

ᵃThere is some question whether this effect is available at all levels above the minimal one.

FIGURE 14-6. INTOXICATION LEVELS, MEMORY PHENOMENA

TABLE 14-1

EFFECTS OF BACKGROUND FACTORS ON MEMORY PHENOMENA

BACKGROUND FACTORS   EFFECTS

More Drug Experience	More frequent:
	  Recall more of
	    material read
	  Good memory for peri-
	    ods of intoxication
	  Easily sidetracked
		Less frequent:
		  Thoughts slip away
		  Think said something
		    when haven't

	More intoxicated for:
	  Forget start of
	    conversation
	  Think said something
	    when haven't
		Less intoxicated for:
		  Mistake fantasy for
		    memory

Older		Less frequent:
		  Easily sidetracked
		  Spontaneously remem-
		    ber long-past events
		  Recall less of material
		    read

More Educated		Less frequent:
		  Easily sidetracked
		  Worse long-term
		    memory
		  Good memory for peri-
		    ods of intoxication
		Less intoxicated for:
		  Easily sidetracked
		  Converse intelligently
		    despite forgetting

Males	More intoxicated for:
	  Forget start of sentence
		Less frequent:
		  Good memory for peri-
		    ods of intoxication

Meditation		Less frequent:
		  Recall less of material
		    read

Therapy & Growth	More frequent:
	  Recall more of
	    material read
		Less frequent:
		  Recall less of material
		    read

get distracted and forget what he set out to do. Moving toward Very Strongly, intermediate-term memory begins to shorten, so that the start of one's conversation may be forgotten before it is finished (although this is generally not felt to impair conversation significantly), and the user may eventually find himself forgetting the beginnings of his sentences. Most of these memory tricks and shortenings are quite apparent to the user, and many users exert effort to compensate for them. At the Very Strong level the user may (rarely) not be aware of the tricks of his memory functioning and temporarily mistake fantasies for actual memories.

MODULATING FACTORS

The effects of relatively linear background factors are summarized in Table 14-1.

Users with more drug experience seem less prone to tricks of memory, experiencing several of them less frequently and at higher levels of intoxication. The older users show a similar trend.

Several effects of background factors were not linear. The younger users were more variable on level of intoxication for worsened long-term memory. The Weekly users can be more intoxicated and still converse intelligently despite memory problems than can the Occasional or Daily users, as well as needing to be more intoxicated to think they've said something when they've only thought about it.

SUMMARY

While very low levels of intoxication may not affect or even may slightly potentiate memory, in the Moderate and higher levels of intoxication there are strong alterations of memory functioning. There is an increasing shortening of memory span, up to the point where a user may forget the start of a sentence he is speaking. Users are generally aware of this span shortening and try to compensate for it in various ways—apparently successfully, as it is a common experience for users to feel they can converse intelligently in spite of this shortening of memory span. State-specific memory is also experienced, i.e., happenings of one intoxication period, which were unrecallable in the subsequent ordinary state of consciousness, are recallable the next time the user again becomes intoxicated.

CHAPTER 15

Cognitive Processes: Thought

THE ABSORBINGNESS, intensity, and peculiarities of thought are highly valued by users of marijuana as a better or more efficient way of thinking; thus the common use of the phrase "being high" for describing marijuana (or other psychedelic drug) intoxication implies that the thoughts and experiences are more profound, more insightful. In this chapter we shall consider the absorbingness of intoxicated thinking, its orientation, the change in the quality of thought, and its experienced consequences.

MAJOR EFFECTS

Absorption in Thought

A common experience is *"I can get so wound up in thoughts or fantasies that I won't notice what's going on around me or won't hear someone talking to me unless they attract my attention forcibly"* (9%, 21%, 40%, 23%, 6%). This is experienced more frequently by the younger users ($p < .05$) and by the College-educated ($p < .01$) and less frequently by Users of Psychedelics ($p < .05$). It generally occurs at the Strong and Very Strong levels of intoxication (3%, 9%, 33%, 32%, 12%), with Light and Moderate Total users experiencing it at lower levels than the Heavy Total users ($p < .05$, overall).

This kind of extreme absorption can apparently occur without some physical actions being stopped: *"I can get so wound up in thoughts or fantasies while doing some physical task or job that I lose awareness of doing it, yet suddenly find that I have finished the physical task even though I lost track of it mentally."* This is also a common experience (17%, 16%, 42%, 21%, 4%), more so among the College-educated than among the Professionals ($p < .05$). When experienced, it begins most frequently at the Strong and Very Strong levels (3%, 11%, 38%, 25%, 5%). Moderate Total users may experience this absorption at somewhat lower levels of intoxication ($p < .05$, overall).

An essentially similar common effect, getting so lost in fantasy that
it takes a while to reorient, has already been mentioned in Chapter
9.

Although these three ways of being lost in thought occur with about
equal frequency, they do form a continuum of absorption with respect
to level of intoxication. Finishing a physical task without awareness of
what one is doing occurs at lower levels than being so absorbed that
others must attract one's attention by rather forcible means, albeit not
significantly so; while having been so absorbed that reorientation is
needed afterwards occurs at higher levels than finishing a task noncon-
sciously ($p < .0005$) or than needing to have one's attention gotten
forcibly ($p < .01$). These differences are shown in Figure 15-1.

Blank Periods

In spite of the absorbingness of thought, and the changes in its
nature discussed below, it also seems possible for thought to cease for
periods: "*I suddenly realize that nothing has been happening for a long
time; my mind has been blank and nothing has been going on.*" This
is an infrequent effect (31%, 33%, 27%, 5%, 0%), especially among Users
of Psychedelics ($p < .05$), which occurs at very high levels (2%, 4%,
18%, 27%, 11%).

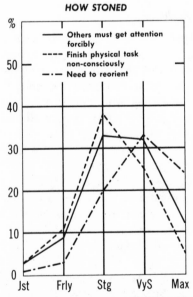

Figure 15-1. INTENSITY OF ABSORPTION IN THOUGHT

Note.—For guide to interpreting the "How Stoned" graph, see note on Figure 6-1.

Occurring significantly less frequently ($p < .0005$) is the rare effect of *prolonged* blank periods: "*My mind goes completely blank for long periods (15 minutes or more); even though I'm not asleep, I have no thoughts or images or anything going on in my mind*" (56%, 27%, 13%, 2%, 0%), also a phenomenon of the very high levels of intoxication for those who could rate it (1%, 2%, 8%, 16%, 13%). Females experience prolonged blank periods more frequently than males ($p < .05$). The young and the College-educated need to be more intoxicated to experience prolonged blanks than the older users ($p < .01$) or the Professionals ($p < .05$).

As discussed in Chapter 20, it is possible that these prolonged blank periods are actually periods of sleep with sudden onsets and terminations, even though the users do not label them as such.

Insights

The content of thought when intoxicated is commonly felt to be insightful into one's own psychological processes and those of others. "Spontaneously, *insights about myself, my personality, the games I play come to mind when stoned and seem very meaningful*" is a characteristic effect (3%, 9%, 31%, 40%, 15%), which begins to occur at Moderate to Strong levels of intoxication (7%, 28%, 37%, 17%, 4%). It is reported as occurring at lower levels of intoxication by Users of Psychedelics ($p < .01$).

One would assume that, if insights characteristically come spontaneously while intoxicated, adding conscious effort to the process would help it. "*If I* deliberately *work on it, I can have important insights about myself, my personality, the games I play,*" while a common effect (6%, 17%, 31%, 23%, 19%), occurs less frequently than spontaneous insights ($p < .05$), as shown in Figure 15-2. Whether this means that the users do not deliberately try to have insights very often or whether they try but it does not work as well as letting insights occur spontaneously is unknown, although my informants' comments incline me to the former hypothesis. Deliberate insights also begin to occur at the Moderate to Strong levels of intoxication (12%, 26%, 34%, 9%, 5%).

Insights into others, mentioned briefly in Chapter 12, are indicated by "*I learn a great deal about psychological processes, what makes people tick, i.e., general knowledge about how the mind works (as opposed to specific insights about yourself).*" This is also a common effect (11%, 16%, 35%, 24%, 12%), which occurs at Moderate to Strong levels (7%, 21%, 39%, 11%, 2%). Heavy Total users experience it at lower levels of intoxication ($p < .05$, overall). As shown in Figure 15-2, it occurs less frequently than spontaneous insights about oneself ($p < .01$), but with the same frequency as deliberate insights into oneself. Levels of intoxication do not differ for these three phenomena.

Orientation of Thought

Let us now consider more specific ways in which cognitive processes alter.

"*I give little or no thought to the future; I'm completely in the here-and-now*" is a characteristic effect (3%, 10%, 34%, 32%, 21%), reported more frequently by Light Total users than by Moderate or Heavy Total users ($p < .01$). It begins to occur at Moderate to Strong levels (11%, 21%, 39%, 17%, 5%), at lower levels for Meditators ($p < .05$, overall).

What may be a consequence of this increased here-and-now-ness is "*I do things with much less thought to possible consequences of my actions than when straight; i.e., I go ahead and do things without thinking first about 'What will people think? How will this affect me?' etc.,*" a common effect (14%, 20%, 29%, 24%, 12%). This is also less frequent among Heavy Total users ($p < .001$, overall). It may occur at Strong levels (9%, 17%, 36%, 17%, 4%), with Users of Psychedelics reporting lower minimal levels ($p < .05$).

Feeling more in the here-and-now occurs more frequently than giving less thought to consequences ($p < .0005$), but at essentially the same

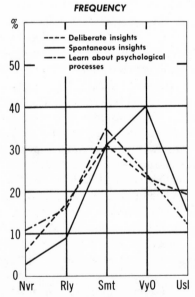

Figure 15-2. INSIGHTS INTO SELF AND OTHERS

levels of intoxication, as shown in Figure 15-3. The shortening of intermediate- and short-term memory is also plotted in Figure 15-3, as it is of interest to see if increased here-and-now-ness results from shortening of memory span. Forgetting the start of the conversation occurs more frequently than increased here-and-now-ness ($p < .05$), and the latter more frequently than forgetting the start of one's sentence ($p < .0005$). Increased here-and-now-ness occurs at lower levels of intoxication than forgetting the start of the conversation ($p < .05$) or of one's sentence ($p < .0005$), so other factors, such as increased attention to intensified sensory input, are partially responsible for increased here-and-now-ness.

Thinking and Problem Solving

Some aspects of alterations in problem-solving activity concern the dropping of steps in problem solving, the switch to more intuitive modes of thought, increased tolerance of contradictions, and increased use of imagery.

"*I think about things in ways that seem intuitively correct, but which do not follow the rules of logic*" is a very common effect (7%, 10%, 36%, 31%, 11%), which begins to occur at Moderate to Strong levels (7%, 26%, 38%, 13%, 3%). Both Meditators and the Therapy and Growth

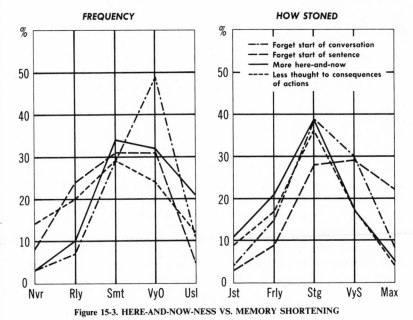

Figure 15-3. HERE-AND-NOW-NESS VS. MEMORY SHORTENING

Note.—For guide to interpreting the "How Stoned" graph, see note on Figure 6-1.

group experience this at lower levels than ordinary users ($p < .05$, overall).

Less frequent than things seeming intuitively correct ($p < .0005$), but at similar levels of intoxication, is "*In thinking about a problem of the sort that normally requires a series of steps to solve, I can get the answer without going through some of the usual intermediate steps; i.e., I can start to think about the problem and then just arrive at what is clearly the answer, without being aware of the steps in the thought process I would normally be aware of.*" This is a common effect (26%, 18%, 39%, 13%, 1%), more so with females ($p < .05$). The modal minimal level of intoxication is Strongly (3%, 16%, 27%, 17%, 5%).

"*I am more willing to accept contradictions between two ideas or two views of the situation than when straight. I don't get up tight because the two things don't make immediate sense*" is a characteristic effect (11%, 8%, 24%, 33%, 17%), which begins to occur at Moderate levels of intoxication (13%, 33%, 23%, 9%, 1%). Light and Heavy Total users experience this more frequently than Moderate Total users ($p < .01$, overall).

"*When thinking about things while stoned, there are visual images that just automatically go along with the thinking; i.e., I think much more in images instead of just abstract thought*" is a very common effect (8%, 15%, 29%, 31%, 15%), which begins to occur at Moderate and Strong levels (7%, 27%, 35%, 15%, 3%).

Efficiency of Thought

Given then that thought commonly is less oriented to the future, is more intuitive, skips intermediate steps, and uses imagery more, is it "higher" or better? The users' feeling about the efficiency of their thought processes while intoxicated were obtained in the next two questions.

"*If I try to solve a problem, it* feels *as if my mind is working much more efficiently than usual (regardless of how you evaluate your solution later)*" is a common effect (13%, 19%, 37%, 17%, 11%), which begins to occur at Moderate to Strong levels of intoxication (12%, 24%, 35%, 9%, 1%)

"*If I try to solve a problem, it* feels *as if my mind is much less efficient than usual (regardless of how you evaluate the solution later)*" is also a common effect (12%, 26%, 40%, 11%, 5%), which begins to occur at Strong levels (3%, 17%, 31%, 22%, 7%). It is experienced less frequently by Heavy and Moderate Total users ($p < .05$, overall), as well as less frequently by Users of Psychedelics ($p < .05$).

One aspect of thinking seeming less efficient is "*I can't think clearly; thoughts keep slipping away before I can quite grasp them*," a common effect (11%, 18%, 50%, 19%, 2%), which begins at the Strong and Very Strong levels (3%, 13%, 24%, 31%, 14%). This inability to grasp thoughts occurs less frequently in the Weekly users than in the Daily or Occasional users ($p < .05$, overall). Users of Psychedelics report this less frequently ($p < .05$). This may be a phenomenon of memory span shortening, rather than of thought per se; i.e., a complex thought may be partially or wholly forgotten before it is completely worked out.

The control of thought, its directability, rather than its graspability, is dealt with in "*I feel as if I lose control over my thoughts; they just go on regardless of what I want (without reference to whether you like this or not).*" This is also a common phenomenon of the Very Strong levels of intoxication, presented fully in Chapter 17.

The relationships between the direction and grasping of thought and the users' feelings about its efficiency are presented in Figure 15-4. Overall differences in frequency of occurrence and level of intoxication are both significant ($p < .001$ and $p << .0005$, respectively). The feeling that thought is more efficient than usual is somewhat more frequent than the other three phenomena, and definitely occurs at lower levels of intoxication. Thoughts slipping away before grasped and losing control of thought begin to occur mainly at the Very Strong level, with thought seeming more efficient beginning at the Moderate and Strong levels.

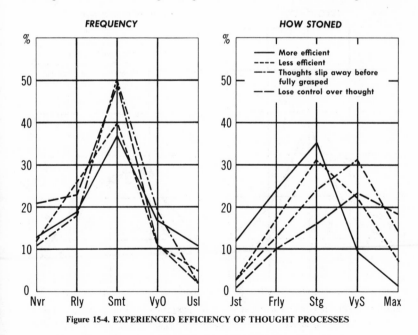

Figure 15-4. EXPERIENCED EFFICIENCY OF THOUGHT PROCESSES

Note.—For guide to interpreting the "How Stoned" graph, see note on Figure 6-1.

The *feeling* that one's thoughts are more or less efficient in problem solving is, as we all know from experience, not necessarily related to actual performance. To get at this distinction, the following two questions were asked.

"*If I work on a problem while stoned, I work* more *accurately than straight, as judged by later real-world evaluation*" is a fairly frequent effect (17%, 29%, 28%, 10%, 3%), which begins to occur at Moderate to Strong levels (13%, 23%, 24%, 7%, 1%). The converse effect, "*If I work on a problem while stoned, I work* less *accurately than straight, as judged by later real-world evaluation*" is a common effect (9%, 15%, 37%, 17%, 8%), which again occurs at Moderate to Strong levels of intoxication (4%, 27%, 25%, 17%, 2%).

The relationships between the mind *feeling* more or less efficient at problem solving and later *evaluations* of accuracy are shown in Figure 15-5. The feeling that the user's mind is working more efficiently occurs slightly more frequently than the feeling that it is working less efficiently, but not significantly so. Later evaluation of work indicates that decreased accuracy is more frequent than increased accuracy ($p < .0005$). Too, the *feeling* of increased efficiency occurs more often than the later evaluations of increased accuracy ($p < .01$), so a certain false confidence is sometimes produced by marijuana intoxication.

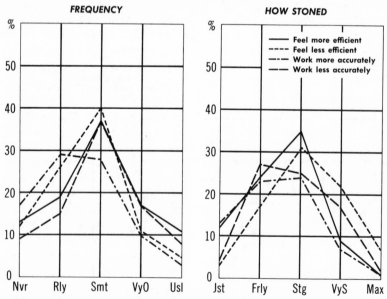

Figure 15-5. EFFICIENCY IN PROBLEM SOLVING: FEELINGS VS. LATER EVALUATION

Note.—For guide to interpreting the "How Stoned" graph, see note on Figure 6-1.

With respect to levels of intoxication, feeling that the mind is more efficient begins at lower levels ($p < .0005$). A similar trend is apparent in later evaluation, where increased accuracy is rated as beginning at lower levels of intoxication ($p < .01$). There is a suggestion in the data ($p < .10$) that decreased accuracy begins to occur at somewhat lower levels of intoxication than the feeling of decreased efficiency.

These relationships suggest that Moderate to Strong levels of intoxication may increase the efficiency of the user in problem solving activity, but higher levels decrease it, judging by both concurrent feelings and retrospective evaluation. A certain amount of false confidence also occurs. Comments by my informants on this indicate that at high levels, what seem to be brilliant chains of thought and insights frequently occur, but are often seen to be false in retrospect. Occasionally they can be very creative, as discussed elsewhere. It is difficult to concentrate and direct thought at these high levels, to keep it centered around a single problem. At low levels direction is relatively easy.

The Sense of Meaning

Although psychologists have never been able to conceptualize it well, thought has dimensions other than being logical or illogical, correct or incorrect by external standards. One of these dimensions is characterized by words such as *depth* and *subtlety*.

"*I appreciate very subtle humor in what my companions say, and say quite subtly funny things myself*" is a characteristic effect of marijuana intoxication (2%, 5%, 38%, 39%, 15%). Moderate Total users report it most frequently ($p < .05$, overall). It begins to occur at Moderate levels of intoxication (12%, 40%, 31%, 10%, 2%).

My informants indicate this sense of subtle humor is very pervasive; two intoxicated users can have a conversation that will be incredibly humorous in this subtle way to them, but it might not seem at all humorous to a straight observer. Or an intoxicated user will see very funny implications and connotations in what a straight person is saying, without the latter being aware of them. This general feeling of being able to "tune in" to deeper levels of understanding and meaning is exemplified by the very common phenomenon, "*Commonplace sayings or conversations seem to have new meanings, more significance*" (4%, 9%, 42%, 35%, 11%), which begins to occur at Strong levels of intoxication (9%, 25%, 43%, 14%, 3%). This is one of the bases of the ability to get involved in very elaborate and subtle social games discussed in Chapter 12.

Another very common effect of marijuana intoxication is "*The ideas that come to my mind when stoned are much more original than usual*"

(5%, 7%, 42%, 33%, 8%). This begins to occur at Moderate to Strong levels (6%, 32%, 41%, 7%, 3%).

A striking example of the apparent facilitation of creative processes in conjunction with marijuana intoxication was offered by one user, a 40-year-old physicist:

> I smoke marijuana once or twice a week for recreation, but a couple of times I've started thinking about my work when stoned and had real breakthroughs as a result. Once, when I had been in the process of setting up a new laboratory for several months, I got stoned one evening and started thinking about things at the lab and suddenly had all these ideas popping into my mind of little things I had to do if the laboratory was to function on schedule, little details about equipment that were unspectacular but essential. I listed about twenty ideas in an hour, and every one of them checked out the next day. They were all sorts of things that had been pushed to the back of my mind by more obvious problems in setting up the laboratory. Another time I got thinking about a problem area in my work, and all sorts of theoretical ideas came popping into my head. They fit together into a coherent theory which looked damned good the next morning—I have since published the theory and organized a lot of research around it, to my great advantage.

Thus users find that marijuana intoxication allows a new depth of thought to be experienced, adding meaning, humor, subtlety, and originality to their thought processes on occasion.[1]

Reading

Reading is a type of thought process that is fundamental to modern technological civilization. A very characteristic effect is *"I find it difficult to read while stoned"* (9%, 6%, 23%, 24%, 33%). This occurs less frequently among Heavy Total users and the Therapy and Growth group ($p <$ .01 and $p <$ .05, overall, respectively). It begins to occur at Moderate and Strong levels of intoxication (11%, 29%, 27%, 13%, 5%). The converse phenomenon, *"It is easier to read than usual while stoned"* is infrequent (43%, 26%, 20%, 1%, 2%) and occurs at Low and Moderate levels (18%, 20%, 7%, 2%, 1%) among those who could rate it. Moderate and Heavy Total users experience reading ease more frequently ($p <$ .05, overall).

---

[1]One of the most intriguing and practically exciting studies of creativity ever carried out (Harman, McKim, Mogar, Fadiman, & Stolaroff, 1966) found a substantial enhancement of creativity, both in terms of psychological tests and actual job performance, when carefully prepared subjects (professionals whose work involved creativity, such as designers and physicists) were given moderate doses of LSD in the proper setting. I strongly suspect marijuana could have the same effect under proper conditions and consider this a high research priority.

The relationships between ease and difficulty of reading are shown in Figure 15-6. Finding reading difficult occurs much more frequently ($p <<< .0005$). Reading ease is a phenomenon that occurs primarily at the lowest levels of intoxication and is then replaced by reading difficulty ($p < .0005$).

As discussed in Chapter 14, recall of what has been read while intoxicated is generally poorer after the period of intoxication is over, although it may be somewhat better at very low levels of intoxication. Note also the common effect of visual imagery automatically accompanying reading (Chapter 6).

Thought and Memory

The process of thinking and problem solving involves continual use of memory functions. Sensory input data must be compared with information in memory for recognition and classification, and compared with stored data (values, desires) to see if the input is congruent with the goals of the person. If not, the person must think about what to do, a process involving comparison of the current situation with memories of past situations and the outcomes of various courses of action in those past situations. Memories must be sorted as to degrees of relevance.

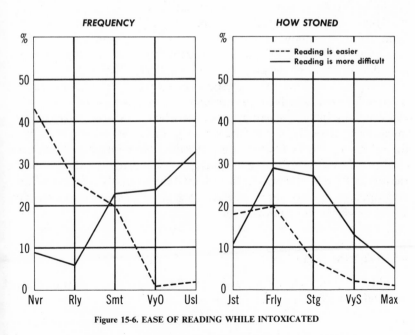

Figure 15-6. EASE OF READING WHILE INTOXICATED

Note.—For guide to interpreting the "How Stoned" graph, see note on Figure 6-1.

The shortening of memory span noted in Chapter 14 clearly affects the thought processes, even though some or much of the shortening may sometimes be overcome with special effort on the user's part. Long-term memories may not be as readily available for comparison with the present situation, or the "wrong" old memory may be retrieved.[2] With shortening of intermediate- and short-term memory, the nature of the current situation may not be grasped clearly throughout problem-solving activity, so the thought processes are no longer guided by the goal of being relevant to the situation. Thus decreased efficiency of thought may be a common effect of marijuana intoxication.

This is very much a matter of level, however. At low levels there is little effect on memory, and users often feel their thought processes are more efficient.

When it comes to a consideration of creativity, the shortening of memory span may be a distinct advantage. To the extent that creativity is defined as unlikely chains of associations, a common pragmatic defini-tion in much research on the subject, the shortening of memory span and the erraticness of retrieval will produce unlikely associations and facilitate the creative process. Whether this will appear "genuinely" cre-ative after the intoxication has ended is another question; we usually require a certain coherence and "fit" with other conceptual systems or reality before we consider something creative. The users generally recog-nize this, enjoying the feeling of creativity that occurs at high levels of intoxication without taking it too seriously until checked out later.

This view of the effects of marijuana on creativity has been ex-pounded in detail elsewhere (Anonymous, 1969).

An intriguing research question then centers around the effects, particularly creative effects, of marijuana intoxication on users who were especially disciplined or had trained themselves to be able to concentrate much more than the normal person. The only account of this sort of thing I know of is by Crowley (in Regardie, 1968), although Krippner's studies of artists influenced by psychedelic drugs is also relevant (Krippner, 1969a, 1969b). Both suggest that a highly disciplined and goal-directed individual can guide a drug experience as he wishes, even at very high levels of intoxication.

ADDITIONAL EFFECTS

Many specific effects of marijuana intoxication on thought processes were offered:

---

[2]"Wrong" is highly situation-specific; retrieving a memory other than the one desired may be seen as non-adaptive, entertaining, or creative, depending on the situation.

"I am aware of multi-leveled thought processes, often not related" (Very Often, Strongly).

"My concentration is longer and stronger" (Usually, Fairly).

"I notice and become engrossed in details" (Usually, Just).

"The ability to see things (society, the world, interpersonal relationships) from a different perspective, unclouded by the fog of our sociological upbringing and the usual ego-trip" (Very Often, Strongly).

"People and irrelevant events seem synchronized" (Very Often, Strongly).

"Considering in ultimate detail every aspect of my own personal involvements" (Usually, Fairly).

"I become very philosophical . . ." (Usually, Strongly).

"I find myself trying to do something ordinary and pay too little attention so that I do it wrong (e.g., dial the wrong phone number for my home telephone)" (Sometimes, Very Strongly).

"Helpful in putting writings or ideas in perspective" (Sometimes, Fairly).

"I can foresee the future possibilities of my life and its patterns" (Usually, Maximum).

"Discover dramatic new ways of looking at problems when stoned" (Very Often, Strongly).

"See subtle harmony and interplay between diverse subjects, e.g., math and music" (Usually, Strongly).

"Able to comprehend the most abstract concepts" (Very Often, Strongly).

"Thought process is very fast, yet you see things as happening slower than they actually are (at least you think you do)" (Rarely, Very Strongly).

"Very complex connections are made between two or more unrelated events or comments or scenes" (Usually, Fairly).

"Everything (sounds, objects, people, total environment) seems to be *just exactly right!* All related and perfectly in place" (Usually, Fairly).

"I have a feeling, during and after, of an integration of thoughts and emotions" (Sometimes, Strongly).

"Grasp of total situation widened and strengthened (seeing things whole)" (Sometimes, Very Strongly).

"I am able to sit still and attend to things carefully if I want to" (Very Often, Fairly).

LEVELS OF INTOXICATION FOR THOUGHT PHENOMENA

The various alterations of thought processes and some of the relevant memory process are arranged by level in Figure 15-7. The overall grouping is highly significant ($p \lll .0005$).

Prolonged blank periods . . . .
SO ABSORBED IN THOUGHT OR FANTASY
THAT NEED TO REORIENT AFTERWARDS .

Type size code:
CHARACTERISTIC
COMMON
INFREQUENT
Rare

LOSE CONTROL OF THOUGHT . . . .
BLANK PERIODS . . . .
FORGET START OF SENTENCE . . . .
ABSORBED, ATTENTION MUST BE FORCIBLY GOTTEN
THOUGHTS SLIP AWAY BEFORE GRASPED . . . . . .
FORGET START OF CONVERSATION . . . .
FINISH TASK EVEN THOUGH MENTALLY LOST TRACK
OF . . . .
MIND FEELS LESS EFFICIENT . . . .
SKIP INTERMEDIATE STEPS IN PROBLEM SOLVING . . . . .
LESS THOUGHT ABOUT CONSEQUENCES OF ACTIONS . . .
MORE HERE-AND-NOW . . . .
INSIGHTS INTO OTHERS . . . .
NEW SIGNIFICANCE TO COMMONPLACE CONVERSATIONS
SPONTANEOUS INSIGHTS INTO SELF . . . .
WORK *LESS* ACCURATELY . . . .
THOUGHT ACCOMPANIED BY VISUAL IMAGES . . . .
THOUGHT MORE INTUITIVE . . . .
HARDER TO READ . . . .
IDEAS MORE ORIGINAL . . . .
DELIBERATE INSIGHTS INTO SELF . . . .
MIND FEELS *MORE* EFFICIENT . ? . ? . ? . ? . ? . ? . ? . ? . ? . ? . ? . [a]
APPRECIATE MORE SUBTLE HUMOR . . . .
PLAY ELABORATE GAMES . . . .
WORK MORE ACCURATELY . . ? . ? . ? . ? . ? . ? . ? . ? . ? . ? . ? . [a]
MORE VISUAL IMAGERY WHEN READING . . . .
ACCEPT CONTRADICTIONS MORE READILY . . . .
EASIER TO READ . . ? . ? . ? . ? . ? . ? . ? . ? . ? . ? . ? . ? . ? . ? . ? . ? . [a]

| Just | Fairly | Strongly | Very Strongly | Maximum |

[a]There is some question whether this effect is available at all levels above the minimal one.

FIGURE 15-7. INTOXICATION LEVELS, THOUGHT PHENOMENA

Beginning at the lowest levels of intoxication, we have a "relaxation" of thought such that contradictions are tolerated and feelings of increased subtlety and efficiency are noticed. Moving toward the Strong level of intoxication, reading becomes difficult and the direction of thought becomes less controllable, but the richness of thought continues to increase; it may seem more intuitive, original, and significant, and is commonly accompanied by more visual imagery than usual. The user begins to feel he is less efficient at problem-solving thought and is more oriented to the here-and-now.

Above the Strong level, shortening of memory span begins to affect thinking, so the user may become completely absorbed in the experience of long chains of what seem brilliant thoughts, but not recall where he started from. The intense pull of enhanced sensations and intensified feelings and fantasies at these high levels makes direction of thought difficult. Rarely, blank periods may occur at the very high levels.

MODULATING FACTORS

The effects of relatively linear background variables are summarized in Table 15-1.

TABLE 15-1

EFFECTS OF BACKGROUND FACTORS ON THOUGHT

BACKGROUND FACTORS	EFFECTS	
More Drug Experience	More frequent: 　More subtle humor 　Easier to read 　Recall more of 　　material read More intoxicated for: 　Absorbed, attention 　　must be gotten 　　forcibly 　Forget start of 　　conversation	Less frequent: 　Mind goes blank 　So absorbed need to 　　reorient afterwards 　More here-and-now 　Less thought to conse- 　　quences of actions 　Mind feels less efficient 　Thoughts slip away 　　before grasped 　Harder to read 　Absorbed, attention 　　must be gotten 　　forcibly Less intoxicated for: 　Spontaneous insights 　Insights into others 　Less thought to conse- 　　quences of actions
Older		Less frequent: 　Absorbed, attention 　　must be gotten 　　forcibly 　Recall less of material 　　read Less intoxicated for: 　Prolonged blank 　　periods
More Educated		Less frequent: 　Absorbed, attention 　　must be gotten 　　forcibly 　Lose track of task, but 　　finish it anyway Less intoxicated for: 　Prolonged blank 　　periods

TABLE 15-1 (*Continued*)

BACKGROUND FACTORS   EFFECTS

Males	More intoxicated for: Forget start of sentence	Less frequent: Prolonged blank periods Skip intermediate steps in problem solving
Meditation		Less frequent: Recall less of material read Less intoxicated for: More here-and-now Think intuitively
Therapy & Growth	More frequent: Recall more of material read	Less frequent: Harder to read Recall less of material read

Several background variables had non-linear effects. Moderate Total users were less intoxicated for the experience of finishing some physical task without realizing it, and they accepted contradictions between ideas less frequently than the Heavy or Light Total users. The Weekly users experienced thoughts slipping away before they could grasp them less frequently than the Occasional or Daily users.

The effects of greater drug experience form a pattern that suggests that more experienced drug users: (1) get into psychological, insightful material at lower levels; (2) have given up the here-and-now-ness orientation to some extent; and (3) have altered a number of effects that might be detrimental to long-term adaptation to the world. With respect to the latter point, the experienced users more frequently find it easier to read and retain what they read, and less frequently experience blank periods, thoughts slipping away, decreased planning (less thought to consequences of actions), and disorientation from hyper-absorption in thoughts and fantasies; also high absorption and memory span shortening shift to higher levels of intoxication.

SUMMARY

Marijuana intoxication can produce intensified awareness of thought processes such that the user can get very absorbed in his thinking, have insights into himself and others, appreciate very subtle humor, and feel his thoughts are more original, intuitive, and profound. At low levels of intoxication, the user may feel his thought processes are more efficient and accurate; but as he becomes more intoxicated, this may be replaced by a feeling of inability to properly direct his thought processes so that he becomes less efficient at problem-solving activities, although creative thought may continue to be enhanced. Shortening of memory span at high levels of intoxication also makes the direction of thought difficult. Users do not feel that this shortening of memory span or difficulty in consciously directing thought is necessarily a hindrance in coping with the world, however, and may consider the more intuitive approach to thought while "high" superior in many situations. More experienced users are less affected by some of the apparently debilitating changes in thought patterns.

CHAPTER *16*

Emotions

MAJOR EFFECTS

Emotional Tone of Intoxication

As might be expected in a group of *experienced* users, i.e., users who repeat the marijuana intoxication experience over and over, it is a very characteristic effect that "*I almost invariably feel good when I turn on, regardless of whether I felt bad before turning on*" (5%, 11%, 19%, 31%, 30%). This effect has begun to occur in most users by Moderate levels of intoxication (21%, 33%, 25%, 7%, 1%). The converse effect, "*I almost invariably feel bad when I turn on, regardless of how I felt before I turned on*" is a rare effect (47%, 36%, 9%, 1%, 1%). In those who could rate it, it generally began at the Moderate level (8%, 15%, 9%, 5%, 7%). Heavy Total users need to be more intoxicated to feel bad ($p < .05$, overall).

Although emotional mood prior to intoxication was overcome in the previous two effects, it is a common effect that "*Whatever mood I was in before turning on becomes greatly amplified, so if I felt down I really feel bad and if I felt good I really feel very good*" (9%, 18%, 36%, 22%, 14%). This occurs more frequently with the Meditators and the Therapy and Growth groups ($p < .05$, overall). It begins to occur at Moderate to Strong levels (19%, 22%, 32%, 11%, 2%).

The relationships of these three phenomena are shown in Figure 16-1. Feeling almost invariably good occurs more frequently than pre-intoxication emotions being amplified ($p < .0005$), and amplified emotions occur more frequently than feeling bad ($p <<< .0005$). Feeling almost invariably bad occurs at higher levels of intoxication than either feeling good ($p < .001$) or emotions being amplified ($p < .01$), primarily because of a few users who indicate Very Strong and Maximum for feeling bad. The difference in levels between feeling good and emotions amplified is not significant.

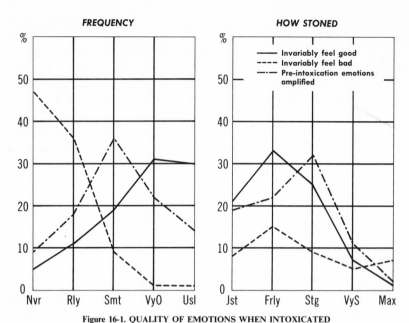

Figure 16-1. QUALITY OF EMOTIONS WHEN INTOXICATED

Note.—For guide to interpreting the "How Stoned" graph, see note on Figure 6-1.

While the graph suggests that feeling good tends to occur at lower levels and feeling bad at very high levels, comments of pilot subjects and informants indicate that this picture is incomplete. There is a general good feeling that comes from marijuana intoxication at all levels, and this will override mild emotional states the user may have just before becoming intoxicated. If the user has a strong negative mood before becoming intoxicated (whether he is consciously completely aware of it or not), the amplification of emotions common to marijuana intoxication will amplify the negative feelings sufficiently to overcome the good feeling that accompanies intoxication, and he will feel very bad indeed. This latter effect is also modulated by a user's ability to control his intoxication effects; he may be able to suppress the effects of a negative pre-intoxication emotion up to a point, usually by concentrating his attention on pleasurable stimuli and/or not giving attention to his negative feelings. If he is so intoxicated that his control is erratic, and/or the negative pre-intoxication emotion is too strong, he will be unsuccessful and experience the negative emotion in amplified form.[1] The material in Chapter 17 on control is very relevant here.

---

[1]Many informants mentioned that when they know they have a difficult emotional situation on their mind, which they do not feel ready or able to deal with, they will deliberately avoid using marijuana or, if they use it, stay at Low to Moderate levels of intoxication so they can stay out of the problem area. An exception to this is the use of intoxication for gaining insight into personal problems, where the user feels the risk of strong negative emotions is worth taking.

Giggling

An aspect of the positive emotional tone characteristically associated with marijuana intoxication is "*I giggle a lot when stoned; I am silly, even though the situation is not that funny.*" This is a very common effect (3%, 23%, 47%, 20%, 7%), which occurs more frequently with Females ($p < .05$). It generally begins to occur at Strong levels (11%, 25%, 36%, 18%, 5%), although Heavy Total users must be more intoxicated to experience it ($p < .05$, overall). Older users begin giggling at lower levels than younger ones ($p < .05$).

Strength of Emotions

A very common effect of marijuana intoxication is "*I feel emotions much more strongly when stoned, so they affect me more*" (6%, 13%, 37%, 27%, 17%). The younger users experience this more frequently ($p < .05$). It begins to occur at the Strong levels (14%, 21%, 39%, 4%).

The converse effect, "*I feel emotions much more weakly when stoned, so they have little effect on me*" is infrequent (35%, 29%, 21%, 7%, 4%), and occurs less frequently than emotions feeling stronger ($p << .0005$). It begins to occur at Moderate to Strong levels (7%, 20%, 21%, 6%, 3%), essentially the same levels as feeling emotions more strongly.

Emotional Crises—"Freaking Out"

Given the effect of intoxication in amplifying emotions, combined with some loss of control at very high levels of intoxication, the possibility of the user's being temporarily overwhelmed by intense negative emotions requires investigation. Users term such an event "freaking out."

The users were asked, "*How many people have you seen 'freak out' on grass, i.e., have such a catastrophic emotional upset that they needed help of some sort? (Not counting yourself).*" Table 16-1 tabulates their answers. It is important to note, however, that these figures cannot be taken as an estimate of the *actual* number of emotional crises among users of marijuana but only as a *maximal* estimate; because the questionnaires were passed from acquaintance to acquaintance in the distribution process, a fair number of users had been intoxicated together and so were probably reporting on the same cases of emotional crises and overestimating the incidence of such crises to an unknown extent. Thus most of the users have never seen an overwhelming emotional reaction in other users, and few (10 percent) have seen three or more.

If one wished to estimate an incidence ratio of emotional crises, the data in Table 16-1 are not useful as we do not know the number of observations on which they are based, i.e., how many intoxicated

TABLE 16-1

NUMBER OF PEOPLE HAVING
EMOTIONAL CRISES (FREAKOUTS)
WITNESSED BY USERS

NUMBER OF PEOPLE HAVING CRISES	PERCENT OF USERS[a]
0	61%
1	17%
2	11%
3 or more	10%

Note.—These figures cannot be taken as an estimate of the *actual* number of emotional crises among users of marijuana but only as a *maximal* estimate because many of the users had been intoxicated together and were probably reporting on the same cases, thus overestimating the incidence of crises to an unknown extent.

[a] 1% of the users were lost in the rounding process here.

people the users have observed altogether. To get at this question, the users were asked as part of the above item, *"What percentage is this compared to all the times you've seen people get stoned?"* The categorized data are presented in Table 16-2.

It is again important to stress that these figures overestimate the incidence to some unknown degree. Nevertheless, the incidence of emotional crises would seem to be very low. Except for 5 percent of the users (one of them a physician), 89 percent of the users estimate the incidence of such reactions as 1 percent or less, and 73 percent as less than a tenth of 1 percent.

Nature of Emotional Crises

Although explanations of the emotional catastrophes were not asked for on the questionnaire, some users added comments. Combining this with various remarks by pilot subjects and informants, it seems that emotional crises fall mainly into two classes. The major one is that of emotionally unstable people or normal people with a major emotional problem on their mind who use marijuana and have their problems amplified. The second, less frequent category is negative emotions of fright and/or confusion, which occasionally result from initial experiences with overdoses of marijuana; i.e., the inexperienced user smokes much more than he knows how to handle and is temporarily confused, disoriented, or frightened by the effects of intoxication. Many users have this happen early in their marijuana-using career. Most apparently learn

TABLE 16-2

PERCENTAGES OF PEOPLE HAVING
EMOTIONAL CRISES
WITNESSED BY USERS

PERCENTAGE OF PEOPLE HAVING CRISES[a]	PERCENT OF USERS
0%	61%
≤ .01%	7%
≤ .1%	5%
≤ 1%	16%
2%-4%	3%
5%-10%	2%

Note.—These figures cannot be taken as an estimate of the *actual* number of emotional crises among users of marijuana but only as a *maximal* estimate because many of the users had been intoxicated together and were probably reporting on the same cases, thus overestimating the incidence of crises to an unknown extent.

[a] The remainder of the users gave verbal answers that were not classifiable. These were: "very small," "super small," "so small," "almost not worth noting," and "very small percent." Note also that 1% of the users were lost in rounding errors.

to control negative effects and/or adapt to unusual effects so as not to be concerned about them; indeed, they come to value them. A few, frightened by the experience, do not use marijuana any more.

Outcome of Emotional Crises

With respect to emotional crises in others, the users were asked, *"What sort of help did they get? How effective was it?"* Of the 53 users answering this question, the majority (64 percent) indicated that friends and other users present simply talked to the disturbed person, reassured him, and calmed him down—a sufficient treatment. Touching the disturbed person was often mentioned in these accounts as particularly effective and reassuring. In 8 percent of the cases the incident simply subsided by itself. In 13 percent some sort of medical or psychological assistance was obtained, although this included such mild treatments as "sleeping it off in the student health center." Miscellaneous methods were used in the other instances.

In one of the above cases the user indicated the help was not effective for the disturbed person, but his disturbance was part of a long-term pattern of personality disorder.

Emotional Crises among the Users

The users were asked, *"Have you ever freaked out in this way? How many times? What sort of help did you get, and how effective was it?"* Because the size of the sample is known, this gives a better estimate of the incidence of this occurrence. Table 16-3 presents the data.

TABLE 16-3

EMOTIONAL CRISES AMONG THE USERS

NUMBER OF CRISES	PERCENT OF USERS
0	77%
1	14%
2	3%
3 or more	3%
No response	3%

Of the 30 users who had had such an experience, 40 percent indicated it had subsided by itself, and 53 percent that they had been "talked down" by friends, with one user indicating that professional help was needed. One of the users indicated he had deliberately provoked a crisis just to see if he could take it!

Thus in the present sample 20 percent of the users reported one or more experiences of emotional crises, almost all of which subsided by themselves or through the support and reassurance of friends. Only one required professional assistance, giving a serious risk ratio of about 1 percent.[2] The caution should be added, however, that this figure of 1 percent applies to populations similar to the present one, i.e., users who are experienced and (by implication) well adapted to handling marijuana intoxication. In an unselected population of non-users, the risk ratio for emotional crisis reactions requiring professional help would probably be somewhat higher, depending on the nature of the situations in which marijuana was used.

Physical Components of Emotion

A common experience is *"I am more aware of the body tensions and feelings that are part of emotions when stoned"* (13%, 11%, 25%, 31%,

---

[2]I use the phrase "serious risk" deliberately here, as I am making a value judgment that being very upset for a few hours is not, per se, a serious risk. Life is full of things that upset us seriously for hours, days, weeks. Requiring professional help to deal with the upset, however, is more serious, and can be considered an indication of "risk."

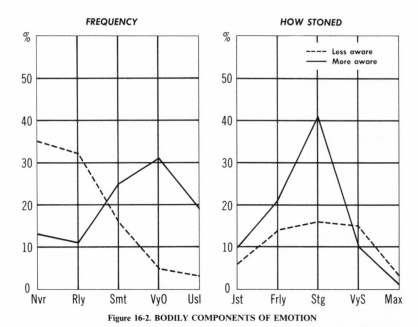

Figure 16-2. BODILY COMPONENTS OF EMOTION

Note.—For guide to interpreting the "How Stoned" graph, see note on Figure 6-1.

19%). This begins to occur at Strong levels of intoxication (10%, 21%, 41%, 10%, 1%). The converse effect, "*I am* less *aware of the body tensions and feelings that are part of emotions when stoned*" is an infrequent effect (35%, 32%, 16%, 5%, 3%), which is more variable with respect to levels of intoxication (6%, 14%, 16%, 15%, 3%) in those who could rate it. As shown in Figure 16-2, being more aware occurs more frequently ($p \ll .0005$) and at lower levels of intoxication ($p < .01$).

ADDITIONAL EFFECTS

"Any hostile action or word is upsetting" (Usually, Fairly).

"Relief of anxiety or restlessness" (Usually, Just).

"Presence of anxiety attacks" (Rarely, Strongly).

"Deep concern with injustices all over the world, regardless of my actual participation" (Very Often, Fairly).

"A feeling of depression when coming down" (Usually).

"Extremely sensitive to remarks or criticism" (Usually, Very Strongly).

"My negative feelings upon being disturbed increase, like the feeling toward an alarm clock in the morning" (Usually, Fairly).

"I cry more easily about appropriate things" (Very Often, Strongly).

"Little emotional fear of pain" (Usually, Just).

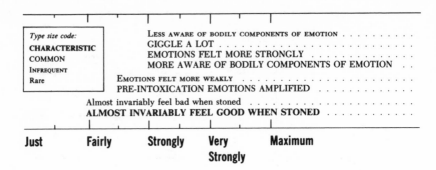

FIGURE 16-3. INTOXICATION LEVELS, EMOTIONAL PHENOMENA

"Annoyed awareness of ego posturings of other stoned people" (Very Often, Fairly).

LEVELS OF INTOXICATION FOR EMOTION

Figure 16-3 groups the various emotional phenomena by levels of intoxication. The overall grouping is highly significant ($p < .001$).

As the user becomes intoxicated, he characteristically feels good, a positive emotional tone that persists through all levels of intoxication unless he has strong emotions from his pre-intoxication state that are amplified in the intoxicated state. As he becomes more intoxicated, emotions are sometimes felt less strongly, but more usually emotions are felt more strongly. At Strong levels of intoxication and higher, the bodily components (muscle tensions, viscera feeling, etc.) of emotions may come into awareness, and the positive emotional tone may result in giggling. At very high levels negative emotions are more likely to overcome the positive emotional tone of intoxication if they are very strong or the user has poor control.

MODULATING FACTORS

All background variables had relatively linear effects on emotional phenomena. They are summarized in Table 16-4.

SUMMARY

Marijuana intoxication characteristically produces a pleasant emotional state in the experienced users in this study. This pleasant feeling tone is sufficient to override the effects of moderate negative emotional states the user may have had just before becoming intoxicated.

TABLE 16-4

EFFECTS OF BACKGROUND FACTORS ON EMOTIONS

BACKGROUND FACTORS	EFFECTS	
More Drug Experience	More intoxicated for: Usually feel bad Giggle a lot	
Meditation	More frequent: Pre-intoxication mood amplified	
Therapy & Growth	More frequent: Pre-intoxication mood amplified	
Males		Less frequent: Giggle a lot
Older		Less frequent Feel emotions more strongly Less intoxicated for: Giggle a lot

The emotions, both positive and negative, noble and selfish, which the user does experience while intoxicated, are usually felt more strongly than in his ordinary state, although the personal and situational triggers for eliciting emotion may alter. At high levels of intoxication, where emotions are felt very strongly and decreased control of intoxication phenomena may sometimes occur, a user with a poor personality structure and/or one otherwise normal but involved in high temporary levels of emotional stress may "freak out," be temporarily overwhelmed by negative emotions. This has occurred to 20 percent of the users, but in only one case was it serious enough to require professional assistance; in others, the disturbance subsided by itself, or the reassurance and support of friends was sufficient to alleviate the user's distress.

CHAPTER 17

Control

MOST CURRENT IDEAS about the nature of marijuana intoxication seem to neglect the fact that since we exercise a fair amount of control over the contents of our minds in ordinary life, it might be expected that control would be similarly exercised by an experienced drug user. This study indicates that much control *is* exercised by experienced users, primarily by altering the direction and focus of attention. Aspects of this control will be discussed under the general headings of the particular phenomena of intoxication to be controlled and the level of intoxication.

CONTROL OF THE PHENOMENA OF INTOXICATION

Need for Control

In understanding the nature of control over the effects of marijuana intoxication, it is important to note that there is less need felt for tight control: "*I find it easy to accept whatever happens; I don't need to control it or feel in control of it.*" This is a very characteristic effect (2%, 7%, 25%, 29%, 35%), generally manifested by the Moderate level of intoxication (19%, 34%, 27%, 10%, 4%).

Concern about and Loss of Control

"*I* worry *about losing control, such that I might do something I wouldn't want to do (regardless of whether you* actually *lose control)*" is a rare phenomenon (36%, 41%, 18%, 4%, 1%), consonant with the characteristic feeling of accepting things. When it occurs, it generally begins at the Very Strong levels for those who could rate it (5%, 7%, 11%, 19%, 15%). Daily users worry about this the least, Weekly users next least, and Occasional users worry the most ($p < .05$, overall), albeit still infrequently.

Some change in behavior that reflects a lowering of normal inhibitions, a change in the criteria for what needs to be controlled, is expressed in the common phenomenon, "*My inhibitions are lowered so that I do things I'm normally too inhibited to do (Note: this does not apply to* antisocial *acts but to acts that are generally acceptable, but that you can't normally do through shyness or the like)*" (11%, 19%, 41%, 21%, 7%). This effect has been well expressed elsewhere: "The decrease of socially reinforced inhibitions also accounts for the actions of users which claim public attention: jumping over fireplugs and parking meters, uninhibited dancing (erotic and non-erotic), and playful behavior (which is subtly taboo in our society) [Anonymous, 1969, p. 348]." It generally begins to occur at Moderate to Strong levels (8%, 26%, 31%, 17%, 5%), with the younger users needing to be more intoxicated for this experience ($p < .05$).

Actual loss of control to the point of antisocial actions was the rarest effect found in the present study: "*I lose control of my actions and do antisocial things (actions that harm other people) that I wouldn't normally do*" (77%, 22%, 1%, 0%, 0%). For the few who could rate this, the mininal

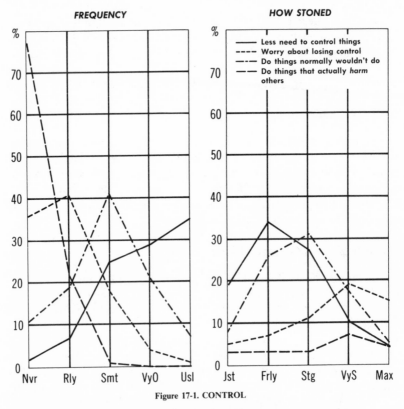

Figure 17-1. CONTROL

Note.—For guide to interpreting the "How Stoned" graph, see note on Figure 6-1.

intoxication levels peaked at Very Strong (3%, 3%, 3%, 7%, 4%).

The relationships of the lessened need for control, concern over control, and losing control to various degrees are plotted in Figure 17-1, with overall differences highly significant ($p <<< .0005$, for frequency, $p < < .0005$ for levels). Feeling less need to be in control of things is most frequent, inhibitions being lowered next most frequent, worrying about loss of control infrequent, and losing control to the point of actions that harm others least frequent. Worrying about losing control and actually losing it to the point of harm are very high level phenomena; inhibitions being lowered is a Moderate to Strong level phenomenon, and feeling less need to control things, a Low to Moderate level phenomenon.

Directions of Fantasies and Thoughts

Prolonged fantasies, enriched with spectacular imagery and intensely absorbing, often seeming as real as nocturnal dreams or life itself, are a main pleasure of marijuana intoxication when the user indulges in them. What sort of control over these can the user exercise, if he is not content to let them develop spontaneously?

"*I have little or no control over my fantasies; i.e., they flow along spontaneously, and even if I try, I can't change what I'm fantasying about*" is an infrequent effect (24%, 29%, 31%, 11%, 3%), albeit more frequent among the College-educated ($p < .05$) and the younger users ($p < .05$). It generally begins to occur at the Strong to Very Strong levels of intoxication (3%, 7%, 25%, 19%, 15%).

The converse effect, "*I have excellent control over my fantasies: I can make them go in whatever direction I want*" is a common effect (6%, 18%, 31%, 27%, 15%), also more frequent among the College-educated ($p < .01$). It generally begins to occur at Moderate to Strong levels (13%, 21%, 36%, 14%, 3%). A similar effect, "*I feel as if I lose control over my thoughts; they just go on regardless of what I want (without reference to whether you like this or not)*" occurs with essentially the same frequency and beginning at the same levels of intoxication as not having control over fantasy (21%, 23%, 39%, 11%, 2% for frequency and 1%, 10%, 16%, 23%, 18% for levels).[1]

It is of interest to compare these feelings of control over fantasy with feeling of efficiency of the mind in problem solving (Chapter 15),

---

[1]It is important to note that loss of control can be very pleasurable, according to many of my informants, depending on the personality of the user. They enjoy the spontaneous entertainment quality, the surprise of the unexpected and exotic places their thoughts and fantasies travel to. One informant expressed the enjoyment of loss of control as being analogous to riding a roller coaster; if you're sure the machine is in safe operating condition, you climb on and enjoy the thrills of the ride. Once you're on, it's no longer a question of your control. Thus if the user feels his personality is in good operating condition, he trusts himself to become intoxicated and let the intoxicated state take him where it will.

where ability to direct thought properly is important. Figure 17-2 relates these four phenomena.

Excellent control over fantasies is reported more frequently than the mind's feeling more or less efficient in problem solving ($p < .05$ in either case) and much more frequently than poor control over fantasy ($p < .0005$). The latter three phenomena occur with about the same frequency. Both excellent control over fantasy and the mind's feeling more efficient are reported at lower levels of intoxication than poor control or inefficiency ($p < .0005$ in each case). Poor control over fantasy occurs at somewhat higher levels than the mind's feeling inefficient ($p < .05$). Thus there is a general feeling of decreasing control at higher levels.

Control of Emotional States

The general ability of users to control emotional states in order to produce a generally pleasant, even ecstatic experience, discussed in Chapter 16, should be mentioned again. As discussed above, there is generally little felt need to control emotions as they are usually pleasant. When control is necessary, it is easier at lower levels of intoxication than at the very high levels.

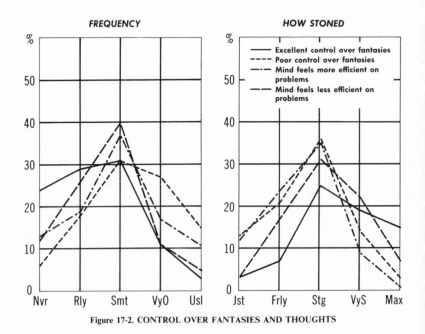

Figure 17-2. CONTROL OVER FANTASIES AND THOUGHTS

Note.—For guide to interpreting the "How Stoned" graph, see note on Figure 6-1.

Control of Pain

In Chapter 11 it was reported that pain was easy to tolerate if the user directs his attention elsewhere, but it was also a common effect for pain to be more intense if the user concentrated on it. This not only emphasizes the importance of directing attention in the control of intoxication effects, but the changes in criteria for what to control. Ordinarily most of us go to great lengths to avoid pain; in the intoxicated state, many users find the new experience that comes from concentrating on pain worth the discomfort, at least enough to try it once to see what it's like.

External Tasks

A characteristic effect of intoxication is "*I often forget to finish some task I've started, or get sidetracked more frequently than when straight*" (4%, 9%, 33%, 44%, 9%). This effect begins to occur at Strong levels (7%, 24%, 43%, 16%, 3%). It is experienced more frequently by the younger users ($p < .05$), the College-educated ($p < .05$), and the Users of Psychedelics ($p < .05$). It begins at higher levels for the College-educated ($p < .05$) and Users of Psychedelics ($p < .05$).

The converse effect, "*I can work at a necessary task with extra energy, absorption, and efficiency*" is a common effect (12%, 22%, 38%, 17%, 7%), which begins to occur at Moderate levels (17%, 33%, 24%, 5%, 1%). It is experienced more frequently by Users of Psychedelics ($p < .001$) and begins at higher levels for Heavy Total users ($p < .05$, overall).

Figure 17-3 shows the relationships between these two levels of control over external tasks. Getting sidetracked is more frequent ($p < .0005$), while having extra energy and being absorbed in a task occurs at lower levels of intoxication ($p < .0005$).

Possession

The experience of "possession," the temporary displacement of a person's mind by some outside "spirit" or force, is as old as mankind. Our culture generally rejects the notion of independently existing spirits able to possess someone and control his body; but, phenomenologically, possession is a real experience to those to whom it happens, even though we would consider the "spirit" as simply a manifestation of some split-off part of the person's personality. Two questions dealing with possession were included in the questionnaire as validity scale items, since I had not heard of the phenomenon in pilot interviews. As a number of users reported this phenomenon, the data are given here, as well as a related effect, the user's body seeming to move by itself.

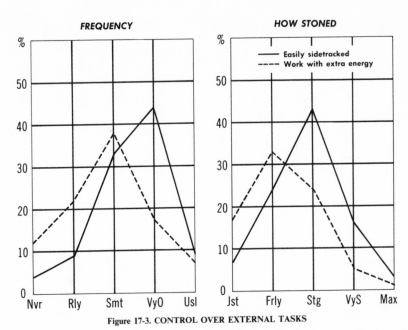

Figure 17-3. CONTROL OVER EXTERNAL TASKS

Note.—For guide to interpreting the "How Stoned" graph, see note on Figure 6-1.

"*I have lost control and been 'taken over' by an outside force or will, which is hostile or evil in intent, for a while*" is a rare effect (79%, 14%, 4%, 0%, 0%), which occurs at Very Strong and Maximal levels for the few who could rate it (1%, 1%, 1%, 5%, 9%).

"*I have lost control and been 'taken over' by an outside force or will, which is good or divine, for a while*" is also a rare effect (63%, 16%, 9%, 5%, 1%), which occurs at very high levels of intoxication (1%, 3%, 9%, 9%, 7%). The Therapy and Growth group has experienced this more frequently ($p < .05$, overall).

The extent to which the users may be reporting experiences more aptly classified as "inspiration" rather than the feeling of possession is unknown.

"*Parts of my body have moved on their own volition, have done something which I did not will*" is also a rare effect (57%, 22%, 13%, 5%, 1%), which occurs more frequently among females than males ($p < .05$). When it occurs, it generally begins at the very high levels (1%, 3%, 7%, 14%, 10%).

Although the levels of intoxication for these three possession phenomena were all very high and did not differ significantly, their frequency of occurrence did, as shown in Figure 17-4.

Parts of the body moving by themselves and being possessed by a good force occur with about equal frequency, and both occur more

FREQUENCY

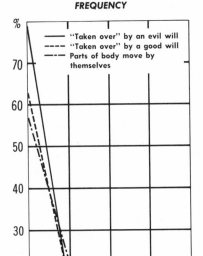

Figure 17-4. "POSSESSION" PHENOMENA

frequently than being possessed by an evil or hostile force ($p < .0005$ and $p < .05$, respectively).

CONTROL OF THE LEVEL OF INTOXICATION

While users often are not concerned with what level of intoxication they will reach in any given session, especially if they have no problems on their minds, there are occasions on which a user will not want to get very intoxicated, e.g., if he expects to have to deal with some situation he is not sure he can handle while intoxicated. On the other hand, if the user does not expect to have to deal with straight people or perform complex tasks, he may wish to get as intoxicated as possible. If he wishes to control his level of intoxication, he may do so by controlling the amount of marijuana he smokes[2] and/or by using various psychological

---

[2]With respect to controlling level of intoxication, smoking marijuana is preferred to eating it, as the user can control his level of intoxication very rapidly and precisely. If it is eaten, about three times as much is required for a given level, onset is much slower, duration is longer, offset is longer, and altering level by eating more is risky because of these time delays. Many of the cases of overdosing that my informants knew of resulted from eating marijuana.

techniques to decrease his level (bringing himself "down") or increase his level (bringing himself "up"). The psychological techniques are particularly important when a situation unexpectedly occurs that makes the user feel he should come down.

Desire to Get Higher

Sometimes users at a given level of intoxication feel an intense need to become even more intoxicated: *"I get a rather compulsive desire to get even higher after a certain stage: I will smoke much more if I can."* This is an infrequent effect (26%, 27%, 27%, 15%, 4%), which begins to occur at Moderate to Strong levels (11%, 22%, 24%, 12%, 3%). This desire occurs more frequently among younger users ($p < .05$), the College-educated ($p < .05$), Heavy Total users ($p < .01$, overall), and Daily users ($p < .05$). The young experience this at lower levels ($p < .05$).

Comments by my informants suggest that the primary motivation behind this effect is the anticipation of greater pleasure from being more intoxicated.

Experience with LSD

The users were asked, *"Since taking LSD (or mescaline, peyote, psilocybin, or another major psychedelic drug), I am able to get much higher on grass than I was before."* Of the 104 users answering this, 56 said yes and 48 said no, so a substantial portion of users feel their experiences with more powerful psychedelic drugs have enabled them to have more experiences when subsequently using marijuana. Informants commented to the effect that psychedelic drug experiences showed them that certain types of experiences were possible; knowing this, they have then been able to direct attention toward them and attain them with marijuana. This nicely illustrates the nature of potential effects, discussed in Chapter 2, as an underlying model for drug intoxication states.

Other Drugs Used to Raise the Level of Intoxication

The users were asked to explain any yes answers to *"I have special ways of getting higher besides smoking more grass: (1) other drugs + grass; and (2) special mental techniques."* For the first part of this question, 23 percent answered yes, 67 percent no, and 10 percent skipped it. Some users mentioned several drugs they had used in conjunction with marijuana.

Ten mentions were made of taking other psychedelic drugs, such as LSD or DMT, in addition to marijuana, and six mentions were made of using hashish, the more potent form of marijuana. That more powerful psychedelics than marijuana should potentiate its effect is not surprising, but one may wonder why the users bother to smoke marijuana if the more powerful drug is available, unless the marijuana effects add some special quality to the more powerful psychedelic.

There were eight mentions of amphetamines for potentiating the marijuana state. Although the method of administration was not mentioned, it is likely that it was by mouth.

Alcohol was mentioned as a potentiator in seven cases, often with indications that the ratio of the two drugs had to be just right, usually a small amount of alcohol with the usual quantity of marijuana smoked.

Among miscellaneous drugs mentioned were amyl nitrate (2) and opium (2).[3]

Mental Techniques for Raising the Level of Intoxication

Thirty-nine percent of the users indicated they had special mental techniques for getting higher. I have classified them into eleven types, with examples of each given below. The number of times various techniques were mentioned in the users' explanations is presented in Table 17-1.

TABLE 17-1

MENTAL TECHNIQUES FOR GETTING HIGHER

TYPE OF TECHNIQUE	NUMBER OF TIMES MENTIONED
Focusing, concentrating on current activity	9
Contact with intoxicated companions	7
Meditation	7
Direct willing to get higher	7
Breathing techniques	6
Music	4
Letting go, non-striving, relaxation	4
Fantasy	4
Inducing positive emotions	4
Hypnosis	2
Miscellaneous	15

[3]Some of the users' experience with other drugs used to potentiate or alter the nature of marijuana intoxication results from the fact that some of the marijuana sold in the United States is adulterated with these drugs, either because some customers prefer it (although most of my informants do not like the idea of their marijuana being adulterated with unknown ingredients) or to "potentiate" marijuana that is otherwise too weak in active ingredients to be salable.

Focusing, concentrating on current activity, refers to putting all of one's attention on what one is doing or a sensory stimulus one is receiving, e.g., " . . . staring at one object or some other spot of interest . . . ," or "cutting out extraneous concerns with past or future, remaining in here-and-now and digging it (grooving). . . ."

Contact with intoxicated companions refers to the speech and actions of the intoxicated persons' serving to remind the user of higher-level phenomena so that he can experience them, e.g., "thinking like whomever I'm with who's higher," or "talking to stoned people and being with them for a while." "Contact highs," when a user is straight at the time but feels many of the phenomena of intoxication simply by being in close contact with an intoxicated person, were also reported as a common effect (Chapter 12).

Meditation refers to actual use of this word by the user to describe his technique such as "Kundalini yoga—as energy flows up spine and reaches brain, I get higher . . . ," or *"Mantra* chanting, zazen."[4]

Direct willing to get higher refers to reports of simply willing to reach a high level of intoxication without any specific mechanisms of such willing being described; e.g., "I move mentally through the same plane as a grass session, and then an LSD session, and finally, beyond both into a higher series of energy levels . . ."; or "Once fairly stoned I can get as high almost as I like with only the will and the knowledge ('You can fly, Wendy!' said Peter)."

Breathing techniques are illustrated in such comments as "Center on my breathing, close my eyes, and concentrate on getting higher"; or "I hold my breath for 30 seconds at a time and stare at a fixed point of light. . . ." Several users specifically mentioned hyperventilating, but noted it produced only a transient alteration in level of intoxication.

Music, especially if it is about other states of consciousness, can be used to get higher; e.g., "Listen to music and relax—especially Donovan—can get high without anything"; or "Listen to music, especially with stereo earphones; all else blocked out, get especially high."

Letting go, non-striving, relaxation are illustrated by "Just let mind loose," or ". . . allowing same thought processes to develop as when on acid. . . ," or " . . . just relaxing into it, like floating, not striving."

Fantasy refers to imagining specific events that lead into a higher state, such as " . . . guided daydream[5]. . . ," or "Sometimes smoke a regular cigarette and pass it around pretending it's a joint."

Inducing positive emotions to get higher is illustrated by "I think

---

[4]*Mantras* are special sounds for meditating on (see Govinda, 1960, e.g.), and *zazen* refers to the practice of Zen meditation (Suzuki, 1959).

[5]The guided daydream is a psychotherapeutic technique for evoking deep levels of imagery. It is used primarily in Europe but is increasingly used in the United States. See Assagioli (1965), Desoille (1965), and Gerard (1961).

happy . . . ," or ". . . remind myself how incredible it is just to be alive
in the first place. . . ."

Hypnosis was mentioned by two users, without further explanation.
Aaronson's work (1969) in inducing psychedelic-like states through hypnosis, and Baumann's (1970) technique of training adolescents to reex-
perience many of the pleasures of marijuana intoxication through hypnotic regression is relevant here.

Lowering the Level—"Coming Down"

"*I can 'come down' at will if I need to be straight for a minute to
deal with some complicated reality problem (circle the point of highness
above which* can't *do this*)" is an extremely characteristic effect of marijuana intoxication (5%, 3%, 18%, 21%, 49%).[6] It is more frequent among
males ($p < .05$), the Professionals ($p < .01$), and Users of Psychedelics
($p < .01$). Light Total users report it less frequently than Moderate
or Heavy users ($p < .05$, overall), and the Daily users report it more
frequently than the Weekly or Occasional users ($p < .05$, overall).

The Very Strong and Maximal levels were the main ones the users
could not come down from at will (2%, 8%, 11%, 33%, 24%). Female
users and Users of Psychedelics indicated being able to come down
temporarily from higher levels of intoxication ($p < .05$ and $p < .01$,
respectively).

A similar question was asked later in the questionnaire in opposite
form, namely, "*There is a certain degree of being stoned from above which
I* cannot *come down quickly if I* must *come down to deal adequately
with reality (circle level).*" This is a fairly frequent effect (23%, 27%,
21%, 10%, 8%), more so with females ($p < .05$) and Non-users of Psychedelics ($p < .05$). The levels above which the user cannot come down
quickly are almost exclusively the Very Strong and Maximal levels (0%,
1%, 3%, 21%, 37%), with a higher level being indicated by the Moderate
Total users than the Light or Heavy Total users ($p < .05$, overall).

As shown in Figure 17-5, feeling able to come down at will is far
more frequent than feeling unable to ($p << .0005$). Being unable to
come down quickly when desired is rated as occurring at higher levels
of intoxication than the point where the user can come down at will
($p < .0005$).

---

[6]This widespread ability to "come down," i.e., suppress many of the effects of intoxication at
will, raises an interesting methodological question for laboratory studies of the effect of marijuana
or its derivatives on various performance measures. If the user believes, as a result of the demand
characteristics of the experiment (Orne, 1962; Rosenthal, 1966), that he should do as well as possible,
he may come down and try to perform as he would straight. On the other hand, if he thinks it
important to perform as an intoxicated person should, he may not only *not* suppress effects, he may
exaggerate them. If the demands are not clear to the subjects, great variability in performance will
occur that could wipe out real effects. If the demands have consistent effects on the subjects, but
are not clear to the experimenter or the readers of the report on the experiment, error will result
from confusing one of many potential effects (drug plus particular demands) with "natural" effects.

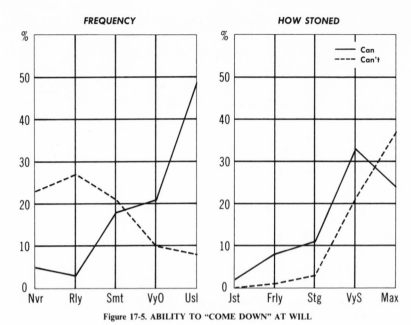

Figure 17-5. ABILITY TO "COME DOWN" AT WILL

Note.—For guide to interpreting the "How Stoned" graph, see note on Figure 6-1.

Techniques for Coming Down

Twenty-nine percent of the users answered yes to the question *"I have special technique(s) for coming down rapidly if I need to be straight quickly (please describe)"*. Of those answering no, a number offered comments to the effect that they had never experienced a situation they couldn't handle adequately when intoxicated, and so had no need of techniques for coming down.

I have classified the 52 techniques described by users in Table 17-2, and illustrated the techniques in each category below.

Direct willing, concentration refers to simply willing oneself to be normal; e.g., "Just tell myself to straighten up and it works!"; or " . . . just telling myself *straighten out!!!. . .*" A number of the techniques put in the miscellaneous category may also have been instances of direct willing, but it was not completely clear that they were.

Inducing negative emotions indicates techniques of frightening oneself and consequently coming down almost immediately, as "I 'freak' myself by imagining the consequences if I 'blow it' "; or "Think of cops and being busted and my family—if that doesn't do it, nothing will"; or "Bug my partner, who then bums my trip: I snap back in a flash!"

Intense focus on current situation is illustrated by ". . . concentrate on the straight task which requires attention"; or "Concentration, deep

TABLE 17-2

TECHNIQUES FOR "COMING DOWN" RAPIDLY

TYPE OF TECHNIQUE	NUMBER OF TIMES MENTIONED
Direct willing, concentration	13
Inducing negative emotions	9
Intense focus on current situation	8
Acting normal, straight, putting on everyday role	5
Fantasy, suggestion	2
Drugs	2
Miscellaneous	13

concentration on the matter at hand can make one straight enough to cope with the situation." Focus on the situation was also used to increase the level of intoxication, but it was a different quality of focus, one of the "suchness" of things rather than the reality demands they make on the user.

Acting normal, straight, putting on everyday role includes techniques of faking normality or putting on an everyday personality, which then brings the user down. Examples are ". . . put on my work-a-day intellectual persona"; or "By standing up . . . and lighting up a cigarette (more natural-looking, gives me something to hold my attention) and above all making a determined effort to appear 'straight.' "

Fantasy and suggestion involve creating an image or suggestion that alters the state of consciousness to normal, namely, "I pretend I am walking out of a fog or scene into another scene"; and "Wendy, you're on the ground."

Drugs, Thorazine and Niacin, were mentioned by an engineering student and a psychiatrist. respectively.

ADDITIONAL EFFECTS

"Presence of compulsive behavior or thoughts" (Rarely, Strongly).

"I syncopate rhythm when playing the guitar, sometimes unintentionally. This happens only stoned. I find syncopating intentionally difficult" (Very Often, Maximum).

"I get totally absorbed in the process of laughing for minutes at a time; I overreact to any sort of humor" (Usually, Fairly).

"I am suddenly aware of the unreality of my and other's behavior and become convulsed with laughter" (Usually, Fairly).

"Confidence and self-faith are plentiful" (Usually, Just).

"Cannot stop from smiling" (Usually, Fairly).

"I enjoy acting out fantasies when stoned" (Very Often, Strongly).

"Incessant flowing of verbiage—talking to myself, not out loud" (Very Often, Strongly).

LEVELS OF INTOXICATION FOR CONTROL

Various effects of marijuana intoxication on control are plotted by level of intoxication in Figure 17-6. The overall grouping is highly significant ($p \lll .0005$).

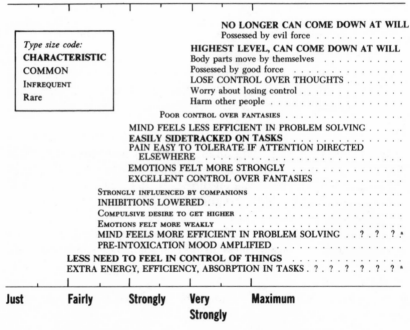

NO LONGER CAN COME DOWN AT WILL
Possessed by evil force . . . .

Type size code:
CHARACTERISTIC
COMMON
INFREQUENT
Rare

HIGHEST LEVEL, CAN COME DOWN AT WILL
Body parts move by themselves . . . .
Possessed by good force . . . .
LOSE CONTROL OVER THOUGHTS . . . .
Worry about losing control . . . .
Harm other people . . . .

POOR CONTROL OVER FANTASIES . . . .
MIND FEELS LESS EFFICIENT IN PROBLEM SOLVING . . . . .
EASILY SIDETRACKED ON TASKS . . . .
PAIN EASY TO TOLERATE IF ATTENTION DIRECTED
  ELSEWHERE . . . .
EMOTIONS FELT MORE STRONGLY . . . .
EXCELLENT CONTROL OVER FANTASIES . . . .

STRONGLY INFLUENCED BY COMPANIONS . . . .
INHIBITIONS LOWERED . . . .
COMPULSIVE DESIRE TO GET HIGHER . . . .
EMOTIONS FELT MORE WEAKLY . . . .
MIND FEELS MORE EFFICIENT IN PROBLEM SOLVING . . ? . ? . ? [a]
PRE-INTOXICATION MOOD AMPLIFIED . . . .

LESS NEED TO FEEL IN CONTROL OF THINGS . . . .
EXTRA ENERGY, EFFICIENCY, ABSORPTION IN TASKS . ? . ? . ? . ? . ? . ? . ? [a]

| Just | Fairly | Strongly | Very Strongly | Maximum |

[a]There is some question whether this effect is available at all levels above the minimal one.

FIGURE 17-6. INTOXICATING LEVELS, CONTROL

Beginning at the Moderate and Moderate-to-Strong levels, there is characteristically a decreased need to feel in control of things, an increased willingness to trust the situation and let things happen. Some ordinarily inhibited thoughts and behaviors will be allowed, and the user feels his mind is working very efficiently, a feeling that probably reinforces the lessening of need to control things. At the Strong level the user may feel his mind works less efficiently in dealing with problems, and he is easily sidetracked when working on external tasks. His emotions are generally felt more strongly, but he usually feels he has excellent

TABLE 17-3

EFFECTS OF BACKGROUND FACTORS ON CONTROL

BACKGROUND FACTORS	EFFECTS	

More Drug Experience	More frequent:
	  Easily sidetracked
	  Extra efficiency, energy
	    for tasks
	  Can come down at will
	  Compulsive desire to
	    get higher
	
	More intoxicated for:
	  Easily sidetracked
	  Extra efficiency, energy
	    for tasks
	  Can come down at will
		Less frequent:
		  Worry about losing
		    control
		  Can't come down at
		    will

Older	More intoxicated for:
	  Compulsive desire to
	    get higher
		Less frequent:
		  Poor fantasy control
		  Easily sidetracked
		  Compulsive desire to
		    get higher
		
		Less intoxicated for:
		  Inhibitions lowered

More Educated	More frequent:
	  Can come down at will
		Less frequent:
		  Poor fantasy control
		  Good fantasy control
		  Easily sidetracked
		  Compulsive desire to
		    get higher
		
		Less intoxicated for:
		  Easily sidetracked

Males	More frequent:
	  Can come down at will
		Less frequent:
		  Body parts move by
		    themselves
		  Can't come down at
		    will
		
		Less intoxicated for:
		  Can come down at will

Therapy & Growth	More frequent:
	  Possessed by good
	    force or will	

control over his fantasies and so can guide his experiences in very plea-surable directions. Moving up to the Very Strongly intoxicated level, the user may begin to feel lessened control over his thoughts and, less frequently, lessened control over his fantasies, but most users still feel they can come down at will if required. At the highest levels users sometimes feel that they cannot come down at will. They may also, very rarely, feel "possessed" by an external force or will, more often good than evil.

MODULATING FACTORS

The effects of relatively linear background variables are summarized in Table 17-3. Users with more drug experience are less troubled with worries about losing control, and can come down more frequently and from higher levels than other users.

One background variable had a non-linear effect. Moderate Total users indicated a higher level above which they could not come down quickly than either Light or Heavy Total users.

SUMMARY

Although they feel less need to be in control of things and are more willing to trust the situation, experienced marijuana users are able to control the nature of their intoxication experiences to a high degree. Direction of attention is the main way in which this is done; if one concentrates on a desired effect, it may very well occur, while directing concentration away from an undesired effect will frequently allow that effect to fade away.

Control is good through most of the range of intoxication, but begins to get poorer for some users at the very high levels.

Most users can generally come down at will from even the Very Strong level of intoxication. Various techniques for coming down include direct willing. inducing fear, or intense focusing on the reality situation that they need to deal with. Many users also can increase their level of intoxication by mental techniques: direct willing, meditating, or associ-ating with others who are more intoxicated. These factors illustrate the importance of situational and psychological variables, over and above drug dosage, in determining level of intoxication at any given time. Also, more experienced drug users have more control of intoxication in general.

CHAPTER 18

Identity

EACH OF US feels he is a unique person, an integrated whole, with long- and short-term values, likes, dislikes, and goals, and a unique set of memories, which constitute our personal history. Above and beyond these components, there is a certain sense of what we might call "I-ness," an immediate feeling quality added to experience that makes it *my* experience. Important changes can occur in this feeling of identity during marijuana intoxication.

MAJOR EFFECTS

Openness

"*I feel more childlike, more open to experience of all kinds, more filled with wonder and awe at the nature of things*" is one of the most characteristic effects of marijuana intoxication (5%, 4%, 22%, 39%, 29%). Females experience it more frequently than males ($p < .05$). It begins to occur at Moderate to Strong levels (11%, 27%, 39%, 13%, 3%). This is in marked contrast to the infrequent effect "*I feel isolated from things around me . . .*" discussed in Chapter 12. Isolation occurs far less frequently ($p << .0005$) and at higher levels ($p < .0005$) than openness, as shown in Figure 18-1.

Loss of Separateness

Two experiences represent an even greater dropping of the feeling of separation from others and the world.

"*I have been so absorbed in looking at or contemplating an object or person that I felt as if I were that object or person; i.e., temporarily the split between it-and-me or they-and-me was transcended*" is an infrequent effect (31%, 30%, 29%, 7%, 2%), which begins to occur, among those who could rate it, at Very Strong to Maximal levels (1%, 4%, 13%, 21%, 21%). The Meditators have experienced this more frequently

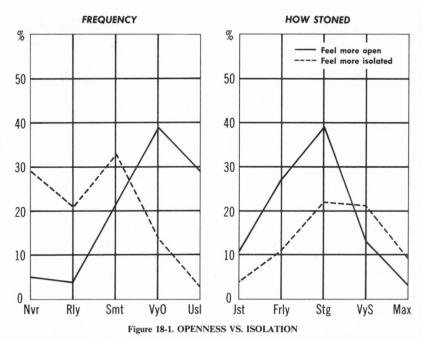

Figure 18-1. OPENNESS VS. ISOLATION

Note.—For guide to interpreting the "How Stoned" graph, see note on Figure 6-1.

($p < .01$, overall). The young and the College-educated need to be more intoxicated to experience this merging ($p < .05$ in each case).

"*I lose all sense of self, of being a separate ego, and feel at one with the world*" is a common effect (19%, 25%, 31%, 21%, 3%), again more so with the Meditators ($p < .01$). It begins to occur at Strong to Very Strong levels (1%, 8%, 23%, 20%, 17%).

An effect quite different from diminution of the ego sense and at-oneness with the world is the enhancement of the feeling of uniqueness, differentness. "*I feel completely unique; there is no one like me; I feel as if I am much better than ordinary people when stoned*" is an infrequent effect (25%, 25%, 29%, 10%, 7%). It generally begins to occur at the Strong levels (7%, 15%, 22%, 19%, 5%).

The relationships between these three phenomena are shown in Figure 18-2. Feeling at one with the world occurs more frequently than merging with the contemplated object or person ($p < .01$), but the latter phenomenon and feeling unique occur about equally. Merging and feeling at one with the world occur at about equally high levels of intoxication, and both are at significantly higher levels than feeling unique ($p < .0005$ and $p < .001$, respectively).

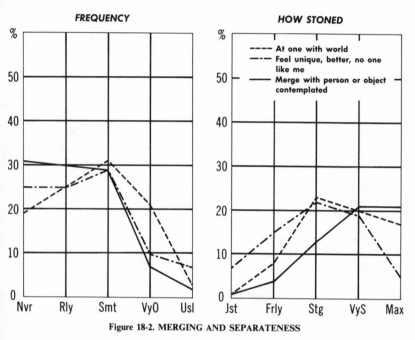

FREQUENCY

HOW STONED

- - - - At one with world
- · - · Feel unique, better, no one like me
——— Merge with person or object contemplated

Figure 18-2. MERGING AND SEPARATENESS

Note.—For guide to interpreting the "How Stoned" graph, see note on Figure 6-1.

Alteration of Identity

A common experience is "*I feel very powerful, capable, and intelligent when stoned*" (16%, 11%, 49%, 16%, 7%), more so with Heavy Total users ($p < .05$, overall). This generally begins to occur at the Strong level of intoxication (7%, 18%, 35%, 16%, 3%), with Heavy Total users and Daily users experiencing this at lower levels ($p < .01, p < .05$, overall, respectively).

A much more dramatic change is represented by: "*Some events become archetypal, part of the basic way Man has always done things. That is, instead of me (John Doe, ego) doing something, it is just Man Doing What Man Has Always Done. That is, my actions become part of the pattern that man has always been part of, instead of me, a particular individual, carrying out a particular act at a particular moment in space/time.*" This is a common effect (23%, 19%, 38%, 16%, 3%), experienced more frequently by Users of Psychedelics ($p < .05$). It begins to occur at Strong and Very Strong levels (4%, 5%, 25%, 25%, 10%), with Males having to be more intoxicated than Females for this experience ($p < .05$).

This effect is highly valued by many users; they feel they can temporarily transcend the limitations of their ego, their hangups (neurotic problems), and their culture, and can participate in a more fundamental, natural way of existence. This effect is related to some of those discussed in Chapter 19 on Spiritual Experiences.

"My personality changes a lot temporarily while I'm stoned, so that in many important ways I am a different person for that time" is an infrequent effect (23%, 32%, 25%, 13%, 3%), which may begin to occur at the Strong to Very Strong levels (1%, 11%, 20%, 21%, 13%). The Occasional users experience it less frequently than the Weekly or Daily users ($p < .05$, overall). A related, infrequent effect, the feeling that the location of consciousness has moved within the body, has been presented in Chapter 11.

ADDITIONAL EFFECTS

"I become very introspective, trying to see who I am, what I'm doing" (Usually, Fairly).

"I feel as though myself and one other person (usually my lover) form a sort of island around which all other action flows" (Usually, Fairly).

"I feel as though I and/or the group I am with are the only people in the world" (Very Often, Very Strongly).

"I feel 'more like myself,' the quintessence of me" (Sometimes, Strongly).

"My whole self seems to be standing inside my skull, leaning forward and looking out through the eye-holes" (Sometimes, Very Strongly).

"When stoned I get very introspective and see the 'real' me" (Very Often, Maximum).

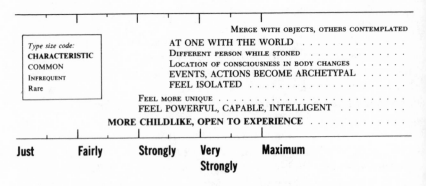

FIGURE 18-3. INTOXICATION LEVELS, IDENTITY PHENOMENA

LEVELS OF INTOXICATION FOR IDENTITY

The various effects on identity of marijuana intoxication are arranged by level in Figure 18-3. The overall ordering is highly significant ($p \ll .0005$).

Beginning in the Moderate to Strong range, the user becomes more childlike, open to experience, interested in all sorts of things that might ordinarily be regarded as unimportant. As he reaches the Strong level, the user often begins to feel more powerful, capable, intelligent, and may feel especially unique and special, a kind of ego enhancement.

TABLE 18-1

EFFECTS OF BACKGROUND FACTORS ON IDENTITY

BACKGROUND FACTORS	EFFECTS	
More Drug Experience	More frequent: Events become arche- typal Personality changes Feel powerful, capable	
		Less intoxicated for: Feel powerful, capable
More Educated		Less intoxicated for: Merge with others Location of conscious- ness in body changes
Older		Less intoxicated for: Merge with others
Males		Less frequent: More childlike, open
	More intoxicated for: Events become arche- typal	
Meditators	More frequent: Merge with others At one with world Feel isolated	
Therapy & Growth	More frequent: Possessed by a good force	

As he moves up toward the very high levels of intoxication, however, the sense of ego often fades, and the user often finds his experiences and actions less unique or individual and more archetypal, with a feeling of at-one-ness with the universe frequently replacing the ordinary sense of separation. Near Maximal levels this may sometimes include the feeling of merging with others.

MODULATING FACTORS

The relatively linear effects of various background variables are summarized in Table 18-1. As might be expected, Meditators have more frequent experiences of transcending the limitations of the individual ego.

SUMMARY

Marijuana intoxication characteristically produces a childlike openness to experience and a sense of wonder and awe, in contrast to the usual businesslike manner in which we classify events and people strictly in terms of their importance to us. At moderate levels of intoxication this may also be accompanied by feelings of ego enhancement, of feeling powerful, capable, unique. At the high levels of intoxication, however, the sense of separateness, of being an individual ego, is often replaced by feelings of oneness with the world, of actions and experiences becoming archetypal, and occasionally, of merging with people or objects. These high level effects are greatly valued by users and are one of the important reasons why they consider marijuana intoxication a "higher" state of consciousness.

CHAPTER 19

Spiritual Experiences

IN DEALING WITH spiritual experiences it is important to remember that the sample consists primarily of young college students of the West Coast, a very idealistic, serious, and religiously unconventional group. To many such students religion is not a question of going to church on Sunday but a seeking after mystical experience and a daily living of religious principles, many of which are derived from Oriental religions and philosophies (an excellent reference on the impact of the new religions is Needleman, 1970).

MAJOR EFFECTS

Contact with the Divine

"*I feel in touch with a Higher Power or a Divine Being to some extent when stoned; I feel more in contact with the 'spiritual' side of things*" is an infrequent effect (39%, 13%, 24%, 12%, 10%), which begins to occur primarily at Strong to Very Strong levels of intoxication (1%, 7%, 18%, 17%, 9%) in those able to rate this. Meditators and the Therapy and Growth group experience it less frequently than Ordinary Users ($p <$ .01, overall), the College-educated ($p <$ .05) and Users of Psychedelics ($p <$ .01) more frequently.

Meditation

A number of users feel they can meditate[1] more effectively when intoxicated: "*I am able to meditate more effectively than when straight (if yes, please describe what sort of meditation you do on the back of this page).*" This is an infrequent effect (46%, 10%, 13%, 7%, 9%). As might be expected, it is more frequent among Meditators ($p <$ .05, overall). Daily users also experience it more frequently ($p <$ .01, overall).

---

[1]For readers interested in the psychology of meditation, I recommend Ornstein and Naranjo's (1971) new book highly.

Users of Psychedelics do not have to be as intoxicated to experience meditating more effectively ($p < .05$). This effect peaks at the Strong level of intoxication (5%, 5%, 15%, 7%, 1%). Note that many more users than the number formally classified as Meditators are giving positive responses here with respect to their occasional or informal meditation practice.

Most of the comments offered by Meditators on this item simply repeated the name of the type of meditation they regularly did, but a few were more specific concerning *how* marijuana intoxication affected their meditation. These comments are given below.

A 21-year-old masseuse who practices T'ai-Chi[2] and Hatha Yoga[3] writes:

> At times I have felt that I have gotten a better feeling for T'ai-Chi while stoned. I have felt the *chi*[4] more fully and have been able to let it flow through me in a way that enabled my mind to give up control of my body. I have not actually meditated while stoned. But I have experienced while stoned the mindless serenity that I hope to be able to attain through zazen sitting.

A male artist who practices Subud[5] writes:

> Pot allows me to empty out, to drop the ego and immediate mundane concerns. A peace ensues and a rapport with eternity arises. It is as if a pressure valve was opened, and I am able to slough off the tensions and considerations of this three-dimensional "reality" and experience what seems to be a four-dimensional state of essentials, with flexible time and space. Pot is a sacrament when such cleansing states are reached. It is also religious (4-D) in that it goes from the most base to the sublime, from microcosm to macrocosm, Yin to Yang.

---

[2] T'ai-Chi is an ancient Chinese discipline of moving the body in certain ways while practicing mental centering and direction of psychic energy (*chi, ki, prana*). Descriptions may be found in Chang and Smith (1967) and Feng and Kirk (1970).

[3] Hatha yoga, as distinguished from other branches of yoga, is primarily concerned with development and control of the physical body. Some of the unusual-looking positions used by its practitioners have been the basis of the popular stereotype of yogis as people who are contortionists. It may be practiced alone for its health benefits, but in terms of the overall yoga system it is considered a basic and beginning form of yoga; it is necessary to strengthen and control the physical body so it will not be a source of distraction during more advanced meditation. The reader interested in yoga may see Behanan (1937), Blofeld (1970), Chang (1963), Evans-Wentz (1958), Garrison (1964), Johnston (1968), Muses (1961), Wood (1954), and Yeats-Brown (1958).

[4] *Chi* is the spiritual energy that the practitioner attempts to direct through his body. See the discussion of experiences of energy in Chapter 11.

[5] Subud is a modified form of Sufism (See Shah, 1964, 1968 for general information on Sufism), which uses a form of opening meditation (Ornstein and Naranjo, 1971) known as the *latihan* for direct contact with higher forces (Needleman, 1970).

A 19-year-old male student who practices meditation on mandalas[6] writes that when intoxicated he experiences "long perceptual jags of continuous absorption into and penetration of the perceived field."

A 29-year-old electrical technician who describes his meditation practice as an eclectic mixture of early Christian and oriental techniques writes: "I find my ability to center in while stoned is increased. This is also the factor of 'letting go' which is enhanced during meditation. To me getting stoned is a communion of sorts with the God-head."

A number of users mentioned that they practiced Zen[7] meditation exercises on occasion and that marijuana intoxication occasionally helped. This opinion would probably not be shared by regular practitioners of Zen.

Spiritual Experiences

"*I have spiritual experiences, discrete experiences which have had a powerful, long-term religious effect on me, while stoned (If so, please describe)*" was answered yes by 33 percent of the users. Meditators answered yes and no in the ratio of two to one, while for Ordinary users the ratio was one to three ($p < .0005$).

These figures overestimate the occurrence of religious experiences with marijuana intoxication per se because some users indicated in their answers that they were referring to experiences induced by LSD or similar powerful psychedelics. Subtracting these, we have 25 percent of the users reporting significant spiritual experience while intoxicated with marijuana.

The distribution of several categories of spiritual experience is shown in Table 19-1, with experiences resulting from LSD rather than marijuana shown in a separate column. Examples of experiences in each category are given below.

Unity refers to the experience of feeling at one with the universe, God, others, the overall plan of things. Examples are: ". . . death would be a process by which I allowed myself to be absorbed into the light; at that point I felt as if a large part of me was the light. This experience gave me a lasting, more positive feeling about death and giving up the ego"; or "Mystical one with the all-knowing."

Stimulation of long-term interest in religion refers to reports where the emphasis was put not on the experience itself, although it may have

---

[6]The mandala is a visual meditation symbol whose essentials consist of a center and a patterned periphery. The overall symbol may be very simple or exceptionally complex. It embodies certain symbolic principles in its design as well as forming a fixation point for the meditator. See Arguelles and Arguelles (in press), Tucci (1969), and Wilhelm and Jung (1962).

[7]Good introductions to Zen Buddhism may be found in Suzuki (1959, 1962) and Watts (1957).

TABLE 19-1

SPIRITUAL EXPERIENCES WHILE INTOXICATED

TYPE OF EXPERIENCE	NUMBER OF USERS REPORTING	
	Marijuana	LSD
Unity	10	3
Stimulation of long-term interest in religion	7	2
Contact with divine beings	4	2
Long-term positive changes in life-style	3	3
Deep peace, joy	2	0
Miscellaneous	6	2

been impressive, but on the fact that it forced the user to confront basic religious questions and resulted in a long-term involvement in religious practices. Examples are: "Not really religious—but more like an *important* thing because it can mellow people down make them think about what they're doing. In this way hostility can be decreased; people appreciate each other more and can generally get their heads and hearts together. I guess that's kind of religious at that!"; or "I experienced the Kundalini force[8] twice when stoned; this has influenced me to begin seriously studying Indian sacred writings. . . ."

Contact with divine beings is illustrated by "I have seen Christ and spoken to Him; He's the one who knows me and I need Him"; or "Powerful feelings of the presence of a loving, powerful, helpful being, often. I should say, at this point I do not believe these effects occur because of the grass; I think they are experiences, which are sharper because of less surface noise and anxiety (grass seems very often to make concentration easier and more lasting)."

Long-term positive changes in life-style of the type highly valued in religious teachings are illustrated by "Usually assumes form of a high degree of 'spiritual' empathy with others present"; or ". . . the communion and God-contact has caused me to alter my life-style; e.g., I don't lock our house, although there is expensive sound equipment, records, books, and art supplies in it. A willingness to share our food and home with people. Not saying no to people who ask for time and help. A

---

[8]The *Kundalini force* refers to the ancient Indian idea of a special sort of power (*prana, ki, chi*—see Chapter 11) which is stored in a special center at the base of the spine. Certain meditation exercises or drugs are supposed to be able to liberate this energy so it can flow up the spinal column, activating various *chakra* centers on the way and finally producing a state of consciousness conducive to liberation and enlightenment in the *properly prepared* yogi. It is considered highly dangerous to release the *Kundalini force* without proper training under the guidance of a master. See Garrison (1964), Govinda (1960), Krishna (1970), and Woodruffe (1931).

calmer, serene attitude on life, but filled with more positive action, e.g., teaching sensory awareness to the Free University set."

Deep peace, joy, represented by ". . . on pot I have experienced peace and joy from God"; and "Mostly the experiences are of a nature concerning a peaceful state of mind."

Among the more interesting miscellaneous cases is one of purported recall of past life: ". . . strong identification with ocean led to doctrines of reincarnation[9]—also sound experiences of previous lives."

Another interesting case was a humbling experience which also would qualify as a classical account of an out-of-the-body (OOBE) experience, although the user did not classify it as such in the earlier item dealing with such experiences (Chapter 10). Such experiences frequently lead the experiencer to a deep belief in the immortality of his own soul, usually expressed in the form that he no longer *believes* in survival of death, he *knows* it to be true because he has experienced being alive while "out" of his physical body. This does not logically follow, but the logic of it is usually not important to someone who has had the experience. The experience of this 19-year-old student was as follows.

> I had quite an interesting experience while camping. I got stoned on grass, and as I was about to go to sleep, I came completely awake and aware of my surroundings. It was pitch black in the tent, yet I could see as if it were daylight. I felt as if my body were covered with eyes and I could see in all directions. I slowly floated up through the top of the tent, looking at the whole area. I got farther away, moving towards space. I got very realistic views of the earth. I kept moving up until I could see half of the earth, then the earth and the moon, continuing until I stood at the edge of space, inspecting the whole universe. I was all of a sudden struck by man's insignificance. Then I proceeded to move until I could see hundreds of universes glinting like stars. None of these universes was any larger than the head of a pin. It was incredibly beautiful. I began laughing almost hysterically because now our own universe, immense as it seems to us, was no bigger than the head of a pin and one among millions besides. I described the whole experience as it happened to several other people; and I believe from the reactions I got, I thoroughly scared the hell out of them.

Experiences Sometimes Interpreted as Spiritual

A number of the intoxication experiences already reported on in other chapters are sometimes interpreted by users as manifestations of

---

[9]Beliefs about the idea of reincarnation in the West are generally so distorted as to be ludicrous. The reader interested in some accurate presentations of Eastern ideas and an introduction to the scant scientific literature on the subject should see Chari (1967), Ducasse (1960), Head and Cranston (1967), and Stevenson (1966).

higher forces or spiritual forces, or as the workings of the user's own dormant spiritual nature.

Auras around people (Chapter 6) may be considered manifestations of spiritual energy perceptible by psychic sight or, in the cases of saints and holy men, sometimes visible to ordinary people.

Ostensible paranormal phenomena, namely, *telepathy, precognition,* and *magical operations,* discussed in Chapter 10 may also be interpreted as budding spiritual faculties.

Out-of-the-body experiences may be considered by users as direct proof of the existence of the soul and budding spiritual faculties, especially when coupled with mystical experiences of the sort reported above.

Floating in limitless space may be interpreted in the same manner as OOBEs and have a humbling effect.

Sexual intercourse seeming more a *union of souls* (Chapter 13) may seem a way of being more in accordance with the divine plan.

Possession (Chapter 17), especially by a force which seems good, is a classic religious phenomenon.

At-one-ness with the world and *archetypal experience* (Chapter 18) may be seen in religious terms as greater attunement with the way of the divine, as can *increased openness, childlikeness* (". . . except ye be as little children . . .").

Readers further interested in the effect of psychedelic drugs in inducing mystical experience under proper conditions should see Pahnke's classic study (Pahnke, 1966; Pahnke and Richards, 1969) and Huxley's *The Doors of Perception* (1954). An interesting contrast to Huxley is Zaehner's experience of completely suppressing the effects of mescaline intoxication in order to prove that Huxley was wrong (Zaehner, 1957)!

RELIGIOUS SIGNIFICANCE OF BECOMING INTOXICATED

Although not all users who had had spiritual experiences while intoxicated felt this had made getting intoxicated an act of religious significance for them, 22 percent of the users did: "*Getting stoned has acquired a religious significance for me.*" Another 4 percent indicated LSD use, rather than marijuana, had acquired religious significance.

The Meditators indicated much more frequently than ordinary users that getting intoxicated had acquired a religious significance for them ($p < .01$).

The reasons given for this were quite varied. The simplest sorts of explanations were on the order of "I now pray daily and have faith and a need for religion, which I didn't feel a year ago"; or "Grass is a way to reach God"; or "Very simply, I can talk to God." The more complex explanations of yes answers indicated that the insights and experiences arrived at while intoxicated had led to the formulation of a set of religious beliefs; e.g., "In many ways I feel that when stoned I have released myself from some of the hassling of the 'real' world and can be more at one with what is lasting or ultimate—that is, I feel I have more of a chance of considering it. . . . It's an analytical contemplation tool—see deeply if not broadly—any answers found must check out down in the 'real' world. . . . The view of myself and the world I get is also much more peaceful, less filled with petty distractions. . . ."

Many users also indicated that using marijuana was religious to them, but not in the conventionally understood meaning of the term; e.g., "Grass can definitely serve as a sacrament for me; that is, I frequently feel more religious after smoking and will often smoke to achieve this effect. I doubt if this would work in the same way if I simply smoked and then went to church; feeling religious is something personal that you cannot turn on every Sunday morning." Or, "When I am stoned, I am more *aware* of who I am spiritually. Grass has helped along the way of self-realization, and in this sense it is a sacrament."

ADDITIONAL EFFECTS

"Everything in nature appears to be good. I have great feelings for all of nature and feel that all things (plants, bugs, people, etc.) are of the same substance and makeup, doing the best they can in their struggle to hold onto life and find happiness. Everything takes on this 'struggle for existence' theme and meaning, and this is all very beautiful" (Usually, Strongly).

"Am able to experience the blinding white light[10] of universal soul" (Rarely, Maximum).

"Zen, Tea Ceremony, ritual charm apparent for the first time" (no specification of frequency or level).

"Feeling of reaching 'it,' white void or infinity, or point where yin/yang, life/death, yes/no meet" (Usually, Very Strongly).

LEVELS OF INTOXICATION FOR SPIRITUAL EXPERIENCES

Figure 19-1 orders various spiritual experiences and related phenomena by level of intoxication. The overall ordering is highly significant ($p \lll .0005$).

---

[10]The perception of the clear light or the white light is an advanced type of mystical experience sought after in many Oriental approaches to liberation. See Blofeld (1970), Govinda (1960), or Leary, Metzner, and Alpert (1964).

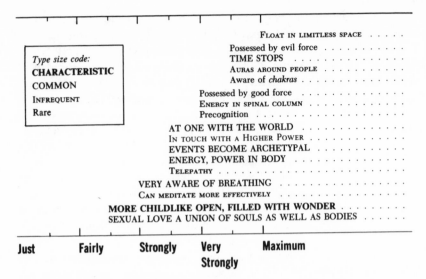

FIGURE 19-1. INTOXICATION LEVELS, SPIRITUAL EXPERIENCES

At the Moderate to Strong levels, spiritual experiences tend to be concerned with the way the world is perceived, such as being open and childlike, being closer to one's sexual partner. Meditation may begin to seem more effective. Moving toward the Very Strong level, the nature of the perceived world begins to change, so that events may become archetypal, the user may feel at one with the world or in touch with a higher power, and psychic or spiritual events may begin to occur. Going higher, time begins to be transcended by stopping in many cases or by ostensible precognition in rare cases. The user may feel himself possessed by outside forces on rare occasions, and the ordinary world may be completely left behind. Mystical experiences may occur at these very high levels that the users cannot describe for lack of words.

MODULATING FACTORS

Table 19-2 summarizes the relatively linear effects of various background variables.

A general pattern of more frequent spiritual experiences for the Meditators and those with more drug experiences is clear.

SUMMARY

For some users, important spiritual experiences have taken place while they were intoxicated with marijuana, or as a result of marijuana use. Some of these have been spontaneous, others deliberately sought

TABLE 19-2

EFFECTS OF BACKGROUND FACTORS ON SPIRITUAL EXPERIENCES

BACKGROUND FACTORS	EFFECTS	

More Drug Experience	More frequent:
	  In touch with Higher
	    Power
	  Meditate more
	    effectively
	  Events archetypal
	  Sex a union of souls
	  Perform magic
	  Precognition
	  Telepathy
	  Auras around people
		Less intoxicated for:
		  Meditate more
		    effectively
		  Sex a union of souls

Meditation	More frequent:
	  In touch with a Higher
	    Power
	  Meditate more
	    effectively
	  Spiritual experiences
	  Religious significance
	    to getting intoxicated
	  At one with the world	

Therapy & Growth	More frequent:
	  In touch with a Higher
	    Power
	  OOBEs
	  Multiple OOBEs
	  Possessed by good
	    force	

More Educated		Less frequent:
		  Sex a union of souls
		  In touch with a Higher
		    Power

Older		Less intoxicated for: Float in limitless space

Males	More frequent:
	  Multiple OOBEs
	
	More intoxicated for:
	  Events archetypal
		Less frequent:
		  OOBEs
		  Childlike, open

through meditation, which many users feel is enhanced by intoxication. Because of these experiences, the use of marijuana has acquired a religious significance to some users.

Whether these drug-induced spiritual experiences are "genuine" is a question that academics and theologians can argue about forever. The best experimental data on this question are Pahnke's (1966), which indicated that the characteristics described for drug-induced mystical experiences did not differ significantly from those of naturally-occurring mystical experiences, but that study dealt with much more powerful psychedelics than marijuana.

Certainly some of the users have made marijuana or LSD use a religious sacrament for themselves, and two respectable churches in the United States have considerable experience in the sacramental use of the more powerful psychedelics (Aiken, 1970; Clark, 1970; Osmond, 1970; Watts, 1970).

My informants, who have extensive drug experience and have devoted much time to serious spiritual interests, note, however, the use of psychedelic drugs for spiritual growth has both advantages and disadvantages. The advantages center around the possibility of the drug experience serving as an "opening," an experience of possibilities and potentialities. The spiritual possibilities seen must be developed and worked with in the user's everyday life, however. Constantly seeking to reinduce these spiritual experiences with drugs may lead to a substitution of thrilling experiences for real work.

CHAPTER 20

Sleep and Dreams

MAJOR EFFECTS

Falling Asleep

One of the most characteristic effects of marijuana intoxication is *"I find it very easy to go to sleep at my usual bedtime when stoned"* (3%, 7%, 7%, 19%, 57%), which begins to occur at the lowest level of intoxication (28%, 27%, 19%, 5%, 5%). The linked opposite effect, *"I find it very difficult to get to sleep when stoned, even if it's my usual bedtime"* (45%, 23%, 14%, 5%, 8%) occurs far less frequently ($p < .001$), and from Strong to Maximal levels (4%, 5%, 14%, 12%, 11%), as shown in Figure 20-1 below. Ease of going to sleep is generally associated with a much lower minimal level of intoxication ($p < .001$) than is difficulty, also shown in Figure 20-1, although many (53 percent) of the users could not rate the minimal level of intoxication of the latter effect.

The Professionals indicate somewhat lower levels of intoxication for ease in falling asleep, compared to the College-educated ($p < .05$).

Early drowsiness is very common: *"I get very drowsy even though it's not late or otherwise close to my usual bedtime,"* (2%, 13%, 45%, 25%, 12%). The modal minimal degree of intoxication for this is Strongly, with 76% of the users rating this in the Fairly to Very Strongly Stoned range (9%, 17%, 38%, 21%, 7%). Several background factors strongly affect the level of intoxication for this phenomenon.

Heavy Total users have Very Strongly/Maximum as modal response categories of intoxication levels, while Medium and Light Total users have Fair/Strong as modal categories ($p < .001$, overall). A similar finding occurs when frequency of use in the last six months is the background factor ($p < .01$, overall), the Daily users again indicating Very Strongly/Maximum as modal levels, the Weekly users indicating Fairly and Strongly modally (with Very Strongly and Maximum also quite frequent), and the Occasional users having a mode at Fairly/Strongly.

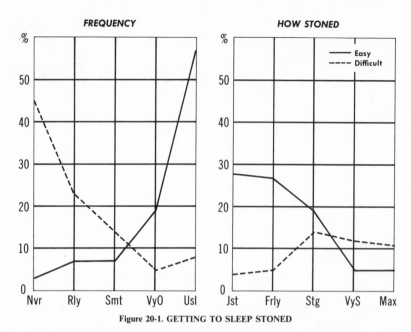

Figure 20-1. GETTING TO SLEEP STONED

Note.—For guide to interpreting the "How Stoned" graph, see note on Figure 6-1.

Meditators experience early evening drowsiness at lower levels of intoxication ($p < .001$).

A related, rare phenomenon dealt with fully in Chapter 15 is "*My mind goes completely blank for long periods (15 minutes or more); even though I'm not asleep, I have no thoughts or images or anything going on my mind.*" It may very well be that this high-level phenomenon actually represents sudden periods of sleep overwhelming the user.

Quality of Sleep

The effect of marijuana intoxication on ease or difficulty of going to sleep is paralleled by the reported effects on the quality of sleep: "*My sleep is particularly refreshing if I go to bed stoned,*" (7%, 7%, 35%, 20%, 26%) is very common, while the linked opposite, "*My sleep is restless and poor if I go to bed stoned,*" (49%, 28%, 13%, 4%, 3%) is rare ($p < .001$). Figure 20-2, below, presents the distributions for frequency of occurrence and minimal level of intoxication for these effects. Disturbed sleep usually begins at higher levels of intoxication ($p < .001$); levels are 17%, 27%, 33%, 5%, 1% for refreshing sleep and 4%, 7%, 13%, 13%, 8% for disturbed sleep.

The refreshing quality of sleep is affected by frequency of use;

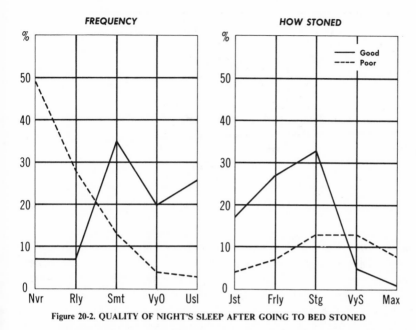

Figure 20-2. QUALITY OF NIGHT'S SLEEP AFTER GOING TO BED STONED

Note.—For guide to interpreting the "How Stoned" graph, see note on Figure 6-1.

Weekly and Daily users have somewhat higher minimal levels of intoxication for this than Occasional users ($p < .05$, overall).

Dreaming

Two questions dealt with the effect of marijuana on recalled dreaming. "*My dreams are more vivid if I go to bed stoned*" is common (23%, 18%, 23%, 16%, 12%), but its opposite, "*My dreams are less vivid or forgotten if I go to bed stoned*" (23%, 27%, 21%, 7%, 13%) occurs about as frequently. Both effects have the same distribution of minimal intoxication levels (7%, 18%, 28%, 9%, 2% and 11%, 23%, 17%, 10%, 3%, respectively). Thus the effects of marijuana on the dreaming process must be modulated by immediate situational and psychological factors rather than dosage *per se*. Heavy Total users rate Fairly/Strongly and Very Strongly/Maximum about equally for less vivid dreaming, while Low and Moderate Total users peak sharply at Fairly/Strongly ($p < .05$).

LEVELS OF INTOXICATION FOR SLEEP PHENOMENA

The effects of marijuana intoxication on sleeping and dreaming are ordered by level of intoxication in Figure 20-3. Overall differences between levels are highly significant ($p <<< .0005$). At the lower levels

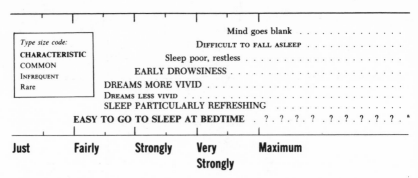

FIGURE 20-3. INTOXICATION LEVELS, SLEEP AND DREAM PHENOMENA

we find ease of falling asleep at bedtime. As we go up a level, effects on dreams may manifest and a refreshing quality may be added to sleep. The next higher level indicates possible early evening drowsiness, and the next two levels above that possible poor sleep and difficulty in going to sleep, respectively. Unrecognized sleep attacks may occasionally occur at the highest levels. Early evening drowsiness being in the midrange of the intoxication levels might indicate a change in the nature of intoxication from a tranquilizing or sedative effect to a predominantly excitatory effect at high levels.[1]

MODULATING FACTORS

All the background factors affecting sleep and dream phenomena had relatively linear effects. They are summarized in Table 20-1.

In general, more experience with drugs tends to push some of the disagreeable phenomena of marijuana intoxication to higher levels of intoxication.

SUMMARY

In general, users report that marijuana frequently produces early drowsiness, ease of going to sleep at bedtime, and an especially refreshing sleep. Given the widespread existence of problems of sleeping in this country, reflected in immense sales of both proprietary and prescription medications for aiding sleep, further investigation of the sedative effects of marijuana is called for. Further, most of the effective sleeping medications available as prescription drugs have undesirable side effects, such

---

[1]Note that these effects are for the level of intoxication at the time of going to sleep. Since most users smoke marijuana early in the evening, they may experience high level effects for the first couple of hours, but have come down to a lower level by bedtime, avoiding the problem of the adverse effects of high levels of intoxication on sleep.

TABLE 20-1

EFFECTS OF BACKGROUND FACTORS ON SLEEP AND DREAMS

BACKGROUND FACTORS	EFFECTS	
More Drug Experience	More intoxicated for: Early drowsiness Sleep particularly refreshing Dreams less vivid	
Older		Less intoxicated for: Mind goes blank
More Educated		Less intoxicated for: Easy to go to sleep at bedtime
Meditation		Less intoxicated for: Early drowsiness
Males		Less frequent: Mind goes blank

as lethargy the following morning.[2] Although not specifically dealt with on the questionnaire, my informants have indicated that lethargy following an evening of marijuana intoxication is rare and usually associated with very high levels of intoxication.

The general effects of drowsiness, ease or difficulty of going to sleep, and quality of sleep are modulated by a number of factors, which suggest a general dimension of control over the marijuana state. In the intoxicated state a great deal of mental activity and experience is occurring, more so at higher levels of intoxication. With too much mental activity, drowsiness is warded off, and sleep may be poor. Also, as emotional states tend to be amplified by marijuana, and unpleasant emotional state may demand more attention, be harder to inhibit. Thus users who have more experience generally with marijuana or other psychedelic drugs apparently acquire more familiarity with the working of the state and more ability to control its manifestation, and so are not troubled as frequently with negative effects such as difficulty with sleep, except at higher levels of intoxication where control is more difficult.

---

[2]Numerous studies have found that effective sedative drugs uniformly disrupt the natural sleep-dream cycle (see Kales, 1969, for some recent summaries of these effects). No data is available at the time of this writing on whether marijuana does this also.

CHAPTER 21

"Desirable" and "Undesirable" Effects

BASIS OF CLASSIFICATION

Non-Objectivity of Classification

Classifying the 214 possible effect descriptions[1] as "desirable" or "undesirable" is the least objective analysis of the entire study, and probably represents my personal values as much as or more than any general standards of what is desirable and undesirable.

For example, are visual hallucinations—seeing things that aren't there—(Chapter 6) per se undesirable? Many persons, especially those influenced by traditional medical models of disease, would say yes, yet my pilot subjects and informants indicated that this was usually a pleasurable and interesting effect. To sit at home, know that you are under the influence of marijuana, and see, for example, a flowing, colored ball floating in the air is most interesting, if not joyful.

What about emotional crises, "freaking out" (Chapter 16)? Again, comments by the users in describing their experiences and comments of informants indicated that while this may have been quite unpleasant at the time, it may also be highly valued in retrospect as providing necessary catharsis and/or insights into problem areas.

Criteria for "Undesirable" Effects

The criteria I finally chose for selecting what I hoped would be *unequivocally* negative effects, i.e., effects which no one would value, were that: (1) the effect is clearly unpleasant to experience; and (2) it has no later redeeming value, other than the user probably learns to avoid it in the future. Of the 214 effects, 19 met these criteria.

Others will include more or fewer in their own "undesirable" list, depending on their own values.

---

[1]This includes the regular 206 items plus 8 validity scale items which were reported on in the text because of their inherent interest.

LEVELS OF INTOXICATION FOR "UNDESIRABLE" EFFECTS

The 19 "undesirable" effects are plotted with respect to level of intoxication in Figure 21-1. Descriptions will not be repeated here as they have all been presented in other chapters. Question numbers are given in the figure if the reader wishes to refresh himself on the exact wording of the question. The overall ordering of effects is highly significant ($p \lll .0005$).

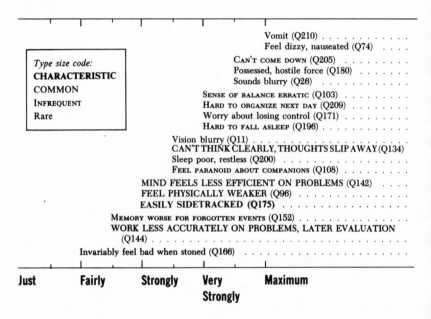

FIGURE 21-1. "UNDESIRABLE" EFFECTS AND LEVELS OF INTOXICATION

Undesirable effects are not frequent. Of the 19 effects, one was characteristic, four were common, six were infrequent, and eight were rare. For the other 184 effects, which could be rated for frequency of occurrence and which were pleasant, emotionally interesting, or *equivocally* undesirable, 29 were characteristic, 91 were common, 51 were infrequent, and 13 were rare. The clearly undesirable effects thus occur much less frequently ($p < .0005$) than the general run of effects. This is, of course, not surprising, as selecting experienced marijuana users for the present study assures getting a sample for whom pleasant effects predominate over unpleasant ones.

TABLE 21-1

EFFECTS OF BACKGROUND FACTORS ON "UNDESIRABLE" EFFECTS

BACKGROUND FACTORS	EFFECTS	
More Drug Experience	More frequent: Get sidetracked	Less frequent: Feel paranoid Thoughts slip away before fully grasped Mind feels less efficient Worry about losing control Hard to organize next day Can't come down when necessary
	More intoxicated for: Vision blurry Invariably feel bad Get sidetracked	
Older	More frequent: Hard to organize next day	Less frequent: Get sidetracked
	More intoxicated for: Sense of balance erratic	
More Educated		Less frequent: Memory worse Get sidetracked
		Less intoxicated for: Get sidetracked Hard to organize next day
Males		Less frequent: Vision blurry Sense of balance erratic Can't come down when necessary
Meditators		Less intoxicated for: Feel paranoid

As Figure 21-1 shows, the relatively frequent "undesirable" effects, four dealing with decreased efficiency on problem solving[2] and one with feeling physically weak, begin to occur around the Strong level of intoxication. All the undesirable effects beginning at Very Strong and higher are infrequent or rare.

MODULATING FACTORS

The relatively linear effects of various background factors[3] are summarized in Table 21-1.

Moderate Total users indicated higher levels for not being able to come down when necessary than either Light or Heavy Total users.

It is of interest to note that many of the undesirable effects of intoxication in inexperienced users may be transitional ones that fade out with greater experience. Of the 19 effects, almost half are either significantly less frequent or occur at significantly higher levels for more experienced drug users.

SUMMARY

Less than 10 percent of the effects of intoxication investigated in this study seemed unequivocally "undesirable" in nature, and these effects were primarily infrequent and rare. With greater drug experience, almost half of these became even less frequent or were shifted to very high levels of intoxication. The pleasures of intoxication far outweigh the drawbacks in reports of experienced users.

---

[2]One of my more sophisticated informants suggests that it is misleading to classify difficulty in problem solving as an unequivocally "undesirable" effect. This is so in a situation where the user is strongly intoxicated and suddenly forced to work on conventional problems, but ordinarily the user will not get intoxicated if he expects to have to work on conventional problems. He may get moderately intoxicated to work on a problem requiring much deliberate work and original points of view, or very strongly intoxicated if originality of solution but not sustained concentration on the problem is required.

[3]For statistical reasons, the background analyses are not very sensitive here. Since most of the "undesirable" effects were infrequent or rare, only very large differences would show up in the background analyses.

CHAPTER 22

Aftereffects

A FEW OF THE ITEMS dealt with possible aftereffects of marijuana intoxication, even though aftereffects were seldom mentioned in the pilot interviews.

MAJOR AFTEREFFECTS

Memory for Periods of Intoxication

Two questions (158 and 159), already discussed in Chapter 14, dealt with memory for the period of intoxication. Both improved and worsened memory were common effects, occurring with equal frequency, but worsened memory tended to begin at the higher levels of intoxication.

Memory for material read while intoxicated was discussed in the same chapter. Poor memory was a common effect, improved memory an infrequent one. Levels of intoxication did not differ significantly, although comments from informants suggested that the very lowest levels of intoxication were associated with improved memory, but all levels above this with worsened memory for read material.

Changes in Religious, Philosophical Values

In Chapter 19 we found that 25 percent of the users reported spiritual experiences that had had a long-term religious effect on them, and 22 percent reported that getting intoxicated with marijuana had acquired a religious significance. Other users indicated their dislike of the term "religious" but indicated that insights about themselves and the world during intoxication had greatly affected their philosophy of life.

Sleep

As discussed in Chapter 20, ease in going to sleep after being intoxicated for an evening is a characteristic effect, and having an especially refreshing night's sleep is very common. The converse effects were infrequent and rare, respectively, and occurred at much higher levels of intoxication.

Trembling

"*I tremble a lot in my hands for a while* after *having been stoned*" was added to the questionnaire as a validity scale item, as I had never heard of such an effect in pilot interviews. It turned out to be a rare effect in this sample (71%, 20%, 7%, 0%, 1%), associated with Very Strong levels of intoxication among the few who rated it (1%, 1%, 7%, 9%, 7%).

Next Day's Activity

"*I find it very hard to get organized or accomplish anything I want to the day after smoking grass. (Circle lowest level at which this occurs)*" is an infrequent effect (39%, 27%, 23%, 6%, 3%), which mainly begins to occur at the Very Strong level for those who could rate it (0%, 6%, 15%, 19%, 15%). It is reported as occurring more frequently by older users ($p < .05$), and less frequently by Heavy Total users ($p < .05$, overall and Users of Psychedelics ($p < .01$). The College-educated indicate higher levels of intoxication for this aftereffect ($p < .05$).

LEVELS OF INTOXICATION FOR AFTEREFFECTS

Figure 22-1 orders the various aftereffects by level of intoxication. The overall ordering is highly significant ($p <<< .0005$).

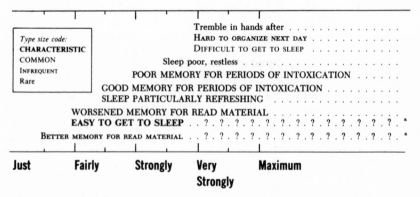

Type size code:
CHARACTERISTIC
COMMON
INFREQUENT
Rare

Tremble in hands after . . . .
HARD TO ORGANIZE NEXT DAY . . . .
DIFFICULT TO GET TO SLEEP . . . .
Sleep poor, restless . . . .
POOR MEMORY FOR PERIODS OF INTOXICATION . . . . . .
GOOD MEMORY FOR PERIODS OF INTOXICATION . . . .
SLEEP PARTICULARLY REFRESHING . . . .
WORSENED MEMORY FOR READ MATERIAL . . . .
EASY TO GET TO SLEEP . . ? . ? . ? . ? . ? . ? . ? . ? . ? . ? . ? . ? . ? . [a]
BETTER MEMORY FOR READ MATERIAL . . ? . ? . ? . ? . ? . ? . ? . ? . ? . ? . ? . ? . [a]

| Just | Fairly | Strongly | Very Strongly | Maximum |

[a]There is some question whether this effect is available at all levels above the minimal one.

FIGURE 22-1. INTOXICATION LEVELS, AFTEREFFECTS

At the lower levels, we have some aftereffects that can be characterized as desirable, namely, ease of going to sleep, particularly refreshing sleep, and good memory for periods of intoxication. Poor recall of material read is the major exception to this.

At the Strong level we have the only other common aftereffect beginning to occur, poor memory for periods of intoxication.

At the higher levels there are a number of undesirable aftereffects, all infrequent or rare.

TABLE 22-1

EFFECTS OF BACKGROUND FACTORS ON AFTEREFFECTS

BACKGROUND FACTORS   EFFECTS

Background Factors	Effects	
More Drug Experience	More frequent: Good memory for period of intoxication Good memory for read material More intoxicated for: Sleep particularly refreshing	Less frequent: Hard to organize next day
Older	More frequent: Hard to organize next day	Less frequent: Poor memory for read material
More Educated		Less frequent: Good memory for period of intoxication Less intoxicated for: Hard to organize next day Easy to go to sleep
Males		Less frequent: Good memory for period of intoxication
Meditation	More frequent: Spiritual experiences while intoxicated Religious significance to getting intoxicated	Less frequent: Poor memory for read material
Therapy & Growth	More frequent: Good memory for read material	Less frequent: Poor memory for read material

MODULATING FACTORS

The relatively linear effects of various background factors on aftereffects of intoxication are summarized in Table 22-1.

SUMMARY

There are very few aftereffects reported for marijuana intoxication, and many of these occur infrequently or rarely.

There is nothing comparable to the hangover of alcohol intoxication, although finding it hard to get organized and accomplish things the next day infrequently follows intoxication at the very high levels. This occurs less frequently among more experienced users.

It is easy to get to sleep and sleep is usually very refreshing following periods of intoxication.

The aftereffect hardest to assess is the long-term alteration of religious and philosophical beliefs of the users. Insights and spiritual experiences occurring during intoxication initiate many such changes.

CHAPTER 23

Miscellaneous Effects

SEVERAL EFFECTS that did not fit with any of the categories used to organize other chapters are reported here. No overall comparison of intoxication levels or modulating factors will be made.

COMMON EFFECTS

Involvement

"*I get much more involved in ordinary tasks than when I'm straight; they're completely absorbing*" is a very common effect (7%, 11%, 33%, 33%, 14%), which begins to occur at Moderate to Strong levels (7%, 27%, 42%, 12%, 1%). It is experienced more frequently by the College-educated ($p < .01$) and at somewhat lower levels of intoxication by the Heavy Total users ($p < .05$).

Optimism-Pessimism

"*I feel that the world is all right, that everything is pretty much the way it should be when stoned (except for the marijuana laws)*" is a common effect (14%, 19%, 33%, 13%, 16%), which generally begins to occur at Moderate to Strong levels (9%, 27%, 29%, 11%, 3%). Meditators are highly variable on the level for this ($p < .01$, overall), while the Therapy and Growth group and the ordinary users peak sharply at the Fairly/Strongly level.

The converse effect, "*I feel the world is in pretty bad shape, that all sorts of changes need to be made in the social order to make it a decent place to live in (for things besides the marijuana laws)*" is also a common effect (8%, 17%, 26%, 23%, 19%), which occurs at the lowest levels (25%, 25%, 23%, 4%, 3%). The College-educated and the older users experience this more frequently ($p < .05$ in each case).

Both optimism and pessimism occur with about equal frequency, but optimism begins to occur at higher levels ($p < .01$).

Reality of Fantasies

"*With my eyes closed, my inner visions and fantasies become extremely real, as real as nighttime dreams.*" This is a common effect (11%, 19%, 27%, 27%, 14%) that begins to occur at the Strong and Very Strong levels (1%, 15%, 23%, 31%, 12%). The College-educated experience it more frequently ($p < .05$), but Daily users experience it less frequently than Weekly or Occasional users ($p < .05$, overall).

An even greater intensity of experience is expressed by "*Some of my inner trips, eyes-closed fantasies, have been so vivid and real that, even though I know logically they couldn't be real, they feel real; they are as real as ordinary waking-life experience.*" This is also a common experience (21%, 19%, 35%, 15%, 7%), which occurs at Very Strong levels (0%, 7%, 20%, 29%, 15%). The Professionals need to be more intoxicated for this ($p < .05$). It occurs less frequently than fantasies being as real as dreams ($p < .01$), but at essentially the same levels.

Going Up

Although users usually feel a smooth, continuous increase in level of intoxication as they smoke more marijuana, this is not always the case. "*I move up to higher levels of consciousness in jumps, sudden increases, rather than smoothly*" is a common experience effect (19%, 18%, 39%, 14%, 5%). This is experienced more often by Heavy Total users ($p < .05$, overall) and by Users of Psychedelics ($p < .01$).

ADDITIONAL EFFECTS

Included here are all miscellaneous effects volunteered by the users at the end of the questionnaire, which have not already been mentioned in previous chapters.

"Hashish produces a clear, cleaner, and more mental high than even high quality grass, like the difference between beer and 100 proof vodka" (Usually, Strongly).

"My nose runs and sinuses clear if I have a cold" (Usually, Fairly).

"Heat, like in a sauna bath, heightens the psychedelic experience" (Rarely, Very Strongly).

"I take grass to get away from a painful situation, to escape for a while" (Rarely, Strongly).

"Stomach tranquilizer" (Very Often, Fairly).

"My nose gets stopped up" (Usually, Just).

"Fantastic vortices of energy form around me. Time/space warp, dissolve into quietude as I relax" (Rarely, Maximum).

"Creates interest and motivation in my work" (Usually, Just).

"A need to be surrounded by aesthetically beautiful surroundings all the time" (Usually, Just).

"Everyday events and experiences, such as riding in a car, walking, etc., take on a much greater meaning and pleasure" (Usually, Fairly).

"I love to look at natural, living things in great depth for a long time, even more than when I'm straight" (Usually, Just).

"All antinomies are reconciled in a march back toward an absolute" (Very Often, Just).

"Walking along a street becomes magical" (Sometimes, Fairly).

"I can close my eyes and shut out the world, i.e., it ceases to exist" (Usually, Strongly).

PART III

RELATIONSHIPS

CHAPTER 24

Levels of Intoxication

THIS CHAPTER will summarize the data on minimal levels of intoxication for the various effects of marijuana intoxication. The first three sections will deal with overall views of the material, and the final section will present a detailed summary of *all* effects by minimal level of intoxication.

THE MINIMAL LEVEL MODEL AND TOTAL EFFECTS

The basic model of marijuana intoxication effects, discussed at length in Chapter 2, assumed that any given effect became available for the user to experience once he was intoxicated to some certain minimal degree *and* when the variables other than level of intoxication assumed necessary configurations. Above this minimal level, the model assumes that the effect is always available as long as the other variables maintain the necessary configurations.

Examination of the present data, combined with interviews with informants, has convinced me that this model is valid for the vast majority of the effects presented. In a few cases, however, it seems that at some level higher than the minimal level the effect may no longer be available. Ease of reading is an example; at the low levels of intoxication an increased fluency of reading may be experienced, but this drops out above the Moderate level and is replaced by reading difficulty (Chapter 15).

Further discussions will assume the general validity of the minimal level model unless otherwise noted.

An important consequence of the minimal level model is that the nature of the marijuana experience at any one time becomes more variable at higher levels of intoxication. That is, at higher levels of intoxication more and more effects are *potentially* available. In terms of experimental studies of intoxication, this means that non-drug variables (personality, set and setting, etc.) become increasingly important at high doses.

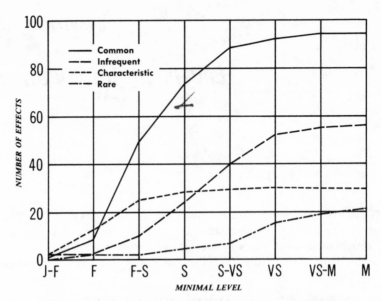

**Figure 24-1. CUMULATIVE DISTRIBUTIONS: TYPES OF EFFECTS
BY MINIMAL LEVELS OF INTOXICATION**

This is illustrated in Figure 24-1, a plot of the cumulative distributions of various types of effects by the minimal level of intoxication presented earlier for each individual effect.

At the Just to Fair levels, only five effects are available; by the time the Maximum level is reached, over two hundred effects are potentially available.

Looking at types of effects, we see that Characteristic Effects almost all become available by the Fairly/Strongly level, Common Effects by the Strongly/Very Strongly level, Infrequent Effects by the Very Strongly level, and Rare Effects at the Very Strongly/Maximum level. Thus the experiences of a user who is mildly intoxicated are fairly predictable from this knowledge of level alone, but predictability drops off rapidly with increasing level.

LEVELS OF INTOXICATION AND CHARACTERISTIC EFFECTS

The 30 effects rated as occurring so frequently they were called *characteristic* (at least 50 percent of users rated them Very Often or Usually) are ordered by minimal level of intoxication in Figure 24-2. They range from the lowest level, Just/Fairly,[1] up to the Very Strongly

---

[1]No effect was commonly rated as beginning at the Just level.

level. Most characteristic effects begin at the Fairly and Fairly/Strongly levels.

Characteristic effects come as close as we can presently get to indicating what the "pure drug effects" of marijuana might be. That is, because they occur so commonly, either they must result from very powerful effects of the drug that manifest regardless of other determining factors, *or* the necessary configuration of non-drug factors on which they depend for manifestation is extremely common within our culture. To some extent, then, Figure 24-2 represents the relationship of relatively "pure drug effects" to level of intoxication.

Marijuana users usually test the quality of the marijuana they are buying. This is done either by smoking a fixed amount of it and rating the level of intoxication reached or by smoking until a desired level of intoxication is reached and noting how much marijuana was required.

FORGET START OF CONVERSATION . . . .

New qualities to sexual orgasm . . . .

Easily sidetracked . . . .

More here-and-now . . . .

Type size code:
CHARACTERISTIC
COMMON
Infrequent
Rare

SEE PATTERNS IN NORMALLY AMBIGUOUS VISUAL MATERIAL . .

TIME PASSES MORE SLOWLY . . . .

DISTANCE IN WALKING CHANGED . . . .

Spontaneous insights about self . . . .

MORE CHILDLIKE, OPEN TO EXPERIENCE . . . .

DIFFICULT TO READ . . . .

PHYSICALLY RELAXED . . . .

New qualities to touch . . . .

Movement exceptionally smooth when dancing . . . .

TOUCH MORE EXCITING, SENSUAL . . . .

GREATER SPATIAL SEPARATION BETWEEN MUSICAL INSTRUMENTS

Deep insights into others . . . .

VISUAL IMAGERY MORE INTENSE . . . .

Appreciate very subtle humor . . . .

HARD TO PLAY ORDINARY SOCIAL GAMES . . . .

Less noisy at parties than when straight . . . .

LESS NEED TO FEEL IN CONTROL OF THINGS . . . .

More tolerant of contradictions . . . .

INVARIABLY FEEL GOOD FROM TURNING ON . . . .

TASTE SENSATIONS HAVE NEW QUALITIES . . . .

EASY TO GET TO SLEEP AT BEDTIME . . ? . ? . ? . ? . ? . ? . ? . ? . ? . [a]

UNDERSTAND WORDS OF SONGS BETTER . . . .

ENJOY EATING A LOT . . . .

LESS NOISY AT PARTIES THAN WHEN TIPSY OR DRUNK . . . .

NEW, SUBTLE QUALITIES TO SOUNDS . . . .

CAN COME DOWN AT WILL . . . .

Just	Fairly	Strongly	Very Strongly	Maximum

[a]There is some question whether this effect is available at all levels above the minimal one.

FIGURE 24-2. LEVELS OF INTOXICATION, CHARACTERISTIC EFFECTS

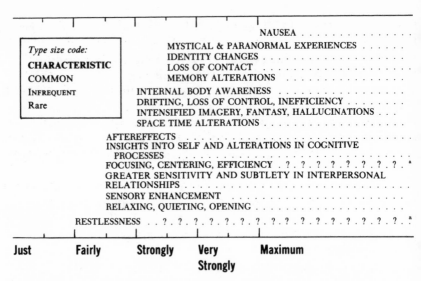

Type size code:
CHARACTERISTIC
COMMON
INFREQUENT
Rare

NAUSEA . . . .
MYSTICAL & PARANORMAL EXPERIENCES . . . . . .
IDENTITY CHANGES . . . .
LOSS OF CONTACT . . . .
MEMORY ALTERATIONS . . . .
INTERNAL BODY AWARENESS . . . .
DRIFTING, LOSS OF CONTROL, INEFFICIENCY . . . .
INTENSIFIED IMAGERY, FANTASY, HALLUCINATIONS . . .
SPACE TIME ALTERATIONS . . . .
AFTEREFFECTS . . . .
INSIGHTS INTO SELF AND ALTERATIONS IN COGNITIVE
    PROCESSES . . . .
FOCUSING, CENTERING, EFFICIENCY . ? . ? . ? . ? . ? . ? . ? . ? . [a]
GREATER SENSITIVITY AND SUBTLETY IN INTERPERSONAL
    RELATIONSHIPS . . . .
SENSORY ENHANCEMENT . . . .
RELAXING, QUIETING, OPENING . . . .
RESTLESSNESS . . ? . ? . ? . ? . ? . ? . ? . ? . ? . ? . ? . ? . ? . ? . ? . [a]

Just   Fairly   Strongly   Very   Maximum
                                        Strongly

[a]There is some question whether this effect is available at all levels above the minimal one.

FIGURE 24-3. TYPES OF EFFECTS AND MINIMAL LEVEL OF INTOXICATION

While each marijuana user probably has certain idiosyncratic effects he uses to judge how intoxicated he is, some of the characteristic effects presented in Figure 24-2 probably function commonly as a guide to level and thus to the potency of the marijuana.

Because so few characteristic effects have a minimal level above the Strong level, Figure 24-2 does not provide useful information about what else, in addition to these characteristic effects, may occur at the higher levels of intoxication. Such data is found in the final two sections of this chapter.

LEVELS OF INTOXICATION AND TYPES OF EFFECTS

To determine what sorts of effects may begin to occur at each of the eight levels of intoxications distinguished in this study, one could tabulate the effects beginning for each level, and this has been done in the next section. This is a cumbersome procedure, however, and it also tends to overwhelm the general reader with material, even if very useful for the researcher.

I have condensed most of the effects reported on earlier into sixteen general categories, explained below. I then determined the minimal level of intoxication where at least 50 percent of the effects in the category had begun.[2] These categories and their average minimal levels are plotted in Figure 24-3. No attempt was made to include frequency of occurrence information in this graph, as was done in earlier graphs of this sort.

Restlessness includes six effects[3] indicating restlessness, a desire to move about to do things. Comments by informants indicated that these types of effects probably do not fit the minimal level model; i.e., restlessness is often a transitory phenomenon of the very low levels of intoxication and is replaced by relaxation and lethargy as soon as the user becomes more intoxicated. This is indicated by the use of question marks on the graph.

Relaxing, quieting, opening includes 52 effects indicating feeling physically relaxed, content, open to whatever happens, less striving, less active.

Sensory enhancement includes 72 items dealing with new, enhanced, or more subtle qualities of sensory perceptions of the external world.

Greater sensitivity and subtlety in interpersonal relationships includes 26 items dealing with feelings of insights into others, increased empathy with them, and the ability to interact in very subtle and sensitive ways, to play subtle "games."

Focusing, centering, efficiency includes 28 items dealing with focusing more clearly on tasks at hand, being more here-and-now, being centered in oneself in a situation rather than pulled off balance, and feeling more capable and efficient at tasks. This is another category of effects that probably does not fit the minimal level model in all respects, with feelings of inefficiency being more likely at the higher levels of intoxication.

Insights into self and alteration of cognitive processes includes 32 items dealing with heightened awareness of one's mental processes and one's personality characteristics, often including the awareness of alteration in functioning of these processes.

Aftereffects includes some 14 effects occurring the day following a session of marijuana intoxication, without regard as to whether these are desirable or undesirable.

Space/time alterations includes 37 effects dealing with changes in perception of space, spatial relationships, and time.

Intensified imagery, fantasy, hallucinations includes 41 effects indicating greatly intensified imagery in all sensory modalities, intensified

---

[2]I shall not present the methods for this tabulation in any detail, as it involved a good deal of my personal judgment, and I am not certain others would classify individual effects the same way. Figure 24-3 is offered more as a suggestion to research than as a final account.

[3]Note that the number of times constituting a given category has no necessary relation to the commonness of such effects; it was determined by the construction of the questionnaire.

and more absorbing fantasy activity, synesthesia, and visual hallucination.

Drifting, loss of control, inefficiency includes 36 effects reflecting an inability to concentrate, to perform tasks well, or to recall desired memories.

Internal body awareness includes 65 effects dealing with enhanced awareness of sensations and processes inside one's body.

Memory alterations includes some 19 effects concerned with false memories, *déjà vu*, alterations in memory retrieval, state-specific memory, and the like. Simple worsening or bettering of recall has been included in the inefficiency or efficiency categories above.

Loss of contact includes 29 effects dealing with loss of contact with the external environment or one's own body, often resulting from absorption in internal activities.

Identity changes includes 9 effects dealing with temporary changes in personality, archetypal qualities to events, and changes in the relationship of self-concept to the body.

Mystical and paranormal experiences includes 12 effects dealing with spiritual experiences and ostensibly paranormal effects such as telepathy.

Nausea includes 2 effects dealing with the feeling of nausea and actual vomiting.

Considering the relation of types of effects to minimal level of intoxication as a whole, then, we see the following:

At the lowest levels there may be a mild restlessness, but this is replaced with relaxation, calmness, and quieting at only slightly higher levels. Sensory enhancement begins at low levels, coupled with feelings of being centered and efficient. While this sensory enhancement persists through all levels, feelings of efficiency may be replaced by those of inefficiency, inability to concentrate on a task, at Strong levels.

The Fairly/Strongly level also is characterized with feelings of insight into one's own and others' psychological processes, so that both thought and social interaction seem very subtle, clever, and different. Some aftereffects the next day follow intoxication at the Fairly/Strongly level, increasingly so at the very high levels.

At the Strong level major alterations in the perception of space and time may occur, and the user can become very absorbed in an inner world of thought, fantasy, and intensified bodily sensations, although social interaction is still easily possible.

At the Strongly/Very Strongly level and higher, memory is altered in its functioning, and the user may become so absorbed in inner experience that he temporarily loses contact with his own body and/or the environment. Mystical and ostensibly paranormal experiences sometimes occur.

Nausea and vomiting (both rare effects) may occur at the maximal level.

LEVELS OF INTOXICATION: DETAILED DATA

The following table presents all the effects of the present study classified by the average minimal level of intoxication. Within the table, the effects are ordered by the arithmetic mean of intoxication level ratings, with the effect having the lowest mean at the bottom.

Frequency data are given by type style in the usual convention; i.e., characteristic effects in boldface, infrequent effects in small caps, and rare effects in lower case. The question number of each effect is also given after the item as an aid to the reader.

TABLE 24-1

EFFECTS BY MINIMAL LEVEL OF INTOXICATION

Effects Beginning at the Just/Fairly Level:

HIGHER PEOPLE GET ME HIGHER (Q121)
LESS NOISY AT PARTIES THAN WHEN DRUNK (Q110)
REMEMBER MORE OF WHAT IS READ (Q20)
HEAR MORE SUBTLE CHANGES IN SOUNDS (Q24)
EASIER TO READ THAN WHEN STRAIGHT (Q19)

Effects Beginning at the Fairly Level:

LEARN A LOT ABOUT PSYCHOLOGICAL PROCESSES (Q138)
Invariably feel bad when intoxicated (Q166)
Colors get duller (Q2)
HARD TO PLAY ORDINARY SOCIAL GAMES (Q106)
CONTOURS GET SHARPER (Q10)
LESS NOISY AT PARTIES THAN WHEN STRAIGHT (Q109)
EASIER TO ACCEPT WHATEVER HAPPENS, LESS NEED TO CONTROL (Q170)
EASIER TO ACCEPT CONTRADICTIONS (Q137)
CRAVE SWEET THINGS TO EAT (Q46)
REMEMBER LESS OF WHAT IS READ (Q21)
TALK A LOT MORE THAN WHEN STRAIGHT (Q117)
WORK AT TASKS WITH EXTRA ENERGY AND ABSORPTION (Q179)
INVARIABLY FEEL GOOD WHEN INTOXICATED (Q165)
NEW QUALITIES TO TASTE (Q39)
FEEL THE WORLD IS IN BAD SHAPE (Q215)
EASY TO GO TO SLEEP AT BEDTIME (Q197)
UNDERSTAND THE WORDS OF SONGS BETTER (Q25)
MORE SOCIABLE (Q115)
ENJOY EATING AND EAT A LOT (Q44)

Effects Beginning at the Fairly/Strongly Level:

DISTANCES SEEM GREATER (Q52)
MEMORY FOR OTHERWISE FORGOTTEN EVENTS IS WORSE (Q152)
SEE PATTERNS, FORMS IN OTHERWISE AMBIGUOUS VISUAL MATERIAL (Q13)
TIME PASSES MORE SLOWLY (Q58)
LESS SOCIABLE (Q116)
PICTURES ACQUIRE A THIRD DIMENSION OF DEPTH (Q4)
STRONGLY INFLUENCED BY COMPANIONS (Q120)
TALK A LOT LESS (Q118)
DISTANCES IN WALKING CHANGED (Q51)
SPONTANEOUSLY HAVE INSIGHTS ABOUT MYSELF (Q139)
WORK ON TASKS LESS ACCURATELY, JUDGED BY LATER EVALUATION (Q144)
INHIBITIONS LOWERED (Q173)
SMELL HAS NEW QUALITIES (Q47)
VISUAL IMAGES AUTOMATICALLY ACCOMPANY THINKING (Q148)
SMELLS RICHER, MORE UNIQUE (Q48)
THINK IN A MORE INTUITIVE FASHION (Q149)
SURFACES SEEM ROUGHER, FORM INTERESTING PATTERNS (Q34)
BETTER PERSON TO MAKE LOVE WITH WHEN STONED (Q127)
PLEASANT, WARM TINGLING INSIDE BODY (Q81)
DREAMS MORE VIVID (Q201)
PAIN MORE INTENSE IF CONCENTRATED ON (Q89)
MORE INVOLVED IN ORDINARY TASKS (Q217)
OBJECTS SEEM HEAVIER (Q35)
FEEL MORE CHILDLIKE, OPEN TO EXPERIENCE (Q207)
CLOSER MENTAL CONTACT WITH PARTNER WHEN MAKING LOVE (Q125)
MORE DIFFICULT TO READ (Q18)
PLAY CHILDISH GAMES (Q105)
FEEL THE WORLD IS IN GOOD SHAPE (Q214)
PHYSICALLY RELAXED (Q99)
IDEAS MORE ORIGINAL, CREATIVE THAN WHEN STRAIGHT (Q145)
INSIGHTS ABOUT MYSELF IF I DELIBERATELY TRY TO HAVE THEM (Q140)
MEMORY FOR OTHERWISE FORGOTTEN EVENTS BETTER (Q151)
MOVEMENTS VERY SMOOTH, COORDINATED (Q100)
NEW QUALITIES TO TOUCH (Q31)
COMPULSIVE DESIRE TO GET HIGHER (Q176)
SURFACES FEEL SMOOTHER, SILKIER (Q33)
FEEL EMOTIONS MORE WEAKLY (Q162)
EVENTS AND THOUGHTS FLOW MORE SMOOTHLY (Q61)
TOUCH MORE EXCITING, SENSUAL (Q32)
DREAMS LESS VIVID (Q202)
NEED FOR SEX GOES UP (Q122)
GOOD MEMORY FOR PERIOD OF INTOXICATION (Q158)
GET PHYSICALLY RESTLESS, WANT TO MOVE AROUND (Q98)
GREATER SEPARATION BETWEEN INSTRUMENTS WHEN LISTENING TO STEREO (Q29)
EMPATHIZE STRONGLY WITH OTHERS (Q114)
FEELS AS IF MIND IS WORKING MORE EFFICIENTLY (Q141)
VIVID TASTE IMAGERY (Q45)
DEEP INSIGHTS INTO OTHERS (Q113)
SAY MORE PROFOUND THINGS (Q111)
AUDITORY IMAGERY MORE VIVID (Q27)
VISUAL IMAGERY MORE VIVID (Q8)
APPRECIATE MORE SUBTLE HUMOR (Q146)
MOOD BEFORE INTOXICATION AMPLIFIED BY INTOXICATION (Q160)
PLAY VERY ELABORATE GAMES (Q147)
WORK ON TASKS MORE ACCURATELY, JUDGED BY LATER EVALUATION (Q143)
NEW COLORS, SHADES OF COLOR (Q1)
SALIVATE A LOT (Q42)
MARKED INCREASE IN SEXUAL DESIRE *IF* SITUATION IS APPROPRIATE (Q124)
GROUP TAKES ON A SENSE OF UNITY WHEN STONED (Q112)
SLEEP MORE REFRESHING THAN USUAL (Q199)
MORE VISUAL IMAGERY WHILE READING (Q22)
RETASTE FOOD WHEN BELCHING (Q43)

Effects Beginning at the Strongly Level:

BODY FEELS LIGHT, FLOATY (Q79)
BODY FEELS HEAVY (Q80)
LOSE AWARENESS OF BODY UNLESS STRONG STIMULUS OCCURS(Q70)
VISUAL DEPTH MAGNIFIED (Q14)
SPACE BECOMES AN AUDITORY SPACE (Q30)
Others seem dead, lifeless (Q119)
POOR MEMORY FOR PERIOD OF INTOXICATION (Q159)
DÉJÀ VU (Q63)
FEELS AS IF MIND IS WORKING LESS EFFICIENTLY (Q142)
LONG TIME DELAY BETWEEN CHEWING AND TASTING (Q41)
Less desire for sex (Q123)
VIVID TACTUAL IMAGERY (Q37)
EVENTS AND THOUGHTS FOLLOW JERKILY (Q62)
SKIP INTERMEDIATE STEPS IN PROBLEM SOLVING (Q133)
TIME PASSES MORE RAPIDLY (Q59)
VERY AWARE OF BREATHING (Q73)
SOUND OF OWN VOICE CHANGES (Q28)
FOCUSED SIGHTS VERY REAL, OTHERS DIM—VISUAL CENTRALITY (Q12)
World looks flat, lacks depth (Q5)
MOVEMENTS AWKWARD (Q101)
DROWSY EARLY IN EVENING (Q198)
FEEL WEAKER (Q96)
DISTANCES SEEM SHORTER (Q53)
FEEL UNIQUE, NO ONE IS LIKE ME (Q188)
THINGS IN PERIPHERY LOOK DIFFERENT (Q9)
AWARE OF HEART BEATING (Q92)
FEEL STRONGER (Q95)
SPONTANEOUSLY REMEMBER THINGS LONG FORGOTTEN (Q150)
LESS AWARE OF BODILY COMPONENTS OF EMOTION (Q164)
VIVID SMELL IMAGERY (Q50)
NEW QUALITIES TO TEMPERATURE (Q38)
PAIN EASY TO TOLERATE IF ATTENTION DIVERTED (Q88)
GIVE LESS THOUGHT TO CONSEQUENCES OF ACTIONS (Q131)
FEEL VERY POWERFUL, CAPABLE (Q190)
NEW QUALITIES TO SEXUAL ORGASM (Q128)
OBJECTS SEEM LIGHTER (Q36)
CAN MEDITATE MORE EFFECTIVELY (Q193)
EASILY SIDETRACKED, FORGET TO FINISH TASKS (Q175)
MORE HERE-AND-NOW (Q136)
GIGGLE A LOT (Q174)
NEW MEANING TO COMMONPLACE SAYING, EVENTS (Q135)
FEEL EMOTIONS MORE STRONGLY (Q161)
EXCELLENT CONTROL OF FANTASIES (Q178)
MORE AWARE OF BODILY COMPONENTS OF EMOTION (Q163)

Effects Beginning at the Strongly/Very Strongly Level:

SPACE TAKES ON A 'SOLID' QUALITY (Q56)
AWARE OF INTERNAL ORGANS NORMALLY UNAWARE OF (Q75)
FORGET START OF SENTENCE (Q154)
LOSE SENSE OF SEPARATE SELF, AT ONE WITH WORLD (Q189)
MUSCLES DEVELOP A TREMOR (Q86)
PERSONALITY CHANGES A LOT WHILE STONED (Q185)
IN TOUCH WITH A HIGHER POWER (Q177)
POOR CONTROL OF FANTASIES (Q177)
LOCATION OF CONSCIOUSNESS IN BODY SHIFTS (Q77)
SO ABSORBED IN FANTASY THAT ATTENTION MUST BE GOTTEN FORCIBLY (Q129)
VISION BLURRY (Q11)
CAN'T THINK CLEARLY, THOUGHTS SLIP AWAY BEFORE GRASPED (Q134)
EVENTS BECOME ARCHETYPAL (Q191)
INNER VISIONS AS REAL AS NOCTURNAL DREAMS (Q218)
THINK I'VE SAID SOMETHING WHEN I'VE ONLY THOUGHT ABOUT IT (Q156)
THINGS GET NEAR OR FURTHER AS I LOOK AT THEM—DEPTH JIGGLE (Q15)

VIBRATION OR TINGLING IN BODY, NOT PHYSICAL TREMOR (Q85)
VERY AWARE OF INTERNAL ORGANS WHILE DEFECATING OR URINATING (Q78)
BODY FEELS LARGER (Q90)
BODY FEELS SMALLER (Q91)
Sleep poor and restless (Q200)
POWER, FORCE, ENERGY SENSATIONS IN BODY (Q82)
FEEL ISOLATED FROM THINGS AROUND ME (Q107)
CAN CONVERSE INTELLIGENTLY DESPITE SHORTENED MEMORY SPAN (Q155)
Smell sensations broken into components (Q49)
FORGET START OF CONVERSATION (Q153)
FINISH PHYSICAL TASK EVEN THOUGH MENTALLY LOST TRACK OF (Q130)
BODY PART ATTENDED TO STANDS OUT MUCH MORE (Q71)
SENSUAL QUALITY TO VISION (Q3)
FEEL ISOLATED FROM PARTNER WHILE MAKING LOVE (Q126)
OTHERS HAVEN'T NOTICED I'M STONED (Q212)
FEEL PARANOID, SUSPICIOUS ABOUT OTHERS WITH ME (Q108)
SO AWARE OF PEOPLE'S THOUGHTS IT MUST BE TELEPATHY (Q65)
TASTE SENSATIONS DIVIDED INTO COMPONENTS (Q40)

Effects Beginning at the Very Strongly Level:

CAN'T COME DOWN QUICKLY ABOVE THIS LEVEL (Q205)
BODY NUMB (Q76)
GET SO LOST IN FANTASY IT TAKES A WHILE TO REORIENT AFTER (Q55)
ANOTHER PERSON'S FACE WILL CHANGE AS I WATCH IT (Q16)
CAN COME DOWN AT WILL IF NECESSARY (Q184)
OBJECTS VIBRATE OR PULSE AS IF THEY HAD A LIFE OF THEIR OWN (Q17)
Parts of body have moved by themselves (Q182)
SENSE OF BALANCE ERRATIC (Q103)
Tremble a lot in hands after having been stoned (Q102)
HARD TO GET ORGANIZED NEXT DAY (Q209)
Can perform magical operations to affect things or people (Q68)
AURAS AROUND OBJECTS (Q7)
INNER TRIPS, FANTASIES AS REAL AS REALITY (Q208)
Possessed by a good force (Q181)
LOSE CONTROL OVER THOUGHTS (Q183)
OTHERS HAVE NOTICED I ACT DIFFERENTLY WHEN STONED (Q211)
PROLONGED BLANK PERIODS (Q219)
FELT SHAPE OF BODY DOESN'T CORRESPOND TO ACTUAL FORM (Q69)
SYNESTHESIA: SOUNDS HAVE VISUAL IMAGES ASSOCIATED (Q216)
Worry about losing control (Q171)
Aware of energy flowing in spine (Q83)
THINK SOMETHING IS A MEMORY THAT TURNS OUT TO BE A FANTASY (Q157)
DIFFICULT TO GET TO SLEEP AT BEDTIME (Q196)
Do antisocial things that hurt others (Q172)
Precognition, able to fortell future (Q66)

Effects Beginning at the Very Strongly/Maximum Level:

Possessed by an evil force (Q180)
MERGE WITH OBJECT OR PERSON CONTEMPLATED (Q186)
HAVE LOST ALL CONSCIOUSNESS OF BODY DURING FANTASY TRIPS (Q94)
TIME SEEMS TO STOP (Q60)
AURAS AROUND PEOPLE (Q6)
HALLUCINATIONS (Q23)
Aware of *chakra* centers along spine (Q84)
Sounds are blurry, indistinct (Q26)

Effects Beginning at the Maximum Level:

Felt nauseated and vomited (Q210)
Felt dizzy or nauseated (Q74)
LOST ALL CONSCIOUSNESS OF BODY, FLOATED IN LIMITLESS SPACE (Q93)

CHAPTER 25

Experience in Using Drugs

THE 150 USERS had a wide range of experience in drug use. Marijuana use ran from less than six months experience to more than eleven years use. Seventy-two percent had tried major psychedelic drugs such as LSD.

Three background analyses for drug use were carried out, namely, by total amount of use of marijuana, frequency of use of marijuana in the six months immediately preceding filling out the questionnaire, and use or non-use of major psychedelics.

Total marijuana use was divided, according to the method described in Chapter 5, so as to yield three groups, termed Heavy Total users, Moderate Total users, and Light Total users. Frequency of use in the preceding six months also produced three groups, the Daily, Weekly, and Occasional users. Users of Psychedelics were those who had tried any major psychedelic drug at least once.

The number of significant comparisons for each of these background variables is presented in Table 25-1, below. While Frequency of Use yielded only a few more significant comparisons than might be expected by chance, Total Use and Psychedelic Use yielded many more, and so are highly significant factors affecting marijuana intoxication.

TABLE 25-1

NUMBER OF SIGNIFICANT COMPARISONS, VARIOUS
BACKGROUND VARIABLES

SIGNIFICANCE LEVEL	TOTAL USE	FREQUENCY OF USE	USE OF PSYCHEDELICS	EXPECTED BY CHANCE
$\leq .05$	42	21	33	19
$\leq .01$	9	7	13	4
$\leq .001$	5	1	4	0

TABLE 25-2

EFFECTS MORE FREQUENT IN USERS WITH MORE DRUG EXPERIENCE

CATEGORY	INTOXICATION EFFECT[a]	SIGNIFICANCE LEVEL
Vision	SENSUAL QUALITY TO VISION, T	.01
	AURAS AROUND PEOPLE, P	.0005
	AURAS AROUND OBJECTS, T, P	.05, .05
	FACE CHANGES, P	.01
	VISUAL HALLUCINATIONS, T	.05
Hearing	SPACE BECOMES AN AUDITORY SPACE, P	.05
Touch	VIVID TACTILE IMAGERY, T	.05
Taste	SALIVATE A LOT, T	.01
	RETASTE FOOD WHEN BELCHING, T	.05
Smell	NEW QUALITIES TO SMELL, T	.05
	SMELLS, RICHER, MORE UNIQUE, T, P	.05, .05
Space/Time	TIME PASSES RAPIDLY, T	.05
Paranormal	TELEPATHY, T	.01
	Precognition, T, F	.05, .001
	Magical operations, F	.01
Body	AWARE INTERNAL ORGANS IN DEFECATING, T	.05
	FEELINGS OF ENERGY IN BODY, P	.05
	Feel energy in spine, P	.05
	Aware of *chakra* centers, T	.05
	BODY FEELS SMALLER, T	.05
	FEEL STRONGER, T	.01
	MOVEMENTS AWKWARD, UNCOORDINATED, T, F, P	.05, .05, .01
Social	**LESS NOISY AT PARTIES THAN WHEN STRAIGHT, F**	.05
Sex	MORE NEED FOR SEX IF SITUATION APPROPRIATE, P	.05
	CLOSER TO SEXUAL PARTNER, UNION OF SOULS, P	.0005
Thought	ABSORBED, ATTENTION MUST BE GOTTEN FORCIBLY, P	.05
	MORE SUBTLE HUMOR, T	.05
	EASIER TO READ, T	.05
Memory	RECALL MORE OF MATERIAL READ, T, F, P	.001, .05, .05
	GOOD MEMORY FOR PERIODS OF INTOXICATION, F	.01
Control	**EASILY SIDETRACKED, P**	.05
	COMPULSIVE DESIRE TO GET HIGHER, T, F	.01, .05
	EXTRA ENERGY, EFFICIENCY FOR TASKS, T	.001
	CAN COME DOWN AT WILL, T, F, P	.05, .05, .01
Identity	PERSONALITY CHANGES TEMPORARILY, F	.05
	FEEL POWERFUL, CAPABLE, INTELLIGENT, T	.05
	EVENTS, ACTIONS ARCHETYPAL, P	.05
Spiritual	IN TOUCH WITH A HIGHER POWER, P	.01
	MEDITATE MORE EFFECTIVELY, F	.01
Miscellaneous	GO UP IN JUMPS, T	.05

[a] The letter T (Total Use), F (Frequency of Use), or P (Use of Psychedelics) following each effect indicates which background variables were the significant ones.

As detailed descriptions of the effects of each of the three background variables have been presented with each item description, this chapter will summarize these effects on a dimension of greater or lesser drug experience. That is,Users of Psychedelics have more drug experience than Non-users, Heavy Total users more than Moderate Total users, Weekly users more than Occasional users, etc. Most of the three category comparisons (Total Use and Frequency of Use) showed a linear trend, i.e., the Heavy or Daily category users showing the greatest frequency or highest minimal level, the Moderate or Weekly next highest, and the Light or Occasional users the least. Thus the summary statements in the following tables that "users with more drug experience report effect x more or less frequently or at higher or lower levels than users with less drug experience" generally adequately summarizes a finding.

TABLE 25-3

EFFECTS LESS FREQUENT IN USERS WITH MORE DRUG EXPERIENCE

CATEGORY	INTOXICATION EFFECT	SIGNIFICANCE LEVEL
Vision	PERIPHERAL VISION CHANGES, P	.01
Hearing	**UNDERSTOOD WORDS OF SONGS BETTER, T, P**	.05, .01
Touch	OBJECTS SEEM HEAVIER, MASSIVE, P	.05
Taste	DELAY BETWEEN CHEWING AND TASTING, P	.01
	ENJOY EATING AND EAT A LOT, P	.05
Space/Time	LOSE TRACK, NEED TO REORIENT, P	.05
Body	LOSE AWARENESS OF BODY PARTS NOT FOCUSED, P	.0005
	PAIN MORE INTENSE IF CONCENTRATED ON, P	.05
	LOSE ALL CONSCIOUSNESS OF BODY DURING FANTASY TRIPS, F	.01
	MOVEMENT EXCEPTIONALLY SMOOTH, P	.01
Social	**HARD TO PLAY ORDINARY SOCIAL GAMES, T**	.0005
	FEEL PARANOID, P	.01
Thought	LESS THOUGHT TO CONSEQUENCES OF ACTIONS, T	.001
	THOUGHTS SLIP AWAY BEFORE GRASPED, F, P	.05, .05
	HERE AND NOW, T	.01
	MIND FEELS LESS EFFICIENT, T, P	.05,.05
	HARDER TO READ, T	.01
	MIND GOES BLANK, P	.05
Memory	THINK SAID SOMETHING WHEN HAVEN'T, T, P	.05
Control	Worry about losing control, F	.05
	CAN'T COME DOWN AT WILL, P	.05
Aftereffects	HARD TO ORGANIZE NEXT DAY, T, P	.05,.01
Miscellaneous	INNER VISIONS AS REAL AS NOCTURNAL DREAMS, F	.05

Ten percent of the significant differences were not linear: the Moderate or Weekly users showed the highest or lowest value. These non-linear effects, mostly from the Frequency of Use analyses, are shown in a separate table.

Table 25-2 summarizes 40 effects experienced more frequently by users with greater drug experience. Overall frequency of occurrence is summarized in the usual type style code.

One would expect that users with more drug experience would have experienced a wider variety of effects. Three rare effects and 18 infrequent effects are indeed experienced more frequently by users with more drug experience.

Table 25-3 summarizes 23 effects experienced less frequently by the more experienced users; Table 25-4, the 20 effects for which more experienced users have a higher minimal level of intoxication; and Table 25-5, the 18 effects for which they have a lower minimal level.

TABLE 25-4

EFFECTS THAT USERS WITH MORE DRUG EXPERIENCE MUST BE MORE INTOXICATED TO EXPERIENCE

CATEGORY	INTOXICATION EFFECT	SIGNIFICANCE LEVEL
Vision	PERIPHERAL VISION CHANGES, P	.05
	BLURRINESS OF VISION, F	.05
	MORE CENTRALITY OF VISION, F	.05
	PULSING OF VISION, P	.05
Hearing	SPACE BECOMES AN AUDITORY SPACE, T	.05
Space/Time	**TIME PASSES MORE SLOWLY, T**	.05
	EVENTS FOLLOW EACH OTHER JERKILY, P	.05
Social	TALK MORE, P	.01
	PEOPLE HAVEN'T NOTICED I'M STONED, T, P	.05,.05
Thought	ABSORBED, ATTENTION MUST BE GOTTEN FORCIBLY, T	.05
Memory	**FORGET START OF CONVERSATION, T**	.05
	THINK I'VE SAID SOMETHING WHEN HAVEN'T, P	.05
Emotion	Usually feel bad when stoned, T	.05
	GIGGLE A LOT, T	.05
Control	**EASILY SIDETRACKED, P**	.05
	EXTRA ENERGY, EFFICIENCY FOR TASKS, T	.05
	CAN COME DOWN AT WILL, P	**.01**
Sleep	EARLY EVENING DROWSINESS, T, F	.001, .01
	SLEEP PARTICULARLY REFRESHING, F	.05
	DREAMS LESS VIVID OR FORGOTTEN, T	.05

TABLE 25-5

EFFECTS THAT USERS WITH MORE DRUG EXPERIENCE CAN

EXPERIENCE AT LOWER LEVELS OF INTOXICATION

CATEGORY	INTOXICATION EFFECT	SIGNIFICANCE LEVEL
Vision	SENSUAL QUALITY TO VISION, T	.05
Taste	VIVID TASTE IMAGERY, P	.05
Space/Time	TIME STOPS, P	.05
Paranormal	TELEPATHY, P	.05
Body	PAIN MORE INTENSE IF CONCENTRATED ON, T	.05
Social	**LESS NOISY AT PARTIES THAN WHEN STRAIGHT, P**	.05
	SAY MORE PROFOUND THINGS, P	.05
	People seem like robots, P	.05
	PLAY ELABORATE GAMES, T, P	.05, .05
Sex	MORE NEED FOR SEX, P	.0005
	CLOSER TO SEXUAL PARTNER, T, F	05, .05
Thought	LESS THOUGHT TO CONSEQUENCES OF ACTIONS, P	.05
	INSIGHTS INTO OTHERS, T	.05
	SPONTANEOUS INSIGHTS INTO SELF, P	.01
Memory	MISTAKE FANTASY FOR MEMORY, T	.05
Identity	FEEL POWERFUL, CAPABLE, INTELLIGENT, T, F	.01, .05
Spiritual	MEDITATE MORE EFFECTIVELY, P	.05
Miscellaneous	MORE INVOLVED IN ORDINARY TASKS, T	.05

In the basic model of drug intoxication set forth in Chapter 2, it was hypothesized that increasing experience with drug-induced states of consciousness would generally result in the user's experiencing fewer negative, unpleasant effects and/or that such negative effects would be pushed to higher levels of intoxication. This is generally confirmed by the data. Of the 19 unequivocally "undesirable" effects (discussed fully in Chapter 21), about half are experienced significantly less frequently or have higher minimal levels for the users with more drug experience, with only one comparison being significant in the opposite direction.

It was also hypothesized that increased drug experience would generally lead to increased control of the intoxicated state. This is also confirmed by the data. Experienced users worry less frequently about losing control, find less frequently that they can't come down if necessary, most be more intoxicated to be sidetracked, and can come down at will more frequently and from higher levels. The one finding contrary to this hypothesis is that they experienced being easily sidetracked more frequently.

A heavy marijuana user would also have many more occasions on which he had to function in ordinary (non-drug subculture) situations with ordinary people. A number of background differences, in addition to increased control, would seem to reflect this need to function frequently in ordinary situations, namely, increased frequency of ease in reading and good memory for periods of intoxication; decreased frequency of losing track and needing to reorient, finding it hard to play ordinary social games, feelings of paranoia about companions, giving less thought to consequences of actions, here-and-now-ness (too much would interfere with planning), and thinking you've said something when you haven't.

TABLE 25-6

NON-LINEAR EFFECTS OF TOTAL USE AND FREQUENCY OF USE

CATEGORY	INTOXICATION EFFECT: WEEKLY OR MODERATE USERS	SIGNIFICANCE LEVEL
More frequently experience:		
Space/Time	SPACE, AIR TAKES ON 'SOLID' QUALITY, F	.05
Social	**LESS NOISY AT PARTIES THAN WHEN DRUNK, T**	.05
	STRONGLY INFLUENCED BY COMPANIONS, F	.05
Less frequently experience:		
Thought	**MORE WILLING TO ACCEPT CONTRADICTIONS, T**	.01
Must be *more* intoxicated to experience:		
Vision	VISUAL JIGGLE, T, F	.05, .01
	IMAGERY WHILE READING, F	.05
Body	**PHYSICALLY RELAXED, DON'T WANT TO MOVE, F**	.05
	MOTIONS EXCEPTIONALLY SMOOTH, F	.05
Thought	FINISH TASK EVEN THOUGH MENTALLY LOST TRACK OF, T	.05
Memory	CONVERSE INTELLIGENTLY DESPITE SHORTENING OF MEMORY SPAN, F	.05
	THINK SAID SOMETHING WHEN HAVEN'T, F	.01
Need be *less* intoxicated to experience:		
Hearing	SPACE BECOMES AN AUDITORY SPACE, T	.05
Taste	CRAVE SWEET THINGS, T	.05

The thirteen non-linear effects of background variables are summarized in Table 25-6.

CHAPTER 26

Meditation and Growth

THE QUESTIONNAIRE asked whether the users regularly practiced any sort of meditation or non-drug discipline for spiritual or personal growth. Sixteen percent indicated regular practice of some form of Oriental or Occidental meditation. Seven percent indicated they were or had been regularly involved in some form of conventional psychotherapy (2 percent) or growth discipline (5 percent), such as psychoanalysis, Gestalt therapy, sensitivity training, encounter groups, etc. Users indicating irregular practice were not included in either the Meditation group or the Therapy and Growth group.

Overall, the three-way chi-square analyses comparing the Meditators and the Therapy and Growth group against all other users were quite significant. Twenty-eight analyses were significant at the .05 level (19 expected by chance), 14 at the .01 level (4 expected by chance) and 2 at the .001 level (none expected by chance).

In most analyses, either the Meditators or the Therapy and Growth group were clearly higher or lower than Ordinary Users. Occasionally both these groups were higher or lower than the Ordinary Users, and in such cases both groups have been indicated in the summary tables as significantly different from Ordinary Users.[1]

Most often the Meditators were clearly higher or lower on various effects than the Therapy and Growth group or the Ordinary users. Tables 26-1 and 26-2 summarize significant differences for the Meditators. The Meditators more frequently experience a variety of effects, which we would expect in such a group of fairly disciplined[2] people.

Table 26-3 summarizes significant differences for the Therapy and Growth group. This is a rather mixed group in terms of disciplines followed, making the results difficult to interpret.

---

[1]One consequence of this is that there are more significant effects listed in the tables, because of duplication, than are reported below.

[2]Given the generally young age of the sample, the Meditation group should not be considered representative of what sorts of results might be gotten with *highly* trained meditators.

TABLE 26-1

MEDITATION AND FREQUENCY OF VARIOUS INTOXICATION EFFECTS

CATEGORY	INTOXICATION EFFECT	SIGNIFICANCE LEVEL

Meditators *more* frequently experience:

CATEGORY	INTOXICATION EFFECT	SIGNIFICANCE LEVEL
Vision	FACE OF ANOTHER PERSON CHANGES	.05
Taste	RETASTE FOOD WHEN BELCHING	.01
Space/Time	AIR, SPACE BECOMES SOLID	.05
Paranormal	ªOOBEs before beginning marijuana use	.01
Body	ENERGY FEELINGS IN BODY	.05
	Energy in spine	.05
	Aware of *chakra* centers	.01
Emotion	PRE-INTOXICATION MOOD AMPLIFIED	.05
Identity	MERGE WITH OBJECT OR PERSON CONTEMPLATED	.01
	AT ONE WITH THE WORLD	.01
Spiritual	IN TOUCH WITH A HIGHER POWER	.01
	MEDITATE MORE EFFECTIVELY	.05
	ªSpiritual experiences while intoxicated	.0005
	ªReligious significance to getting intoxicated	.01

Meditators *less* frequently experience:

CATEGORY	INTOXICATION EFFECT	SIGNIFICANCE LEVEL
Hearing	AUDITORY IMAGERY BETTER	.01
Taste	VIVID TASTE IMAGERY	.05
Space/Time	JERKINESS OF FLOW OF EVENTS	.05
Social	FEEL ISOLATED	.01
	TALK MORE	.05
Sex	NEW QUALITIES TO ORGASM	.01
Thought	RECALL LESS OF MATERIAL READ	.05

ªNot coded as to frequency of occurrence by type style.

TABLE 26-2

MEDITATION AND LEVELS OF INTOXICATION FOR VARIOUS EFFECTS

CATEGORY	INTOXICATION EFFECT	SIGNIFICANCE LEVEL

Meditators must be *more* intoxicated to experience:

CATEGORY	INTOXICATION EFFECT	SIGNIFICANCE LEVEL
Hearing	AUDITORY IMAGERY ENHANCED	.05
Social	LESS SOCIABLE	.05
Miscellaneous	FEEL THE WORLD IS ALL RIGHT	.01

Meditators need be *less* intoxicated to experience:

CATEGORY	INTOXICATION EFFECT	SIGNIFICANCE LEVEL
Hearing	AUDITORY SPACE	.05
Touch	NEW QUALITIES TO TOUCH	.05
	TOUCH MORE SENSUAL	.01
Taste	VIVID TASTE IMAGERY	.01
Space/Time	WALKING DISTANCE CHANGED	.01
Body	HYPERAWARENESS OF BREATHING	.01
Social	FEEL PARANOID	.05
Thought	MORE HERE-AND-NOW	.05
	THINK MORE INTUITIVELY	.05
Sleep	EARLY EVENING DROWSINESS	.001

Table 26-3

Therapy and Growth Group and Frequency of Various Intoxication Effects

CATEGORY	INTOXICATION EFFECT	SIGNIFICANCE LEVEL
Therapy & Growth Group *less* frequently experiences:		
Vision	NEW COLORS	.05
Thought	**HARDER TO READ**	.05
Memory	RECALL LESS OF MATERIAL READ	.05
Therapy & Growth Group *more* frequently experience:		
Paranormal	ªOOBEs	.05
	ªMultiple OOBEs	.05
Body	AWARE OF INTERNAL ORGANS WHEN DEFECATING	.05
Memory	RECALL MORE OF MATERIAL READ	.05
Emotion	PRE-INTOXICATION MOOD AMPLIFIED	.05
Identity	Possessed by a good force or will	.05
Spiritual	IN TOUCH WITH A HIGHER POWER	.01
Therapy & Growth Group must be *more* intoxicated to experience:		
Space/Time	EVENTS FLOW SMOOTHLY	.05
Therapy & Growth Group need be *less* intoxicated to experience:		
Space/Time	**WALKING DISTANCE CHANGED**	.01
Sex	MORE NEED FOR SEX	.05

ªIndicates not coded as to frequency of occurrence by type style.

CHAPTER 27

Age, Sex, and Educational Level

AGE

BECAUSE MOST RESPONDENTS were young, only two age ranges could be used for analysis purposes, namely, those younger than 25 (72 percent of the sample) and those 25 or older (28 percent of the sample).

Overall, the age variable was not particularly significant. Twenty-three analyses were significant at the .05 level, where about 19 would be expected by chance; and 5 were significant at the .01 level, when 4 would be expected by chance. None were significant at the .001 level. This may result from the restricted range. Thus many of the differences summarized below are probably artifactual. These differences must be regarded primarily as possible guides to further research, rather than as solid findings.

Table 27-1 summarizes significant differences in frequency of occurrence of 18 various effects, and Table 27-2 summarizes 10 significant differences in minimal level of intoxication. General frequency of occurrence data is also presented in the usual type style code.

MALE AND FEMALE

Forty-nine percent of the respondents were males, 27 percent were females. The rest could not be classified because of a clerical error that omitted the sex blank on some of the questionnaires.

Overall, the sex variable was not very significant. Twenty-five analyses were significant at the .05 level when about 19 would be expected by chance, and only one was significant at the .01 level, when about four would be expected by chance. The differences summarized in Table 27-3 and 27-4 should be taken only as guidelines for further research.

Overall frequencies of occurrence are coded in the tables by the usual type style convention.

TABLE 27-1

AGE AND FREQUENCY OF VARIOUS INTOXICATION EFFECTS

CATEGORY	INTOXICATION EFFECT	SIGNIFICANCE LEVEL

Older users (25+) *more* frequently experience:

Hearing	AUDITORY IMAGERY MORE VIVID	.05
Social	OTHERS HAVEN'T NOTICED I'M STONED	.01
Aftereffects	HARD TO GET ORGANIZED NEXT DAY	.05

Older users (25+) *less* frequently experience:

Vision	AURAS AROUND OBJECTS	.05
	THINGS IN PERIPHERY LOOK DIFFERENT	.05
	HALLUCINATIONS	.01
Hearing	QUALITY OF OWN VOICE CHANGES	.05
Paranormal	ªOOBE's *after starting to use marijuana*	.05
Body	BODY SEEMS VERY HEAVY	.05
	PAIN MORE INTENSE IF CONCENTRATED ON	.01
	GET PHYSICALLY RESTLESS	.05
Thought	ABSORBED, ATTENTION MUST BE FORCIBLY GOTTEN	.05
Memory	SPONTANEOUSLY RECALL THINGS LONG FORGOTTEN	.05
	REMEMBER LESS OF WHAT IS READ	.01
Emotion	FEEL EMOTIONS MORE STRONGLY	.05
Control	**EASILY SIDETRACKED ON TASKS**	.05
	COMPULSIVE DESIRE TO GET HIGHER	.05
	POOR CONTROL OVER FANTASIES	.05
Miscellaneous	FEEL WORLD IS IN BAD SHAPE	.05

ªNot coded for frequency of occurrence by type style. (See Chapter 10.)

TABLE 27-2

AGE AND LEVELS OF INTOXICATION FOR VARIOUS EFFECTS

CATEGORY	INTOXICATION EFFECT	SIGNIFICANCE LEVEL

Older users (25+) must be *more* intoxicated to experience:

Body	PAIN MORE INTENSIVE IF CONCENTRATED ON	.05
Control	COMPULSIVE DESIRE TO GET HIGHER	.05

Older users (25+) need be *less* intoxicated to experience:

Body	LOSE AWARENESS OF BODY UNLESS STRONG STIMULUS DEMANDS ATTENTION	.05
	LOSE CONSCIOUSNESS OF BODY, FLOAT IN LIMITLESS SPACE	.05
	SENSE OF BALANCE ERRATIC	.05
Thought	Prolonged blank periods	.01
Memory	WORSE LONG-TERM MEMORY	.05
Control	INHIBITIONS LOWERED	.05
Identity	MERGE WITH CONTEMPLATED OBJECT OR PERSON	.05

TABLE 27-3

SEX AND FREQUENCY OF VARIOUS INTOXICATION EFFECTS

CATEGORY	INTOXICATION EFFECT	SIGNIFICANCE LEVEL
Males more frequently experience:		
Paranormal	ᵃ*Multiple OOBEs*	.05
Body	BODY GETS NUMB	.05
Social	STRONGLY INFLUENCED BY COMPANIONS	.05
Control	**CAN COME DOWN AT WILL**	.05
Females more frequently experience:		
Vision	VISION BLURRY	.05
Touch	OBJECTS SEEM HEAVIER	.05
Paranormal	ᵃ*OOBEs per se*	.05
Space/Time	TIME PASSES RAPIDLY	.05
	TIME STOPS	.05
Body	AWARE OF HEART BEATING	.05
	MOVEMENTS EXCEPTIONALLY SMOOTH AND COORDINATED	.05
	SENSE OF BALANCE ERRATIC	.05
Thought	Prolonged blank periods	.05
	SKIP INTERMEDIATE STEPS IN PROBLEM SOLVING	.05
Memory	GOOD MEMORY FOR PERIODS OF INTOXICATION	.05
Emotion	GIGGLE A LOT	.05
Control	Body parts move by themselves	.05
	CAN'T COME DOWN AT WILL	.05
Identity	**MORE CHILDLIKE, OPEN TO EXPERIENCE**	.05

ᵃNot coded for frequency of occurrence by type style.

TABLE 27-4

SEX AND LEVELS OF INTOXICATION FOR VARIOUS EFFECTS

CATEGORY	INTOXICATION EFFECT	SIGNIFICANCE LEVEL
Males must be more intoxicated to experience:		
Hearing	SYNESTHESIA	.05
	MORE AWARE OF INTERNAL ORGANS	.05
Body	BODY GETS NUMB	.01
	BODY FEELS SMALLER	.05
Memory	FORGET START OF SENTENCE	.05
Identity	EVENTS BECOME ARCHETYPAL	.05
Females must be more intoxicated to experience:		
Control	**CAN COME DOWN AT WILL**	.05

EDUCATIONAL LEVEL

Seventy-two percent of the users were in college or had a bachelor's degree of some sort. Twenty-one percent were in graduate school or had advanced degrees (M.A., M.S., M.D., Ed.D., or Ph.D.). These are the College-educated and the Professional groups, respectively, in our analysis. Seven percent of the users were in various educational level groups too small to be analyzable.

Educational level was a significant background variable. Thirty-four analyses were significant at the .05 level instead of the 19 expected by chance, and 11 at the .01 level, rather than the four expected by chance. Thus many of the differences summarized in the following two tables are potentially replicable findings as well as guides to research.

TABLE 27-5

EDUCATIONAL LEVEL AND FREQUENCY OF VARIOUS INTOXICATION EFFECTS

CATEGORY	INTOXICATION EFFECT	SIGNIFICANCE LEVEL
Professionals more frequently experience:		
Control	**CAN COME DOWN AT WILL**	.01
College-educated more frequently experience:		
Vision	SENSUAL QUALITY TO VISION	.05
	PATTERNS IN VISUALLY AMBIGUOUS MATERIAL	.05
Touch	SURFACES FEEL ROUGH, INTERESTING	.01
	NEW QUALITIES TO TEMPERATURE	.01
Body	HYPERAWARE OF BREATHING	.05
	BODY FEELS LIGHT	.01
	PAIN MORE INTENSE IF CONCENTRATED ON	.05
	BODY FEELS SMALLER	.05
	PHYSICALLY RESTLESS	.01
Social	**HARD TO PLAY ORDINARY SOCIAL GAMES**	.05
Sex	CLOSER TO SEXUAL PARTNER, UNION OF SOULS	.05
	NEW QUALITIES TO ORGASM	.01
Thought	ABSORBED, ATTENTION MUST BE GOTTEN FORCIBLY	.01
	LOSE MENTAL TRACK OF TASK BUT FINISH IT ANYWAY	.05
Memory	WORSENED LONG-TERM MEMORY	.05
	GOOD MEMORY FOR PERIODS OF INTOXICATION	.05
Control	**EASILY SIDETRACKED**	.05
	COMPULSIVE DESIRE TO GET HIGHER	.05
	POOR FANTASY CONTROL	.05
	GOOD FANTASY CONTROL	.05
Spiritual	IN TOUCH WITH A HIGHER POWER	.05
Miscellaneous	WORLD SEEMS IN PRETTY BAD SHAPE	.05
	MORE INVOLVED IN ORDINARY TASKS	.01
	INNER FANTASIES AS REAL AS NOCTURNAL DREAMS	.05

Tables 27-5 and 27-6 summarize significant differences in frequency of occurrence and minimal level of intoxication, respectively. General frequency of occurrence data is preserved in the type style code.

Although it is risky to comment on the overall patterning of results when a fair number of them may be due to chance, there is a general pattern of the College-educated having more sensory enhancement types of experiences.

TABLE 27-6

EDUCATIONAL LEVEL AND LEVELS OF INTOXICATION FOR VARIOUS EFFECTS

CATEGORY	INTOXICATION EFFECT	SIGNIFICANCE LEVEL
Professionals need to be more intoxicated to experience:		
Vision	Colors get duller	.05
Touch	OBJECTS SEEM MORE MASSIVE	.05
Space/Time	AIR, SPACE TAKES ON SOLID QUALITY	.05
Body	MOVEMENTS AWKWARD, UNCOORDINATED	.05
Miscellaneous	SOME INNER TRIPS SEEM COMPLETELY REAL	.05
College-educated need to be more intoxicated to experience:		
Hearing	SPACE BECOMES AN AUDITORY SPACE	.05
Touch	SURFACES FEEL SMOOTHER, SILKIER	.05
	SURFACES FEEL ROUGH, INTERESTING	.01
Space/Time	DISTANCES SEEM SHORTER	.05
Body	LOCATION OF CONSCIOUSNESS CHANGES	.01
	AWARE OF HEARTBEAT	.05
Social	TALK MORE	.05
Sex	Need sex less	.05
	BETTER LOVER WHEN STONED	.05
Thought	Prolonged blank periods	.05
Memory	CONVERSE INTELLIGENTLY DESPITE FORGETTING START OF WHAT I SAID	.05
Control	**EASILY SIDETRACKED**	.05
Sleep	**EASY TO GO TO SLEEP AT BEDTIME**	.05
Aftereffects	HARD TO GET ORGANIZED NEXT DAY	.05
Identity	MERGE WITH OBJECT OR PERSON CONTEMPLATED	.05

CHAPTER 28

Alcohol and Marijuana

THE 150 USERS had been drinking alcohol longer than they had used marijuana, but for the six months preceding their filling out the questionnaire, they had been using marijuana with greater frequency. Given a free choice, 43 percent would never use alcohol, and 37 percent would use alcohol in preference to marijuana less than a quarter of the time (see Chapter 4).

To the question, *"Could you compare the effects of alcohol and marijuana on yourself? When do you prefer to use the one, when the other?"*, eighty-three percent of the users volunteered answers, from very short ones ("Alcohol makes my mind fuzzy, and I prefer not to use it anymore") to long and detailed comparisons. I shall report the major comparisons in several categories, giving a ratio in each case (M/A) where the first number is the number of users mentioning the effect for marijuana and the second the number mentioning it for alcohol.

COMPARATIVE EFFECTS

Sensory and Bodily Effects

Alcohol was more frequently reported to worsen sensory perception and appreciation (0/29), produce unpleasant physical sensations such as nausea (2/19), and have negative aftereffects (0/27). Marijuana was more frequently reported as enhancing sensory perception (27/3). Effects mentioned with about equal frequency were pleasant physical sensations (4/4), relaxed or sleepy feelings (17/20), or energetic feelings (5/6).

Interpersonal Relations

Alcohol was reported to more frequently induce chatter and laughter in groups (1/7), as well as boisterous aggression and violence (0/9) and childishness (1/15). Group effects mentioned with about equal frequency for marijuana and alcohol were extroversion (9/12), serious conversation (2/1), and enhanced sexual desire (6/5).

Cognitive Effects

Marijuana was reported to improve cognitive processes (31/1), and lead to personal and spiritual insights (17/0), while alcohol was reported to worsen cognitive processes (2/11).

Emotional Effects

Marijuana and alcohol were mentioned as inducing pleasant emotions equally frequently (16/15), and unpleasant emotions equally frequently (3/4).

Control

Marijuana was generally praised because the user did not lose control of himself and could "sober up" immediately if necessary (9/1).

Situations

The users indicated that alcohol was best used in large or impersonal groups as a social lubricant (3/25), but that marijuana was best for getting intoxicated alone or in small, intimate groups (14/4).

Legal Consequences

Concern with being arrested was mentioned as an effect of marijuana intoxication but not for alcohol (9/1).

OTHER DATA

Several years before the present study, with the aid of Carl Klein, I carried out a survey of the incidence of marijuana use at a West Coast university. Many of the users of the present study were later obtained from the same university. These students were asked, in the questionnaire of the earlier study, to describe the major effects of alcohol and marijuana on themselves. As they were rushed for time, most of them gave very brief answers. Comparisons of qualities reported for alcohol and marijuana in that (unpublished) study are summarized in Table 28-1. The table summarizes answers from 150 students who had used alcohol, 86 of whom also had used marijuana at least once.

These older data are generally consistent with the present data.

SUMMARY

People who have used both alcohol and marijuana to intoxicate themselves perceive the effects as different in a number of ways.

Marijuana is preferred for becoming intoxicated alone or in small intimate groups, and reportedly leads to enhancement of sensation, pleasant physical sensations, both improved and worsened interpersonal relations, improved cognitive processes, personal and spiritual insights, and fears about being arrested more frequently than for alcohol.

Alcohol is preferred for large and impersonal group situations and reportedly leads to worsened sensory perception, unpleasant physical sensations, childishness and lowering of inhibitions, violence, worsened cognitive processes, and more unpleasant aftereffects than marijuana.

Users generally choose marijuana if given a free choice and/or tend to restrict their use of alcohol to small amounts.

TABLE 28-1

COMPARISON OF ALCOHOL AND MARIJUANA INTOXICATION
Tart-Klein Study, 1968

EFFECT	ALCOHOL	MARIJUANA	SIGNIFICANCE OF DIFFERENCE[a]
Sensory & Bodily Effects:			
Sensory enhancement	1%	35%	.001
Sensory worsening	13%	0%	.001
Pleasant physical sensations	2%	8%	.05
Unpleasant physical sensations	13%	7%	NS
Interpersonal Relations:			
Improved	3%	9%	.05
Worsened	1%	10%	.01
Inhibitions lowered	15%	2%	.01
Cognitive Effects:			
Improved cognitive processes	2%	21%	.001
Worsened cognitive processes	10%	5%	NS
Personal insights	1%	8%	.01
Spiritual experiences	0%	2%	NS
Emotional Effects:			
Pleasant mood	18%	31%	NS
Unpleasant mood	5%	13%	NS
Fear of being arrested	0%	6%	.01

Note.—The percentages in this table do not add up to exactly 100% due to rounding errors and/or some users' skipping the question.

[a] Because of the brief answers given in this earlier study, the figures in the various categories represent one answer per student and were therefore amenable to statistical tests of the significance of the differences.

CHAPTER 29

More Powerful Psychedelics (LSD) and Marijuana

MANY USERS of both marijuana and the more powerful psychedelic drugs such as LSD believe that the drugs are qualitatively different. Others believe that all or some of the effects from marijuana can also be experienced with the more powerful psychedelics along with many other effects, which cannot be experienced with marijuana.

This chapter provides some data on similarities and differences between marijuana intoxication effects and those of more powerful psychedelics.

The instructions for the questionnaire (Chapter 3) explained that:

> . . . There is one other category on the "How Stoned" scale marked "LSD." You are to circle this category *only* if you have experienced that effect after having taken one of the very powerful psychedelic drugs like LSD, DMT, DET, mescaline, peyote, psilocybin, or STP. Thus there will probably be a number of things described that you've never experienced with pot but have with one of the more powerful psychedelics (if you've had one of the more powerful psychedelics).

Seventy-two percent of the sample (108 users) had used more powerful psychedelics at least once, and of this group, 54 were classified as *heavy* psychedelic users in that they had used one or more of the more powerful psychedelic drugs at least half a dozen times. This heavy psychedelic use group may be presumed to have had reasonable opportunity to experience a variety of effects with the more powerful psychedelics. The percentage of them experiencing the various effects while intoxicated with the more powerful psychedelics provides some interesting data to compare with the marijuana data.

Note that these data cannot be more than suggestive, for two reasons. First, the measure of percentage of users experiencing something *at all* for the more powerful psychedelics is not the same as the frequency of occurrence ratings of the same effects for marijuana. Second, Users of Psychedelics differed from Non-users on frequency of occurrence on marijuana for many items (Chapter 25), so there is a lack of statistical independence between the measures.[1] Nevertheless, a look at what effects are frequent for the more powerful psychedelics while infrequent for marijuana, and vise versa, is of considerable interest.

Complete data of this sort of users of psychedelics per se as well as the heavy users of psychedelics are presented in Appendix 1. Here we shall deal only with the heavy psychedelic user group.

Table 29-1 lists the common and characteristic effects of marijuana intoxication, which are *not* frequent for more powerful psychedelics in that less than 10 percent of the heavy psychedelic user group reports them as having been experienced while intoxicated on the more powerful drugs.

Many of these effects may not be frequent with the more powerful psychedelics because the user intoxicated on them avoids many ordinary

TABLE 29-1

COMMON AND CHARACTERISTIC EFFECTS OF MARIJUANA INTOXICATION
NOT FREQUENT WITH MORE POWERFUL PSYCHEDELICS

INTOXICATION EFFECT	PERCENTAGE OF USERS EXPERIENCING THIS WITH MORE POWERFUL PSYCHEDELICS
CONVERSE INTELLIGENTLY DESPITE FORGETTING (Q155)	9%
FINISH PHYSICAL TASK EVEN THOUGH LOSE TRACK OF IT MENTALLY (Q130)	9%
PAIN MORE INTENSE IF CONCENTRATED ON (Q89)	9%
ENJOY EATING AND EAT A LOT (Q44)	9%
GET MORE INVOLVED IN ORDINARY TASKS (Q217)	7%
DREAMS MORE VIVID (Q201)	7%
GOOD MEMORY FOR PERIODS OF INTOXICATION (Q158)	7%
PLAY VERY ELABORATE GAMES WITH OTHERS (Q147)	7%
LESS NOISY AT PARTIES THAN WHEN STRAIGHT (Q109)	7%
VIVID VISUAL IMAGERY WITH READING (Q22)	6%
EASY TO GO TO SLEEP AT BEDTIME (Q197)	6%
WORK LESS ACCURATELY BY LATER EVALUATION (Q144)	6%
OBJECTS SEEM HEAVIER (Q35)	6%
RECALL LESS OF MATERIAL READ (Q21)	6%
SLEEP PARTICULARLY REFRESHING (Q199)	4%
EARLY EVENING DROWSINESS (Q198)	4%
EXTRA ENERGY, ABSORPTION IN TASKS (Q179)	4%
HIGHER PEOPLE GET ME HIGHER (Q121)	4%
LESS NOISY AT PARTIES THAN WHEN DRUNK (Q110)	4%
CRAVE SWEET THINGS TO EAT (Q46)	4%
VIVID TASTE IMAGERY (Q45)	2%

---

[1]This relation would seem practically impossible to avoid, as it would be difficult to find people with much experience with more powerful psychedelics and little with marijuana.

situations and tasks that seem too trite or too difficult for his state of consciousness. Eating, going to parties, working on tasks, seem a waste of time to many users; if they are intoxicated with LSD, they are too involved in feelings of profound insights and the like to waste time on such things.

The difficulties with sleep probably are due to the much longer lasting effects of most of the more powerful psychedelics, so the user is still experiencing many drug effects at his usual bedtime, which prevent him from sleeping well.

Table 29-2 presents 25 effects, which at least 20 percent of the Heavy user group have experienced with more powerful psychedelics, but which are infrequent or rare effects for marijuana intoxication. These include a variety of more exotic effects, such as telepathy, hallucinations, and feelings of contact with a Higher Power, as well as several effects reflecting concern about control.

TABLE 29-2

EFFECTS FAIRLY FREQUENT WITH MORE POWERFUL PSYCHEDELICS BUT INFREQUENT OR RARE WITH MARIJUANA

INTOXICATION EFFECT	PERCENTAGE OF USERS EXPERIENCING THIS WITH MORE POWERFUL PSYCHEDELICS
PULSING OF VISION (Q17)	56%
FACE OF ANOTHER CHANGES AS WATCHED (Q16)	52%
VISUAL HALLUCINATIONS (Q23)	48%
LOSE TOUCH WITH BODY, FLOAT IN LIMITLESS SPACE (Q93)	46%
CAN'T COME DOWN AT WILL (Q205)	43%
DIFFICULT TO GET TO SLEEP (Q196)	41%
AURAS AROUND PEOPLE (Q6)	41%
ACT DIFFERENTLY ACCORDING TO OTHERS (Q211)	39%
AURAS AROUND OBJECTS (Q7)	39%
FEEL IN TOUCH WITH A HIGHER POWER (Q211)	37%
MERGE WITH OBJECT OR PERSON CONTEMPLATED (Q186)	37%
AWARE OF INTERNAL ORGANS NORMALLY UNAWARE OF (Q75)	30%
Feel dizzy, nauseated (Q74)	30%
FELT SHAPE DOESN'T CORRESPOND TO ACTUAL BODY (Q69)	30%
VISUAL JIGGLE (Q15)	30%
POOR CONTROL OF FANTASIES (Q177)	26%
Worry about losing control (Q171)	26%
Sleep following intoxication poor, restless (Q200)	24%
TELEPATHY (Q65)	24%
PERSONALITY CHANGES A LOT TEMPORARILY (Q185)	22%
Prolonged blank periods (Q132)	20%
MUSCLES DEVELOP VISUALLY OBSERVABLE TREMORS (Q86)	20%
AWARE OF INTERNAL ORGANS WHEN DEFECATING (Q78)	20%
BODY NUMB (Q76)	20%
SPACE, AIR SOLID, "FILLED" (Q56)	20%

CHAPTER 30

Factor Analysis: Dimensions
of Intoxication

ALL THE DATA on marijuana intoxication presented so far have been based on how experienced users describe their experiences; i.e., it is primarily descriptive. One naturally wonders if there are more basic dimensions of the intoxication experience that could account for the many different specific effects, that would reduce many effects to a smaller, more basic number.

Factor analysis is a statistical technique that begins to answer such questions. All the different items of information are correlated with each other; a factor analysis then ascertains whether some sets of items form natural groupings that might represent more basic dimensions.

The data format of the present study is not well suited to factor analysis; the five-point frequency scale is rather limited, is not normally distributed, and does not constitute an interval or ratio scale. Thus the data given below are the weakest of the present study and are presented only for the sake of completeness and the guidance of other investigators.

In order to reduce the number of items to a level the computerized factor analysis program of the University of California at Berkeley's Computer Center could handle, every other item, starting with Q1, was selected. This included two items (Q67 and Q167) that were not answered in the same form as the others and so are not considered in interpreting the factors. Thus the analysis is based on 104 frequency of occurrence items.

RESULTS

The principal components analysis revealed one main factor (Eigen-values for the first twelve factors were 13.953, 4.842, 3.956, 3.489, 3.191, 2.927, 2.758, 2.673, 2.443, 2.377, 2.255, and 2.171). Items loading .400 or greater on this first factor are presented in Table 30-1. The usual type-style code for overall frequency of occurrence is used. As principal component rotations are primarily of mathematical rather than psychological interest, no interpretation of this factor will be made.

TABLE 30-1

First Factor, Principal Components

LOADING	Q#	BRIEF DESCRIPTION
.613	191	EVENTS BECOME ARCHETYPAL
.612	111	SAY MORE PROFOUND THINGS
.610	141	MIND FEELS MORE EFFICIENT IN PROBLEM SOLVING
.587	15	VISUAL JIGGLE
.582	133	SKIP INTERMEDIATE STEPS IN PROBLEM SOLVING
.563	65	TELEPATHY
.560	151	BETTER LONG-TERM MEMORY
.538	113	**INSIGHTS INTO OTHERS**
.527	3	SENSUAL QUALITY TO VISION
.526	49	Different smell components at different locations
.519	45	VIVID TASTE IMAGERY
.514	37	VIVID TACTUAL IMAGERY
.514	147	PLAY ELABORATE GAMES
.506	139	**SPONTANEOUS INSIGHTS INTO SELF**
.498	95	FEEL STRONGER
.486	17	PULSING OF VISION
.484	163	MORE AWARE OF BODILY COMPONENTS OF EMOTION
.471	143	WORK MORE ACCURATELY ON PROBLEMS
.486	145	IDEAS MORE ORIGINAL
.467	89	PAIN MORE INTENSE IF CONCENTRATED ON
.462	13	**PATTERNS, MEANING IN AMBIGUOUS VISUAL MATERIAL**
.459	149	THOUGHT MORE INTUITIVE
.459	63	DÉJÀ VU
.459	47	NEW QUALITIES TO SMELL
.452	85	VIBRATION IN BODY THAT IS NOT MUSCLE TREMOR
.445	125	CLOSER CONTACT WITH PARTNER IN MAKING LOVE
.444	135	NEW SIGNIFICANCE TO COMMONPLACE CONVERSATIONS
.438	91	BODY FEELS SMALLER
.431	216	SYNESTHESIA
.424	218	INNER VISIONS AS REAL AS NOCTURNAL DREAMS
.421	189	AT ONE WITH WORLD
.404	193	MEDITATE MORE EFFECTIVELY
.402	27	AUDITORY IMAGES MORE VIVID

A Varimax rotation for 12 factors revealed one small-sized factor and eleven others that were not too much smaller. The proportion of the total communality accounted for by each factor was .078, .048, .044, .035, .033, .032, .031, .030, .028, .028, and .025. Each factor is described in Table 30-2.

Factor I seems to consist mainly of feelings of competence, perceptiveness, and intuitive-archetypal approaches to the environment. We might call it "Being High," as it fits many descriptions by users of the virtues of marijuana intoxication.

Factor II reflects enhancement of touch, taste, and smell sensations and imagery. It has been tentatively called "Enhancement of Non-dominant Senses," as these senses generally play a minor role compared to vision and hearing in most of our transactions with the world. One could also consider these as close-up or "intimate" senses, as contrasted with the functioning of vision and hearing at much greater distances.

Factor III deals primarily with increased awareness of various internal processes, such as body tensions, dreams, feelings of the location of consciousness, and thoughts. It has tentatively been named "Enhanced Internal Awareness."

Factor IV consists of items describing increased absorption in internal processes and a (consequent) loss of contact with the external world. It has tentatively been called "Internalization of Awareness."

Factor V does not seem to have a common theme, and Factor VI has only three items loading heavily enough to define it. It seems to represent unpleasant, dysphoric effects. Factor VII seems to represent perceptual instability in the visual system.

Factor VIII does not show any clear pattern, unless it be memory decrement. Factor IX also seems to represent memory decrement, although it is defined by only two items. The remaining three factors that were analyzed for in the Varimax rotation show no particular patterns that can readily be named.

TABLE 30-2

VARIMAX ROTATION FACTORS

LOADING	Q#	BRIEF DESCRIPTION

Factor I.   *"Being High"*

.698	191	EVENTS BECOME ARCHETYPAL
.682	111	SAY MORE PROFOUND THINGS
.599	113	**INSIGHTS INTO OTHERS**
.592	151	BETTER LONG-TERM MEMORY
.553	141	MIND FEELS MORE EFFICIENT IN PROBLEM SOLVING
.547	115	MORE SOCIABLE
.526	147	PLAY ELABORATE GAMES
.520	189	AT ONE WITH WORLD
.511	135	NEW SIGNIFICANCE TO COMMONPLACE CONVERSATIONS
.489	143	WORK MORE ACCURATELY ON PROBLEMS
.487	117	TALK MORE
.483	95	FEEL STRONGER
.482	133	SKIP INTERMEDIATE STEPS IN PROBLEM SOLVING
.481	145	IDEAS MORE ORIGINAL
.440	127	BETTER LOVER THAN WHEN STRAIGHT
.430	163	MORE AWARE OF BODILY COMPONENTS OF EMOTION
.424	65	TELEPATHY
.411	125	CLOSER CONTACT WITH PARTNER IN MAKING LOVE
.401	27	AUDITORY IMAGES MORE VIVID
.400	161	FEEL EMOTIONS MORE STRONGLY

Factor II.   *"Enhancement of Non-dominant Senses"*

.707	31	**NEW QUALITIES TO TOUCH**
.649	33	**SURFACES FEEL SMOOTHER, SILKIER**
.599	47	NEW QUALITIES TO SMELL
.539	37	VIVID TACTUAL IMAGERY
.553	45	VIVID TASTE IMAGERY
.432	49	Different smell components at different locations
.430	39	**NEW QUALITIES TO TASTE**

TABLE 30-2

VARIMAX ROTATION FACTORS (CONTINUED)

LOADING	Q#	BRIEF DESCRIPTION

Factor III. "Enhanced Internal Awareness"

.552	193	MEDITATE MORE EFFECTIVELY
.534	183	LOSE CONTROL OVER THOUGHTS
.469	197	EASY TO GO TO SLEEP AT BEDTIME
.448	75	MORE AWARE OF INTERNAL ORGANS GENERALLY
.448	201	DREAMS MORE VIVID
.444	163	MORE AWARE OF BODILY COMPONENTS OF EMOTION
.435	216	SYNESTHESIA
.419	77	LOCATION OF CONSCIOUSNESS IN BODY CHANGES

Factor IV. "Internalization of Awareness"

.543	129	ABSORBED, ATTENTION MUST BE FORCIBLY GOTTEN
.521	55	SO ABSORBED IN THOUGHT NEED TO REORIENT AFTERWARDS
.491	93	LOSE TOUCH WITH BODY, FLOAT IN LIMITLESS SPACE
.462	89	PAIN MORE INTENSE IF CONCENTRATED ON
.437	73	VERY AWARE OF BREATHING
.429	123	Less need for sex
.416	23	VISUAL HALLUCINATIONS

Factor V.   No common theme apparent

.673	171	Worry about losing control
.579	208	SOME INNER TRIPS SEEM REAL, EVEN THOUGH THEY COULDN'T BE REAL
.544	137	ACCEPT CONTRADICTIONS MORE READILY
.487	61	EVENTS FLOW MORE SMOOTHLY
.468	165	INVARIABLY FEEL GOOD WHEN STONED

Factor VI. "Dysphoria"

.600	5	World looks flat
.534	101	MOVEMENTS AWKWARD, UNCOORDINATED
.531	119	People seem dead, like robots

Factor VII. "Visual Instability"

.575	9	PERIPHERAL VISION CHANGES
.450	103	SENSE OF BALANCE ERRATIC
.410	7	AURAS AROUND OBJECTS
—.423	185	DIFFERENT PERSON WHILE STONED

Factor VIII.   No common theme apparent

.680	175	EASILY SIDETRACKED
.565	105	PLAY CHILDISH GAMES
.458	210	Gotten nauseated, vomited
.420	153	FORGET START OF CONVERSATION

Factor IX.   No common theme apparent

.650	21	REMEMBER LESS OF WHAT IS READ
.462	153	FORGET START OF CONVERSATION

TABLE 30-2

VARIMAX ROTATION FACTORS (CONTINUED)

LOADING	Q#	BRIEF DESCRIPTION

Factors X, XI, and XII.   No common themes apparent

Factor X:

.612	59	TIME PASSES RAPIDLY
.444	11	VISION BLURRY
.428	85	VIBRATION IN BODY THAT IS NOT MUSCLE TREMOR

Factor XI:

.470	25	**UNDERSTAND WORDS OF SONGS BETTER**
.452	205	CAN'T COME DOWN AT WILL
.440	99	**PHYSICALLY RELAXED, DON'T WANT TO MOVE**
—.468	121	HIGHER PEOPLE GET ME HIGHER (CONTACT HIGH)

Factor XII:

.513	214	FEEL WORLD IS OK
—.495	177	POOR CONTROL OVER FANTASIES
—.400	19	EASIER TO READ

CHAPTER *31*
Summary

THE NATURE OF MARIJUANA INTOXICATION

ALTHOUGH MARIJUANA has been known to man for countless centuries, our scientific knowledge of its effects is meager. A major source of confusion that has hindered research has been the general failure to recognize that most effects of marijuana are *potential* effects rather than inherent properties of the drug itself. That is, a variety of non-drug factors can markedly influence which potential effects manifest at any given time (see Chapter 2). Thus most laboratory studies and personal anecdotes are of limited value, because the limited range of laboratory conditions and the particular personality characteristics of the writers, acting on the state of consciousness produced by marijuana, produced only some of the potential effects and inhibited others. The personal anecdotes often tell us more about the writer than anything else, and the laboratory studies have produced effects generally unrepresentative of those found in ordinary marijuana use.

THE PRESENT STUDY

The aim of the present study was to find out the total range of potential effects that could be experienced and described by experienced users of marijuana. By systematically asking them about their experiences over a six-month period, the non-drug factors, which determine the manifestation of potential effects, would have assumed practically all possible combinations of values many times, thus eliciting the total range of effects. By asking the users about the frequency of various effects, it was possible to classify various potential effects as characteristic, common, infrequent, or rare, under conditions of ordinary marijuana use. Similar questioning about minimal level of intoxication (see Chapter 2 for details of this model) allowed rough classification of effects by the level of intoxication above which most experienced users could experience them (if the various non-drug factors assumed the right configurations).

THE USERS

The 150 experienced users who returned satisfactory questionnaires (see Chapter 4) had all used marijuana at least a dozen times in order to be eligible for the study. Thus the effects of learning to cope with the unfamiliarity of marijuana intoxication were deliberately eliminated from the present study (although worthy of study in their own right), and the results presented here should not be applied to naïve users.

Our 150 users are a predominantly young, highly educated group of Californians, primarily students, but with a fair number of older persons and professionals among them. Overall they have a high interest in self-improvement (meditation or therapy), considerable experience with more powerful psychedelic drugs like LSD, and little experience with hard narcotics. Most of them used marijuana once a week or more during the six-month period of the present study. By combining various self-reports on marijuana use, we can estimate that they have used marijuana about 37,000 times, for a total of 421 years of experience.

The remainder of this summary chapter will cover the major effects of marijuana intoxication (in terms of the users' self-reported experiences) under five major headings, namely, the perception of the external environment, interpersonal relations, internal mental processes, the perceiver (self-concept and identity of the user), and levels of intoxication. To keep this chapter brief, I shall not summarize the various miscellaneous effects of Chapters 20 to 23 nor the analyses of various relationships and background factors covered in Part III.

PERCEPTION OF THE EXTERNAL ENVIRONMENT

Vision

With respect to vision, *seeing forms, meaningful patterns in visual material that normally is ambiguous,* and *finding visual imagery more vivid than usual* are characteristic effects. Common effects include *contours seeming sharper, seeing new shades of color, having visual imagery automatically accompany thoughts and reading, being able to see a third dimension in pictures,* and *experiencing a sensual quality to vision.*

Hearing

For hearing, *hearing more subtle qualities of sound* is one of the most characteristic effects found, as well as *understanding the words of songs better* and *finding a greater spatial separation between sound sources.* Common effects include *auditory images being more vivid, finding that space becomes organized according to sound characteristics rather than visual characteristics,* and *synesthesia,* or sounds producing visual images in the user's mind.

Touch, Taste, Smell

The sense of *touch taking on new qualities* and *becoming more sensual* are characteristic, and experiencing *vivid tactual imagery* is common. *New qualities to taste* and *enjoying eating very much* are characteristic effects. Again, *taste imagery is markedly enhanced* is a common effect, as well as *craving for sweet things*. It is also common for the *sense of smell to become enhanced and richer*.

The Senses in General

In looking at the sensory changes, we should remember that sensory perception is not, as we commonly assume, a passive process of "seeing what's there," but an active process of constructing percepts from the physical stimuli that come in. The level of this constructive or pattern-making process is generally optimal in terms of providing a good signal-to-noise ratio; i.e., we make few mistakes about what is there. I suspect what marijuana is doing is increasing the level of functioning of this patterning activity, making it work in a more active way. This may result in a genuine increase in the ability to pick signals out of noisy backgrounds, but it probably also increases the number of mistakes; i.e., it organizes things that are not actually related in the real world into a coherent percept.

The Space/Time Matrix

Perceptions of the external environment are not isolated percepts; they occur in the context of the space/time matrix. This space/time matrix is normally background for perceptions—we take it for granted. Marijuana intoxication can cause some radical changes in the way the space/time matrix is perceived. For example, *greater separation between sound sources* as, say, a pair of stereo speakers, has already been mentioned as a characteristic effect, and the *distance experienced in walking some place being radically changed* is also characteristic. Common effects on space are for *distances per se to seem greater or shorter*, and *for near things to seem even nearer and for far things to seem even farther*, a depth-magnification effect. Infrequently, *air or space may take on a "solid" quality*, or the user may *completely lose track of his physical body* and *seem to float in limitless space*.

Changes in time perception are striking. Characteristically, *time seems to pass more slowly*, and the user feels *much more in the here-and-now*, totally immersed in the present situation without thinking about its relation to the past or its possible future developments. Commonly, *events seem to flow more smoothly in time*, although *they may flow rather jerkily* at higher levels. *Déjà vu*, the feeling that one has done this before, may be experienced, and *time may seem to stop*, i.e., it's not just that things take longer but certain experiences are simply timeless; they seem to occur "outside" of time. At high levels of intoxication, particularly, the users' experiences are less and less structured by the ordinary physical space/time matrix. Events and experiences become more and more difficult to communicate as their relationship to the usual space/time matrix is lost.

Paranormal Perception

Another mode of perceiving the environment is by experiences of ostensible extrasensory perception, phenomena such as telepathy, clairvoyance, and precognition. The users believed that they had experienced a great many ostensible paranormal phenomena. Seventy-six percent of them believed in the reality of extrasensory perception. *Feeling so aware of what other people were thinking that the users thought it was telepathy* was a fairly frequent effect, with only 30 percent of the users saying they had never experienced this. *Precognition*, foretelling the future by more than a logical inference, was a rare effect, but not absent.

An even more exotic ostensible paranormal phenomenon was *out-of-the-body experiences*, which 44 percent of the users indicated they had experienced at least once, although not always in conjunction with marijuana. This incidence of out-of-the-body experiences is much higher than has ever been reported for any other population sample, so marijuana use is probably instrumental in promoting this experience.

INTERPERSONAL RELATIONS

Marijuana intoxication is seldom a solitary activity, where the user just sits around perceiving the external world and his own body. Users feel it is a social drug *par excellence.* What does it do to social interaction?

Social Interaction

Characteristic effects on social interaction are *being less noisy at parties than when either straight or drunk* on alcohol, *finding ordinary social games hard to play*, picking up on and *saying much more subtly humorous things*, and having *feelings of great insights into others.* Other common effects are *feeling more sociable* at low levels of intoxication, *less sociable* at higher levels, *talking more* at low levels and *talking less* at higher levels, having *more feeling of group solidarity*, *playing either very childish or very elaborate and involved games with others*, *saying things that seem more profound and appropriate*, and *having a great deal of empathy with others. Giggling a lot* is also a common effect.

It seems as if marijuana acts as a potentiator of social interaction from Low to Moderate levels of intoxication. At high levels, marijuana may have two quite different effects on social interaction because of the great intensification of inner experiences. The user may become less social and withdraw from group interaction in order to fully appreciate his inner experiences. If, on the other hand, he continues to interact with others, he may feel this interaction to be particularly profound, occasionally including such things as feelings of *merging with the other person* or feeling so aware of them that he believes it to be a kind of *telepathic interaction.*

Sexuality

One of the most intimate kinds of interaction possible with another person is sexual love. The majority of the users indicated that marijuana greatly enhances sexual pleasure. Relevant characteristic effects were: *new qualities to touch and taste* (with *new smell qualities* being common)—what one might consider the intimate senses—and *new, pleasurable qualities to orgasm.* It was common for the user to *feel more need and desire for sex,* and, particularly, to *feel more sexual desire if the situation was appropriate.* That is, marijuana is not an aphrodisiac in the sense of *forcing* sexual drive, but rather it makes sex more desirable if there is already an initial attraction. It was common for the users to feel that they were *better lovers when intoxicated,* to have *much closer contact with their partner in making love,* it being much more a union of souls rather than just of bodies, and to be much more responsive to the sexual partner. Some users described making love at high levels of marijuana intoxication as so ecstatic as to be beyond words in many respects, a blending and fusing of essence and energy that took them beyond the bounds of space and time, and into one another.

It should be noted, however, that one quarter of the users thought they were *worse lovers* when intoxicated than when straight, for, they reported, they became so immersed in their own intensified and pleasurable sensations that they paid little attention to their lovers.

INTERNAL MENTAL PROCESSES

Memory

A characteristic effect of marijuana intoxication on memory is to *forget the start of a conversation;* that is, there is a decrement in memory for things occurring over the last few minutes. Nevertheless, it is a common effect for users to feel that they *can converse intelligently despite this shortening of their memory span.* It is also common to have a *good memory for events in general occurring during the period of intoxication,* but *poor memory for this period* is also just as common, depending on unknown psychological factors. *Long-forgotten events commonly pop into memory.* At high levels of intoxication it is common to *forget even the start of one sentence,* and *thoughts may slip away before being fully grasped.* Users often make special efforts, apparently successfully, to continue to function well in spite of this large loss of memory.

State-specific memory occurs; intoxication experiences apparently forgotten can be recalled the next time the user is intoxicated.

Thought

There are many effects of marijuana on thought processes. Characteristic effects are: *accepting contradictions more readily,* not getting upset just because things do not make immediate sense, and having *spontaneous insights into one's own personal functioning,* as well as *being more here-and-now.* It is also characteristic to find it *harder to read,* and to *appreciate more subtle humor,* as mentioned earlier. It is common to feel that *one has ideas that are much more original than usual,* to feel *thinking is more intuitive,* to find *thought automatically accompanied by visual images,* to *see new significance in things that ordinarily seem dull or commonplace,* to *skip intermediate steps in problem-solving,* and to *get so absorbed in thought that one's attention must be forcibly gotten.* At Low levels of intoxication, it is common for the user to feel his *mind is working more efficiently on problem-solving activities,* but at higher levels it is common to feel that *the mind begins to work less efficiently.*

Emotion

The only characteristic effect of marijuana on emotional mood is to *almost invariably feel good,* which is what we would expect in a group of experienced marijuana users. It is common to *feel emotions more strongly,* to be *more aware of bodily components of emotion* (muscle tensions, heartbeat, etc), and *to have one's mood just before becoming intoxicated considerably amplified.* For these experienced users, there is a generally good emotional tone to being intoxicated that can override mildly negative emotions just before becoming intoxicated. If they are in a very negative mood, however, there is a chance of this emotion being greatly amplified and producing a very bad trip. Most of the users had never had a *severe negative emotional crisis* while intoxicated. Of those users who had experienced such a crisis, most indicated it had subsided by itself or that they had been talked down by friends, with only one user needing professional help. In retrospect, some of the users felt their emotional crises had been a good thing in making them aware of aspects of themselves they had not wanted to face.

Control

To what extent can experienced users control the effects of marijuana intoxication sufficiently well to generally avoid negative experiences? It is characteristic that *users feel less need to be in control of things*, and that *they can come down at will*, i.e., suppress most of the effects of intoxication when necessary. Experienced users have a wide variety of psychological techniques for increasing their level of intoxication at will. Experienced users feel that most of the instances of strong negative effects of marijuana are due to rigid, overcontrolled, or unstable people trying it and not being able to tolerate the change in their experiences.

THE PERCEIVER

Experiences do not just happen; they happen to and are caused by a unique individual with likes and dislikes, a past and hopes. How might a user's feeling of who he is change during marijuana intoxication?

The Body

One of the most important sources of sensory input that provides a frame of reference for our identity is our own body. Although there are many effects here, only two were characteristic: the user gets *very physically relaxed and is disinclined to move about*, and if he does move about, his *movements seem exceptionally smooth and coordinated.* The direction of attention is important in how the body is perceived, a common effect being *"if I am paying attention to some particular part of my body the rest of my body fades away a lot. . . ."* Getting *so absorbed in thinking or fantasies that all perception of the body is lost* is also common. With respect to pain, it is common for *pain to be easier to tolerate if attention is turned elsewhere* and for *pain to be more intense if concentrated on.* It is also common for the *body to feel particularly light.*

A number of common effects deal with becoming aware of internal processes in the body to a greatly enhanced extent, such as feeling a *pleasant warmth in the body, being very aware of the beating of one's heart*, and being *hyper-aware of breathing.* Another common experience that does not seem to be simply an enhancement of ordinary sensations is getting *feelings in the body that are described as energy or force of some sort flowing.*

Sense of Identity

Marijuana intoxication has a number of effects on a person's feeling of identity per se. For example, a characteristic effect is for the user *to feel more childlike, more open to experience,* more filled with wonder and awe at the nature of things than he is ordinarily. Common effects on identity include *feeling particularly powerful, capable, and intelligent, feeling a lack of separation between oneself and the world,* an at-one-ness with the world, and *feeling that one's actions and events become archetypal.* That is, instead of John Smith doing a particular thing with Mary Jones at a certain time, it becomes Man interacting with Woman in the Way Man has always interacted with Woman.

Spiritual Experiences

This shift in identity to archetypal levels takes us to a number of experiences, which may be considered spiritual, that is, dealing with the ultimate nature and destiny of man. Some of the users have had important spiritual experiences take place while they were intoxicated, others have had experiences occurring later but considered a result of their marijuana use. Some of these were spontaneous, others were deliberately sought through meditation techniques practiced while intoxicated. Thus 22 percent of the users felt that *using marijuana had acquired a religious significance* for them. Particular experiences included visions, ostensible paranormal experiences, the infrequent experience of *feeling directly in touch with a Higher Power,* and some other experiences already discussed but given a spiritual connotation, such as sexual love seeming a union of souls, being more childlike and open to the universe, and the space/time matrix radically changing.

LEVELS OF INTOXICATION

Practically all the potential effects of marijuana intoxication seem to fit the model (Chapter 2) of the minimal level of intoxication; i.e., after a certain threshold of intoxication has been reached for a given effect, it is potentially available at all levels above that. One consequence of this is that more and more variability as to which effects are experienced at a given time occurs with higher levels of intoxication. Most of the characteristic effects, for example, have common minimal thresholds in the Fair to Strong range (See Chapter 24).

Categories of potential effects available as we go from Fair up toward Maximal levels of intoxication may be described as follows (these are graphed in Figure 24-3, page 246).

Beginning at fair levels of intoxication, there may be a number of phenomena, which depict a sort of *restlessness.* This is one of the few categories of phenomena which does not seem to meet the minimal level model noted earlier; these phenomena generally seem to disappear once the user gets more strongly intoxicated rather than staying potentially available at all levels above the minimal one.

Going somewhat higher, the user may experience a variety of effects that we might call *relaxing, quieting, or opening.* These involve a general calming down and being receptive to things. *Sensory enhancement* in the various senses may begin at this level, as well as feelings of *greater sensitivity to others* and *subtlety in interpersonal relationships.* At these Low-to-Moderate levels, we may also have the beginnings of *feelings of efficiency,* being able to focus well on things, being centered in oneself, and being able to work well. This last category is the one other type of effect that also does not seem to meet the minimal level model, but rather to exist only at these Moderate levels and to be later replaced by feelings of inefficiency. *Insights into oneself, realization of changes in cognitive processes,* and *aftereffects,* such as finding it somewhat hard to get organized the next day, may begin at this Moderate to Strong intoxication level.

As the user smokes enough to get up to the Strong levels of intoxication, *alterations in his perception of the space/time matrix* of existence may begin to occur. *Imagery* in all sensory modalities may be greatly intensified, fantasy may become extremely real, and it may be possible to experience fantasies so real as to almost be hallucinations. At the Strong level and above we may also begin to get *feelings of drifting, losing control* of the situation, and, if problem-solving activity is pressed upon a user, feelings that the mind works inefficiently. Greatly *enhanced awareness of internal body processes* that normally cannot be sensed may start to come in at this level also.

As the user becomes even more intoxicated, he may begin to experience *alterations in memory functions,* such as forgetting what he started to talk about, remembering things other than what he is trying to recall, or state-specific memory. *Loss of contact* with the environment becomes possible, and the user may become absorbed in internal experiences. *Identity may change* in the ways discussed above, and the infrequent *mystical and paranormal experiences* may occur at this level.

Jumping up to the Maximal level, *nausea* may occur, albeit very rarely. Note again that practically all lower-level phenomena are potentially available at higher levels as well.

IMPLICATIONS FOR FUTURE RESEARCH

What are some major questions for future research?

First, how can we get an even better understanding of the nature of marijuana intoxication? Replication and extension of the present study is called for. With such a design, we could devise better questions to ask, better in terms of having more specific meaning to both users and investigators and better in terms of psychometric properties that would allow more sophisticated statistical analyses. Similar studies could be carried out with different populations and tell us valuable things about how cultural factors shape experience; I doubt that the young black in the ghetto has the same spectrum of effects with marijuana as the white college student or professional.

Still within the systematic questioning format, we could investigate the interrelationships of intoxication phenomena within a single individual, trying to do justice to the uniqueness of individual experience. From such case studies one could then compare individuals and possibly find similar types of users, i.e., there might be very little overlap between the experiences of some users, even though all their experiences fall within the total spectrum of potential effects of marijuana intoxication. The reasons for these individual differences could tell us a good deal about the functioning of the mind.

The results of the present study and replications of it can also be used to guide laboratory research and perhaps avoid many of the pitfalls that have plagued previous laboratory studies. Many questions can be studied in the laboratory that are not very suitable for the field study approach. For example, how well do users' ratings of their level of intoxication correlate with actual amount of marijuana or THC consumed? Which is more useful for predicting other aspects of intoxication, experience or behavior, self-report of level or knowledge of amount of chemical consumed? Undoubtedly, some users will not be able to rate the amount of THC well, whereas others will do so very well. What makes for good raters and poor raters? Does the ability to "come down at will" or have a "contact high" make knowledge of THC levels meaningless? How does a new user "learn" to become intoxicated? How do experienced users "learn" new effects? Could completely new effects be produced under the special conditions possible in a laboratory setting? Could a "disciplined" use of drugs be taught, say in conjunction with bio-feedback techniques, making entirely new intoxication effects available?

A second important direction for future research is understanding other states of consciousness in general and eventually, consciousness itself. The type of overall look presented in this book for the phenomenology of marijuana intoxication has not been carried out for the other states of consciousness, yet many people make facile assertions such as, "Meditation is just a form of self-hypnosis," based only on surface knowledge of different states of consciousness.

This lack of data on other states of consciousness makes it impossible to answer some important questions about marijuana intoxication, e.g., what effects of marijuana intoxication can be identically experienced in other states of consciousness? Might we learn to experience some of the desirable effects of being stoned in our ordinary state?

A third important direction for future research is on the practical uses and benefits of marijuana intoxication. Obviously, pleasure is the main benefit of marijuana for most users most of the time. But does it really aid creative thinking? Might it have specific applications in personal growth or psychotherapy through its many effects on thought, emotions, memory, identity? Might there be useful medical applications in selected cases, such as a tranquilizer or sedative in low doses?

Finally, a good deal of research is needed on what the *real* costs or dangers of occasional or chronic marijuana use might be. So much propaganda has been put out, officially and unofficially, on this question that the waters are very muddied. I think it unlikely that we ever get something for nothing, but let's find out the actual physiological or psychological costs of marijuana use so we can weigh them against the benefits and make an intelligent decision about whether the benefits are worth the cost.

Effects of More Powerful Psychedelic Drugs

For each possible effect description, users were asked to circle "LSD" if they had also experienced that effect at least once while intoxicated with one of the more powerful psychedelic drugs (LSD, mescaline, psilocybin, STP, MDA, harmaline, etc).

The table below presents, for every question, two items of information: (1) the percentage of *all* users of the more powerful psychedelics who circled "LSD" on this question; and (2) the percentage of *heavy* users of the more powerful psychedelics who circled the "LSD" response. Heavy users were defined as those who had had a more powerful psychedelic drug six or more times.

Question Number	% Psychedelic Users Who Circled "LSD"		Question Number	% Psychedelic Users Who Circled "LSD"	
	Heavy Users	Total Users [a]		Heavy Users	Total Users
1	27	32	16	38	52
2	5	9	17	47	56
3	16	17	18	13	22
4	26	26	19	3	2
5	10	11	20	3	4
6	36	41	21	3	6
7	29	39	22	7	7
8	18	22	23	39	48
9	12	20	24	16	20
10	15	17	25	8	15
11	11	17	26	10	13
12	15	20	27	8	15
13	24	32	28	19	28
14	13	13	29	10	17
15	20	30	30	16	22

[a]Note that these are percentages of the 108 respondents who had used psychedelic drugs, *not* of the total 150 marijuana users.

Question Number	% Psychedelic Users Who Circled "LSD"		Question Number	% Psychedelic Users Who Circled "LSD"	
	Heavy Users	Total Users		Heavy Users	Total Users
31	19	28	67C	24	33
32	14	20	68	3	4
33	13	20	69	24	30
34	12	17	70	15	22
35	6	6	71	13	20
36	7	11	72	8	13
37	10	13	73	12	19
38	12	19	74	23	30
39	17	24	75	18	30
40	8	13	76	11	20
41	6	9	77	7	11
42	6	9	78	15	20
43	2	4	79	13	19
44	7	9	80	7	11
45	2	2	81	9	17
46	2	4	82	25	37
47	9	15	83	11	19
48	8	13	84	9	15
49	5	9	85	17	26
50	4	6	86	12	20
51	19	22	87	1	2
52	14	22	88	11	13
53	11	15	89	7	9
54	7	13	90	4	4
55	29	37	91	7	7
56	15	20	92	9	15
57	10	17	93	35	46
58	20	26	94	29	35
59	10	13	95	10	13
60	37	50	96	10	13
61	13	24	97	4	6
62	9	13	98	19	24
63	13	13	99	11	17
64	N.A.	N.A.ᵃ	100	8	11
65	19	24	101	8	13
66	7	11	102	7	11
67A	N.A.	63	103	16	19
67B	N.A.	N.A.	104	N.A.	N.A.

ᵃN.A., not applicable, indicates that information about LSD was not asked for on this question.

Question Number	% Psychedelic Users Who Circled "LSD"		Question Number	% Psychedelic Users Who Circled "LSD"	
	Heavy Users	Total Users		Heavy Users	Total Users
105	8	11	144	4	6
106	17	20	145	15	22
107	10	15	146	7	13
108	12	13	147	5	7
109	5	7	148	10	15
110	3	4	149	13	20
111	7	13	150	15	22
112	8	11	151	9	17
113	13	20	152	5	9
114	12	19	153	11	17
115	8	15	154	15	22
116	14	20	155	8	9
117	8	13	156	10	15
118	11	19	157	7	15
119	5	7	158	7	7
120	2	4	159	7	15
121	3	4	160	8	11
122	7	11	161	13	19
123	9	15	162	5	9
124	8	13	163	7	11
125	12	19	164	6	11
126	7	9	165	9	15
127	6	11	166	3	4
128	17	30	167	N.A.	N.A.
129	13	22	167B	N.A.	N.A.
130	7	9	168	N.A.	N.A.
131	10	15	169A	N.A.	N.A.
132	10	20	169B	12	N.A.
133	8	15	170	12	20
134	19	28	171	22	26
135	15	22	172	6	9
136	19	24	173	12	20
137	11	19	174	10	17
138	17	26	175	11	20
139	19	28	176	5	6
140	15	20	177	17	46
141	13	24	178	7	11
142	11	20	179	3	4
143	6	7	180	8	11

Question Number	% Psychedelic Users Who Circled "LSD"		Question Number	% Psychedelic Users Who Circled "LSD"	
	Heavy Users	Total Users		Heavy Users	Total Users
181	11	11	202	3	6
182	9	15	203	N.A.	N.A.
183	23	33	204-1	30	N.A.
184	36	37	204-2	37	41
185	18	22	205	41	43
186	26	37	206	32	41
187	5	9	207	20	26
188	9	13	208	24	32
189	37	50	209	18	17
190	11	19	210	12	15
191	30	43	211	29	39
192	26	37	212	18	24
193	7	7	213	N.A.	N.A.
194	42	48	214	9	15
195	33	43	215	7	13
196	29	41	216	26	35
197	3	6	217	6	7
198	2	4	218	22	30
199	2	4	219	4	7
200	13	24	220	N.A.	N.A.
201	5	7			

Questionnaire Used in
This Study*

NO NAMES!

Age _____ Occupation _____ (if a student, what do you plan?)

Sex _____ Marital Status _____ Education: degree or highest grade completed

---

Do you have any children? _____ Political affiliation _____

Religious affiliation _____

Ever been arrested? _____ For what? _____
                        Were you convicted? _____

Do you regularly practice any sort of meditation or other non-drug discipline for   45
spiritual or personal growth? _____
If so, what? _____

How long have you been smoking pot or hash? _____
In *all* this time, what has been your
average frequency of use?   _____ Almost every day or more
(ignore this question if you've been   _____ Once/week or more
turning on less than 6 months)   _____ Once/month or more
                                    _____ Occasionally

During the last *six months*, what
has been your frequency of use?   _____ Almost every day or more
                                    _____ Once/week or more
                                    _____ Once/month or more
                                    _____ Occasionally

How often have you used any of the following major psychedelics: LSD, mescaline,
peyote, psilocybin, DMT, or DET? —
                    Before you started   _____ More than 6 (how many?)
                    smoking pot?   _____ One to five times
                                      _____ Never

---

*This is a reproduction of the questionnaire used for collecting the data of the present study.
The instructions for filling out the questionnaire and the covering letter that went out with
it are reproduced in Chapter 3.

†For the reader's convenience I have added the page number on which individual questions
are discussed in this book.

After you started   _____ More than 6 (how many?)
smoking pot?   _____ One to five times
                         _____ Never

Within the last   _____ More than 6 (how many?)
six months?   _____ One to five times
                         _____ Never

Please make the same ratings (before, after, last 6 months) by putting three numbers
(N-N-N) after each of the drugs below you have tried:
Amphetamine or methadrine (by mouth)
Amphetamine or methadrine (by injection)
STP   MDA
PEACE   Others (what?)

Do you think your experiences (if any) with any of these other psychedelic drugs
have affected or changed the quality of your experiences with pot? If yes, how?

How long have you been drinking alcoholic beverages in sufficient quantity to
change your consciousness (i.e., drinking to get "tipsy" or drunk, rather than just
having a little wine or beer with meals for the taste)?

In *all* this time, what has been your average frequency of use?

During the last six months, what has been your average frequency of use?

If pot were as available legally as alcohol, about what percentage of the time would
you choose alcohol to alter your state of consciousness rather than pot?

VISION SENSE: *Page*

1. I can see new colors or more subtle shades of color than when I'm straight.   *60*
   Frequency?   Never   Rarely   Sometimes   Very Often   Usually
   How Stoned? Just   Fairly   Strongly   Vy Strongly   Maximum   LSD

2. Colors get duller, not as vivid.   *60*
   Frequency?   Never   Rarely   Sometimes   Very Often   Usually
   How Stoned? Just   Fairly   Strongly   Vy Strongly   Maximum   LSD

3. There is a sensual quality to vision, as if I were somehow "touching" the   *63*
   objects or people I am looking at.
   Frequency?   Never   Rarely   Sometimes   Very Often   Usually
   How Stoned? Just   Fairly   Strongly   Vy Strongly   Maximum   LSD

4. When I look at *pictures* they may acquire an element of visual depth, a third-   *61*
dimensional aspect that they don't have when straight.
Frequency? Never   Rarely   Sometimes   Very Often   Usually
How Stoned? Just   Fairly   Strongly   Vy Strongly   Maximum   LSD

5. The world looks flat; it lacks the third dimension of depth.   *62*
Frequency? Never   Rarely   Sometimes   Very Often   Usually
How Stoned? Just   Fairly   Strongly   Vy Strongly   Maximum   LSD

6. I see fringes of colored light around *people* (not objects), what people have   *65*
called the "aura."
Frequency? Never   Rarely   Sometimes   Very Often   Usually
How Stoned? Just   Fairly   Strongly   Vy Strongly   Maximum   LSD

7. I see fringes of colored light around *objects* (not people), what people have   *64*
called the "aura."
Frequency? Never   Rarely   Sometimes   Very Often   Usually
How Stoned? Just   Fairly   Strongly   Vy Strongly   Maximum   LSD

8. If I try to visualize something, form a visual image, I see it in my mind's   *64*
eye more intensely, more sharply than when straight.
Frequency? Never   Rarely   Sometimes   Very Often   Usually
How Stoned? Just   Fairly   Strongly   Vy Strongly   Maximum   LSD

9. Things outside the center of my visual field, things in the periphery of my   *62*
vision look different when I'm not looking directly at them than when I look
directly at them. E.g., I might see a door as open when I'm not looking directly
at it, but when I look directly at it, it is closed.
Frequency? Never   Rarely   Sometimes   Very Often   Usually
How Stoned? Just   Fairly   Strongly   Vy Strongly   Maximum   LSD

10. Things seen are seen more sharply in that their edges, contours stand out   *59*
more sharply against the background.
Frequency? Never   Rarely   Sometimes   Very Often   Usually
How Stoned? Just   Fairly   Strongly   Vy Strongly   Maximum   LSD

11. My vision tends to be somewhat blurry, if I try to examine something visually,   *59*
I can't focus quite as sharply as when straight.
Frequency? Never   Rarely   Sometimes   Very Often   Usually
How Stoned? Just   Fairly   Strongly   Vy Strongly   Maximum   LSD

12. My visual perception of the space around me is changed so that what I'm   *62*
looking at is very real and clear, but everything else I'm not focusing on visually
seems further away or otherwise less real or clear.
Frequency? Never   Rarely   Sometimes   Very Often   Usually
How Stoned? Just   Fairly   Strongly   Vy Strongly   Maximum   LSD

13. I can see patterns, forms, figures, meaningful designs in visual material that   *59*
does not have any particular form when I'm straight, that is just a meaningless
series of lines or shapes when I'm straight.
Frequency? Never   Rarely   Sometimes   Very Often   Usually
How Stoned? Just   Fairly   Strongly   Vy Strongly   Maximum   LSD

14. Visual depth perception changes, so that near objects seem much nearer and   *62*
far objects seem much further away.
Frequency? Never   Rarely   Sometimes   Very Often   Usually
How Stoned? Just   Fairly   Strongly   Vy Strongly   Maximum   LSD

15. Objects or people may seem to get visually nearer or further *as I look at*   62
them without their actually moving at all.
Frequency?   Never   Rarely   Sometimes   Very Often   Usually
How Stoned?   Just   Fairly   Strongly   Vy Strongly   Maximum   LSD

16. The face of another person will change even as I watch it, so he keeps changing   *133*
from one different person to another.
Frequency?   Never   Rarely   Sometimes   Very Often   Usually
How Stoned?   Just   Fairly   Strongly   Vy Strongly   Maximum   LSD

17. Everything I look at seems to vibrate or pulse, as if it had a life of its own.   64
Frequency?   Never   Rarely   Sometimes   Very Often   Usually
How Stoned?   Just   Fairly   Strongly   Vy Strongly   Maximum   LSD

18. I find it difficult to read while stoned.   *159*
Frequency?   Never   Rarely   Sometimes   Very Often   Usually
How Stoned?   Just   Fairly   Strongly   Vy Strongly   Maximum   LSD

19. It is easier to read than usual while stoned.   *159*
Frequency?   Never   Rarely   Sometimes   Very Often   Usually
How Stoned?   Just   Fairly   Strongly   Vy Strongly   Maximum   LSD

20. If I read while stoned, I remember *more* of what I've read hours later than   *159*
if I had been straight.
Frequency?   Never   Rarely   Sometimes   Very Often   Usually
How Stoned?   Just   Fairly   Strongly   Vy Strongly   Maximum   LSD

21. If I read while stoned, I remember *less* of what I've read hours later than   *159*
if I had been straight.
Frequency?   Never   Rarely   Sometimes   Very Often   Usually
How Stoned?   Just   Fairly   Strongly   Vy Strongly   Maximum   LSD

22. I have more imagery than usual while reading; images of the scenes I'm reading   64
about just pop up vividly.
Frequency?   Never   Rarely   Sometimes   Very Often   Usually
How Stoned?   Just   Fairly   Strongly   Vy Strongly   Maximum   LSD

23. With my eyes open, I can see things that aren't there, i.e., for which there   65
is no real visual basis. For example, if you look at stains on a wall and see
a design, that's an illusion; you are altering something there. This question
deals with seeing something when there's *nothing* there, such as seeing a pattern
or object on a perfectly blank wall.
Frequency?   Never   Rarely   Sometimes   Very Often   Usually
How Stoned?   Just   Fairly   Strongly   Vy Strongly   Maximum   LSD

                                                                               Page
HEARING SENSE:

24. I can hear more subtle changes in sounds; e.g., the notes of music are purer   *71*
and more distinct, the rhythm stands out more.
Frequency?   Never   Rarely   Sometimes   Very Often   Usually
How Stoned?   Just   Fairly   Strongly   Vy Strongly   Maximum   LSD

25. I can understand the words of songs which are not clear when straight.   *71*
Frequency?   Never   Rarely   Sometimes   Very Often   Usually
How Stoned?   Just   Fairly   Strongly   Vy Strongly   Maximum   LSD

26. I have difficulty hearing things clearly; sounds are blurry and indistinct.   *37-39,*
Frequency?   Never   Rarely   Sometimes   Very Often   Usually   *71*
How Stoned?   Just   Fairly   Strongly   Vy Strongly   Maximum   LSD

27. If I try to have an auditory image, hear something in my mind, remember   *74*
    a sound, it is more vivid than when straight.
    Frequency?   Never   Rarely   Sometimes   Very Often   Usually
    How Stoned? Just   Fairly   Strongly   Vy Strongly Maximum   LSD

28. The sound quality of my own voice changes, so that I sound different to myself   *74*
    when I talk.
    Frequency?   Never   Rarely   Sometimes   Very Often   Usually
    How Stoned? Just   Fairly   Strongly   Vy Strongly Maximum   LSD

29. When listening to stereo music or live music, the spatial separation between   *72*
    the various instruments sounds greater, as if they were physically further apart.
    Frequency?   Never   Rarely   Sometimes   Very Often   Usually
    How Stoned? Just   Fairly   Strongly   Vy Strongly Maximum   LSD

30. With my eyes closed and just listening to sounds, the space around me becomes   *72*
    an *auditory* space, a place where things are arranged according to their sound
    characteristics instead of visual geometrical characteristics.
    Frequency?   Never   Rarely   Sometimes   Very Often   Usually
    How Stoned? Just   Fairly   Strongly   Vy Strongly Maximum   LSD

TOUCH SENSE: *Page*

31. Touch sensations take on new qualities that they don't have when straight.   *79*
    Frequency?   Never   Rarely   Sometimes   Very Often   Usually
    How Stoned? Just   Fairly   Strongly   Vy Strongly Maximum   LSD

32. My sense of touch is more exciting, more sensual, when stoned.   *79*
    Frequency?   Never   Rarely   Sometimes   Very Often   Usually
    How Stoned? Just   Fairly   Strongly   Vy Strongly Maximum   LSD

33. Some surfaces feel much smoother, silkier than when straight.   *79*
    Frequency?   Never   Rarely   Sometimes   Very Often   Usually
    How Stoned? Just   Fairly   Strongly   Vy Strongly Maximum   LSD

34. Some surfaces feel much rougher, more irregular, than when straight; the   *79*
    roughness or graininess forms interesting patterns.
    Frequency?   Never   Rarely   Sometimes   Very Often   Usually
    How Stoned? Just   Fairly   Strongly   Vy Strongly Maximum   LSD

35. Objects seem heavier, more massive, when I lift them when stoned.   *80*
    Frequency?   Never   Rarely   Sometimes   Very Often   Usually
    How Stoned? Just   Fairly   Strongly   Vy Strongly Maximum   LSD

36. Objects seem lighter, less massive, when I lift them.   *80*
    Frequency?   Never   Rarely   Sometimes   Very Often   Usually
    How Stoned? Just   Fairly   Strongly   Vy Strongly Maximum   LSD

37. I can experience vivid tactual imagery, imagine what things feel like and feel   *79*
    their texture very vividly in my mind.
    Frequency?   Never   Rarely   Sometimes   Very Often   Usually
    How Stoned? Just   Fairly   Strongly   Vy Strongly Maximum   LSD

38. The *temperature* of things, their warmth or coldness, takes on new qualities.   *80*
    Frequency?   Never   Rarely   Sometimes   Very Often   Usually
    How Stoned? Just   Fairly   Strongly   Vy Strongly Maximum   LSD

TASTE SENSE: *Page*

39. Taste sensations take on new qualities that they don't have when straight.   *81*
    Frequency?   Never   Rarely   Sometimes   Very Often   Usually
    How Stoned? Just   Fairly   Strongly   Vy Strongly   Maximum   LSD

40. Tastes become divided into several components, instead of an overall taste.   *83*
    E.g., a bite of bread may taste salty on one part of your tongue and sour
    on another part at the same time.
    Frequency?   Never   Rarely   Sometimes   Very Often   Usually
    How Stoned? Just   Fairly   Strongly   Vy Strongly   Maximum   LSD

41. There is an exceptionally long time delay between starting to chew food and   *83*
    the time the taste actually reaches my consciousness.
    Frequency?   Never   Rarely   Sometimes   Very Often   Usually
    How Stoned? Just   Fairly   Strongly   Vy Strongly   Maximum   LSD

42. I salivate quite a lot when stoned.   *37-39,*
    Frequency?   Never   Rarely   Sometimes   Very Often   Usually   *83*
    How Stoned? Just   Fairly   Strongly   Vy Strongly   Maximum   LSD

43. If I belch, I retaste the food in my stomach, and it tastes very good.   *83*
    Frequency?   Never   Rarely   Sometimes   Very Often   Usually
    How Stoned? Just   Fairly   Strongly   Vy Strongly   Maximum   LSD

44. I enjoy eating very much and eat a lot.   *82*
    Frequency?   Never   Rarely   Sometimes   Very Often   Usually
    How Stoned? Just   Fairly   Strongly   Vy Strongly   Maximum   LSD

45. If I try to imagine what something tastes like, I can do so very vividly.   *82*
    Frequency?   Never   Rarely   Sometimes   Very Often   Usually
    How Stoned? Just   Fairly   Strongly   Vy Strongly   Maximum   LSD

46. I crave *sweet* things to eat, things like chocolate, more than other foods.   *82*
    Frequency?   Never   Rarely   Sometimes   Very Often   Usually
    How Stoned? Just   Fairly   Strongly   Vy Strongly   Maximum   LSD

SMELL SENSE: *Page*

47. Smell sensations take on new qualities that they don't have when straight.   *85*
    Frequency?   Never   Rarely   Sometimes   Very Often   Usually
    How Stoned? Just   Fairly   Strongly   Vy Strongly   Maximum   LSD

48. Smells become much richer and more unique when stoned.   *85*
    Frequency?   Never   Rarely   Sometimes   Very Often   Usually
    How Stoned? Just   Fairly   Strongly   Vy Strongly   Maximum   LSD

49. When I smell something, different components of the smell seem to register   *86*
    at different physical locations in my nose.
    Frequency?   Never   Rarely   Sometimes   Very Often   Usually
    How Stoned? Just   Fairly   Strongly   Vy Strongly   Maximum   LSD

50. If I try to imagine what something smells like, I can do so much more vividly   *86*
    than when straight.
    Frequency?   Never   Rarely   Sometimes   Very Often   Usually
    How Stoned? Just   Fairly   Strongly   Vy Strongly   Maximum   LSD

SPACE/TIME PERCEPTION: *Page*

51. When I walk someplace, my experience of the distance covered is quite changed   *89*
(e.g., not being aware of the space between, just seeming to suddenly be there
or, conversely, feeling that it takes an immense number of steps to cover the
distance).

Frequency?	Never	Rarely	Sometimes	Very Often	Usually	
How Stoned?	Just	Fairly	Strongly	Vy Strongly	Maximum	LSD

52. Distances between me and things or me and other people seem to get greater;   *89*
they are further away.

Frequency?	Never	Rarely	Sometimes	Very Often	Usually	
How Stoned?	Just	Fairly	Strongly	Vy Strongly	Maximum	LSD

53. Distances between me and other things or people seem to get shorter; they   *89*
are closer.

Frequency?	Never	Rarely	Sometimes	Very Often	Usually	
How Stoned?	Just	Fairly	Strongly	Vy Strongly	Maximum	LSD

54. Objects seem to tilt toward the left.   *37-39*

Frequency?	Never	Rarely	Sometimes	Very Often	Usually	
How Stoned?	Just	Fairly	Strongly	Vy Strongly	Maximum	LSD

55. I get so lost in fantasy or similar trips in my head that I completely forget   *90*
where I am, and it takes a while to reorient after I come back and open
my eyes.

Frequency?	Never	Rarely	Sometimes	Very Often	Usually	
How Stoned?	Just	Fairly	Strongly	Vy Strongly	Maximum	LSD

56. The space or air around me takes on a solid quality; it is no longer "empty"   *91*
space.

Frequency?	Never	Rarely	Sometimes	Very Often	Usually	
How Stoned?	Just	Fairly	Strongly	Vy Strongly	Maximum	LSD

57. The force of gravity seems to alternate between pushing me up and pushing *37-39*
me down.

Frequency?	Never	Rarely	Sometimes	Very Often	Usually	
How Stoned?	Just	Fairly	Strongly	Vy Strongly	Maximum	LSD

58. Time passes very slowly; things go on for the longest (e.g., one side of a record   *92*
seems to play for hours).

Frequency?	Never	Rarely	Sometimes	Very Often	Usually	
How Stoned?	Just	Fairly	Strongly	Vy Strongly	Maximum	LSD

59. Time passes very rapidly; things finish almost before they seem to have gotten   *92*
started.

Frequency?	Never	Rarely	Sometimes	Very Often	Usually	
How Stoned?	Just	Fairly	Strongly	Vy Strongly	Maximum	LSD

60. Time seems to stop; it's not just that things take longer, but certain experiences   *92*
seem outside of time, are timeless.

Frequency?	Never	Rarely	Sometimes	Very Often	Usually	
How Stoned?	Just	Fairly	Strongly	Vy Strongly	Maximum	LSD

61. Events and thoughts flow more smoothly; the succession of events in time   *93*
is smoother than usual.

Frequency?	Never	Rarely	Sometimes	Very Often	Usually	
How Stoned?	Just	Fairly	Strongly	Vy Strongly	Maximum	LSD

62. Events and thoughts follow each other jerkily; there are sudden changes from   *93*
one thing to another.

Frequency?	Never	Rarely	Sometimes	Very Often	Usually	
How Stoned?	Just	Fairly	Strongly	Vy Strongly	Maximum	LSD

63. *While* something is happening, I get the funny feeling that this sequence has   *94*
happened before, in exactly the same way. Even though I logically know it
couldn't have happened before, it feels strange, as if it's repeating exactly
(this is called a *déjà vu* experience and should not be confused with a false
memory).

Frequency?	Never	Rarely	Sometimes	Very Often	Usually	
How Stoned?	Just	Fairly	Strongly	Vy Strongly	Maximum	LSD

EXTRASENSORY PERCEPTION: *Page*

64. I believe in the existence of extrasensory perception (ESP), i.e., that people   *99*
can sometimes acquire knowledge about things happening at a distance in
space or time, or about other people's thoughts, when there is no possibility
of this knowledge having been acquired through the known senses (sight,
hearing, etc.).

    _____ Believe strongly
    _____ Believe somewhat
    _____ Haven't made up my mind
    _____ Disbelieve somewhat
    _____ Disbelieve strongly

65. I feel so aware of what people are thinking that it must be telepathy, mind   *100*
reading, rather than just being more sensitive to the subtle cues in their behavior.

Frequency?	Never	Rarely	Sometimes	Very Often	Usually	
How Stoned?	Just	Fairly	Strongly	Vy Strongly	Maximum	LSD

66. I can foretell the future by some kind of precognition, more than just predicting   *100*
logically from present events.

Frequency?	Never	Rarely	Sometimes	Very Often	Usually	
How Stoned?	Bust	Fairly	Strongly	Vy Strongly	Maximum	LSD

67. Have you ever had the experience of feeling "located" outside your physical   *103*
body, i.e. of *you* being at a different location in space than the one you knew
your body was at? Dreams aren't included here, or situations where you just
lose consciousness of your body. This is where you consciously feel located
at a different place and know *at the time* that you are conscious but at a
different location. Has this happened to you:

At all _____ (if so please describe on rear)
While stoned? _____happened before started smoking grass.
                                  after

68. I can perform magical operations that will affect objects or people while stoned.   *10?*
(Please describe on rear)

Frequency?	Never	Rarely	Sometimes	Very Often	Usually	
How Stoned?	Just	Fairly	Strongly	Vy Strongly	Maximum	LSD

PERCEPTION OF THE BODY: *Page*

69. My perception of how my body is shaped gets strange; the "felt" shape or   *116*
form doesn't correspond to its actual form (e.g., you may feel lopsided, or
parts of your body feel heavy while others feel light).

Frequency?	Never	Rarely	Sometimes	Very Often	Usually	
How Stoned?	Just	Fairly	Strongly	Vy Strongly	Maximum	LSD

70. I lose awareness of most of my body unless I specifically focus my attention *109*
there, or some particularly strong stimulus demands my attention there.
Frequency? Never Rarely Sometimes Very Often Usually
How Stoned? Just Fairly Strongly Vy Strongly Maximum LSD

71. If I am paying attention to some particular part of my body, the rest of my *109*
body fades away a lot so the part I'm attending to stands out more sharply.
Frequency? Never Rarely Sometimes Very Often Usually
How Stoned? Just Fairly Strongly Vy Strongly Maximum LSD

72. When there is any trembling in my body, the upper half of my body trembles *37-39*
much more than the lower half.
Frequency? Never Rarely Sometimes Very Often Usually
How Stoned? Just Fairly Strongly Vy Strongly Maximum LSD

73. I become very aware of my breathing and can feel the breath flowing in and *118*
out of my throat as well as filling my lungs.
Frequency? Never Rarely Sometimes Very Often Usually
How Stoned? Just Fairly Strongly Vy Strongly Maximum LSD

74. I get dizzy or nauseated, so much so that I wonder if I will get sick. *120*
Frequency? Never Rarely Sometimes Very Often Usually
How Stoned? Just Fairly Strongly Vy Strongly Maximum LSD

75. I become aware of parts of my body that I am normally unaware of, can't *117*
become aware of when straight, such as internal organs.
Frequency? Never Rarely Sometimes Very Often Usually
How Stoned? Just Fairly Strongly Vy Strongly Maxieum LSD

76. My body gets very numb, without feeling. *117*
Frequency? Never Rarely Sometimes Very Often Usually
How Stoned? Just Fairly Strongly Vy Strongly Maximum LSD

77. The location of my consciousness, the physical locale of the part of *me* that *117*
seems most me, has moved to different parts of my physical body from those
it occupies while straight.
Frequency? Never Rarely Sometimes Very Often Usually
How Stoned? Just Fairly Strongly Vy Strongly Maximum LSD

78. When defecating or urinating, I become aware of the internal organ processes *118*
involved that I can't be aware of when straight.
Frequency? Never Rarely Sometimes Very Often Usually
How Stoned? Just Fairly Strongly Vy Strongly Maximum LSD

79. With my eyes closed, my body may feel very light or even feel as if I float *111*
up into the air when stoned.
Frequency? Never Rarely Sometimes Very Often Usually
How Stoned? Just Fairly Strongly Vy Strongly Maximum LSD

80. My body feels abnormally heavy, as if it weighed much much more. *111*
Frequency? Never Rarely Sometimes Very Often Usually
How Stoned? Just Fairly Strongly Vy Strongly Maximum LSD

81. I feel a lot of pleasant warmth inside my body. *117*
Frequency? Never Rarely Sometimes Very Often Usually
How Stoned? Just Fairly Strongly Vy Strongly Maximum LSD

82. I get feelings in my body that are best described as energy, force, power of   *118*
    some sort flowing.
    Frequency?   Never   Rarely   Sometimes   Very Often   Usually
    How Stoned?   Just   Fairly   Strongly   Vy Strongly   Maximum   LSD

83. I become very aware of my spine and feel energy flowing through it.   *119*
    Frequency?   Never   Rarely   Sometimes   Very Often   Usually
    How Stoned?   Just   Fairly   Strongly   Vy Strongly   Maximum   LSD

84. I become aware of *chakra* centers along my spine and feel changes in my   *119*
    state of consciousness as energy flows through the *chakras*.
    Frequency?   Never   Rarely   Sometimes   Very Often   Usually
    How Stoned?   Just   Fairly   Strongly   Vy Strongly   Maximum   LSD

85. I feel a vibration or tingling sensation in some or all of my body that I can   *118*
    tell is *not* an actual muscle tremor by looking at my body.
    Frequency?   Never   Rarely   Sometimes   Very Often   Usually
    How Stoned?   Just   Fairly   Strongly   Vy Strongly   Maximum   LSD

86. My muscles develop actual physical tremors (large enough to see visually).   *113*
    Frequency?   Never   Rarely   Sometimes   Very Often   Usually
    How Stoned?   Just   Fairly   Strongly   Vy Strongly   Maximum   LSD

87. My scalp itches a lot if I have smoked too much grass.   *37-39*
    Frequency?   Never   Rarely   Sometimes   Very Often   Usually
    How Stoned?   Just   Fairly   Strongly   Vy Strongly   Maximum   LSD

88. Pain is easy to tolerate if I keep my attention elsewhere.   *110*
    Frequency?   Never   Rarely   Sometimes   Very Often   Usually
    How Stoned?   Just   Fairly   Strongly   Vy Strongly   Maximum   LSD

89. Pain is more intense if I concentrate on it.   *110*
    Frequency?   Never   Rarely   Sometimes   Very Often   Usually
    How Stoned?   Just   Fairly   Strongly   Vy Strongly   Maximum   LSD

90. My body feels larger than usual.   *112*
    Frequency?   Never   Rarely   Sometimes   Very Often   Usually
    How Stonedu   Just   Fairly   Strongly   Vy Strongly   Maximum   LSD

91. My body feels smaller than usual.   *112*
    Frequency?   Never   Rarely   Sometimes   Very Often   Usually
    How Stoned?   Just   Fairly   Strongly   Vy Strongly   Maximum   LSD

92. I am much more aware of the beating of my heart.   *117*
    Frequency?   Never   Rarely   Sometimes   Very Often   Usually
    How Stoned?   Just   Fairly   Strongly   Vy Strongly   Maximum   LSD

93. I have lost all consciousness of my body and the external world, and just   *110*
    found myself floating in limitless space (not necessarily physical space).
    Frequency?   Never   Rarely   Sometimes   Very Often   Usually
    How Stoned?   Just   Fairly   Strongly   Vy Strongly   Maximum   LSD

94. I have lost all consciousness of my body during fantasy trips, i.e., gotten so   *90,*
    absorbed in what was going on in my head that my body might as well not   *110*
    have existed for a while.
    Frequency?   Never   Rarely   Sometimes   Very Often   Usually
    How Stoned?   Just   Fairly   Strongly   Vy Strongly   Maximum   LSD

MOVEMENT: *Page*

95. I *feel* much stronger when stoned (regardless of whether actually physically   *113*
    stronger or weaker).
    Frequency?   Never   Rarely   Sometimes   Very Often   Usually
    How Stoned? Just   Fairly   Strongly   Vy Strongly   Maximum   LSD

96. I *feel* much weaker when stoned (regardless of whether actually physically   *113*
    stronger or weaker).
    Frequency?   Never   Rarely   Sometimes   Very Often   Usually
    How Stoned? Just   Fairly   Strongly   Vy Strongly   Maximum   LSD

97. My non-dominant hand (left if you're right-handed and vice-versa) becomes *37-39*
    partially paralyzed, unusable.
    Frequency?   Never   Rarely   Sometimes   Very Often   Usually
    How Stoned? Just   Fairly   Strongly   Vy Strongly   Maximum   LSD

98. I get physically restless so that I want to move around a lot.   *114*
    Frequency?   Never   Rarely   Sometimes   Very Often   Usually
    How Stoned? Just   Fairly   Strongly   Vy Strongly   Maximum   LSD

99. I get physically relaxed and don't want to get up or move around.   *114*
    Frequency?   Never   Rarely   Sometimes   Very Often   Usually
    How Stoned? Just   Fairly   Strongly   Vy Strongly   Maximum   LSD

100. When I move about or dance, my motions seem exceptionally smooth and   *114*
     well coordinated.
     Frequency?   Never   Rarely   Sometimes   Very Often   Usually
     How Stoned? Just   Fairly   Strongly   Vy Strongly   Maximum   LSD

101. When I move about or dance, my motions seem awkward and uncoordinated.   *114*
     Frequency?   Never   Rarely   Sometimes   Very Often   Usually
     How Stoned? Just   Fairly   Strongly   Vy Strongly   Maximum   LSD

102. I tremble a lot in my hands for a while *after* having been stoned.   *37-39,*
     Frequency?   Never   Rarely   Sometimes   Very Often   Usually   *234*
     How Stoned? Just   Fairly   Strongly   Vy Strongly   Maximum   LSD

103. My sense of balance gets very erratic, making it seem difficult to walk or   *115*
     even maintain a sitting position.
     Frequency?   Never   Rarely   Sometimes   Very Often   Usually
     How Stoned? Just   Fairly   Strongly   Vy Strongly   Maximum   LSD

104. Smoking grass makes me cough hard while inhaling and holding my breath. *37-39,*
     Frequency?   Never   Rarely   Sometimes   Very Often   Usually   *113*
     How Stoned? Just   Fairly   Strongly   Vy Strongly   Maximum   LSD

RELATIONS WITH OTHER PEOPLE: *Page*

105. When stoned with others, I play "childish" games; i.e., we interact with each *132*
     other in ways which are very enjoyable but which people would ordinarily
     consider childish.
     Frequency?   Never   Rarely   Sometimes   Very Often   Usually
     How Stoned? Just   Fairly   Strongly   Vy Strongly   Maximum   LSD

106. I find it very hard to play *ordinary* social games when stoned.   *132*
     Frequency?   Never   Rarely   Sometimes   Very Often   Usually
     How Stoned? Just   Fairly   Strongly   Vy Strongly   Maximum   LSD

107. I feel isolated from things around me, as if there were some kind of barrier   *135*
or glass wall between me and the world, muting everything coming in and
partially isolating me.
Frequency?   Never   Rarely   Sometimes   Very Often   Usually
How Stoned?   Just   Fairly   Strongly   Vy Strongly   Maximum   LSD

108. I get somewhat paranoid about the people with me; I am suspicious about   *135*
what they're doing.
Frequency?   Never   Rarely   Sometimes   Very Often   Usually
How Stoned?   Just   Fairly   Strongly   Vy Strongly   Maximum   LSD

109. I am less noisy and boisterous at parties than when straight.   *127*
Frequency?   Never   Rarely   Sometimes   Very Often   Usually
How Stoned?   Just   Fairly   Strongly   Vy Strongly   Maximum   LSD

110. I am less noisy and boisterous at parties than when drunk or tipsy on alcohol.   *127*
Frequency?   Never   Rarely   Sometimes   Very Often   Usually
How Stoned?   Just   Fairly   Strongly   Vy Strongly   Maximum   LSD

111. I feel the things I say in conversation when stoned are more profound, more   *134*
appropriate to the conversation, more interesting.
Frequency?   Never   Rarely   Sometimes   Very Often   Usually
How Stoned?   Just   Fairly   Strongly   Vy Strongly   Maximum   LSD

112. When stoned with a group of people, the group takes on a much greater   *134*
sense of unity, of real social relationship, than when straight; i.e., I feel much
more part of a *group* instead of one person simply in the presence of other
people.
Frequency?   Never   Rarely   Sometimes   Very Often   Usually
How Stoned?   Just   Fairly   Strongly   Vy Strongly   Maximum   LSD

113. I have feelings of deep insights into other people, how they tick, what their   *133*
games are, when stoned (regardless of whether they check out later).
Frequency?   Never   Rarely   Sometimes   Very Often   Usually
How Stoned?   Just   Fairly   Strongly   Vy Strongly   Maximum   LSD

114. I empathize tremendously with others; I feel what they feel; I have a tremen-   *133*
dous intuitive understanding of what they're feeling.
Frequency?   Never   Rarely   Sometimes   Very Often   Usually
How Stoned?   Just   Fairly   Strongly   Vy Strongly   Maximum   LSD

115. I become more sociable; I want to be with and interact with people more.   *128*
Frequency?   Never   Rarely   Sometimes   Very Often   Usually
How Stoned?   Just   Fairly   Strongly   Vy Strongly   Maximum   LSD

116. I become less sociable; I want to be by myself.   *128*
Frequency?   Never   Rarely   Sometimes   Very Often   Usually
How Stoned?   Just   Fairly   Strongly   Vy Strongly   Maximum   LSD

117. I talk a lot more than when straight.   *128*
Frequency?   Never   Rarely   Sometimes   Very Often   Usually
How Stoned?   Just   Fairly   Strongly   Vy Strongly   Maximum   LSD

118. I talk a lot less than when straight.   *128*
Frequency?   Never   Rarely   Sometimes   Very Often   Usually
How Stoned?   Just   Fairly   Strongly   Vy Strongly   Maximum   LSD

119. Other people seem dead, lifeless, as if they were robots when I'm stoned.   *135*
Frequency?   Never   Rarely   Sometimes   Very Often   Usually
How Stoned?   Just   Fairly   Strongly   Vy Strongly   Maximum   LSD

120. I am very strongly influenced by the social situation set up by my companions,   *135*
so I will do whatever they are doing even if it is something I don't want
to do or wouldn't do normally.

| Frequency? | Never | Rarely | Sometimes | Very Often | Usually | |
| How Stoned? | Just | Fairly | Strongly | Vy Strongly | Maximum | LSD |

121. Being with people who are much higher than I am (as from their being on   *134*
acid or much more stoned on grass) gets me higher even though I don't smoke
any more grass.

| Frequency? | Never | Rarely | Sometimes | Very Often | Usually | |
| How Stoned? | Just | Fairly | Strongly | Vy Strongly | Maximum | LSD |

SEXUAL ACTIVITY: *Page*

122. My sexual drive goes up when stoned; I have more *need* for sex.   *141*

| Frequency? | Never | Rarely | Sometimes | Very Often | Usually | |
| How Stoned? | Just | Fairly | Strongly | Vy Strongly | Maximum | LSD |

123. I have much less sexual drive when stoned; it's difficult to arouse me even   *141*
in a situation which would normally arouse me.

| Frequency? | Never | Rarely | Sometimes | Very Often | Usually | |
| How Stoned? | Just | Fairly | Strongly | Vy Strongly | Maximum | LSD |

124. I have no increase in sexual feelings unless it's a situation that I would normally   *141*
be sexually aroused in, and then the sexual feelings are much stronger and
more enjoyable.

| Frequency? | Never | Rarely | Sometimes | Very Often | Usually | |
| How Stoned? | Just | Fairly | Strongly | Vy Strongly | Maximum | LSD |

125. When making love, I feel I'm in much closer mental contact with my partner;   *142*
it is much more a union of souls as well as bodies.

| Frequency? | Never | Rarely | Sometimes | Very Often | Usually | |
| How Stoned? | Just | Fairly | Strongly | Vy Strongly | Maximum | LSD |

126. When making love, I feel rather isolated from my partner; I'm wrapped up   *142*
in my intensified sensations and not really very aware of my partner's reactions
and feelings.

| Frequency? | Never | Rarely | Sometimes | Very Often | Usually | |
| How Stoned? | Just | Fairly | Strongly | Vy Strongly | Maximum | LSD |

127. I feel as if I'm a better person to make love with when stoned. Why? (Please   *146*
answer on back.)

| Frequency? | Never | Rarely | Sometimes | Very Often | Usually | |
| How Stoned? | Just | Fairly | Strongly | Vy Strongly | Maximum | LSD |

128. Sexual orgasm has new qualities, pleasurable qualities, when stoned.   *143*

| Frequency? | Never | Rarely | Sometimes | Very Often | Usually | |
| How Stoned? | Just | Fairly | Strongly | Vy Strongly | Maximum | LSD |

THOUGHT PROCESSES: *Page*

129. I can get so wound up in thoughts or fantasies that I won't notice what's   *163*
going on around me or won't hear someone talking to me unless they attract
my attention forcibly.

| Frequency? | Never | Rarely | Sometimes | Very Often | Usually | |
| How Stoned? | Just | Fairly | Strongly | Vy Strongly | Maximum | LSD |

130. I can get so wound up in thoughts or fantasies while doing some physical   *163*
     task or job that I lose awareness of doing it, yet suddenly find that I have
     finished the physical task even though I lost track of it mentally.
     Frequency?   Never   Rarely   Sometimes   Very Often   Usually
     How Stoned? Just   Fairly   Strongly   Vy Strongly   Maximum   LSD

131. I do things with much less thought to possible consequences of my actions   *166*
     than when straight, i.e., I go ahead and do things without thinking first about
     "What will people think? How will this effect me?" etc.
     Frequency?   Never   Rarely   Sometimes   Very Often   Usually
     How Stoned? Just   Fairly   Strongly   Vy Strongly   Maximum   LSD

132. My mind goes completely blank for long periods (15 minutes or more); even   *37-39,*
     though I'm not asleep, I have no thoughts or images or anything going on   *165*
     in my mind.
     Frequency?   Never   Rarely   Sometimes   Very Often   Usually
     How Stoned? Just   Fairly   Strongly   Vy Strongly   Maximum   LSD

133. In thinking about a problem of the sort that normally requires a series of   *168*
     steps to solve, I can get the answer without going through some of the usual
     intermediate steps; i.e., I start to think about the problem and then just arrive
     at what is clearly the answer, without being aware of the steps in the thought
     process I would normally be aware of.
     Frequency?   Never   Rarely   Sometimes   Very Often   Usually
     How Stoned? Just   Fairly   Strongly   Vy Strongly   Maximum   LSD

134. I can't think clearly; thoughts keep slipping away before I can quite grasp   *168*
     them.
     Frequency?   Never   Rarely   Sometimes   Very Often   Usually
     How Stoned? Just   Fairly   Strongly   Vy Strongly   Maximum   LSD

135. Commonplace sayings or conversations seem to have new meanings, more   *171*
     significance.
     Frequency?   Never   Rarely   Sometimes   Very Often   Usually
     How Stoned? Just   Fairly   Strongly   Vy Strongly   Maximum   LSD

136. I give little or no thought to the future; I'm completely in the here-and-now. *166*
     Frequency?   Never   Rarely   Sometimes   Very Often   Usually
     How Stoned? Just   Fairly   Strongly   Vy Strongly   Maximum   LSD

137. I am more willing to accept contradictions between two ideas or two views   *168*
     of the situation than when straight. I don't get up tight because the two things
     don't make immediate sense.
     Frequency?   Never   Rarely   Sometimes   Very Often   Usually
     How Stoned? Just   Fairly   Strongly   Vy Strongly   Maximum   LSD

138. I learn a great deal about psychological processes, what makes people tick,   *165*
     i.e., general knowledge about how the mind works (as opposed to specific
     insights about yourself).
     Frequency?   Never   Rarely   Sometimes   Very Often   Usually
     How Stoned? Just   Fairly   Strongly   Vy Strongly   Maximum   LSD

139. *Spontaneously*, insights about myself, my personality, the games I play come *165*
     to mind when stoned, and seem very meaningful.
     Frequency?   Never   Rarely   Sometimes   Very Often   Usually
     How Stoned? Just   Fairly   Strongly   Vy Strongly   Maximum   LSD

140. If I *deliberately* work on it I can have important insights about myself, my   *165*
     personality, the games I play.
     Frequency?   Never   Rarely   Sometimes   Very Often   Usually
     How Stoned? Just   Fairly   Strongly   Vy Strongly   Maximum   LSD

141. If I try to solve a problem, it *feels* as if my mind is working much more   *168*
efficiently than usual (regardless of how you evaluate your solution later).
Frequency?   Never   Rarely   Sometimes   Very Often   Usually
How Stoned?   Just   Fairly   Strongly   Vy Strongly   Maximum   LSD

142. If I try to solve a problem it *feels* as if my mind is much less efficient than   *168*
usual (regardless of how you evaluate the solution later).
Frequency?   Never   Rarely   Sometimes   Very Often   Usually
How Stoned?   Just   Fairly   Strongly   Vy Strongly   Maximum   LSD

143. If I work on some problem while stoned, I work *more* accurately than straight,   *170*
as judged by *later* real-world evaluation.
Frequency?   Never   Rarely   Sometimes   Very Often   Usually
How Stoned?   Just   Fairly   Strongly   Vy Strongly   Maximum   LSD

144. If I work on some problem while stoned, I work *less* accurately than straight,   *170*
as judged by *later* real-world evaluation.
Frequency?   Never   Rarely   Sometimes   Very Often   Usually
How Stoned?   Just   Fairly   Strongly   Vy Strongly   Maximum   LSD

145. The ideas that come to my mind when stoned are much more original than   *171*
usual.
Frequency?   Never   Rarely   Sometimes   Very Often   Usually
How Stoned?   Just   Fairly   Strongly   Vy Strongly   Maximum   LSD

146. I appreciate very subtle humor in what my companions say, and say quite   *171*
subtly funny things myself.
Frequency?   Never   Rarely   Sometimes   Very Often   Usually
How Stoned?   Just   Fairly   Strongly   Vy Strongly   Maximum   LSD

147. I can play elaborate games and get very involved in the games.   *132*
Frequency?   Never   Rarely   Sometimes   Very Often   Usually
How Stoned?   Just   Fairly   Strongly   Vy Strongly   Maximum   LSD

148. When thinking about things while stoned, there are visual images that just   *64*
automatically go along with the thinking; i.e., I think much more in images
instead of just abstract thoughts.
Frequency?   Never   Rarely   Sometimes   Very Often   Usually
How Stoned?   Just   Fairly   Strongly   Vy Strongly   Maximum   LSD

149. I think about things in ways that seem intuitively correct, but which do not   *167*
follow the rules of logic.
Frequency?   Never   Rarely   Sometimes   Very Often   Usually
How Stoned?   Just   Fairly   Strongly   Vy Strongly   Maximum   LSD

MEMORY FUNCTIONING: *Page*

150. I *spontaneously* remember things I hadn't thought of in years, more so than   *153*
straight (does not apply to consciously *trying* to remember things.)
Frequency?   Never   Rarely   Sometimes   Very Often   Usually
How Stoned?   Just   Fairly   Strongly   Vy Strongly   Maximum   LSD

151. My memory for otherwise forgotten events is much better than straight when   *153*
I consciously *try* to remember.
Frequency?   Never   Rarely   Sometimes   Very Often   Usually
How Stoned?   Just   Fairly   Strongly   Vy Strongly   Maximum   LSD

152. My memory for otherwise forgotten events is much worse than when straight   *153*
when I *try* to remember.
Frequency?   Never   Rarely   Sometimes   Very Often   Usually
How Stoned?   Just   Fairly   Strongly   Vy Strongly   Maximum   LSD

153. My memory span for conversations is somewhat shortened, so that I may forget   *154*
what the conversation is about even before it has ended (even though I may
be able to recall it if I make a *special* effort).
Frequency?   Never   Rarely   Sometimes   Very Often   Usually
How Stoned? Just   Fairly   Strongly   Vy Strongly Maximum   LSD

154. My meory span for conversations is very shortened, so that I may forget what   *154*
the start of a sentence was about even before the sentence is finished (although
I may be able to recall it if I make a *special* effort).
Frequency?   Never   Rarely   Sometimes   Very Often   Usually
How Stoned? Just   Fairly   Strongly   Vy Strongly Maximum   LSD

155. I can continue to carry on an intelligent conversation even when my memory   *155*
span is so short that I forget the beginnings of what I started to say; e.g.,
I may logically complete a sentence even as I realize I've forgotten how it
started.
Frequency?   Never   Rarely   Sometimes   Very Often   Usually
How Stoned? Just   Fairly   Strongly   Vy Strongly Maximum   LSD

156. I think I've said something when actually I've only *thought* about saying it,   *156*
more so than when straight.
Frequency?   Never   Rarely   Sometimes   Very Often   Usually
How Stoned? Just   Fairly   Strongly   Vy Strongly Maximum   LSD

157. I think something is a memory when it turns out to be a fantasy, something   *156*
I just made up, but fooled myself into thinking was a memory at the time.
(not the same as *déjà vu*.)
Frequency?   Never   Rarely   Sometimes   Very Often   Usually
How Stoned? Just   Fairly   Strongly   Vy Strongly Maximum   LSD

158. My memory of what went on while I was stoned is good afterwards, better   *158*
than if I had been straight all the time.
Frequency?   Never   Rarely   Sometimes   Very Often   Usually
How Stoned? Just   Fairly   Strongly   Vy Strongly Maximum   LSD

159. My memory of what went on while I was stoned is poor afterwards compared   *158*
to what I would have remembered had I been straight.
Frequency?   Never   Rarely   Sometimes   Very Often   Usually
How Stoned? Just   Fairly   Strongly   Vy Strongly Maximum   LSD

EMOTIONS: *Page*

160. Whatever mood I was in before turning on becomes greatly amplified, so   *181*
if I felt down I really feel bad and if I felt good I really feel very good.
Frequency?   Never   Rarely   Sometimes   Very Often   Usually
How Stoned? Just   Fairly   Strongly   Vy Strongly Maximum   LSD

161. I feel emotions much more strongly when stoned, so they affect me more.   *183*
Frequency?   Never   Rarely   Sometimes   Very Often   Usually
How Stoned? Just   Fairly   Strongly   Vy Strongly Maximum   LSD

162. I feel emotions much more weakly when stoned, so they have little effect   *183*
on me.
Frequency?   Never   Rarely   Sometimes   Very Often   Usually
How Stoned? Just   Fairly   Strongly   Vy Strongly Maximum   LSD

163. I am *more* aware of the body tensions and feelings that are part of emotions   *186*
when stoned.
Frequency?   Never   Rarely   Sometimes   Very Often   Usually
How Stoned? Just   Fairly   Strongly   Vy Strongly Maximum   LSD

164. I am *less* aware of the body tensions and feelings that are part of emotions   *187*
when stoned.

| Frequency? | Never | Rarely | Sometimes | Very Often | Usually | |
| How Stoned? | Just | Fairly | Strongly | Vy Strongly | Maximum | LSD |

165. I almost invariably feel good when I turn on, regardless of whether I felt   *181*
bad before turning on.

| Frequency? | Never | Rarely | Sometimes | Very Often | Usually | |
| How Stoned? | Just | Fairly | Strongly | Vy Strongly | Maximum | LSD |

166. I almost invariably feel bad when I turn on, regardless of how I felt before   *37-39,*
I turned on.   *181*

| Frequency? | Never | Rarely | Sometimes | Very Often | Usually | |
| How Stoned? | Just | Fairly | Strongly | Vy Strongly | Maximum | LSD |

167. How many people have you seen "freak out" on grass, i.e., have such a   *183-4*
catastrophic emotional upset that they needed help of some sort? (Not counting
yourself.) _____ No. of People
What percentage is this compared to *all* the times you've seen people get stoned?

168. What sort of help did they get? How effective was it?   *185*

169. Have *you* ever freaked out in this way? ____Yes   ____No   *186*
How many times? _____
What sort of help did you get, and how effective was it?

SELF-CONTROL: *Page*

170. I find it easy to accept whatever happens; I don't need to control it or feel   *191*
in control of it.

| Frequency? | Never | Rarely | Sometimes | Very Often | Usually | |
| How Stoned? | Just | Fairly | Strongly | Vy Strongly | Maximum | LSD |

171. I *worry* about losing control, such that I might do something I wouldn't want   *191*
to do (regardless of whether you *actually* lose control).

| Frequency? | Never | Rarely | Sometimes | Very Often | Usually | |
| How Stoned? | Just | Fairly | Strongly | Vy Strongly | Maximum | LSD |

172. I lose control of my actions and do *antisocial* things (actions that harm other   *136,*
people) that I wouldn't normally do.   *192*

| Frequency? | Never | Rarely | Sometimes | Very Often | Usually | |
| How Stoned? | Just | Fairly | Strongly | Vy Strongly | Maximum | LSD |

173. My inhibitions are lowered so that I do things I'm normally too inhibited   *192*
to do (Note: this does not apply to *antisocial* acts but to acts that are generally
acceptable, but that you can't normally do through shyness or the like).

| Frequency? | Never | Rarely | Sometimes | Very Often | Usually | |
| How Stoned? | Just | Fairly | Strongly | Vy Strongly | Maximum | LSD |

174. I giggle a lot when stoned; I am silly, even though the situation is not that   *183*
funny.

| Frequency? | Never | Rarely | Sometimes | Very Often | Usually | |
| How Stoned? | Just | Fairly | Strongly | Vy Strongly | Maximum | LSD |

175. I often forget to finish some task I've started, or get sidetracked more frequently   *195*
than when straight.

| Frequency? | Never | Rarely | Sometimes | Very Often | Usually | |
| How Stoned? | Just | Fairly | Strongly | Vy Strongly | Maximum | LSD |

176. I get a rather *compulsive* desire to get even higher after a certain stage; I will   *198*
smoke much more if I can.

| Frequency? | Never | Rarely | Sometimes | Very Often | Usually | |
| How Stoned? | Just | Fairly | Strongly | Vy Strongly | Maximum | LSD |

177. I have little or no control over my fantasies; i.e., they flow along spontaneously   *193*
and even if I try I can't change what I'm fantasying about.

| Frequency? | Never | Rarely | Sometimes | Very Often | Usually | |
| How Stoned? | Just | Fairly | Strongly | Vy Strongly | Maximum | LSD |

178. I have excellent control over my fantasies; I can make them go in whatever   *193*
direction I want.

| Frequency? | Never | Rarely | Sometimes | Very Often | Usually | |
| How Stoned? | Just | Fairly | Strongly | Vy Strongly | Maximum | LSD |

179. I can work at a necessary task with extra energy, absorption, and efficiency.   *195*

| Frequency? | Never | Rarely | Sometimes | Very Often | Usually | |
| How Stoned? | Just | Fairly | Strongly | Vy Strongly | Maximum | LSD |

180. I have lost control and been "taken over" by an outside force or will, which   *37-39,*
is hostile or evil in intent, for a while.   *196*

| Frequency? | Never | Rarely | Sometimes | Very Often | Usually | |
| How Stoned? | Just | Fairly | Strongly | Vy Strongly | Maximum | LSD |

181. I have lost control and been "taken over" by an outside force or will, which   *37-39,*
is good or divine, for a while.   *196*

| Frequency? | Never | Rarely | Sometimes | Very Often | Usually | |
| How Stoned? | Just | Fairly | Strongly | Vy Strongly | Maximum | LSD |

182. Parts of my body have moved on their own volition, have done something   *196*
which I did not will.

| Frequency? | Never | Rarely | Sometimes | Very Often | Usually | |
| How Stoned? | Just | Fairly | Strongly | Vy Strongly | Maximum | LSD |

183. I feel as if I lose control over my thoughts; they just go on regardless of   *169,*
what I want (without reference to whether you *like* this or not).   *193*

| Frequency? | Never | Rarely | Sometimes | Very Often | Usually | |
| How Stoned? | Just | Fairly | Strongly | Vy Strongly | Maximum | LSD |

184. I can "come down" at will if I need to be straight for a minute to deal with   *201*
some complicated reality problem (circle the point of highness above which
you *can't* do this).

| Frequency? | Never | Rarely | Sometimes | Very Often | Usually | |
| How Stoned? | Just | Fairly | Strongly | Vy Strongly | Maximum | LSD |

IDENTITY: *Page*

185. My personality changes a lot temporarily while I'm stoned, so that in many   *210*
important ways I am a different person for that time.

| Frequency? | Never | Rarely | Sometimes | Very Often | Usually | |
| How Stoned? | Just | Fairly | Strongly | Vy Strongly | Maximum | LSD |

186. I have been so absorbed in looking at or contemplating an object or person   *207*
that I felt as if I *were* that object or person, i.e., temporarily the split between
it-and-me or they-and-me was transcended.

| Frequency? | Never | Rarely | Sometimes | Very Often | Usually | |
| How Stoned? | Just | Fairly | Strongly | Vy Strongly | Maximum | LSD |

187. When stoned I lose most of my sense of ego identity and usually take on *37-39* the identity of my like-sexed parent (father for males, mother for females).
Frequency? Never Rarely Sometimes Very Often Usually
How Stoned? Just Fairly Strongly Vy Strongly Maximum LSD

188. I feel completely unique; there is no one like me; I feel as if I am much *208* better than ordinary people when stoned.
Frequency? Never Rarely Sometimes Very Often Usually
How Stoned? Just Fairly Strongly Vy Strongly Maximum LSD

189. I lose all sense of self, of being a separate ego, and feel at one with the world. *208*
Frequency? Never Rarely Sometimes Very Often Usually
How Stoned? Just Fairly Strongly Vy Strongly Maximum LSD

190. I feel very powerful, capable, and intelligent when stoned. *209*
Frequency? Never Rarely Sometimes Very Often Usually
How Stoned? Just Fairly Strongly Vy Strongly Maximum LSD

191. Some events become archetypal, part of the basic way Man has always done *209* things. That is, instead of me (John Doe, ego) doing something, it is just Man Doing What Man Has Always Done. That is, my actions become part of the pattern that man has always been part of, instead of me, a particular individual, carrying out a particular act at a particular moment in space/time.
Frequency? Never Rarely Sometimes Very Often Usually
How Stoned? Just Fairly Strongly Vy Strongly Maximum LSD

SPIRITUAL EXPERIENCES: *Page*

192. I feel in touch with a Higher Power or a Divine Being to some extent when *213* stoned; I feel more in contact with the "spiritual" side of things.
Frequency? Never Rarely Sometimes Very Often Usually
How Stoned? Just Fairly Strongly Vy Strongly Maximum LSD

193. I am able to meditate more effectively than when straight (if yes, please describe *213* what sort of meditation you do on the back of this page).
Frequency? Never Rarely Sometimes Very Often Usually
How Stoned? Just Fairly Strongly Vy Strongly Maximum LSD

194. I have spiritual experiences, discrete experiences which have had a powerful, *215* long-term religious effect on me while stoned. (If so, please describe on rear.)
____ Yes ____ No

195. Getting stoned has acquired a religious significance for me. *218*
____ Yes ____ No (If yes, in what way? Explain on back.)

SLEEP: *Page*

196. I find it very difficult to get to sleep if I'm stoned, even if it's my usual bedtime. *223*
Frequency? Never Rarely Sometimes Very Often Usually
How Stoned? Just Fairly Strongly Vy Strongly Maximum LSD

197. I find it very easy to go to sleep at my usual bedtime when stoned. *223*
Frequency? Never Rarely Sometimes Very Often Usually
How Stoned? Just Fairly Strongly Vy Strongly Maximum LSD

198. I get very drowsy even though it's *not* late or otherwise close to my usual *223* bedtime.
Frequency? Never Rarely Sometimes Very Often Usually
How Stoned? Just Fairly Strongly Vy Strongly Maximum LSD

199. My sleep is particularly refreshing if I go to bed stoned.   *224*
Frequency?   Never   Rarely   Sometimes   Very Often   Usually
How Stoned?   Just   Fairly   Strongly   Vy Strongly   Maximum   LSD

200. My sleep is restless and poor if I go to bed stoned.   *224*
Frequency?   Never   Rarely   Sometimes   Very Often   Usually
How Stoned?   Just   Fairly   Strongly   Vy Strongly   Maximum   LSD

201. My dreams are more vivid if I go to bed stoned.   *225*
Frequency?   Never   Rarely   Sometimes   Very Often   Usually
How Stoned?   Just   Fairly   Strongly   Vy Strongly   Maximum   LSD

202. My dreams are less vivid or forgotten if I go to bed stoned.   *225*
Frequency?   Never   Rarely   Sometimes   Very Often   Usually
How Stoned?   Just   Fairly   Strongly   Vy Strongly   Maximum   LSD

SPECIAL TECHNIQUES: *Page*

203. Since taking LSD (or mescaline, peyote, psilocybin, or another major psychede-   *198*
lic drug), I am able to get much higher on grass than I was before.
           _____ Yes
           _____ No
           _____ Not applicable—haven't had LSD

204. I have special ways of getting higher besides smoking more grass with: *198*
1.   Other drugs + grass   ____ Yes ____ No
2.   Special mental techniques   ____ Yes ____ No
(Please explain any yes answer on rear)

205. There is a certain degree of being stoned from above which I can*not* come   *201*
down quickly if I *must* come down to deal adequately with reality. (circle
level)
Frequency?   Never   Rarely   Sometimes   Very Often   Usually
How Stoned?   Just   Fairly   Strongly   Vy Strongly   Maximum   LSD

206. I have special technique(s) for coming down rapidly if I need to be straight   *202*
quickly.
____ Yes ____ No   (If yes, please describe on rear)

MISCELLANEOUS: *Page*

207. I feel more childlike, more open to experience of all kinds, more filled with   *207*
wonder and awe at the nature of things.
Frequency?   Never   Rarely   Sometimes   Very Often   Usually
How Stoned?   Just   Fairly   Strongly   Vy Strongly   Maximum   LSD

208. Some of my inner trips, eyes-closed fantasies have been so vivid and real   *238*
that, even though I know logically they couldn't be real, they feel real; they
are as real as ordinary waking-life experience.
Frequency?   Never   Rarely   Sometimes   Very Often   Usually
How Stoned?   Just   Fairly   Strongly   Vy Strongly   Maximum   LSD

209. I find it very hard to get organized or accomplish anything I want to the   *234*
day after smoking grass (Circle lowest level at which this occurs.)
Frequency?   Never   Rarely   Sometimes   Very Often   Usually
How Stoned?   Just   Fairly   Strongly   Vy Strongly   Maximum   LSD

210. I have gotten very nauseous and vomited.   *120*
Frequency?   Never   Rarely   Sometimes   Very Often   Usually
How Stoned?   Just   Fairly   Strongly   Vy Strongly   Maximum   LSD

211. Others (who were straight at the time) have told me that I act very differently *131*
when I'm stoned. (Circle highest level at which this has happened.)
Frequency?   Never   Rarely   Sometimes   Very Often   Usually
How Stoned?   Just   Fairly   Strongly   Vy Strongly   Maximum   LSD

212. Others (who were straight at the time) have not noticed that I've been stoned *130*
(applies to other people who were your friends and would have told you if
they'd noticed). (Circle highest level at which this has happened.)
Frequency?   Never   Rarely   Sometimes   Very Often   Usually
How Stoned?   Just   Fairly   Strongly   Vy Strongly   Maximum   LSD

213. Could you compare the effects of alcohol and marijuana on yourself on the
back of this page? When do you prefer to use the one, when the other?

214. I feel that the world is all right, that everything is pretty much the way it *237*
should be when stoned (except for the marijuana laws)
Frequency?   Never   Rarely   Sometimes   Very Often   Usually
How Stoned?   Just   Fairly   Strongly   Vy Strongly   Maximum   LSD

215. I feel the world is in pretty bad shape, that all sorts of changes need to be *237*
made in the social order to make it a decent place to live in (for things besides
the marijuana laws).
Frequency?   Never   Rarely   Sometimes   Very Often   Usually
How Stoned?   Just   Fairly   Strongly   Vy Strongly   Maximum   LSD

216. Sounds have visual images or colors associated with them, synchronized with *74*
them.
Frequency?   Never   Rarely   Sometimes   Very Often   Usually
How Stoned?   Just   Fairly   Strongly   Vy Strongly   Maximum   LSD

217. I get much more involved in ordinary tasks than when I'm straight; they're *237*
completely absorbing.
Frequency?   Never   Rarely   Sometimes   Very Often   Usually
How Stoned?   Just   Fairly   Strongly   Vy Strongly   Maximum   LSD

218. With my eyes closed, my inner visions and fantasies become extremely real, *238*
as real as nighttime dreams.
Frequency?   Never   Rarely   Sometimes   Very Often   Usually
How Stoned?   Just   Fairly   Strongly   Vy Strongly   Maximum   LSD

219. I suddenly realize that nothing has been happening for a long time; my mind *164*
has been blank and nothing was going on.
Frequency?   Never   Rarely   Sometimes   Very Often   Usually
How Stoned?   Just   Fairly   Strongly   Vy Strongly   Maximum   LSD

220. I move up to higher levels of consciousness in jumps, sudden increases, rather *238*
than smoothly.
Frequency?   Never   Rarely   Sometimes   Very Often   Usually
How Stoned?   Just   Fairly   Strongly   Vy Strongly   Maximum   LSD

What important or characteristic things happen to you when you're stoned that
haven't been described above? Could you describe each one and rate it in the
same way below? Use the back of this sheet if needed.

221.
Frequency?   Never   Rarely   Sometimes   Very Often   Usually
How Stoned?   Just   Fairly   Strongly   Vy Strongly   Maximum   LSD

222.

Frequency?	Never	Rarely	Sometimes	Very Often	Usually	
How Stoned?	Just	Fairly	Strongly	Vy Strongly	Maximum	LSD

223.

Frequency?	Never	Rarely	Sometimes	Very Often	Usually	
How Stoned?	Just	Fairly	Strongly	Vy Strongly	Maximum	LSD

224.

Frequency?	Never	Rarely	Sometimes	Very Often	Usually	
How Stoned?	Just	Fairly	Strongly	Vy Strongly	Maximum	LSD

Comments?

References

THE FOLLOWING reference list is not intended to be a comprehensive bibliography on marijuana. For reasons discussed in Chapter 2, much of the voluminous older literature on marijuana is of little value to most readers and so has not been included here. The occasional reader interested in a comprehensive guide to the literature on marijuana may see Gamage and Zerken, 1969.

Most of the references below are to various exotic subjects that are not generally familiar to Western readers but are useful in understanding some of the phenomena of marijuana intoxication.

Aaronson, B. Hypnosis, depth perception, and the psychedelic experience. In C. Tart (Ed.), *Altered states of consciousness: A book of readings.* New York: John Wiley & Sons, 1969. Pp. 263–270.

Aaronson, B., & Osmond, H. *Psychedelics: The uses and implications of hallucinogenic drugs.* Garden City, New York: Doubleday, 1970.

Aiken, J. The church of the awakening. In B. Aaronson & H. Osmond (Eds.), *Psychedelics: The uses and implications of hallucinogenic drugs.* Garden City, New York: Doubleday, 1970. Pp. 165–181.

Andrews, G., & Vinkenoog, S. (Eds.) *The book of grass: An anthology of Indian hemp.* New York: Grove, 1967.

Anonymous, Spontaneous phenomena surveyed in Holland. *Newsletter Parapsychol. Found.*, 1958, *5*, No. 4, 3–4.

Anonymous. The effects of marijuana on consciousness. In C. Tart (Ed.), *Altered states of consciousness: A book of readings.* New York: John Wiley & Sons, 1969. Pp. 335–356.

Arguelles, J., & Arguelles, M. *Mandala.* Berkeley, Calif.: Shambala Publications, in press.

Assagioli, R. *Psychosynthesis: A manual of principles and techniques.* New York: Hobbs, Dorman & Co., 1965.

Baumann, F. Hypnosis and the adolescent drug abuser. *Amer. J. clin. Hypnosis*, 1970, *13*, 17–21.

Becker, H. Becoming a marijuana user. *Amer. J. Sociol.*, 1953, *59*, 235–243.

Behanan, K. *Yoga: A scientific evaluation.* New York: Dover, 1937.

Blofeld, J. *The Tantric mysticism of Tibet.* New York: Dutton, 1970.

Bloomquist, E. *Marijuana.* New York: Glencoe, 1968.

Broad, C. *Lectures on psychical research.* London: Routledge & Kegan Paul, 1962.

Chang, G. *The teachings of Tibetan yoga.* New Hyde Park, New York: University Books, 1963.

Chang, M., & Smith, R. *T'ai-chi.* Rutland, Vermont: Charles Tuttle, 1967.

Chair, C. Reincarnation: New light on an old doctrine. *Inter. J. Parapsychol.,* 1967, *9,* 217–222.

Cheek, F., Newell, S., & Joffe, M. Deceptions in the illicit drug market. *Science,* 1970, *167,* 1276.

Clark, W. The psychedelics and religion. in B. Aaronson & H. Osmond (Eds.), *Psychedelics: The uses and implications of hallucinogenic drugs.* Garden City, New York: Doubleday, 1970. Pp. 182–197.

Crancer, A., Dille, J., Delay, J., Wallace, J., & Haykin, M. Comparison of the effects of marijuana and alcohol on simulated driving performance. *Science,* 1969, *164,* 851–854.

Crookall, R. *The study and practice of astral projection.* London: Aquarian Press, 1961.

Crookall, R. *More astral projections: Analyses of case histories.* London: Aquarian Press, 1964. (a)

Crookall, R. *The techniques of astral projection.* London: Aquarian Press, 1964. (b)

deRopp, R. *Drugs and the mind.* New York: Grove, 1967.

Desoille, R. The directed daydream. *Bull. Soc. Recherches Psychotherapiques de Langue Francaise,* 1965, *3,* 27–42. Translation by Frank Haronian, Psychosynthesis Research Foundation, New York.

Drake, B. *The cultivator's handbook of marijuana.* Eugene, Oregon: Augur, 1970. Available from the author, Box 2447, Eugene, Oregon 97402.

Ducasse, C. The doctrine of reincarnation in the history of thought. *Inter. J. Parapsychol.,* 1960, *3,* 61–80.

Eastman, M. Out-of-the-body experiences. *Proc. Soc. Psychical Res.,* 1962, *53,* 287–309.

Ebin, D. (Ed.) *The drug experience.* New York: Orion Press, 1961.

Ellison, A. Some recent experiments in psychic perceptivity. *J. Soc. Psychical Res.,* 1962, *41,* 355–365.

Evans-Wentz, W. *Tibetan Yoga and secret doctrine.* London: Oxford Univ. Press, 1958.

Feng, G., & Kirk, J. *T'ai-chi: A way of centering and I Ching.* New York: Collier, 1970.

Frager, R. On vital energy: Some Eastern and Western conceptions. Paper presented at the World Conference on Scientific Yoga, New Delhi, December, 1970.

Frankenhaeuser, M. Effects of nitrous oxide on subjective and objective variables. *Scand. J. Psychol.,* 1963, *4,* 37–43.

Gamage, J., & Zerkin, E. *A comprehensive guide to the English-language literature on cannabis (marihuana).* Beloit, Wisconsin: STASH Press, 1969. Available from the Student Association for the Study of Hallucinogens, 638 Pleasant Street, Beloit, Wis., 53511.

Garrison, O. *Tantra: The yoga of sex.* New York: Julian Press, 1964.

Gerard, R. Symbolic visualization: A method of psychosynthesis. Paper, Fifth Inter. Cog. Psychotherapy, Vienna, 1961.

Goode, E. (Ed.) *Marijuana.* New York: Atherton, 1969.

Govinda, A. *Foundations of Tibetan mysticism.* New York: Dutton, 1960.

Green, C. Report on enquiry into spontaneous cases. *Proc. Soc. Psychical Res.,* 1960, *53*, 97.

Green, C. Spontaneous "paranormal" experiences in relation to sex and academic background. *J. Soc. Psychical Res.,* 1966, *43*, 357–361.

Green, C. *Out-of-the-body experiences.* Oxford, England: Institute of Psychophysical Research, 1968.

Gurney, E., Meyers, F., & Podmore, F. *Phantasms of the living.* London: Trubner & Co., 1866.

Harman, W., McKim, R., Mogar, R., Fadiman, J., & Stolaroff, M. Psychedelic agents in creative problem solving: A pilot study. *Psychol. Rep.,* 1966, *19*, 211–227. Reprinted in C. Tart (Ed.), *Altered states of consciousness: A book of readings.* New York: John Wiley & Sons, 1969. Pp. 445–461.

Head, J. & Cranston, S. *Reincarnation in world thought.* New York: Julian Press, 1967.

Heywood, R. *The sixth sense: An inquiry into extrasensory perception.* London: Chatto & Windus, 1959.

Hollander, C. (Ed.) *Background papers on student drug involvement.* Washington, D.C.: U. S. National Students Association, 1967.

Huxley, A. *The doors of perception.* New York: Harper & Bros., 1954.

Johnson, R. *The imprisoned splendor.* New York: Harper & Bros., 1953.

Johnston, C. *The Yoga sutras of Patanjali.* London: Stuart & Watkins, 1968.

Kales, A. (Ed.) *Sleep: physiology and pathology.* Philadelphia: Lippincott, 1969.

Kaplan, J. *Marijuana: The new prohibition.* New York: World, 1970.

Kilner, W. *The human aura.* New Hyde Park, New York: University Books, 1965.

Krippner, S. Marijuana and Viet Nam: Twin dilemmas for American youth. Paper, Brooklyn Psychological Assn., 1968. Also in R. Parker (Ed.), *The emotional stress of war, violence, and peace.* Pittsburgh: Stanwix Press, 1971.

Krippner, S. The psychedelic state, the hypnotic trance, and the creative act. In C. Tart (Ed.), *Altered states of consciousness: A book of readings.* New York: John Wiley & Sons, 1969. Pp. 271–290. (a)

Krippner, S. The influence of "psychedelic" experience on contemporary art and music. Paper, Student Association for the Study of Hallucinogens, Beloit, Wis., 1969. (b)

Krishna, G. *Kundalini: The evolutionary energy in man.* Berkeley, California: Shambala, 1970.

Kuhn, T. *The structure of scientific revolutions.* Chicago: Univ. Chicago Press, 1962.

Leary, T., Metzner, R., & Alpert, R. *The psychedelic experience.* New Hyde Park, New York: University Books, 1964.

Lyons, J. The hidden dialogue in experimental research. *J. Phenomenological Psychol.*, 1971, in press.

Manheimer, D., Mellinger, G., & Balter, M. Marijuana use among urban adults. *Science*, 1969, *166*, 1544-1545.

Maslow, A. *The psychology of science: A reconnaissance.* New York: Harper & Row, 1966.

Mechoulam, R. Marihuana chemistry. *Science*, 1970, *168*, 1159-1166.

Membership Committee. The American Society for Psychical Research Membership Survey. *J. Amer. Soc. Psychical Res.*, 1967, *61*, 146-154.

Mesmer, A. *Memoire sur la decourverte du Magnetisme Animal.* Geneva: 1774. Available in *Mesmerism by Doctor Mesmer: Dissertation on the discovery of animal magnetism, 1779.* Trans. by V. Myers. London: Macdonald, 1948.

Muldoon, S., & Carrington, H. *The projection of the astral body.* London: Rider & Co., 1956.

Murphy, G. *The challenge of psychical research.* New York: Harper & Bros., 1962.

Muses, C. (Ed.) *Esoteric teachings of the Tibetan Tantras.* Switzerland: Falcon's Wing Press, 1961.

Needleman, J. *The new religions.* New York: Doubleday, 1970.

Orne, M. The nature of hypnosis: Artifact and essence. *J. abnorm. soc. Psychol.*, 1959, *58*, 277-299.

Orne, M. On the social psychology of the psychological experiment: With particular reference to demand characteristics and their implications. *Amer. Psychologist*, 1962, *17*, 776-783.

Orne, M., & Scheibe, K. The contributions of nondeprivation factors in the production of sensory deprivation effects: The psychology of the "panic button." *J. abnorm. soc. Psychol.*, 1964, *68*, 3-12.

Ornstein, R., & Naranjo, C. *On the psychology of medatation.* New York: Viking, 1971.

Osmond, H. Peyote night. In B. Aaronson & H. Osmond (Eds.), *Psychedelics: The uses and implications of hallucinogenic drugs.* Garden City, New York: Doubleday, 1970. Pp. 67-85.

Pahnke, W. Drugs and mysticism. *Inter. J. Parapsychol.*, 1966, *8*, 295-320.

Pahnke, W., & Richards, W. Implications of LSD and experimental mysticism. In C. Tart (Ed.), *Altered states of consciousness: A book of readings.* New York: John Wiley & Sons, 1969. Pp. 399-428.

Pearlman, S. A select bibliography on drug usage in colleges and universities. *College Student Survey: An interdisciplinary Journal of Attitude Research,* 1968, *2*, 5-7.

Perls, F., Hefferline, R., & Goodman, P. *Gestalt therapy: Excitement and growth in the human personality.* New York: Julian Press, 1951.

Polanyi, M. *Personal knowledge.* Chicago: Univ. of Chicago Press, 1958.

Prasad, J., & Stevenson, I. A survey of spontaneous psychical experiences in school children of Uttar Pradesh, India. *Int. J. Parapsychol.*, 1968, *10*, 241-261.

Priestley, J. *Man and time.* New York: Doubleday, 1964.

Rao, R. *Experimental parapsychology: A review and interpretation.* Springfield, Illinois: Charles C. Thomas, 1966.

Regardie, I. *Roll away the stone: An introduction to Aleister Crowley's essays on the psychology of hashish.* Saint Paul, Minn.: Llewellyn, 1968.

Rosenthal, R. *Experimenter effects in behavioral research.* New York: Appleton-Century-Crofts, 1966.

Rosevear, J. *Pot: A handbook of marihuana.* New Hyde Park, New York: University Books, 1967.

Schutz, W. *Joy: Expanding human awareness.* New York: Grove, 1967.

Shah, I. *The Sufis.* New York: Doubleday, 1964.

Shah, I. *The way of the Sufi.* London: Jonathan Cape, 1968.

Sidgwick, H., Sidgwick, E., Meyers, F. W. H., Meyers, A. T., Podmore, F., & Johnson, A. Report on the census of hallucinations. *Proc. Soc. Psychical Res., 1894 10,* 25–422.

Simmons, J. *Marihuana: Myths and realities.* North Hollywood, Calif.: Brandon House, 1967.

Smith, D. (Ed.), *The new social drug: Cultural, medical, and legal perspectives on marijuana.* Englewood Cliffs, N.J.: Prentice-Hall, 1970.

Solomon, D. (Ed.) *The marihuana papers.* New York: Bobbs-Merrill, 1966.

Sommer, R. *Personal space.* Englewood Cliffs, New Jersey: Prentice-Hall, 1969.

Stevenson, I. Twenty cases suggestive of reincarnation. *Proc. Amer. Soc. Psychical Res.,* 1966, *26,* 1–362.

Suzuki, D. *The training of the Zen Buddhist monk.* New Hyde Park, New York: University Books, 1959.

Suzuki, D. *The essentials of Zen Buddhism.* New York: Dudton, 1962.

Tart, C. A second psychophysiological study of out-of-the-body experiences in a gifted subject. *Inter. J. Parapsychol.,* 1967, *9,* 251–258.

Tart, C. A psychophysiological study of out-of-the-body experiences in a selected subject. *J. Amer. Soc. Psychical Res.,* 1968, *62,* 3–27.

Tart, C. (Ed.) *Altered states of consciousness: A book of readings.* New York: John Wiley & Sons, 1969.

Tart, C. Self-report scales of hypnotic depth. *Inter. J. clin, exp. Hypnosis,* 1970, *18,* 105–125. (a)

Tart, C. Marijuana intoxication: Common experiences. *Nature,* 1970, *226,* 701–704. (b)

Tart, C. Measuring the depth of an altered state of consciousness, with particular reference to self-report scales of hypnotic depth. In Erika Fromm and Ronald E. Shor (Eds.), *Current trends in hypnosis research.* Chicago: Aldine-Atherton, in press.

Tart, C., & Klein, C. Marijuana, alcohol, and psychedelic (hallucinogenic) drug use in a student population. Unpublished paper, University of California at Davis, 1968.

Tucci, G. *The theory and practice of the mandala.* London: Rider & Co., 1969.

von Reichenbach, K. *The odic force: Letters on Od and magnetism.* New Hyde Park, New York: University Books, 1968.

Warmke, H., & Davidson, H. Polyploidy investigations. In *Carnagie Institute of Washington Yearbook,* 1941–43, No. 41.

Warmke, H., & Davidson, H. Polyploidy investigations. In *Carnagie Institute of Washington Yearbook,* 1942–43, No. 42.

Warmke, H., & Davidson, H. Polyploidy investigations. In *Carnagie Institute of Washington Yearbook,* 1943–44, No. 43.

Watts, A. *The way of Zen.* New York: Pantheon, 1957.

Watts, A. Psychedelics and religious experience. In B. Aaronson & H. Osmond (Eds.), *Psychedelics: The uses and implications of hallucinogenic drugs.* Garden City, New York: Doubleday, 1970. Pp. 131–144.

Weil, A. Cannabis. *Science Journal,* 1969, *5A*, No. 3, 36–42.

Weil, A., & Zinberg, N. Acute effects of marihuana on speech. *Nature,* 1969, *222*, 434–437.

Weil, A., Zinberg, N., & Nelsen, J. Clinical and psychological effects of marihuana in man. *Science,* 1968, *162*, 1234–1242.

West, D. *Psychical research today.* London: Duckworth, 1954.

Westbrook, A., & Ratti, O. *Aikido and the dynamic sphere,* Rutland, Vermont: Charles Tuttle, 1970.

Wilelm, R., & Jung, C. *The secret of the golden flower.* New York: Harcourt, Brace, & World, 1962.

Wolstenholme, G. (Ed.) *Hashish: Its chemistry and pharmacology.* Boston: Little, Brown & Co., 1965.

Wood, E. *Great systems of yoga.* New York: Philosophical Publishing House, 1954.

Woodruffe, Sir John. *The serpent power.* Madras, India: Ganesh, 1931.

Yeats-Brown, F. *Yoga explained: A simple approach to a fuller and richer life.* New York: Vista House, 1958.

Zaehner, R. *Mysticism: Sacred and profane.* Oxford: Oxford univ. Press, 1957.

Index

329

Spontaneity, 166
State of consciousness, 3, 11-29, 29, 30, 46, 47, 158, 254, 285, 294. *See also* specific state names
Statistical techniques, 52, 54, 279-283
Stereo separation, 72, 73, 245, 250
STP (DOM) (2,5-dimethoxy-4-methylampheta-mine), 33, 46, 52
Strength, 113, 147, 251, 255
Stroboscopic effects, 65
Subliminal suggestion, 101
Subtlety, 71, 134, 138, 139, 171, 172, 176, 245-248, 250, 255, 293. *See also* Meaning, sense of
Subud, 42, 214
Suggestion, 203. *See also* Hypnosis
Sweets, craving for, 82, 84, 249, 259
Synesthesia, 74-76, 247, 252, 286

T'ai-Chi, 214
Talking, 128, 138, 139, 186, 249, 250
Taste, 81-85, 92, 145, 149, 245, 249, 250-252, 255, 256, 258, 259, 262, 263, 286
Telepathy, 100, 102, 107, 108, 133, 137-140, 218, 220, 252, 255, 258, 277, 288
Temperature, 79-83, 121, 251
Tension, 123, 186, 187, 188, 214
Terminology, 50, 51
Tetrahydrocannabinol. *See* THC
Texture, 79, 83, 96
THC, 5, 14, 120, 294
Theory of states of consciousness, 11, 12
Thorazine, 203
Thought, 163-179, 230, 231, 248, 250, 252, 255-259, 262-264, 266-269, 290
Tilting of visual field, 37
Time, 11, 21, 92-98, 245, 250, 251, 252
Tingling, 81, 118-120, 250, 252
Tolerance, 136, 195, 204, 245, 251, 291
Touch, 79-81, 91, 144, 145, 148, 149, 150, 185, 245, 250, 255, 256, 286
Tranquilizing drugs. *See* specific drug names
Tranquilizing effect, 226, 238, 295

Transcendence. *See* Merging; Archetypal experiences; Spiritual experiences
Trembling, 37, 234, 252
Tremors, 113, 119, 251

Undesirable effects, 14, 15, 18, 206, 226, 229-232, 254, 281
Union with another. *See* Merging
Uniqueness, 11, 12, 22, 208, 210-212, 251, 294
of smells, 87, 255
Unity experience, 134, 138, 142, 147, 148, 210, 215, 216, 218, 220, 221, 250, 255, 292
Urination, 118, 123, 252
Use. *See* Frequency

Validity, 35, 36
Variability of effects, 19, 22
Vibration, sensations of, 118, 120, 122, 123, 252
Violence, 136, 273
Visions. *See* Fantasies; Hallucinations
Visual depth jiggle, 62, 66-68, 91, 95, 251, 259
Visual effects, 22, 59-69, 145, 149, 150, 250, 252, 255-259, 262, 264, 266-269, 281, 282, 286
Voice quality, 74, 76, 251
Void experience, 219
Volition. *See* Willing; Concentration
Vomiting, 120, 122, 123, 230, 248, 252

Walking, 239
Warmth, 80, 81, 117, 123, 250
Water pipe, 5, 113
Weakness, 113, 230, 232, 251
Weight, 111, 112, 123-125, 250, 251
White light experience, 219
Willing, 199, 206. *See also* Concentration
Withdrawal. *See* Isolation

Yoga, 3, 119, 120, 214

Zazen, 200
Zen Buddhism, 200, 215, 219